POINTS OF CONTACT

Points of Contact

The Shared Intellectual History of Vocalisation in Syriac, Arabic, and Hebrew

Nick Posegay

Semitic Languages and Cultures 10.

ISSN (print): 2632-6906
ISSN (digital): 2632-6914

ISBN Paperback: 9781800642966
ISBN Hardback: 9781800642973
ISBN Digital (PDF): 9781800642980
DOI: 10.11647/OBP.0271

Cover image: MS Cambridge University Library, Taylor-Schechter Arabic 53.1 (anonymous Masoretic treatise on vowels and accents). Courtesy of the Syndics of the Cambridge University Library.

Cover design: Anna Gatti

For Andrew, Amanda,

Emma, and Noah

CONTENTS

ACKNOWLEDGEMENTS

The research and open access publication of this book were supported by the Bill & Melinda Gates Foundation through a Gates Cambridge Scholarship [OPP1144], as well as the Leverhulme and Isaac Newton Trusts through an Early Career Fellowship. I could not have completed it without the help of a great many incredible people.

First, thank you to Fred Donner for introducing me to the Middle East, to Jim Robinson for starting me on a path to Cambridge, and to Nichole Fazio-Veigel for making that journey possible. Thank you to all my teachers over the years—from Chicago to Cambridge and Amman to Tangier—this would not have been possible without you.

Thank you to everyone who helped in some way with research, editing, or proofreading, including: Roger-Youssef Akhrass, Sebastian Brock, François Déroche, Nehemia Gordon, Ben Kantor, Jonathan Loopstra, Johan Lundberg, Elvira Martin-Contreras, Kara McCauley, Seth Musser, Jordan Ng, Amanda Posegay, Andrew Posegay, Dana Rodriguez, Lev Tsypin, Hannah Weller, and Peggy Xu. Thank you to Aaron Hornkohl for his assistance in revising and copyediting, Anna Gatti for the cover design, and Alessandra Tosi for managing the publication process. Additional thanks to the librarians and registration staff at the FAMES, Parker, and University Libraries in Cambridge; the Oriental Institute Museum in Chicago; the Hill Museum and Manuscript Library in Minnesota; the Museum of Islamic Art in Doha; and the Syriac Orthodox Patriarchal Library in Damascus.

Thank you to the entire staff of the Taylor-Schechter Genizah Research Unit, especially Melonie Schmierer-Lee and Nadia
Vidro, for their expertise and continuous support.

Thank you to George Kiraz, Ben Outhwaite, and Daniel
King for their insightful comments on earlier drafts of this book,
without which it could never have gone to print.

Special thanks to Magdalen Connolly for her kindness, pro-
fessional expertise, and patience in the face of collaboration; to
Noah van Renswoude for wisdom, linguistic knowledge, commis-
eration, and friendship; and to Sophia Johnson for just about everything else.

Finally, most of all, thank you to Geoffrey Khan for his
many years of instruction, guidance, and care.

1. INTRODUCTION

But the Hebrews, Syrians, Persians, Kushites, Elamites, Medes, Phoenicians, Alans, and Arabs, as well as others unknown to us, do not have enough letters to express the sounds that they write in their languages, or to read them correctly, just as they are. Accordingly, they are forced to place dots on the letters, to distinguish the vowels and words from each other, and they are only able to read correctly by an act of divination, by tradition, or by means of much toil. (Elias of Nisibis [d. 1046], *The Correct Form of Syriac Speech* [Gottheil 1887, ‍ܐ])

The Arab expansion out of the Hijaz threw people across the Middle East into a state of linguistic flux. From the seventh century onwards, Arabic-speaking Muslims increasingly came into contact with speakers of other languages, and new converts to Islam brought their own languages with them. This development jeopardised the proper pronunciation of Qurʾānic recitation, as new Muslims in disparate areas learned Arabic for the first time. Conversely, Aramaic-speaking Jews and Syriac Christians gradually began to adopt Arabic as a lingua franca within the growing Islamic empire. As Arabic spread and fewer people mastered Aramaic, those Jewish and Christian communities risked introducing mistakes into their liturgical traditions, both of which required accurate recitation of the biblical text in Hebrew or Syriac. Consequently, by the beginning of the eighth century, Christians, Muslims, and Jews alike needed to take steps to preserve their recitation traditions against the impacts of linguistic change. This situation coincided with an increasing importance in the culture of writing, including the writing of historically oral traditions, between the seventh and ninth centuries (Schoeler 2006, 111–41, esp. 129, 140; Shah 2008; Khan 2017, 270; 2020, I:12; see also, Bloom 2010). However, the Syriac, Arabic, and Hebrew scripts lacked sufficient letters to record every phoneme in the Bible and the Qurʾān, so to transcribe them more accurately would have required wholesale changes to the orthography of sacred texts.

One story that highlights the resistance to changing the holy texts comes from ʿAbd Allah ibn Ṭāhir (d. 845 CE), a ninth-century Abbasid governor of Khurasan (Bosworth 1982). Famously a patron of culture and scholarship, Ibn Ṭāhir once saw a magnificent example of Arabic calligraphy, but rather than admire it—so the story goes—he lamented: "How beautiful this would be, if there were not so much coriander seed scattered over it!" (Hughes 1895, 686). The wayward coriander seeds were the diacritic points that are now essential to the Arabic script, but for Ibn Ṭāhir they were an undesirable innovation. Opinions such as this did not prevent scribes from adding further innovations to the Arabic writing system, but they did direct them to be as non-invasive as possible with respect to modifying the writing of the Qurʾān. Similar attitudes influenced Syriac and Hebrew scribes as they attempted to record the fine details of their recitation while also preserving traditional biblical orthography.

This opposition to change was especially problematic for the issue of vocalisation, as Arabic, Syriac, and Hebrew all lacked dedicated letters for vowels. Theological concerns notwithstanding, it was impossible for scribes to precisely record biblical or Qurʾānic vowel phonology with their abjad scripts alone. Instead, the scribes and scholars of all three languages faced the same challenge: to determine how to record vocalisation without creating new letters or radically amending the text of their scripture. They accomplished this goal first with diacritic points, but between the seventh and eleventh centuries they invented and deployed many other graphical tools for recording vowels. These innovations also prompted medieval linguists to begin writing about vocalisation to explain the function of the new vowel signs. In doing so, they developed novel linguistic theories with technical terminology that merged their pedagogical traditions with the growing fields of Semitic grammar.

This book examines these ideas about Arabic, Syriac, and Hebrew vocalisation as they emerged in the early medieval Middle East. It traces their evolution during the period before 1100, following the story of each tradition as it matured from the first attempts at partial vocalisation to the complete vowel systems known in the modern day. J. B. Segal told a related story in his book, *The Diacritical Point and the Accents in Syriac* (1953), which examines the origin and development of pointing in Syriac. In its preface, he writes: "To have discussed possible points of contact with Hebrew manuscripts or with Arabic would have disrupted the continuity of the story" (Segal 1953, vii). This choice is understandable, given the scope of his project, but none of these linguistic traditions developed in a vacuum. Syriac grammarians and Hebrew Masoretes exchanged theories of vocalisation as early as the seventh or eighth century, and the first Qurʾānic vocalisers adapted their system from Syriac at the same time. From the ninth century onwards, both Syriac and Hebrew scholars also adapted elements of Arabic phonological thought to explain their own languages. It is thus impossible to achieve a comprehensive understanding of any one Semitic vocalisation tradition without placing it in the proper context of its neighbours. The story, so to speak, has many characters, and if any are absent, then its clarity declines dramatically. As such, this book will compare the phonological theories that Syriac, Arabic, and Hebrew linguists used to describe vocalisation in order to demonstrate how their three traditions were linked in the period between 600 and 1100 CE.

1.0. Organisation and Scope

In writing this introduction, I cannot help but think of the preface to Shelomo Morag's book, *The Vocalization Systems of Arabic, Hebrew, and Aramaic* (1961). He begins it by saying:

> This study is not a complete history of the vocalization systems of Arabic, Hebrew, and Aramaic, nor does it pretend to be one. The time for writing a full history of these vocalization systems has not yet come; much work remains to be done in the examination of mss. and printed texts before such a history can be written. (Morag 1961, 5)

Morag wrote this preface in 1959, and his caveat—"[t]he time... has not yet come".—is no longer true. While Morag already had access to some foundational books that remain relevant, including Nabia Abbott's *The Rise of the North Arabic Script* (1939), J. P. P. Martin's *Histoire de la ponctuation* (1875), Theodore Nöldeke's *Compendious Syriac Grammar* (1904), J. B. Segal's *The Diacritical Point and the Accents in Syriac* (1953), and S. Baer and H. L. Strack's *Dikduke ha-Ṭeʿamim des Ahron ben Moscheh ben Ascher*

(1879), these works were insufficient for establishing a clear history of vocalisation. *The Rise of the North Arabic Script*, for example, focused on the history of the Arabic script, to which the vowel signs were merely an accessory that Abbott did not systematically evaluate (Abbott 1939, 21, 39, 65; see Posegay 2021c). Similarly, Nöldeke's discussion of the vowels is almost entirely descriptive, and makes up just a fraction of his grammar (Nöldeke 1904, §§4–21, 40–54). Segal's analysis is more detailed and incorporates more medieval primary sources on vocalisation (Segal 1953, 7–47), but his heart really belonged to the accent signs. Moreover, *Dikduke ha-Teʿamim des Ahron ben Moscheh ben Ascher* has turned out to contain a number of texts that Aharon ben Asher did not actually write (see Dotan 1967). None of these books were comprehensive accounts of vocalisation and could only serve as starting points for Morag—hence the statement in his preface. The result is that his own book is mainly a description of the forms and functions of Arabic, Hebrew, and Aramaic vocalisation systems, not an analysis of their formative principles and connections. However, our understanding of vocalisation has advanced considerably in the last 60 years, with new studies of both manuscripts and medieval philological texts allowing for a more complete reconstruction of the history of vocalisation.

Regarding Arabic, Abbott herself supplemented her conclusions on vocalisation in *The Rise of the North Arabic Script* with *Studies in Arabic Literary Papyri* (1972, 5–11), and her work, plus studies like Geoffrey Khan's *Arabic Papyri* (1992a), have illuminated the origins of vocalisation signs in non-Qurʾanic manuscripts. Meanwhile, books like François Déroche's *Les Manuscrits*

du Coran (1983) and *The Abbasid Tradition* (1992),[1] along with
Alain George's *The Rise of Islamic Calligraphy* (2010, esp. 74–80)
have clarified the early landscape of vocalised Qurʾānic manuscripts. E. J. Revell (1975), Yasin Dutton (1999; 2000), and
George (2015) have also explored the origins and development
of the Arabic dot systems, while scholars like Kees Versteegh
(1977; 1993), A. A. al-Nassir (1993), and Rafael Talmon (1997b;
2003) have surveyed the technical terminology that the first Arabic grammarians used for vocalisation. There are also now many
more published editions of medieval Arabic linguistic texts than
there were in Morag's day, including: *al-Muḥkam fī Naqṭ al-
Maṣāḥif* (1960), *Risāla Asbāb Ḥudūth al-Ḥurūf* (1983), *Kitāb al-
ʿAyn* (1985), *Kitāb Sībawayh* (1986), and *Sirr Ṣināʿa al-Iʿrāb*
(1993). These sources reveal the theoretical principles behind Arabic vocalisation as well as links to Syriac and Greek.

For Syriac, since Morag, a number of authors have examined the use of vowel points in the manuscript tradition of medieval Syriac scribes, as well as the tradition of Syriac grammarians
after the seventh century. In particular, George Kiraz's *Tūrrāṣ
Mamllā: A Grammar of the Syriac Language* (2012) has widened
the view of the Syriac manuscript tradition, and his book *The
Syriac Dot* (2015) has reconstructed the history of the diacritic
dot with somewhat more readability than that of Segal. Jonathan
Loopstra (2009; 2014; 2015; 2019) has also done considerable
work to bring the East Syrian *mashlmɔnutɔ* tradition to the fore.

---

[1] See also, Déroche (2014) and Déroche et al. (2015, 222–24), the latter
of which is only a brief overview, but contains extensive references to
early vocalised Arabic manuscripts.

Similarly, J. F. Coakley (2011) has shown that the 'Western' vowel signs were a fairly late innovation, greatly clarifying the history of the vowel signs, especially as they relate to Jacob of Edessa. Other Syriac scholars have placed great emphasis on Jacob of Edessa as the first and most important source of early medieval Syriac grammar (Revell 1972; Salvesen 2001; ter Haar Romeny 2008; Farina 2018), and rightly so, as Jacob's works remain central to understanding Syriac vocalisation. We also now have a more precise understanding of Classical Syriac morphophonology, thanks to studies like Ebbe Knudsen's *Classical Syriac Phonology* (2015) and Aaron Butts' *Language Change in the Wake of Empire* (2016). Scholars like Adam Becker (2003; 2006; 2010), Aaron Butts, and Simcha Gross (2020) have also investigated the degree of intellectual contact between Jews and Syriac Christians in the late antique and early Islamic periods, a situation which has direct bearing on the early history of vocalisation. Daniel King (2012) and Raphael Talmon (2000a; 2000b) have done similar work comparing Syriac and the early Arabic grammatical tradition. All of this material together means that not only are we in a better position than Morag to chart the history of Syriac vocalisation, but we can also more easily examine its relationships with Hebrew and Arabic.

Morag himself did some further work on Hebrew vocalisation history, particularly examining early Masoretic technical terminology (1973; 1974; 1979), and other scholars have made great strides to advance the understanding of Hebrew vocalisation since then. Aron Dotan has dominated this field, editing a more accurate version of Ben Asher's *Diqduqe ha-Ṭeʿamim* (1967), investigating the origins of Masoretic activity (1974; 1981), and producing one of the most comprehensive summaries of Hebrew vocalisation in his *Encyclopedia Judaica* article, 'Masora' (2007). Israel Yeivin's *Introduction to the Tiberian Masora* (trans. Revell, 1983) condensed the notes of the Tiberian Masora into a digestible form for the first time, and he also wrote what remains the seminal work on Babylonian Masora and vocalisation (1985). As for the Tiberian tradition, Geoffrey Khan's work on Karaite transcriptions of Hebrew in Arabic script (1990; 1992b) and the recovery of additional medieval linguistic texts from the Cairo Genizah have proven essential for understanding its features since Morag's time. Most importantly, nearly the full text of *Hidāya al-Qārī* has emerged from the Firkovich Collection, which Khan utilised for his monumental work, *The Tiberian Pronunciation Tradition of Biblical Hebrew* (2020). Several other scholars have also published medieval Judaeo-Arabic sources, mostly from the Cairo Genizah, that are critical to the history of Hebrew vocalisation, notably Nehemiah Allony (1964; 1965; 1983), Allony and Yeivin (1985), and Ilan Eldar (1981). All of this work allows us to reconstruct much of the history of the Tiberian Masoretes and compare their vocalisation tradition to those of Syriac and Arabic grammarians (e.g., see Talmon 1997a; 2000a).

So while for Morag the time for writing a full history of Arabic, Hebrew, and Aramaic[2] vocalisation had "not yet come," such a history can feasibly be written today. Still, it is not my intention to write that history, at least not in its entirety. This book does not, for example, survey the use of vocalisation signs

---

[2] By which he mainly means Syriac; see Morag (1961, 46–59).

in any manuscript corpora, nor does it exhaustively account for all the signs that saw use during the medieval period. Mostly for reasons of time and space, it also does not take up any sources related to Samaritan vocalisation system, which surely has some bearing on other systems, and it mentions the Babylonian and Palestinian Hebrew systems only occasionally.[3] Instead, it focuses on the phonological concepts that medieval scholars developed to describe the new technology of 'vocalisation signs' in the Arabic, Syriac, and Tiberian Hebrew writing systems. These concepts changed over time, and the history of that evolution is also a record of interchange between scholars of different languages and faiths.

1.1. Summary of Sections

Broadly speaking, medieval Semitic linguists exchanged ideas over the course of three phases in the history of vocalisation. The phases overlap and their duration differs somewhat between languages, but Arabic, Syriac, and Hebrew all follow this same trajectory. First, a 'relative' phase, near the infancy of the graphical vocalisation systems, when people explained vowels by describing their phonetic features in contrast to other vowels. This phase spans the period from the first Syriac diacritic dots to roughly the end of the eighth century. Second, an 'absolute' phase, when the graphical vocalisation systems solidified in their final forms, and grammarians began assigning names to their vowels on an absolute, one-to-one basis. This phase begins with the introduction of

---

[3] For details on these systems, see Morag (1961, 30–41); Dotan (2007, §§5.1–2, 6).

the Arabic red-dot vocalisation system and the eighth-century Arabic scholars who first applied absolute vowel-naming conventions. It continues through the tenth century. Third, a 'consolidation' phase, mainly in the tenth and eleventh centuries, when scholars sought to tie together the disparate theoretical threads that their predecessors created to explain vocalisation. This period is marked by the growing dominance of Arabic in the Middle East and an increase in its influence on the phonological ideas of Syriac and Hebrew.

While the following discussion traces each language through these phases, its main goal is to detect and explore points of contact between different linguistic traditions. The chief method for finding these connections is the identification of technical terms that appear in primary sources across multiple traditions. This study thus includes a wide survey of the technical terminology that Arabic, Syriac, and Hebrew scholars used to explain vowels, aiming to define them as accurately as possible in their native contexts. It then examines the usage of the shared terminology to determine how and when certain terms may have crossed between traditions. Sometimes these terms are direct loan words, but more often they are calques, usually from Syriac, Arabic, or Greek, that were adapted to fit a new purpose in another tradition. From these shared terms it is then possible to analyse the chronology and direction of intellectual exchange among medieval Semitic linguists.

This book addresses the intellectual history of vocalisation in three sections. The first, chapter 2, surveys the different ways that medieval linguists described vowels as a phonological category that was distinct from consonants. It includes three subsections, each addressing a fundamental principle that links Arabic, Syriac, and Hebrew scholars in the field of vowel phonology: the idea of 'sounding' letters (§2.1); the perception of vowels as 'movements' (§2.2); and the dual nature of the *matres lectionis* (§2.3). These principles provide the foundation for further lines of inquiry related to vocalisation.

Chapter 3 examines the phenomenon of 'relative' vocalisation, drawing on some of the earliest sources that address Semitic vowel phonology in the eighth century. Its first subsection describes the similarities between Syriac grammarians and Hebrew Masoretes in the first attempts to distinguish homographs in their versions of the Bible (§3.1). Specifically, it highlights the apparent exchange of a phonological concept of 'height' as it relates to vowel articulation and the placement of vocalisation points. The second subsection then applies the same relative principle to early Arabic vowel phonology, linking it to the names of the Arabic inflectional cases and to the Sībawayhan description of allophones of the letter *'alif* (§3.2).

Chapter 4 follows the transition from relative·vocalisation to the first 'absolute' vowel naming systems in each language, comparing all three histories to show where they intertwine. It first addresses the chronological development of vowel names in Arabic grammar, putting it in context with the Syriac grammatical tradition during the eighth and ninth centuries (§4.1). Next, it traces Syriac vowel names from their earliest occurrence in the late eighth century to the grammars of the eleventh century

(§4.2). It then surveys the various conventions by which Hebrew scholars named their vowels in comparison with both Arabic and Syriac (§4.3). Each of these subsections extends to the attempts of relatively later authors to consolidate earlier ideas about vocalisation, examining conceptual and terminological developments in the late tenth and eleventh centuries.

Altogether, these discussions show that medieval Arabic, Syriac, and Hebrew linguists had many points of contact with each other as they dealt with the problem of vocalisation in their respective languages. The links between them reveal an interconnected, interfaith intellectual landscape between the seventh and eleventh centuries, one that continues to have implications for the modern reading of these three languages.

1.2. Defining Terms

As will soon become apparent, this book is intensely interested in technical terms, and many of its questions would be much easier to resolve if modern vocalisation studies did not maintain a long tradition of vague and confusing terminology. I define my own terms here.

'Vocalisation' refers both to the process of physically adding vowel signs to a text and to the intellectual domain that explains the creation, function, and application of those signs. This application process may also be called 'pointing.' A 'vocalisation system' is a set of signs that represent the vowel inventory of a particular pronunciation tradition. These include the Syriac dot system, the Syriac miniature letter-form system,[4] the Arabic red-dot system, the modern Arabic system, the Tiberian Hebrew system, the Palestinian Hebrew system, and the Babylonian Hebrew system. A 'vocalisation sign' or 'vowel sign' is a point, dot, or other small grapheme that stands for a vowel phoneme, for example: an Arabic red dot, the Syriac *zqɔpɔ* dots, or the Tiberian *qɔmeṣ* symbol. A 'vowel name' is an individual term that refers to a single vowel, although, depending on its context and author, it may refer to either a phoneme or a grapheme. For example, Arabic *fatḥa* 'opening', Syriac *ptɔḥɔ* 'opening', and Hebrew *pataḥ* 'opening' all indicate the phoneme /a/, but may also refer to different graphemes that represent /a/.

By contrast, 'diacritic mark', 'diacritic dot', or 'diacritic sign' refers to a grapheme that is added to a word to clarify the pronunciation of it or one of its letters in some way. These include the Arabic consonantal *ʾiʿjām* dots, the Syriac dots on *rish* and *dalat*, and the Hebrew *dagesh*, as well as signs like *shadda*, *sukūn*, *seyame*, *qushshɔyɔ*, *rafe*, and *mappiq*. This category does not include any graphemes that regularly represent vowels.

'Accents points', 'cantillation signs', and 'reading dots' (Loopstra 2019, 160–61; Kiraz 2015, 114–19) refer to the systems of dots and signs that indicate intonation and cadence in Hebrew

---

[4] Traditionally known as the 'Western' Syriac system (though not limited to Western Syriac), my designation is based on terms that Nabia Abbott ("small-letter vowels" or "letter signs"; Abbott 1972, 9–11) and E. J. Revell ("letter-form signs"; Revell 1975, 180) coined to describe Arabic diacritics and vocalisation.

and Syriac texts of the Bible. They are generally tangential to the discussions below.

'Punctuation' is a troublesome word and I avoid it whenever possible. Nineteenth- and twentieth-century scholars of vocalisation used it ambiguously to refer either to all dots in manuscripts (regardless of their function), or to refer to the process of adding dots (the process which I call 'vocalisation' and 'pointing').[5] These meanings are now slightly archaic, and they have become conflated with the idea of 'punctuation' as the set of signs that separate clauses in English syntax (comma, semicolon, full stop, etc.).

'Relative vocalisation' is a term for a method of vocalisation that identifies vowels relative to other vowels in the same position, often by comparing homographs that have the same consonants but different vowels. It extends to the comparative terminology which some medieval linguists used to differentiate vowels. These systems include the Syriac diacritic dot system, the early Masoretic *milleʿel-milleraʿ* system, and the early Arabic system for describing allophones of *ʾalif*.

'Absolute vocalisation' is my term for vocalisation systems which can mark and name their phonemic vowels on a one-to-one basis. These are the systems that readers of Semitic languages are most familiar with, including the modern Arabic system, the Syriac miniature letter-form system, and the Tiberian pointing system.

A glossary of vocalisation terminology used in primary sources appears at the end of this book.

---

[5] For example, see Nutt (1870).

2.0. Primary Sources

While I am indebted to the many contemporary scholars who have taken up these topics before me, the core of this book relies on readings of primary texts written by medieval linguists. The following is a chronological overview of the sources that make up the bulk of my corpus. This study is limited to authors who were active before the end of the eleventh century, as after that time the main Semitic vocalisation systems were fully developed. These sources do not exhaustively represent the grammatical traditions of their respective languages, but I have chosen them in order to best show the relationships between Arabic, Syriac, and Hebrew within a manageable corpus. Additional minor sources will be introduced as needed throughout. Unless otherwise noted, translations of Semitic sources are my own.

2.1. Sources for Arabic

Our earliest substantial source for Arabic phonological thought is also the oldest extant Arabic lexicon, *Kitāb al-ʿAyn* (*The Book of the ʿAyn*), compiled mainly by al-Layth ibn al-Muẓaffar (d. c. 803) around the year 800 (Makhzumi 1985; Sellheim 2012a; 2012b; Schoeler 2006, 142–63). It contains a sizable introduction by al-Layth's teacher, al-Khalīl ibn Aḥmad al-Farāhīdī (d. 786 or 791), in which al-Khalīl describes the phonetic features of the Arabic alphabet. This introduction is our primary focus, but the definitions of some terms in the lexical portion of the book are also relevant to the discussion, as they contain important early grammatical teachings (Talmon 1997b).

Sībawayh (d. 793 or 796), the most famous of al-Khalīl's students, needs little introduction. He is the most influential Arabic grammarian, and his *Kitāb Sībawayh* (*Sībawayh's Book*), also known simply as the *Kitāb*, was the foundation for the Basran school of Arabic grammar (Sībawayh 1986). No other grammar has matched its comprehensive coverage of the Arabic language, and it contains several sections devoted to Arabic phonology (al-Nassir 1993). The vocalisation terms in these sections persist in Arabic to this day, and they also appear in medieval texts that describe Syriac and Hebrew.

An important source for understanding the theories behind Arabic technical terminology is *al-Īḍāḥ fī 'Illal al-Naḥw* (*Clarification of the Reasons of Grammar*) by Abū al-Qāsim al-Zajjājī (d. 948/949). Al-Zajjājī was a student of the more famous grammarian Abū Isḥāq al-Sarī al-Zajjāj (d. 922/928), and his *Īḍāḥ* explains the reasons behind the naming of the Arabic inflectional system that relates to vocalisation (al-Zajjājī 1959).

Abū al-Fatḥ 'Uthmān ibn Jinnī (d. 1002) was a direct intellectual successor to Sībawayh, and his *Sirr Ṣinā'a al-I'rāb* (*The Secret of Making Proper Arabic*) is critical to understanding the development of Arabic vocalisation (Ibn Jinnī 1993). It is the first comprehensive study of Arabic phonology (Alfozan 1989, 2), and in it, Ibn Jinnī clarifies and expands the principles of vocalisation laid out in *Kitāb Sībawayh*. This book is particularly important for showing the refinement of Arabic vocalisation terminology in the tenth century.

A less grammatical source is the encyclopaedia *Mafātīḥ al-'Ulūm* (*The Keys to the Sciences*), written by Muḥammad ibn

Aḥmad al-Khwārizmī (d. 997) around 977. It is one of the earliest Arabic encyclopaedias (Bosworth 1963, 19; see Fischer 1985; Talmon 1997b, 263–64), and in it al-Khwārizmī—a Persian scholar who was not a grammarian—gathers vowel names from multiple different traditions (al-Khwārizmī 1968). He claims to draw on the work of al-Khalīl, as well as Greek sources, and lists several terms that refer to non-cardinal vowels.

Another source by a non-grammarian is *Risāla Asbāb Ḥudūth al-Ḥurūf* (*The Treatise on the Causes of the Occurrence of Letters*), an essay by Abū ʿAlī ibn Sīnā (d. 1037) (al-Tayyan and Mir Alam 1983). Ibn Sīnā was a polymath, but he made his career as a physician and philosopher, and he analyses Arabic vocalisation through the lens of biomechanics. The first half of the essay is an acoustic study of Arabic, while the second half classifies the Arabic letters, revealing connections to Greek and Syriac phonetic concepts.

Al-Muḥkam fī Naqt al-Maṣāḥif (*The Rules for Pointing the Codices*), by the *tajwīd* scholar Abū ʿAmr al-Dānī (d. 1053), details the history and proper usage of the Arabic vowel points, emphasising the appearance of the dots in manuscripts (al-Dānī 1960). It provides evidence for the evolution of Arabic vocalisation terminology in the eleventh century and explains the relationships between phonetic features and dots.

2.2. Sources for Syriac

The most important sources that explain early Syriac vocalisation are three works by Jacob of Edessa (d. 708), a renowned West Syriac bishop and grammarian (ter Haar Romeny 2008; esp.

Salvesen 2008; Kruisheer 2008).[6] His *Letter on Orthography* explains the significance of the diacritical point to Syriac writing, while the tractate *On Persons and Tenses* (Phillips 1869) links vowel phonology directly to diacritic dots. After these two short works, Jacob also wrote the first true Syriac grammar, the *Turrɔṣ Mamllɔ Nahrɔyɔ* (*The Correct Form of Mesopotamian Speech*). Although it survives only in fragments (Wright 1871),[7] the introduction to this book presents vowel letters in a way that allows us to connect Greek phonology to the Syriac, Arabic, and Hebrew vocalisation traditions.

Other early Syriac sources include the works of Dawid bar Pawlos (fl. c. 770–800), an abbot from northern Mesopotamia who lived during the late eighth and early ninth centuries (Brock 2011; Posegay 2021b, 152–55). He wrote a few fragmentary works on Syriac grammar, including sections on the nature of speech and vocalisation (Gottheil 1893), as well as several letters on philological topics (Barsoum 1987, 325–29; Moosa 2003, 372–76). Dawid's grammatical writings provide important clarifications related to the descriptions of vowels in Jacob of Edessa's work, and they show the importance of poetry in the history of Syriac vocalisation. Also of note is a grammatical *scholion* which

---

[6] See also, Baumstark (1922, 248–56); Barsoum (1987, 291–306); Brock (1997, 57–60); Moosa (2003, 334–50).

[7] On the status of Jacob's extant grammatical works, see Farina (2018). Gorgias Press is about to republish Jacob's grammar with accompanying English translation in a forthcoming reprint of Merx's *De Artis Grammatica*.

he wrote on the *bgdkt* letters, which contains some of the earliest attested Syriac vowel names.[8]

Another early source for absolute vowel names in Syriac is the version of *Ktɔbɔ d-Shmɔhe Dɔmyɔye* (*The Book of Similar Words*) by Ḥunayn ibn Isḥāq (d. 873) (Hoffmann 1880, 2–49). Ḥunayn was a key figure in the Syriac-Arabic translation movement, and he expanded this text from an earlier work by ʿEnani-shoʿ, a seventh-century monk (Childers 2011). Besides *Ktɔbɔ d-Shmɔhe Dɔmyɔye*, Ḥunayn also wrote one of the first Syriac-Arabic lexica. While no longer extant, this lexicon was foundational to further Syriac lexicographic activity during the tenth century.

The first known lexicographer to make use of Ḥunayn's translation work was ʿĪsā ibn ʿAlī (d. c. 900), and his Syriac-Arabic lexicon saw several revisions over the course of the tenth century (Hoffmann 1874; Gottheil 1908; 1928; see Butts 2009). It includes a considerable number of technical terms related to vocalisation, and it offers a terminological link between the work of Ḥunayn and that of the eleventh-century Syriac grammarians.

The second major extant Syriac-Arabic lexicon is that of Ishoʿ bar Bahlul (fl. 942–968) (Duval 1901). This book straddles the line between dictionary and encyclopaedia, and Bar Bahlul frequently cites other lexicographers from the ninth century. It saw several expansions in the centuries after his death, but remains an important source for examining the practical usage of vocalisation terms to describe vowel phonemes and morphology.

---

[8] MS Jerusalem, St. Mark's Monastery (SMMJ) 356, fols 164v–166r and MS Mardin, Dayr al-Zaʿfarān (ZFRN) 192, fols 199r–200r. An edition and French translation of this text will appear in Farina (2021).

It also contains several definitions that connect Syriac phonology to other linguistic traditions.

Another relevant source for vowel naming is MS London, British Library Additional 12138, the well-known codex of East Syriac *mashlmɔnutɔ* completed in 899 (Wright 1870, I:101; Loopstra 2014; 2015, II:XIII, XXXVIII–XXXIX). This text is also sometimes referred to as the East Syriac 'Masora', based on some similarities with the Hebrew Masoretic tradition (Merx 1889, 29–30). It contains several dozen marginal notes, mostly added after the ninth century, that are useful evidence for the detection of early vowel names.

Elias bar Shinɔyɔ of Nisibis (d. 1046), also known as Elias of Ṣoba, was an East Syriac bishop who wrote extensively in both Arabic and Syriac throughout the first half of the eleventh century (Merx 1889, 109; Teule 2011b). His most significant work for the history of Syriac vocalisation is the *Turrɔṣ Mamllɔ Suryɔyɔ* (*The Correct Form of Syriac Speech*) (Gottheil 1887).[9] This grammar draws on the earlier work of scholars like Jacob of Edessa and Ḥunayn ibn Isḥāq while also incorporating concepts from the Arabic grammatical tradition. It is notable for including a set of absolute names for every Syriac vowel.

Another Eastern bishop, Elias of Ṭirhan (d. 1049), was a contemporary of Elias of Nisibis, and he wrote a Syriac grammar known as the *Memrɔ Gramaṭiqɔyɔ* (*The Grammatical Essay*) (Merx 1889, 137, 154–57; Teule 2011a). Elias wrote this book prior to

---

[9] Gottheil's edition includes an English translation. Bertaina (2011, 199–200) summarises the contents of the entire book, which Elias apparently wrote for a deacon who was also a scribe.

his promotion to Catolicos in 1028, adapting substantial elements from the Arabic grammatical tradition to fit Syriac for the benefit of an Arabic-speaking audience. This work is also known as *Turrɔṣ Mamllɔ Suryɔyɔ* (*The Correct Form of Syriac Speech*), based on the title which appears in the main manuscript of Baethgen's edition (1880). However, due to his perception of Elias's work as somewhat ad-hoc in its organisation, Merx argues that the identification given by ʿAbdishɔ is more appropriate (1889, 157); that is, *Memrɔ Gramaṭiqɔyɔ* (*The Grammatical Essay*). Merx seems particularly keen to minimise the importance of Elias of Ṭirhan, due to his status as one of the 'Arabising' grammarians, in contrast to Syriac writers like Elias of Nisibis, who did not adopt as many Arabic grammatical ideas (1889, 112–24, 138, 157). In an effort to reduce the already substantial confusion between Elias of Nisibis and Elias of Ṭirhan, I will refer to the latter's grammatical book as *Memrɔ Gramaṭiqɔyɔ*, but my use of this title is not intended to reinforce Merx's unfair reductionism. This work includes several important sections on vocalisation and uses absolute vowel names that differ from those of Elias of Nisibis.

2.3. Sources for Hebrew

One of the most important sources for Hebrew vocalisation is the corpus of Hebrew and Aramaic word lists from the Tiberian Masora. These include lists that compare homographs that differ in their vowels (Dotan 1974),[10] as well as lists of vowel names and their signs (Steiner 2005). These lists are nearly all anonymous,

---

[10] Several of the lists relevant to this book are published in Ginsburg (1880); see §3.1.2.

but they illuminate the early development of Masoretic vocalisation practices and show remarkable similarities with the work of Syriac grammarians.

Diqduqe ha-Teʿamim (*The Fine Details of the Accents*) by Aharon ben Asher (d. c. 960) is probably the most famous Masoretic treatise (Dotan 1967). It examines difficult sections of the Tiberian recitation tradition with respect to accents, but it also utilises early Hebrew terminology related to vowel names. Ben Asher lived in the tenth century, during a period when most Masoretic treatises were written in Arabic, but *Diqduqe ha-Teʿamim* is in Hebrew, suggesting that some of its material may predate the tenth century (Khan 2020, I:116–17).

Kutub al-Lugha (*The Books of the Language*), the Judaeo-Arabic grammar of Hebrew by Saadia Gaon (d. 942), is one of the earliest true Hebrew 'grammatical' works (Dotan 1997; see Brody 2016; Malter 1921). Its fifth chapter, *al-Qawl fi al-Nagham* (*The Discourse on Melody*), deals directly with Hebrew vocalisation (Skoss 1952). It includes the most complete description of the Hebrew 'vowel scale', a key concept that helps link the Masoretes to Syriac grammarians. Saadia also adopts plenty of Arabic grammatical terminology and additional concepts from Arabic phonology. In 931, sometime after *Kutub al-Lugha*, Saadia wrote his *Commentary on Sefer Yeṣira* (*Commentary on the Book of Creation*), which contains several passages that are also relevant to vocalisation and vowel naming (Lambert 1891, 45, 52 [Arabic]; 76 n. 1 [French]).

Some of the most overlooked sources on Hebrew vocalisation are a subgenre of Masoretic texts which I refer to as *muṣawwitāt* 'vowels' works (see Eldar 1986). These are Judaeo-Arabic treatises on Hebrew vocalisation and accents that preserve terminology that does not appear in the Tiberian Masora, *Diqduqe ha-Teʿamim*, or *Kutub al-Lugha*. They are known mainly from anonymous fragmentary manuscripts in Cairo Genizah collections, most likely written in the tenth or eleventh centuries. This study analyses five such works published by Allony and Yeivin (Allony 1965; 1983; Allony and Yeivin 1985), and occasionally refers to unpublished texts from other manuscripts in the Genizah. They are critical for reconstructing the internal development of Hebrew vocalisation as well as for demonstrating links with the Arabic grammatical tradition.

A similar text from the Genizah that does have a title is *Kitāb Naḥw al-ʿIbrānī* (*The Book of Hebrew Inflection*), probably from the eleventh century (Eldar 1981). Only one fragment is extant, but it contains another version of the Hebrew vowel scale arranged according to the Arabic case system, providing additional data for the development of the scale and Hebrew vowel names. Its version of the scale appears to be an Arabic translation of a Hebrew Masoretic text, known as *Nequdot Omeṣ ha-Miqrɔ* (*The Dots of the Greatness of the Scripture*), found in Baer and Strack's *Dikduke ha-Teʿamim* (1879, 34–36, §36).

Two further tenth-century Arabic sources are *Kitāb al-Tanqīṭ* (*The Book of Pointing*) and *Kitāb al-Afʿal Dhuwāt Ḥurūf al-Līn* (*The Book of Verbs with Soft Letters*) by Judah ben David Ḥayyūj (d. c. 1000), an Andalusī scholar who adopted Arabic grammatical terminology and actively compared Hebrew with Arabic (Nutt 1870; Jastrow 1897; Basal 1999, 227). The former work is a short text that shows the evolution of some early Hebrew vowel-naming conventions, while the latter is a lexicographical account of weak roots in Hebrew, including considerable morphophonological analysis based on concepts from Arabic grammar.

Finally, the most comprehensive medieval source on the Tiberian recitation tradition is *Hidāya al-Qārī* (*The Guide for the Reader*), a Judaeo-Arabic book by Abū al-Faraj Hārūn (d. c. 1050) (Khan 2020, I:119–20; II). He wrote two versions of this work—one long and one short—but this book relies on the long version as a more comprehensive source. It consists of three sections, one each on consonants, vowels, and accents, but naturally the section on vowels is our main interest. It consolidates vowel names from multiple traditions, makes frequent use of Arabic technical terms, and includes another version of the vowel scale divided accorded to Arabic grammatical principles. It is thus an appropriate capstone for the history of vocalisation at the end of the Masoretic period.

Now, with all of that said, we can get to the points.

2. CONCEPTUALISING VOWELS

The discussion on the 'kings'; but if you want to say the discus-
sion on the 'melodies' or the discussion on the 'inflections', then
that has the same meaning. (Abū al-Faraj Hārūn [d. c. 1050],
The Guide for the Reader [Khan 2020, II:117])

Even from our earliest sources, Semitic linguists had long grap-
pled with the differences between vowels and consonants, both
phonetically and in terms of their traditional orthography. The
primary distinction for many was that vowels could be pronounced on their own, whereas consonants required a vowel to
facilitate their articulation. They were ultimately familiar with
this concept due to contact with the Greek grammatical tradition,
and they adopted the ideas of 'sounding' letters and phonetic
'movement' to explain it. Conversely, many linguists also recognised that Semitic writing systems did not clearly delineate vowels and consonants, leading to diverse interpretations as to the
nature and function of the *matres lectionis* letters. These three concepts—sounding letters, movement, and *matres lectionis*—were
fundamental for talking about vocalisation, and their principles
crosscut the Arabic, Syriac, and Hebrew philological traditions.
This section addresses each of them in turn.

1.0. Sounding it Out: Construction of a Vowel
Category

One of the most common ways that medieval Semitic linguists
described vowels was with the concept of 'sounding' letters.
Quite simply, vowels were called 'sounding' because they had

     https://doi.org/10.11647/OBP.0271.02

some inherent sonorous quality, whereas consonants were 'soundless' unless accompanied by a vowel. This idea can be traced back to the Greek linguistic tradition, but entered Semitic linguistics through the Syriac grammarian Jacob of Edessa (d. 708). Jacob first adapted the Greek concept of sounding letters in order to solve a particularly thorny issue in his career: it was impossible to write a satisfactory grammar with only the rudimentary Syriac diacritic system. As a result, he calqued a Greek concept of vowel letters from Dionysius Thrax's *Technē Grammatikē*—*phōnēenta* 'sounded ones'—into Syriac as *qolonoyoto*. Jacob's eighth-century successor, Dawid bar Pawlos (fl. c. 770–800), clarified the meaning of this term (Gottheil 1893), and by the tenth century, Hebrew scholars had adopted the concept as well. The word—now calqued into Arabic as *muṣawwitāt*—appears in phonological contexts in Judaeo-Arabic linguistic texts from this time, including the work of Saadia Gaon (d. 942) and several Masoretic treatises. The division of 'sounding' and 'soundless' letters is also attested in Ibn Sīnā's writing (d. 1037), even as his Syriac contemporary, Elias of Ṭirhan (d. 1049), modified Jacob of Edessa's original *qolonoyoto* model to fit a different Syriac phonological understanding.

These terms—*phōnēenta, qolonoyoto, muṣawwitāt*—are often translated as 'voiced', reflecting modern linguistic terminology (e.g., Talmon 2000b, 250). This is also the etymology of the English word 'vowel', ultimately descended from Latin *vocalis* 'sounding, vocal', itself a calque of Greek *phōnêen*. However, none of the authors discussed below use these terms to refer to the modern concept of linguistic voicing. Instead, they indicate a distinct phonological category which includes the vowels (indeed, all of them 'voiced'), but (generally) not consonants, voiced or otherwise. I translate them as 'sounding' to avoid conflating these concepts.

1.1. The First Sounding Letters

The earliest evidence of Syriac sounding letters comes from Jacob of Edessa (d. 708), a seventh-century bishop and grammarian whose work reflects a combination of Greek concepts and Syrian terminology. Even in the seventh century, Jacob was already part of a Syriac tradition that had dealt with vowel notation for hundreds of years, and had developed a written system of diacritic dots to indicate non-consonantal phonetic information. These dots were placed based on the relative quality of vowels in a given word when compared to a homograph, and were thus a form of relative vowel notation (Segal 1953, 3–6, 9–12, 28; Kiraz 2012, I:12, 20, 64; 2015, 36–37, 94–98). The diacritic system evolved throughout the sixth and seventh centuries, eventually allowing scribes to use multiple dots to mark more than one vowel in a single word, but it did not reach a level of one-to-one correspondence between vowels and signs until the eighth century (Segal 1953, 9, 29–30; Kiraz 2012, I:12, 21, 70–71; 2015, 101–2). Thus, at the end of the seventh century, Jacob of Edessa lacked graphemes for the absolute marking of Syriac vowels. To some extent, it seems that he was content with this writing system, as he composed a short grammatical tractate, *On Persons and Tenses*, which laid out some rules for Syriac morphology as they related to the placement of the dots. He also wrote his *Letter on*

Orthography to one George of Sarug, pointedly detailing instructions for how scribes should use the diacritic dot (Phillips 1869; see also, Farina 2018). However, this relative dot system was insufficient for writing a proper grammar of Syriac, so later in his career Jacob took more drastic measures (Segal 1953, 40; Talmon 2008, 167).

In the introduction to his landmark grammar *Turrɔṣ Mamllɔ Nahrɔyɔ* (*The Correct Form of Mesopotamian Speech*), Jacob explains the process by which the Greeks increased the number of letters in their alphabet from an original seventeen to its full twenty-four (Wright 1871, ܐ; Farina 2018, 176–77). He then addresses an unknown correspondent—their name is lost from the manuscript—who has requested that Jacob create additional letters to complete the Syriac alphabet (see Merx 1889, 51; Segal 1953, 41–43). Whether or not this correspondent was real, the idea of adding new letters to Syriac seems to have weighed on Jacob for some time, and he acquiesces, saying:

> ܐܡܪܢܐ ܕܝܢ ܕܢܬܣܝܡܘܢ ܢܘܡܘܣܐ ܡܚܬܪܝܐ ܠܡܡܠܠܐ ܗܢܐ. ܣܛܪ ܡܢ ܬܘܣܦܬܐ
> ܕܐܬܘܬܐ ܩܠܢܝܬܐ ܗܠܝܢ ܕܢܣܝܢ ܡܢ ܣܦܪܐ ܗܢܐ. ܕܒܐܝܕܝܗܝܢ ܡܬܚܙܐ ܐܝܟ
> ܠܚܘܝܘ ܢܣܝܢܘܬܗܘܢ ܕܗܠܝܢ ܢ̈ܡܘܣܐ. ܘܬܘܪܨܐ ܕܫ̈ܡܗܐ ܘܕܡ̈ܠܐ ܕܒܗܘܢ
> . ܘܒܗ ܡܢ ܬܪ̈ܬܝܗܝܢ ܐܘܪܚܬ: ܡܢ ܫܐܠܬܟ ܘܡܢ ܡܣܬܘܝܘ ܕܐܡܝܢܐ ܕܒܬ̈ܪܝܐ:
> ܗܘ ܕܐܝܟ ܠܟܘܢ ܕܡܢ ܩܕܡ. ܗܕܐ ܐܬܚܫܒܬ. ܕܒܗ ܡܛܠ ܗܢܐ ܘܬܘܩܢܐ
> ܕܠܗܘܢ ܕܩܘܢܝܐ ܕܠܟܘܢ ܡܬܬܩܦܘܢ ܐܬܘܬܐ: ܠܘܬ ܗ̇ܝ ܕܢܩܫܘܢ ܫܘܚܠܦܐ
> ܘܡܦܩܢܐ ܕܠܗܘܢ ܕܟܬܒ ܩܠܐ: ܘܠܐ ܗܘܐ ܡܛܠ ܫܘܚܠܦܐ ܘܬܘܩܢܐ ܕܠܗ
> ܕܣܦܪܐ.

Thus, I say that there should be established accurate [morphological] rules for this speech, without the addition of these 'sounding letters' which this script lacks, [letters] through which one can demonstrate the application of the rules and the proper forms of the nouns and verbs that are

established by them. But I have been compelled by two
things: by your request, and by the danger of the loss of
[previous] books, which is what motivated those who
came before me. This I have considered: that only for the
sake of the meaning [of words] and the construction of
rules are the letters added—insofar as they may show the
change and pronunciation of the sounds—and not for the
sake of perfecting and re-arranging the script. (Wright
1871, ܐ, Bodl. 159 fol. 1a, col. 1)

Diverging from *On Persons and Tenses*, Jacob admits that the Syriac writing system is insufficient for writing a comprehensive
grammar and that the diacritical dots cannot compensate for that
deficit.[1] Consequently, he introduces seven letters of a new
type—ʾatwɔtɔ qɔlɔnɔyɔtɔ 'sounding letters'—solely for grammatical explanations, and he uses them throughout the text to transcribe examples of Syriac morphology. Six of these letters are
novel symbols, likely modified forms of the Greek vowel letters,
and this addition is an imitation of the process that Jacob claims
occurred in the Greek script (Segal 1953, 42).[2] However, he does
retain the ʾalaph to represent a low backed *a*-vowel. He does away

---

[1] Judith Olszowy-Schlanger (2011, 366) and Nabia Abbott (1972, 6–7)
suggest that complete vocalisation systems were prerequisites for the
production of true 'grammars' of Hebrew and Arabic, respectively. Jacob seems to have reached the same conclusion for Syriac.

[2] Note that despite their similarity to the Greek vowels, Jacob's vowel
letters are not the source of the West Syriac vocalisation system that
uses Greek letter-form signs. J. F. Coakley (2011) has shown that these
signs are not attested until approximately the tenth century; see also,
Kiraz (2012, I:79–80); Loopstra (2009, 279).

with the other Syriac *matres lectionis*, with *waw* and *yod* both becoming regular consonants in the classification of sounding letters. Moreover, unlike the Greeks, Jacob only intended for his
letters to be pedagogical tools, not permanent additions to the
Syriac alphabet, and accordingly, they are only used in *Turrɔṣ
Mamllɔ Nahrɔyɔ* and in Bar Hebraeus' discussions of Jacob (Segal
1953, 44; Kiraz 2012, I:73–74).

Strange orthography notwithstanding, the term *ʾatwɔtɔ
qɔlɔnɔyɔtɔ* (sing. *ʾɔtɔ qɔlɔnɔytɔ*) reveals Jacob's conception of vowels as a phonological category. He uses it twice in the extant introduction (Wright 1871, ܐ, Bodl. 159 fol. 1a, and ܒ, Bodl. 159
fol. 2a, col. 1), setting it against the *ʾatwɔtɔ dlɔ qɔlɔ* 'letters without sound' (Wright 1871, ܒ, Bodl. 159 fol. 2a, col. 1), that is, the
consonants. As Rafael Talmon points out, these two categories
are calques of Greek terms for vowels and consonants: *phōnēenta*
'sounded' and *aphōna* 'soundless' (Talmon 2008, 177; 2000b,
250).

Jacob's source for these words is likely the *Technē Grammatikē* (*The Art of Grammar*) of Dionysius Thrax, a Greek grammarian who lived in the second century BCE (Fiano 2011; see
Merx 1889, 9–28, 50–72; Talmon 2000a, 337–38). In it, he classifies the Greek alphabet according to the amount of airflow
through the mouth during the articulation of each letter, saying:
"Of these letters, seven are vowels (*phōnēenta*), α, ε, η, ι, ο, υ, and
ω. They are called *phōnēenta* because they form a complete

sound (*phōnē*) by themselves" (Davidson 1874, 5).[3] The other seventeen letters are consonants, which "are called consonants because by themselves they have no sound, but produce a sound only when they are combined with vowels." The defining feature of a vowel in the *Technē* is thus that it can be pronounced alone, whereas consonants need a vowel to accompany them. The consonants are then further divided into 'half-sounding' (*hēmiphōna*): ζ ξ ψ λ μ ν ρ σ; which "are called *hēmiphōna* because, being less easily sounded than the vowels, when attempted to be pronounced alone, they result in hisses and mumblings" (Davidson 1874, 5–6). That is, these eight consonants are continuants[4] (/z/, /ks/, /ps/, /l/, /m/, /n/, /r/, /s/) which allow the partial passage of air, but cannot be fully articulated without a vowel. Finally, nine consonants are 'soundless' or 'mute' (*aphōna*): β γ δ κ π τ θ φ χ (Davidson 1874, 6). These nine are stop-plosives (/b/, /g/, /d/, /k/, /p/, /t/, /tʰ/, /pʰ/, /kʰ/), which do not allow continuous airflow without an adjacent vowel.

This division of letters into 'sounding', 'half-sounding', and 'soundless' is traceable to Aristotle's *Poetics* (Davidson 1874, 5, n. §), where Aristotle refers to the vowels as *phōnēen*, the continuant liquid consonants (/r/, /l/, /m/, /n/) plus /s/ as *hēmiphōnon*, and the rest of the consonants as *aphōnon* (Morag 1979, 87; see also, Merx 1889, 191). This arrangement differs slightly from that of Dionysius Thrax, but the division is still based on how long a particular phoneme can be held in continuous pronunciation,

---

[3] Greek text published in Bekker (1816, II:629–43). Quotations in this paragraph are from Davidson's (1874, 630–32) translation of §7.

[4] Including the double consonants, i.e., /ks/, /ps/.

similar to the *Technē*'s division according to relative amounts of obstructed airflow. It is more likely that Jacob adapted his terms from the *Technē* than from Aristotle. While Jacob was quite adept at Greek in general, it is clear that Syriac grammarians engaged with the Greek grammatical tradition specifically via the *Technē*, as evidenced by Joseph Huzaya's translation of the text into Syriac in the first half of the sixth century (Talmon 2000a, 337–38; Van Rompay 2011b; King 2012, 191; Farina 2018, 168). Notably, though, Joseph did not translate the phonetic portions of that work, which included the section on sounding letters (Merx 1889, 28–29; King 2012, 191). Additionally, Jacob does not adopt Dionysius Thrax's 'half-sounding' category at all. Instead, he dispenses with the *hēmiphōna* subdivision and separates the Syriac letters into just two groups: either 'sounding' (i.e., vowels) or 'soundless' (i.e., consonants), according to whether or not a letter can be pronounced on its own.[5] As such, Jacob's implementation of Syriac sounding letters is likely his own interpretation of the *Technē*, and not derived from Joseph Huzaya.

This distinction between 'sounding' and 'soundless' letters persisted within the Syriac grammatical tradition, and a fuller explanation of them appears in the work of Dawid bar Pawlos (fl. c. 770–800). A Miaphysite monk and grammarian from the second half of the eighth century (Brock 2011), Dawid is the author of a fragmentary grammatical text, which reads:

---

[5] Later in his *Turrᵒṣ Mamllᵒ*, Jacob does adapt a separate Greek tripartite division of consonants, likely also borrowed from the *Technē* (Talmon 2008, 167–69).

ܗܘܦ̈ܠܟ ܕܢ ܐܬܘܬܐ̈ ܡܬܦܠܓܢ ܠܬܪܬܝܢ : ܐܝܬ ܡܢܗܝܢ ܩܠܢܝܬܐ ܘܩܠܢܝܬܐ ܩܠܐ . ܘܐܝܬ ܡܢܗܝܢ ܕܠܐ ܩܠܐ

*Letters are divided into 'sounding' and 'soundless'. The
sounding are so called because they are a complete sound,
in and of themselves, and do not need partners for the completion of the beats of their sounds. Instead, one of them
is, in and of itself, its own complete syllable, and by combining them with those which are soundless, all units of
sounds are manifested. The poetic metres are measured by
them, and the quantity of the beats of the metres of homi-
lies and hymns are known and revealed by them. Then
those which are called 'soundless' are thus because they
are unable to make complete units of sounds alone, as the
sounding do. (Gottheil 1893, cxvii, lines 5–12)*

He maintains the two-way division of sounds into vowels and
consonants, using the same 'sounding' terminology as his Greek
and Syriac predecessors. For Dawid, just as for Jacob, the distinguishing feature of the ʾatwɔtɔ qɔlɔnɔyɔtɔ is that they can be pronounced alone, each forming a complete syllable without the addition of consonants (the dlɔ qɔlɔ). This feature of vowels was
central to Syriac poetry and prosody, which measured verses according to their number of syllables (Brock 2016, 9–10). As
Dawid points out, each syllable—or 'beat'[6]—necessarily contains

---

[6] In fact, the word 'beat' (nqɔshtɔ) is sometimes used in Syriac grammar
as a general term for 'vowel'; see Segal (1953, 7, 54, 171); Kiraz (2012,
I:59).

a single vowel, and consequently sounding letters are his most basic unit for quantifying metre. However, while this concept of vowel phonology became important in the Syriac linguistic tradition from as early as the seventh century, it appears that early Arabic grammarians adopted a different interpretation of the Greek 'sounding' terminology.

This alternative Arabic conception of phonetic 'soundingness' was related to the Greek divisions of letters, but it did not apply to vowels, and the pathway by which it entered the Arabic tradition is less clear. Talmon argues that due to the dual function of the *matres lectionis* in Arabic, eighth-century grammarians did not perceive vowel letters as a 'sounding' category distinct from the consonants. As such, while they were, to some extent, aware of the three-way Greek division of *phōnēenta* (vowels), *hēmiphōna* (liquids or continuants), and *aphōna* (all other consonants or stop-plosives), they dispensed with the 'vowel' category and adapted the Greek concepts only to describe groups of consonants (Talmon 1997a, 217–21; 1997b, 285). The clearest of these adaptations is from the teachings of the Kufan grammarian al-Farrā' (d. 822), who—at least according to the commentary on *Kitāb Sībawayh* by Abū Saʿīd al-Sīrāfī (d. 979)—described the consonants *ṣād* and *ḍād* as *muṣawwit* 'sounding'. He further describes the consonants *bā'* and *tā'* as *'akhras* 'mute'. In addition to *ṣād* and *ḍād*, al-Sīrāfī suggests that al-Farrā''s *muṣawwit* letters also included *thā'*, *dhāl*, *ẓā'*, and *zāy*. He further equates the *'akhras* category with Sībawayh's *shadīd* 'strong' letters (i.e., *bā'*, *dāl*, *tā'*, *ṭā'*, *jīm*, *kāf*, *qāf*, and *hamza*) (Talmon 1997a, 211–12).

The connection here is that al-Farrā'''s *'akhras* and Sībawayh's *shadīd* letters both describe plosive consonants in Classical Arabic (Semaan 1968, 56, 60–61; Sībawayh 1986, IV:434).[7] These consonants allow no passage of air at the moment of their articulation, and so they are 'mute'. They contrast with the continuous airflow of what Sībawayh calls the letters of *rikhwa* 'softness', namely the fricatives (al-Nassir 1993, 38–39; Brierley et al. 2016, 164), which roughly correspond with al-Sīrāfī's interpretation of *muṣawwit*. Talmon thus suggests that *muṣawwit* 'sounding' and *'akhras* 'mute' were al-Farrā'''s adaptation of the Greek *phōnēenta* and *aphōna*, reapplied to suit an Arabic phonological tradition that did not have a distinct subset of vowel letters (1997a, 212–13). In this understanding, 'sounding' consonants were those that allowed some continuous airflow during articulation, whereas the 'soundless' consonants were those that required the addition of a vowel in order to produce a stream of air.

Talmon also suggests that there is a second interpretation of these terms which is attributed to al-Khalīl ibn Aḥmad al-Farāhīdī (d. 786/91), preserved partly in the lexicon *Kitāb al-ʿAyn* and partly by the later lexicographer al-Azharī (d. 980) (Makhzumi 1985; Arzandeh and Umar 2011). In this system, the consonants are divided into two groups. The first is called *mudhliq* 'smooth', which includes the liquids and labials (*nūn, mīm, lām, rāʾ, bāʾ, fāʾ*). This group may correspond to Aristotle's *hēmi-*

---

[7] Sībawayh also includes *jīm*, which was probably an affricate (Brierley et al. 2016, 160, 172; see also, Ibn Jinnī 1993, 61).

phōnon, which likewise included the liquid consonants. The second group is then called either *ṣutm* 'solid' or *muṣmit* 'silent',
which includes the rest of the consonants, and parallels Aristotle's *aphōnon* group (Talmon 1997a, 215–17; 1997b, 261–62).
Consequently, these three pairs of early phonetic terms—*muṣawwit–ʾakhras*, *shadīd–rikhwa*, and *mudhliq–muṣmit/ṣutm*—may all
be variations of the same Greek linguistic concept of 'sounding'
letters (Talmon 1997a, 221; 1997b, 285; 2000b, 250). However,
that concept seems to have permeated the Arabic grammatical
tradition at several different points, and was not systematically
calqued or applied to vowels during the eighth century.[8] This situation would change during the ninth century, as the Greek-Syriac-Arabic translation movements facilitated a more systematic
transfer of Greek technical language into Arabic.

1.2. Sounds in Translation

From the late ninth century on, the Arabic word *muṣawwita* took
on a meaning much closer to the original 'vowel' meaning of
phōnēenta, although it remained uncommon for Arabic grammarians to use it to describe their vowel phonology. Likely the earliest extant examples of this new usage are in the book known as
al-Muqtaḍab (*The Digest*) by the Basran grammarian al-Mubarrad
(d. 898). He uses the term twice, first writing: "Among the letters
of interchange are the letters of lengthening and softness, and the
sounding [ones], which are *ʾalif, wāw*, and *yāʾ* (فمن حروف البدل

---

[8] On early contact between Arabic and Greek grammatical teaching, see
Versteegh (1977). See also, Talmon (1997a, 209, n. 3); Mavroudi
(2014).

حروف المدّ واللين والمصوتة وهي الألف والواو والياء) . Later on, he says: "If you make a diminutive from a quintiliteral noun and its fourth [radical] is one of the sounding letters—which are *yā'*, *wāw*, and *'alif*—then no part of its plural or diminutive is apocopated (اذا صغرت اسماً على خمسة ورابعه احد الحروف المصوتة وهي الياء والواو والالف فإن جمعه وتصغيره غير محذوف فيهما شيء)" (al-Mubarrad 1965, I:61, 119; Talmon 1997a, 210–11). In both instances, the word 'sounding' (*muṣawwita*) indicates some quality of the three Arabic *matres lectionis*, especially when they act as 'letters of lengthening and softness' (*ḥurūf al-madd wa-al-līn*). That is, when they represent long vowels (see below, present chapter, §3.0). Talmon also notes that each time, al-Mubarrad lists the letters which fall into this 'sounding' category, possibly because he is aware of a foreign origin of the term *muṣawwita* and does not expect his audience to know exactly what it refers to.

Likely the earliest extant example of *muṣawwita* outside of grammar is in the translation of Aristotle's *Poetics* by the Christian philosopher Abū Bishr Mattā (d. 940), which he produced from a Syriac version in the late ninth or early tenth century. Interpreting through the Syriac technical terms of his source text, Abū Bishr ultimately calques *phōnēen*, *hēmiphōnon*, and *aphōnon*, respectively, as *muṣawwit* 'sounding', *niṣf al-muṣawwit* 'half of the sounding', and *lā muṣawwit* 'not sounding' (al-Badawī 1953, 126; Morag 1979, 87). Al-Fārābī (d. 950/951), perhaps the foremost Islamic scholar of Aristotle, also commented on the *Poetics*, although he does not include Aristotle's classification of sounds. Nevertheless, he does use *muṣawwita* to describe "a letter representing a long vowel" in other works (Morag 1979, 88).

Muṣawwita in these contexts is a calque of the Syriac *qɔlɔnɔytɔ* as used by Jacob and Dawid bar Pawlos, and by exten-sion, it is an indirect calque of the Greek *phōnēenta*. Each of these terms is derived from the basic word for 'voice' and 'sound' in its respective language—*ṣawt, qɔlɔ,* and *phōne*—and classifies vowels as a specific phonological group according to their 'sounding' quality. This quality is the fact that they can be pronounced on their own with a continuous and unobstructed airstream. Morag has noted that the Greek *phōnēenta* was "conveyed to Arabic via Syriac (the middle link being missing)" (Morag 1979, 89), but the 'missing link' is the use of *qɔlɔnɔyɔtɔ* among ninth-century Syriac translators.

This transmission of calques occurred amidst the Greek-Syriac-Arabic translation movements of the Abbasid Caliphate, during which time Syriac translators, most famously the Chris-tian physician Ḥunayn ibn Isḥāq (d. 873), used Syriac as a tool for converting Greek technical terms into Arabic. Sebastian Brock describes Ḥunayn's translation process as follows: "having col-lected together the best and oldest Greek manuscripts he could find, he translated from Greek into Syriac and only then from Syriac into Arabic" (Brock 2016, 11–12; see also, Versteegh 1977, 3; Butts 2011). Syrian translators thus assigned Greek terms which already had Syriac calques—for example, *phōnēenta* and *qɔlɔnɔyɔtɔ*—a direct Arabic technical equivalent; in this case, *muṣawwitāt*. The tenth-century lexicographer Ḥasan bar Bahlul (fl. 942–968) confirms this connection in his Syriac-Arabic lexi-con. He gives only one Arabic word to define *qɔlɔnɔyɔtɔ*, and that word is *muṣawwitāt* (Duval 1901, 1794, 1931). Bar Bahlul claims to have compiled much of his lexicon from the lexica of Ḥunayn and another ninth-century scholar, Ḥenanishoʿ bar Serosheway (d. c. 900) (Van Rompay 2011a).[9] He even names Bar Serosheway as his source for the term *muṣawwitāt*, suggesting that it was known by Syriac-Arabic translators well before Bar Bahlul's life-time.

At the same time that *muṣawwitāt* began to appear occa-sionally in Arabic grammatical texts and translations of Greek works (e.g., al-Mubarrad and Abū Bishr), it also saw some use referring to vowels in Masoretic texts that analysed Hebrew pho-netics (Talmon 1997a, 209–10). These texts constitute a subgenre of Masoretic treatises written mainly in Arabic around the tenth century to discuss the functions of the Hebrew vowels and ac-cents. They often classify vowels with the term *muṣawwitāt*, and I refer to treatises of this type as '*muṣawwitāt* texts'.[10]

One of the most significant of these texts is known as *Kitāb al-Muṣawwitāt* (*The Book of the Sounding Ones*), first published by Allony based on a partial manuscript from the Cairo Genizah (Al-lony 1964; 1965).[11] Allony adopts the title *Kitāb al-Muṣawwitāt* for this work and attributes it to Moshe ben Asher, the father of

---

[9] Unfortunately, these other lexica are not extant.

[10] Following the usage of Ilan Eldar, Nehemia Allony, and Israel Yeivin; see below, and also Allony (1965); Allony and Yeivin (1985); Eldar (1986). ·

[11] Allony published a description of the manuscript fragments (Cam-bridge, UL: T-S Ar.32.31 and Paris, AIU: IX.A.24) and their contents in 1964, before publishing the full Arabic text, with Hebrew translation, in 1965. He later discovered another fragment (Cambridge, UL: T-S Ar.33.6), which he argues is also part of this text (Allony 1983).

the famous Tiberian Masorete Aharon ben Asher (d. c. 960) (Allony 1965, 136). He justifies this attribution simply by the appearance of the word *muṣawwitāt* in it along with other medieval references to a lost work by Moshe ben Asher with that same title (Allony 1964, 9–10; Eldar 1986, 52). However, while the extant fragments do include the word *muṣawwitāt* several times, they do not actually contain a title, nor do they indicate that this particular treatise should be associated with Moshe ben Asher.[12] Noting this inconsistency, Eldar undertook a study to ascertain a sturdier provenance for Allony's text. He argues that the use of word *muṣawwitāt* to refer to vowels is more common than Allony initially thought, and thus cannot be used to infer the title of the text. He further suggests that the phrase *kitāb al-muṣawwitāt* may refer to this genre of Arabic-language Masoretic texts that dealt with vowels and accents, rather than to a specific treatise with that title. Consequently, he concludes that it is doubtful Moshe ben Asher wrote this particular *muṣawwitāt* text, and that it is impossible to determine the true author or title without further evidence (Eldar 1986, 53–55).

The first fragment of this text begins with a passage that is reminiscent of Jacob of Edessa's alphabetical struggles:

---

[12] The closest extant text to this title is probably *Kitāb al-Muṣawwitāt al-Watariyya* (*The Book of Stringed Instruments*) by the ninth-century polymath Abū Yūsuf Yaʿqūb al-Kindī (d. 873). It discusses the musical properties of instruments with various numbers of strings and includes an accurate citation of Psalm 33 according to the Septuagint numeration (al-Kindī 1962, 67–92, esp. 90). On early Arabic Bible translations, see Griffith (2013, 106–8).

אבין אן אל[עבר]אנין יסתעמ[ל] מנטיקהם אל ז [אלתי תסתע[מל חרפהם
פליס תזיד עלי אלז שי כאל [אחרף אל[די לא יוגד שי מסת[עמל] אלא
כב [חרף]

...I specify that for the Hebrews,[13] their speech utilises the
seven, which [in turn] utilise their letter[s]. You cannot
increase the seven, just like the letters, for which nothing
is used except twenty-two letters. (Allony 1965, 136, lines
1–3)

'The seven' in this passage refers to the seven vowels of the Tiberian Hebrew recitation tradition (see Khan 2020, I:244), and the author insists that one cannot add to that number.[14] Similarly, there are twenty-two letters in the Hebrew alphabet, and that number is fixed, such that there are two groups—the seven and the twenty-two—that do not overlap. From this point on, the author refers to the seven as *al-muṣawwitāt* 'the sounding ones' (Allony 1965, 138, line 9; 140, lines 24 and 28; 144, line 53), maintaining the same two-category phonological distinction as Jacob of Edessa. The author also refers to the letter *yod* as *al-ṣūra al-muṣawwita*—literally 'the sounding form'—when it functions as a *mater lectionis* representing the vowel /i/ (Allony 1983, 119–20, lines 106–9).

---

[13] Allony notes that the lacuna in this word could allow 'Syrians' (*suriyyāniyyīn*) or 'Babylonians' (*kasdāniyyīn*), though given the rest of the text, 'Hebrews' is the most reasonable reconstruction (1965, 136, n. 1).

[14] Similar descriptions appear in Arabic grammars of Coptic, which refer to the seven Coptic vowels as *ʾaḥruf ṣawtiyya* or *ʾaḥruf nawātiq* (Bauer 1972, 147–48; K. Versteegh 2011).

Allony and Yeivin (1985) published four more of these *muṣawwitāt* texts, and together they show that the idea of distinguishing vowels from consonants according to 'soundingness' was not a rare phenomenon among Masoretes. Two of the four use the word *muṣawwita*, the first of which is T-S Ar.53.1.[15] Most of this fragment is an explanation of Masoretic accents, but the first few lines read, "Know that the *muṣawwitāt* are seven, excluding the *shewa*... (...אלשוא) (אעלם באן אלמצותאת ז מן סוא אלשוא)" (Allony and Yeivin 1985, 91, lines 1–2). It proceeds to list the Tiberian Hebrew vowels. The second fragment is T-S NS 301.62, which discusses the accents and the *bgdkpt* letters, but says in passing, "If two accents are adjacent, then none of the *mulūk*—I mean, the *muṣawwitāt*—may be between them (אן אלתקיא אללחנין לם יכן בינהם שי מן אלמלוך אעני אלמצותאת)" (Allony and Yeivin 1985, 115–16, lines 38–39). *Mulūk* 'kings' was another name for the Hebrew vowels in the medieval period, so this text represents a combination of vocabulary from different sources, and the author does not expect that their reader will necessarily know both terms.

Another of Allony and Yeivin's fragments, T-S Ar.31.28, reads:

אעלם באן אלאחרוף אואכרהא עלי ג אקסאם אלאול הם אליח חרפבעד
אויה כלהא גזם אעני שׁוָא ליס יכרג מנהא שי אלי אלז מלוך

Know that for endings [of words], the letters are according to three groups. The first is those eighteen besides ʾaleph,

---

[15] Baker and Polliack identified this fragment as part of ʿAlī ben Judah ha-Nazir's *Kitāb Uṣūl al-Lugha al-ʿIbrānīyya*, but this designation is unverified (and seems to me unverifiable) since the rest of that book is not extant (Baker and Polliack 2001, no. 7717)

waw, yod, and *heʾ.* All of them are *jazm*; I mean, *shewa.*
Nothing is pronounced from them towards any of the seven
mulūk. (Allony and Yeivin 1985, 101–2, lines 53–58)

While this fragment does not contain the word *muṣawwita*, it is
clearly familiar with the idea that consonants are unique in their
'soundlessness'. The author has adopted the Arabic grammatical
term for the jussive mood, *jazm* 'cutting off' (i.e., a vowelless inflectional ending), to describe the characteristic of the consonants that causes *shewa* to be silent at the end of a word. This
quality is opposed to that of the Hebrew *matres lectionis*, which,
as the text later explains, have more vowel-like effects (Allony
and Yeivin 1985, 103–5). It is worth noting that, in contrast to
Jacob of Edessa, the Masoretic *muṣawwitāt* texts tend to account
for the *matres lectionis* with an additional group of 'letters' which
have characteristics of both vowels and consonants.

Besides these fragments, there is a more well-known Masoretic source which may also be considered a *muṣawwitāt* text: *The
Treatise on the Shewa.* This anonymous tenth-century treatise is
part of a larger work, but the extant portion focuses on the features of the Tiberian *shewa*.[16] It describes the *shewa,* saying:
"Know that the *shewa* [.......], and that is that it serves symbols—
by which I mean the seven kings, which are called *al-muṣawwitāt*

---

[16] Hence the name. See Levy (1936); Khan (2020, I:117–18). Eldar has
argued that this treatise is from the same work as Allony's *Kitāb al-
Muṣawwitāt*, but I am sceptical of this association. The two texts employ
different, somewhat idiosyncratic terminology to name the Hebrew
vowels (see below, chapter 4, §3.0), which suggests that they have different authors. It is possible that the two works share some source material; see Eldar (1988); Khan (2020, I:119).

אעלם אן אלשוא [.....]רה ודלך אנה יבדם סי[מני]ם אעני אלסבעה מלוך אלדّי)
תסמא אלמצותאת)" (Levy 1936, א). This author directly equates the
muṣawwitāt with other categorical terms for Hebrew vowels, including 'symbols' (*simanim*) and 'kings' (*mulūk*). This variation
suggests there was a pluriformity of vowel terms in the *Treatise*'s
Masoretic source material, which includes some Hebrew texts
that are likely from the ninth century.[17] It likewise confirms that
some Masoretes had adopted the idea of *muṣawwitāt* by the tenth
century.

It is clear that the phonological distinction of vowels as
'sounding ones' in contrast to consonants was known to certain
Masoretes, but the concept also extended to other sectors of the
Hebrew linguistic tradition, including Saadia Gaon's (d. 942)
commentary on *Sefer Yeṣira* (The Book of Creation) (see Khan
2020, I:127–29). While Saadia generally favours the term
naghamāt 'melodies, tones' to refer to vowels,[18] he does use
muṣawwitāt a few times in the second chapter of this book (Lambert 1891, 24–28). While explaining the units of speech, Saadia
says that the most basic audible unit is a *ṣawt* 'sound', "and it is
what one does not comprehend, as someone says, *ʾāā* or the rest

---

[17] Hebrew passages and quotations occur frequently throughout the
Treatise. On changes in authorial language in Masoretic sources, see
Khan (2020, I:116–17).

[18] For brief discussions of this term, see below, present chapter, §§2.2
and 4.0.

of the *muṣawwitāt* (المصوتات سائر او اا قائل كقول يعقل لا ما فهو)" (Lambert 1891, 26, lines 11–12).[19] Like Dawid bar Pawlos, Saadia interprets the vowels as the smallest units of pronounceable speech, which can be articulated without the aid of any other letters. Interestingly, Saadia does not use the term *muṣawwitāt* when he describes the vowels in the fifth chapter of his Hebrew grammar, *Kutub al-Lugha* (*The Books of the Language*) (Skoss 1952; Dotan 1997; see Khan 2020, I:124–25). It is not clear if he changed or updated his vocabulary on this topic, but we do know that he wrote the commentary in 931, after *Kutub al-Lugha*.[20] It may be that he drew some connection between *naghama*, which can indicate both the vowels and accents in Hebrew recitation, and the Arabic verb *ṣawwata*, which is a common term in Arabic musicology (Morag 1979, 89–90). Either way, Saadia maintained nearly the same conception of 'sounding' ones that Jacob of Edessa introduced to the Syriac grammatical tradition in the seventh century.

As already discussed, the most likely path by which the concept of 'sounding letters' entered Arabic linguistics was through ninth-century Syriac translators, but how did it reach the

---

[19] Saadia probably wrote this commentary in Hebrew characters, but Lambert transcribed the non-Hebrew portions of the text in Arabic script. My quotations follow Lambert's transcription. Saadia also mentions that the introduction to the "books on *manṭiq* (speech/logic)" is about *al-muṣawwitāt* (Lambert 1891, 26, line 20).

[20] Saadia refers to *Kutub al-Lugha* at least twice in his commentary (Lambert 1891, 45, 52 [Arabic]; 76, n. 1 [French]; see also, Malter 1921, 44, n. 57).

Masoretic tradition? It could have been through contact with Arabic grammarians, but Talmon argues that this explanation is unlikely, as the use of *muṣawwitāt* as a word for vowels remained quite rare in Arabic grammar even in the tenth century (Talmon 1997a, 221). Instead, the similarities between the Masoretic 'sounding' category and the Syriac *qolonoyoto* letters suggest that the Hebrew interpretation is more closely related to Syriac grammar. As we will later see,[21] there is significant evidence of early contact between Masoretes and Syriac grammarians in the realm of vocalisation, but for the case of the *muṣawwitāt* the point of transmission may also be the translation movement. As Syriac translators converted Greek and Syriac texts into Arabic, they became readable not just to Arab grammarians, but also to Masoretes and other Jewish scholars who were native Arabic speakers. Bar Bahlul, the tenth-century lexicographer who recorded the ninth-century use of *muṣawwitāt* to calque *qolonoyoto*, even reports personal contacts with his Jewish contemporaries. In his lexical entry on the Syriac word *broshit* 'in the beginning', he claims to have read a Jewish *tafsīr* 'commentary' before going and asking a Jew to explain the meaning of *reshit* in Hebrew (Duval 1901, 435). This account suggests that Bar Bahlul interacted with educated Jews in the course of his lexicographic work, and these interactions—or similar ones by his predecessors[22]—could have facilitated the transfer of *muṣawwitāt* into Masoretic circles.

---

[21] See below, chapter 3, §1.0.

[22] Another possible contact is Timothy I (d. 823), an Eastern Catolicos who reports the discovery of some Hebrew manuscripts in a cave near Jericho that were read with the assistance of Jews from Jerusalem

Even as the tenth century passed, the term *muṣawwitāt* to describe vowels did not gain popularity among Arabic grammarians. The phonologist Ibn Jinnī (d. 1002) does make a passing reference to *al-ḥurūf al-thalātha al-layyina al-muṣawwita* 'the three soft sounding letters' in his *Kitāb al-Khaṣā'is* (*The Book of Characteristics*) (Talmon 1997a, 210, n. 5; Ibn Jinnī 1952, 44, n. 112), but he does not apply it to their technical usage in his large book on Arabic phonology, *Sirr Ṣināʿa al-Iʿrāb*. He briefly explains *ṣawt* and the verb *ṣawwata* more generally, but this discussion appears unrelated to sounding letters (Ibn Jinnī 1993, 9–11).

The only other Arabic author in our corpus who discusses 'sounding' vocalisation is Ibn Sīnā (d. 1037), a Persian physician and polymath who wrote mostly in Arabic and was more of a philosopher than a grammarian by trade. He produced his own Arabic version of Aristotle's *Poetics*, in which he translates *phōnēen* and *hēmiphōnon* as *muṣawwit* and *niṣf al-muṣawwit*, respectively, like Abū Bishr a century before him (Morag 1979, 87–88). However, he translates *aphōna* not as *lā muṣawwit* (like Abū Bishr), but rather as *ṣāmit* 'soundless, silent', using the same root as al-Khalīl's *muṣmit* category of non-liquid (or non-labial) consonants.

Ibn Sīnā also wrote one work that specifically classifies Arabic vowel phonology: *Risāla Asbāb Ḥudūth al-Ḥurūf* (*The Treatise on the Causes of the Occurrence of Letters*). He wrote this essay near the end of his life, apparently at the request of a grammarian in

---

(Butts and Gross 2020, 18). Timothy also had some contact with the Arabic grammatical tradition (King 2012, 199–201).

Isfahan, to lay out his understanding of speech on both mechanical and phonological levels (al-Tayyan and Mir Alam 1983, 9). As such, the first three sections focus on the physics of sound waves and the anatomy of the mouth and throat (al-Tayyan and Mir Alam 1983, 53–71). Then, in the fourth section, he explains the articulation of each Arabic *ḥarf* 'letter, phoneme' (pl. *ḥurūf*) as it relates to the mechanical principles. Two of these *ḥurūf* are *al-wāw al-ṣāmita* 'the soundless *wāw*' and *al-yāʾ al-ṣāmita* 'the soundless *yāʾ*' (al-Tayyan and Mir Alam 1983, 83–84). He groups them with the other consonants, indicating the quality of *wāw* and *yāʾ* when they are consonantal (i.e., /w/ and /y/, respectively). By contrast, the next three *ḥurūf* are *al-ʾalif al-muṣawwita* 'the sounding *ʾalif*', *al-wāw al-muṣawwita* 'the sounding *wāw*', and *al-yāʾ al-muṣawwita* 'the sounding *yāʾ*' (al-Tayyan and Mir Alam 1983, 84). *Muṣawwita* is thus Ibn Sīnāʾs term for a *mater lectionis* acting as a vowel, similar to the occasional usages found in the works of al-Mubarrad, al-Fārābī, and Ibn Jinnī as well as the 'sounding form' (*al-ṣūra al-muṣawwita*) of *yod* mentioned by at least one Masorete (see Allony 1983, 119–20, lines 106–9; Talmon 1997a, 211 n. 7).

There is a second version of the *Risāla* which contains substantial variations from the first, especially in the sections on phonetics. It is not clear that Ibn Sīnā himself edited or rewrote the text (al-Tayyan and Mir Alam 1983, 13). The extant version begins, "The foremost *shaykh* said… (...قال الشيخ الرئيس)," in reference to Ibn Sīnā, possibly indicating that it was written by someone who heard or studied the original.[23] In any case, the alternate

---

[23] For this type of scholastic transmission, see Schoeler (2006, 32–33).

text of the section on *ṣāmita* and *muṣawwita* letters warrants further discussion. This version places *al-wāw al-ṣāmita* and *al-yā' al-ṣāmita* among the other consonants, according to the order of their articulation points in the mouth, rather than at the end of the alphabet before the vowels (al-Tayyan and Mir Alam 1983, 124). It then introduces the vowel section, saying, "As for the *muṣawwitāt*, their status and influence are problematic for me (اما المصوتات فأمرها وتأثيرها عليّ كالمشكل);" he proceeds to explain "the small and large *'alifs*," "the two *wāws*," and "the two *yā's*" (al-Tayyan and Mir Alam 1983, 128). While *muṣawwita* appeared in the first version of the *Risāla* to describe a few letters, in this version it is a categorical term, indicating a group which contains all of the *matres lectionis* as well as the Arabic short vowels. This usage corresponds to both the *Turrɔṣ Mamllɔ Nahrɔyɔ* and the Masoretic *muṣawwitāt* texts, both of which use 'sounding' to differentiate vowels and consonants as phonological categories. Notably, in Ibn Sīnā's system, *'alif* does not have a *ṣāmita* form, precisely because the Arabic *'alif* has no consonantal quality.[24] This concept may correlate with Jacob's understanding of the Syriac *'alaph*, which he used to represent one of his 'sounding' letters. On the other hand, *ṣāmit* does not mean 'soundless' in the same way as Jacob of Edessa's *dlɔ qɔlɔ*, literally 'without a sound'. Rather, it is an adjective ('soundless, silent'), more immediately similar to Greek *aphōna* 'soundless' and al-Farrā''s *'akhras* 'mute'.

---

[24] Ibn Sīnā gives *hamza* a separate entry, effectively the consonantal form of *'alif* (al-Tayyan and Mir Alam 1983, 72). For the quality of *'alif* in Classical Arabic, see Alfozan (1989, 37); Semaan (1968, 57–58).

C. H. M. Versteegh has noted the similarity between this Arabic terminology and the Greek, pointing out that the *ṣāmitāt* and *muṣawwitāt*—which also appear in Ibn Sīnā's *Fann al-Shiʿr* (*The Art of Poetry*)—are calques of *aphōna* and *phōnēenta*. He further highlights that Ibn Sīnā refers to fricative consonants as those letters which have *niṣf ṣawṭ* 'a half sound', a calque of *hēmiphōna*, the term which Aristotle used for liquids (and /s/) and which the *Technē* used for continuants (Versteegh 1977, 21). It seems that Ibn Sīnā, specialising as a physician and philosopher, was more likely to engage directly with translations of Greek ideas—such as those of Aristotle and Dionysius Thrax—than the Arabic grammarians who preceded him.

Meanwhile, Ibn Sīnā's contemporary, the Syriac grammarian Elias of Ṭirhan (d. 1049), modified Jacob of Edessa's original *qɔlɔnɔyɔtɔ* terminology in his grammar, *Memrɔ Gramaṭiqɔyɔ* (*The Grammatical Essay*). He lays out his understanding of sounding letters explicitly, saying:

> ܘܙܕܩ ܕܝܢ ܠܡܕܥ ܕܐܬܘܬܐ ܩܠܢܝܬܐ. ܬܠܬ ܐܢܝܢ .. ܗ.. ܐ.. ܘ.. ܝ.. ܘܫܪܟ ܕܐܬܘܬܐ ܐܚܪܢܝܬܐ ܠܗܠܝܢ ܢܩܦܝܢ .. ܗܠܝܢ ܐܬܘܬܐ ܠܒܘܢܝܐ ܕܫܡܗܐ ܐܘ ܡܠܐ ܡܫܘܕܥܢܝܬܐ ܥܠ ܣܘܥܪܢܐ ܡܬܬܝܕܥܢܘܬܐ ܐܬܦܪܫܘ ܠܡܦܩܢܘ ܡܢ ܗܠܝܢ ܬܠܬ ܩܠܢܝܬܐ
>
> It is necessary to know that the sounding letters are three, being *ʾalaph*, *wāw*, *yod*, and the rest of the other letters [are pronounced][25] with them. They are the letters for the construction of nouns or verbs (which indicate action), the vocalisations made known by production from these three sounding ones. (Baethgen 1880, ܠܒ, lines 11–15)

---

[25] Baethgen's edition reads ܢܩܦܝܢ 'they cling to', but this is probably an error for ܢܩܫܝܢ 'they are pronounced'.

Even though Eastern Syriac had six distinct vowel qualities (see Segal 1953, 33; Knudsen 2015, 91–99), Elias asserts that only the three Syriac *matres lectionis* are *qɔlɔnɔyɔtɔ*. The implication here is that the sounding ones are the letters *ʾalaph*, *wāw*, and *yod*, and not the vowel phonemes themselves. This explanation contrasts the Masoretic *muṣawwitāt* texts, which consistently list seven 'sounding ones'—the seven unique Tiberian vowel phonemes—and do not refer to any of the twenty-two Hebrew letters as inherently *muṣawwita*. This difference might be traced back to Jacob of Edessa, who referred to his new vowel letters specifically as sounding letters (*ʾatwɔtɔ qɔlɔnɔyɔtɔ*), but it is also similar to Ibn Sīnā's use of the word *muṣawwita* as an adjective for the Arabic *matres lectionis*. Elias' view that the sounding letters are required for the pronunciation of other letters is also consistent with Dawid bar Pawlos and the Masoretic *muṣawwitāt* authors, who all maintained that the vowels were essential to the articulation of the consonants.

With the help of the *ʾatwɔtɔ qɔlɔnɔyɔtɔ*, Elias discusses how the *matres lectionis* function in Syriac orthography, and here he adds a concept that we have not yet seen:

> ܣܡ ܕܝܢ ܠܘܘ ܡܙܘܥܝܢ ܡܬܬܙܝܥܢܘܬ ܚܪܘܪܐ ܩܘܡ.. ܦܪܝܫܐ.. ܚܠܝܡܐ.. ܦܘܪܩܢܐ..
> ܦܪܝܩܐ.. ܡܛܠ ܕܗܠܝܢ ܐܝܬ ܐܬܘܬܐ ܡܩܠܢܝܬܐ .. ܐܘ ܦܠܓܘܬ ܡܩܠܢܝܬܐ .. ܗ..
> ܕܡܫܡܠܝܢ ܡܬܬܙܝܥܢܘܬܐ ܒܡܡܠܠܐ ܣܘܪܝܝܐ. ܘܠܝܠܝܐ.. ܘܡܘܝܐ.. ܗ.. ܘ.. ܝ..
>
> We consider the *waw* [and the *yod*][26] to be the vocalisation of *ḥrure*, *qum*, *prishɔ*; *ḥlimɔ*, *purqɔnɔ*, and *priqɔ*, because these are sounding letters, or half-soundings: those which

[26] This phrase seems to have dropped out of Baethgen's edition, but the following examples imply that Elias also meant *yod* here.

bestow vocalisation in Syriac, Arabic, and Greek speech.
That is, *waw* and *yod.* (Baethgen 1880, ܒܒ, lines 18–21)

The words which Elias lists are usually spelled with *waw* or *yod* as *matres lectionis* representing their internal vowels. Because these letters function as vowels rather than consonants, Elias designates them 'sounding letters', just like Ibn Sīnā does for the Arabic *matres wāw* and *yāʾ*. Elias then adds a Syriac concept that is reminiscent of the Arabic short vowels: the *pelgut qɔlɔnɔyɔtɔ*, literally 'half of the soundings'. These half-soundings can still bestow vocalisation on consonants, but the phrase designates vowels which do not have individual letters. Instead, they are represented by vocalisation points alone. Due to the standard practice in Syriac of nearly always representing *u-* and *i-*vowels with a *mater lectionis*, these 'half-soundings' are most commonly /a/, /e/, and /ɔ/ (Baethgen 1880, ܒܓ, lines 1–2). This half-sounding terminology notably contrasts Ibn Sīnā's idea of letters with 'half of a sound', which are fricative consonants, ultimately derived from the Greek concept of *hēmiphōna* 'half-sounding' liquids or fricatives. It seems that rather than copying this Greco-Arabic category (just as Jacob of Edessa did not adopt it), Elias reapplies the idea of a half-sounding letter to the vowels that do not appear with *matres lectionis*. His description thus diverges from the Greek notion (e.g., from the *Technē*) of a 'half-sounding' being a letter that allows partially-obstructed continuous airflow.

As for the letter *ʾalaph*, Elias grants it even more 'soundingness' than *wāw* and *yod*, again aligning with Ibn Sīnā's interpretation of the *muṣawwitāt*. Shortly after arguing that *ʾalaph* is silent by itself (Baethgen 1880, ܟܒ, lines 3–4),[27] Elias writes:

> ܐܢܕܝܢ ܐܡܪ ܐܢܫ ܗܟܝܠ ܟܕ ܐܡܪܝܢ ܐܠܗܐ ܥܒܕܐ ܒܪܢܫܐ. ܠܐ.. ܗ.. ܕ..
> ܘ..ܡܬܬܙܝܥܢ.. ܐܠܐ.. ܐ.. ܕܫܠܝܐ ܗܝ.. ܐ.. ܣܡܬܘܢ.. ܡܦܣܝܢ.. ܕܐܠܦ ܒܪ
> ܡܠܘܬܐ ܠܡܥܪܢܐܝܬ ܥܒܝܕܐ ܘܗܝܐ ܠܐܬܘܬܐ ܐܚܪܢܝܬܐ ܘܡܩܕܡܐ ܠܫܪܟܐ.. ܘ..
> ܝ.. ܢܩܫܢ ܐܝܟ ܐܠܦ.. ܐ.. ܟܠ ܗܕܐ ܠܐ ܙܕܩ ܠܡܫܘܬܦܘ ܙܘܥܐ ܠܐܚܪܢܝܬܐ

> If someone were to say, "Therefore, when we say *ʾalɔhɔ*, *ʿabdɔ*, and *barnɔshɔ*, the *heʾ*, *dalat*, and *wāw* are not vocalised, but rather the *ʾalaph* [is vocalised], the *ʾalaph* that you assert that is silent." We respond: *ʾalaph* is completely one of the sounding ones. It bestows movement to other letters, and since it precedes the rest [of them], *wāw* and *yod* sound out, just like *ʾalaph*. Therefore, it is not correct to associate movement with the other [letters]. (Baethgen 1880, ܟܓ, lines 10–14)

Elias claims that *ʾalaph* is entirely a sounding letter, and so has no inherent phonetic quality at all—hence, it is silent. Nevertheless, it always provides 'movement' (*zawʿɔ*; i.e., a vowel) to other letters. Meanwhile, *wāw* and *yod* are modelled after *ʾalaph* in that they are sounding letters that can bestow movement, but are not "completely one of the sounding ones." That is, they do not exclusively represent vowels. The idea of *ʾalaph* as the most sounding of the Syriac *matres lectionis* again likely extends back to Jacob of Edessa, who took *ʾalaph* alone from the Syriac alphabet to

---

[27] Arabic grammarians make a similar designation for the *matres lectionis* letters, which are called *sākin* 'still' when they represent long vowels. See present chapter, §§2.0–3.0.

serve as one of his vowel letters. It also corresponds to Ibn Sīnā's description of the Arabic ʾalif, which was a pure *muṣawwita* letter, whereas *wāw* and *yāʾ* had both *muṣawwita* and *ṣāmita* 'soundless' forms. In this way, both Elias' and Ibn Sīnā's views on the sounding letters are distinct from the Masoretic and earlier Syriac understanding, which considered the 'sounding ones' as a category that included all vowel phonemes, rather than just the *matres lectionis* letters.

The notion of sounding letters as an explanation for the difference between vowels and consonants is fundamental to much of medieval Semitic vocalisation, and the comparison of sources from different linguistic traditions reveals a clear continuation of the idea from pre-Islamic sources until the eleventh century. This chain of transmission begins in Greek works, including Aristotle's *Poetics*, but especially the *Technē Grammatikē* of Dionysius Thrax, which categorised letters as *phōnēenta*, *aphōna*, and *hēmiphōna*. From there, early Syriac grammarians, like Jacob of Edessa and Dawid bar Pawlos, adapted these terms to create two categories of Syriac letters: 'sounding' (*qɔlɔnɔyɔtɔ*) vowels and 'soundless' (*dlɔ qɔlɔ*) consonants. At the same time, their Arabic contemporaries did not adopt any 'sounding' categories for vowels, although they did interpret the earlier Greek terminology in different ways to describe groups of consonants. The ninth-century translation of Greek technical terminology did allow for the penetration of 'sounding' vowel phonology into Arabic, but most Arabic grammarians did not adopt it. That said, the translation movement did allow Hebrew Masoretes to write their own *muṣawwitāt* texts in the tenth century, adopting the same 'sounding category as Syriac grammarians to describe their seven vowels. Also building on earlier Syriac foundations, Elias of Ṭirhan adopted the sounding letters for his *Memrɔ Gramaṭiqɔyɔ*, although he modified Jacob of Edessa's original concept to suit his understanding of the *matres lectionis*. Meanwhile, the sounding terminology did see some use among Muslim scholars to describe vowels, but it seems that that use was limited to non-grammatical realms. Evidence of this usage comes from translations by Abū Bishr and al-Fārābī, as well as Ibn Sīnā's discussions of *muṣawwitāt* and *ṣāmitāt*. By contrast, the idea of vowels as 'motion' was much more widespread in the Arabic grammatical tradition, a concept that became practically universal among medieval scholars of Semitic languages, as we will now explore.

2.0. Vowels as Phonetic Motion

The most common and well-known Arabic term for 'vowel' is *ḥaraka* 'movement' (pl. *ḥarakāt*), which somehow describes the phonetic transition between two consonants which are *sākin* 'still'. It appears in the earliest eighth-century Arabic grammatical sources (see Talmon 1997, 135–37), and continues to see use in grammars of modern Arabic. However, the origins of the term are obscure, and other words that translate as 'movement' were used in relation to vowels and recitation in both Greek (*kinesis*) and Syriac (*zawʿɔ/mziʿɔnɔ*) prior to the earliest attestations of *ḥaraka* in Arabic grammar. It is difficult to draw a direct conceptual link between these early terms and the Arabic word, although some scholars have argued for such a connection. That said, both Syriac and Hebrew scholars eventually adapted *ḥaraka* and *sākin* to describe their own respective vowels and consonants.

This section traces the application and development of these words for 'movement' and 'stillness' in the field of vowel phonology. It begins with the origins of the word *ḥaraka* in the Arabic grammatical tradition, discussing the theories of C. H. M. Versteegh and Max Bravmann regarding potential connections between *ḥaraka* 'movement' and the Greek word *kinesis* 'movement'. Next, it addresses the late antique Syriac accent system(s) known from sources like Thomas the Deacon (fl. c. 600) and MS BL Add. 12138 (written 899), placing the accent names *zawʿɔ* 'movement' and *mzi ʿɔnɔ* 'giving movement' in context with *ḥaraka* and *kinesis*. It then explains how terms derived from *ḥaraka* and *sākin* describe vowels in the Arabic grammatical tradition, specifically discussing Sībawayh's (d. 793/796) *Kitāb* and Ibn Jinnī's (d. 1002) *Sirr Ṣināʿa al-Iʿrāb*. Finally, it analyses the ways in which later Syriac and Hebrew grammarians adapted the Arabic concepts of *ḥaraka* and *sākin* to suit their languages. For Syriac, this analysis relies on the lexica of ʿĪsā ibn ʿAlī (d. c. 900) and Ḥasan bar Bahlul (fl. 942–968), as well as the eleventh-century grammars of Elias of Nisibis (d. 1046) and Elias of Ṭirhan (d. 1049). For Hebrew, it relies on *The Treatise on the Shewa*, other *muṣawwitāt* literature, the writings of Saadia Gaon (d. 942), and Abū al-Faraj Hārūn's (d. c. 1050) *Hidāya al-Qārī* (*The Guide for the Reader*).

2.1. Greek Declension, Arabic Vowels, and Syriac Accents

Though the word *ḥaraka* may be an internal invention as the term for 'a vowel' in the Arabic grammatical tradition, it may also be a calque of a technical term from another tradition—namely, Greek or Syriac. However, the connections between *ḥaraka* and potential source words in these languages are tentative at best. While both Greek and Syriac linguistic texts contain technical terms referring to some fashion of 'movement', neither tradition clearly uses those terms to define the phonetic category of 'vowel' before the eighth century.

Versteegh presents potential links between Arabic *ḥaraka* and Greek grammar in his 1977 book, *Greek Elements in Arabic Linguistic Thinking*. He argues that the early Arabic grammatical tradition had contact with a living teaching tradition of Greek logic and grammar before the ninth century. This contact may have been between Greek and Arabic scholars directly, though it may also have been facilitated by Syriac-speaking intermediaries (Versteegh 1977, 6–10, 38–42; see also, King 2012, 203–4; Mavroudi 2014). He adds that such contact need not have resulted in Arabic grammarians systematically copying large swathes of Greek grammatical teaching, but rather that specific technical terms may have passed individually between the Greek and Arabic traditions (Versteegh 1977, 15, 89). We have already seen this sort of ad hoc transfer in the borrowing of 'sounding' terminology in early Arabic grammatical texts, and the same process may have allowed Arabic grammarians to calque the Greek word *kinesis* 'movement' as *ḥaraka*.

Versteegh's two main pieces of evidence that this calquing occurred rely on the scholastic tradition surrounding the *Technē Grammatikē* (*The Art of Grammar*) by Dionysius Thrax (Versteegh 1977, 23–24). He calls attention to the importance of the *scholia* of the *Technē*—that is, its marginal commentaries—in understanding *kinesis* as a grammatical term. First, he notes the similarity between a line in the *scholia* (Hilgard 1901, 383, lines 3–4, and 550, line 24) and a passage in *al-Īḍāḥ fī ʿIllal al-Naḥw* (*Clarification of the Reasons of Grammar*) by the grammarian Abū al-Qāsim al-Zajjājī (d. 938/939) (al-Zajjājī 1959, 72, line 2–3), observing:

> There is a striking terminological similarity between Zajjājī's words 'It (sc. the declension) is a vowel ['movement'] that enters speech after the completion of its phonetic structure' (*hiya ḥaraka dākhila ʿalā ʾl-kalām baʿda kamāl bināʾihi*) and a text in the scholia on Dionysios Thrax where a grammatical case is defined as 'a movement that occurs at the end of a noun' (*onómatos katà to télos ginoménè kinesis*). (Versteegh 1977, 23)

In both texts, the author describes an inflectional ending as a 'movement' added to the end of a word, and the latter suggests that this 'movement' (*kinesis*) was a technical term in the Greek grammatical tradition. Second, Versteegh finds additional evidence for this technical usage of *kinesis* elsewhere in the *Technē*'s *scholia*, remarking that "the Greek word *kineisthai* is used in the sense of 'to be declined,'[28] and the word *akinetos* sometimes has the meaning 'undeclined'" (Hilgard 1901, 427, line 11; Versteegh

---

[28] See Hilgard (1901, 230, line 26).

1977, 24). In this way, Versteegh argues that *ḥaraka* originally also meant 'declension', and its usage eventually expanded to include vowels that did not represent case endings (Versteegh 1977, 24). Notably, the *Technē* itself does not use this *kinesis* terminology, but the parallels between the *scholia* passages and the technical usage of *ḥaraka* in the Arabic grammatical tradition are indeed striking.

Also striking is that the *Technē*, in conjunction with the grammatical teaching tradition surrounding it, is the most likely source for the introduction of the 'sounding' letters to the Syriac grammatical tradition. As discussed above (present chapter, §1.1), Jacob of Edessa (d. 708) probably had in mind Joseph Huzaya's sixth-century Syriac translation of the *Technē* (Merx 1889, 28–29) as well as the Greek vowel term *phoneenta* when he categorised vowels as *ʾatwɔtɔ qɔlɔnɔyɔtɔ* 'sounding letters' in his *Turrɔṣ Mamllɔ*. This term eventually proliferated from Syriac into the Arabic and Hebrew linguistic traditions with the additional calque *muṣawwitāt*, although this transfer did not fully occur until the translation movement. If *ḥaraka* in fact derives from *kinesis*, then it likely emerged in such a Greco-Syro-Arabic linguistic context where the *Technē* was a well-known source.

Versteegh himself hints at this possibility of a connection to *muṣawwitāt*, suggesting that after the translation movement and the broad introduction of Greek logic into Arabic grammar, grammarians reinterpreted the term *ḥaraka* as a signifier of physical movement, rather than inflection. This reinterpretation, he suggests, resulted from an understanding of *muṣawwitu* within the

Stoic framework of aural sound as a 'body' with movement (Versteegh 1977, 24–25; see King 2012, 204–5). He again cites al-
Zajjājī, who describes the Arabic case endings as descriptions of
jaw 'movements' related to their phonetic articulation (al-Zajjājī
1959, 93–94). Another supporting source is Ibn Sīnā's *Risāla Asbāb Ḥudūth al-Ḥurūf*, where he describes the *muṣawwitāt* in terms
of the upward and downward motion of air (al-Tayyan and Mir
Alam 1983, 84–85). As such, the two notions of *ḥaraka* as grammatical 'declension' and of physical 'motion' could have entered
the Arabic grammatical tradition from Greek twice, at two different times.

Versteegh's argument—that *ḥaraka* is derived from a Greek
grammatical term—is itself a response to the earlier theory of Max
Bravmann, who first hypothesised that *ḥaraka* was a metrical
term meant to indicate the musical 'movement' from one station-
ary consonant to the next. As such, *ḥaraka* originally meant 'syllable'. For Bravmann, *ḥaraka* was also a calque of *kinesis*, but it
was based on the Aristotelian logical conception of *kinesis* as "a
specific form of change, namely the realisation of something potential" (Versteegh 1977, 22–23; Bravmann 1934, 12–18). Versteegh takes issue with the possibility that such an Aristotelian
idea could have entered the Arabic intellectual milieu prior to
the ninth-century translation movement, while *ḥaraka* is attested
in Arabic grammar even before al-Khalīl (d. 786/91) and
Sībawayh (d. 793/6). Aristotelian *kinesis*, he reasons, could not
then be the source of *ḥaraka*. Hence his search for a grammatical
usage of the Greek word.

Despite this quest, he does not consider the possibility of whether the word *kinesis* as a grammatical term in the *Technē scholia* could itself have developed from a Greek metrical term or from the Aristotelian idea of 'realising potential', so that grammatical *kinesis* could then appear, now calqued as *ḥaraka*, in eighth-century Arabic sources without any philosophical baggage. In fact, the use of *kinesis* to mean 'declension' or 'inflection' may have both been more widespread and persisted later in Greek grammar than Versteegh thought. The term appears in the Greek grammatical text *Peri tēs tou Logou Suntaxeōs* (*On the Construction of Speech*), written by the ninth-century Patriarch of Jerusalem, Michael Synkellos (d. 846) (Browning and Kazhdan 2005). He produced this work in Edessa around the year 810 and was clearly influenced by the teachings of the *Technē Grammatikē* (Wouters 1983, 321–22; see edition of Donnet 1982).[29]

Versteegh and Bravmann's competing hypotheses are not necessarily mutually exclusive, though neither unequivocally tells the full story of *kinesis* in the early Islamicate Middle East. For despite Versteegh's scepticism, this idea that a vowel is the necessary movement after a consonant, and thus nearly equivalent to 'syllable', almost exactly matches the description that Dawid bar Pawlos (fl. 770–800) gave for the Syriac *qɔlɔnɔyɔtɔ*, even though the term 'movement' does not appear in his grammatical writings. He noted that only the sounding letters can be pronounced "in and of themselves" (Gottheil 1893, cxvii, lines 5–12; see above, present chapter, §1.1). In fact, we have seen that this precise quality, namely for a vowel to be pronounced *in and*

---

[29] I am grateful to Daniel King for drawing my attention to this source.

of itself—the very ability to create a syllable—was the defining characteristic of 'sounding' letters for a number of medieval linguists, including Jacob of Edessa (d. 708), Saadia Gaon (d. 942), and Elias of Ṭirhan (d. 1049).

These 'sounding' principles are directly linked to the Greek grammatical tradition, and their appearance among Semitic authors like Dawid bar Pawlos reinforces the possibility of an intellectual pathway that could convey *kinesis* from Greek into Syriac or Arabic. Additionally, Talmon (2003, 32–33) has shown that Dawid may have had knowledge of early Arabic grammatical principles, and so could be one of the 'Syriac intermediaries' that Versteegh suspects transferred Greek concepts into the pre-Sībawayhan Arabic tradition. Similarly, Daniel King (2012, 199–201) has identified a letter written in 785 by the Catolicos Timothy I, an Eastern patriarch who lamented the success of Arabic grammarians in comparison to contemporary advancements in Syriac, and seems to have had direct interactions with some Arabic scholars. It seems then that some Syriac scholars in the latter half of the eighth century knew of developments within the Arabic linguistic tradition at the time of Sībawayh and al-Khalīl, and could have been conduits between the Greek and Arabic traditions for ideas about vowels and *kinesis*. Conversely, Dawid bar Pawlos' description of the *ʾatwɔtɔ qɔlɔnɔyɔtɔ* could have been influenced by contemporary conceptions of vowels (i.e., *ḥarakāt*) in Arabic. This type of intellectual exchange could have occurred—as Versteegh suggests—around just a few technical terms, with Greek, Syriac, and Arabic scholars all understanding vowels as vocalised 'movements' in similar, if slightly varied, ways. Furthermore, and again in line with Versteegh, this exchange would not have required a full pre-ninth-century importation of Aristotelian logic into Arabic (or even into Syriac), but rather just the description of vowels and syllables as given by Dawid bar Pawlos and a few lines from the *Technē*.

Versteegh briefly revisited the topic of *ḥaraka* and *kinesis* in another book, *Arabic Grammar and Qurʾanic Exegesis* (1993). In it, he simultaneously asserts that there was new evidence of pre-Sībawayhan contact between Arabic scholars and sources of Greek logic (Versteegh 1993, 23–25), while also backtracking on his original claim that *ḥaraka* began as a term for 'declension' on analogy with a Greek *kinesis* term (Versteegh 1993, 32). After analysing the vowel terminology in eighth-century *ḥadīth* (see below, chapter 4, §1.1), he concludes that the Arabic declensional terms *naṣb* 'standing upright', *khafḍ* 'lowering', and *rafʿ* 'rising' were originally names for vowel phonemes, and their use as the names for case endings was a secondary development. Extrapolating from this discovery, Versteegh asserts that the naming of vowels, rather than cases, with these terms precludes *ḥaraka* from originally being a term for 'declension' in the same way as Greek *kinesis*. He goes so far as to admit specifically that he was incorrect when he made that claim in 1977. However, his first idea may actually be more accurate than this revision. It seems to me that there is no reason that the Arabic case names could not have originated as phonetic descriptors of vowels (as Versteegh argues), while the category of vowels in general (i.e., *ḥarakāt*) was derived from a Greek term for declension; or rather, a term for 'sounds at the end of nouns'.

At any rate, Versteegh does not explain why these two separate naming conventions could not coincide. The early use of
the Arabic declensional terms (*naṣb, rafʿ, khafḍ*) as names for
vowels—even as late as the ninth century (Versteegh 1993, 18–
19)—demonstrates that the line between inflection and vocalisation in early Arabic grammar was blurry at best. That fluidity
must have been almost necessary if a Greek term for 'declension'
were to make the leap to meaning 'vowel' in Arabic. Still, while
it remains unclear whether *haraka* was originally a term for 'declension' or 'vowel' (or 'syllable'), in some sense it does not matter for the present discussion. Either way, the most plausible—if
by no means confirmed—source of *haraka* is the Greek word *kinesis*, and it encompassed, to some extent, all of the vowel phonemes that could potentially occur at the ends of Arabic words.

One fact that does seem certain is that in contrast to Arabic,
there is little evidence of a grammatical term of 'movement' being used to define vowels in Syriac before the second half of the
ninth century.[30] This later development was likely a result of continued contact with Arabic grammar, rather than an import from
Greek, and suggests that there may not have been a Syriac 'inter-
mediary' in the transfer of *kinesis* to Arabic. That said, the Syriac
recitation traditions do include the names of certain accent signs
based on the concept of 'movement', a phenomenon curiously
similar to what Bravmann argued for Arabic.

The earliest Syriac accent signs appear in the fifth or sixth
century, and they seem to reflect an early tradition that predates
the split between the East and West Syriac accent systems. These

---

[30] See discussions of Bar Bahlul and Ibn ʿAlī's Syriac lexica below.

include thirteen early signs, possibly invented in part by Joseph Huzaya (fl. c. 500–530) and known from the appendix of MS BL Add. 12138 (written in 899); as well as a few pre-seventh-century manuscripts (see Loopstra 2009, 46; 2014, I:VII–VIII, XIII, L–LVI; Segal 1953, 60–66; see also, Kiraz 2015, 108–19; Loopstra 2019). Segal notes that some of these accents derived their names from Greek (1953, 75), but none of them had names equivalent to 'movement'.

New accents developed in both the East and West Syriac recitation traditions between the seventh and tenth centuries. In the Eastern system, the new signs included *mziˁɔnɔ* 'causing movement', a supralinear dot that appears at the end of a clause to mark a pause with rising tone (Segal 1953, 81). It appears throughout BL Add. 12138 (Loopstra 2014, I:LXVI), so it developed no later than the ninth century, and is likely much earlier. Segal speculates that its name comes from the energy or stress in the noticeable movement of breath or vibration that accompanies this rising tone, although he notes that Elias of Ṭirhan (d. 1049) attributes it to the movement of the tongue (Segal 1953, n. 5). As for the Western tradition, new signs appear in a short work on accents by Thomas the Deacon from the first half of the seventh century (Martin 1869, ܝ–ܗ; Kiraz 2015, 120–21). He refers to *zawˁɔ* 'movement' (Martin 1869, ܟ, lines 15 and 22), a single supralinear dot at the end of a word that originally emphasised a word or phrase in contrast to that which followed it. Over time, the usage of *zawˁɔ* expanded to indicate any emphatic accent with a rising tone, similar to the Eastern *mziˁɔnɔ* (Segal 1953, 122). This accent persisted in the Western tradition as Jacob of Edessa

(d. 708) revised the accent system near the end of the seventh
century, and by the eleventh century Elias of Ṭirhan claims that
the Western *zawⁿ* and Eastern *mziⁿnⁿ* are equivalent (Segal
1953, 145).

Segal points out that the West Syriac linguistic tradition ex-
perienced greater influence from Greek rhetoric than the East
Syriac tradition did, and Western authors match the names of
accents to Aristotelian categories of speech as early as the sixth
century (Segal 1953, 120–21).[31] It would not be surprising if
zawⁿ as a general term for 'final rising tone' was related to *kinesis*
in a similar manner, but it is not clear how or why a Greek term
for 'inflection' might have been adapted to refer to 'accentuation'
in recitation. Moreover, there is no obvious connection between
the Syriac accent names and the word *ḥaraka* in Arabic, except
to say that they could have a common origin in *kinesis*. It is perhaps best to think of the respective Greek, Syriac, and Arabic
conceptions of phonetic 'movement' as the products of an inter-
linked network of contemporaneous grammatical traditions, rather than a single linear pathway whereby terms moved from
Greek to Syriac, and then to Arabic.

To summarise, the Greek word *kinesis* developed a meaning
close to 'declension' in the Greek grammatical tradition of the
late antique world. This word may have begun as a metrical term,
but it came to refer to the inflected vowels at the ends of Greek
nouns in at least some grammatical circles related to the *Technē*
of Dionysius Thrax. This idea may have allowed seventh- or

---

[31] Note especially Thomas the Deacon's use of *paroksotonos* as the name
of an accent (Martin 1869, ‎ܠ).

eighth-century Arabic grammarians to calque *kinesis* as *ḥaraka*, most likely to refer to their own case vowels, but this meaning then expanded to refer to vowels in general. The same use of 'movement' does not appear in the eighth-century Syriac grammatical tradition, so it is not clear that Syriac intermediaries would have been responsible for this transmission of *kinesis* into Arabic. Furthermore, Syriac authors used 'movement' terms (*mziʿɔnɔ* and *zawʿɔ*) to name certain pausal accents in their recitation tradition as early as the seventh century, but the sources examined here suggest no obvious connection between this usage and the technical term *ḥaraka*.

2.2. Movement between Languages: *Ḥaraka* in Hebrew and Syriac

Ḥaraka is so ubiquitous in Arabic grammatical texts that it hardly needs further explanation. It is a categorical term specific to the three short vowel phonemes—/a/, /i/, and /u/—and it appears from grammatical sources in the eighth century. It actually represents one half of a conceptual pair in these Arabic sources, with the 'movement' of a vowel contrasting with the 'motionless' or 'still' (*sākin*) consonants. Syriac and Hebrew authors adapted these phonological concepts by the ninth or tenth century, and modified them to fit their own languages. In the Syriac linguistic tradition, 'moving' and 'still' classifications first appear in lexicographical works from the late ninth century, and they continue into the eleventh-century grammars. In the Hebrew tradition, they appear in Masoretic treatises and grammatical sources during the same timeframe. For all three languages, 'movement' is essential for facilitating speech.

Sībawayh demonstrates the baseline usage of these classifications in his *Kitāb* by describing individual consonants with the adjectives *mutaḥarrik* 'moved' and *sākin* 'motionless, still' (e.g., Sībawayh 1986, IV:144). A letter that immediately precedes a vowel (*ḥaraka*) is considered *mutaḥarrik*, while a letter that does not precede a vowel is *sākin*. In fully vocalised Classical Arabic, every *mutaḥarrik* letter has a *fatḥa*, *kasra*, or *ḍamma* vowel sign, while every letter that does not have a vowel takes the *sukūn* 'stillness' sign. This fact also leads Sībawayh to classify every *mater lectionis* letter *ʾalif*, *wāw*, and *yāʾ* as *sākin*, even though they stand for long vowels, as they cannot ever take *ḥarakāt* signs (al-Nassir 1993, 109). Sībawayh clarifies part of his understanding of *ḥarakāt* by quoting his teacher, al-Khalīl ibn Aḥmad (d. 786/791):

وزعم الخليل أنّ الفتحة والكسرة والضمّة زوائد، وهنّ يلحقن الحرف لِيُوصَل
الى التكلم به. والبناءُ هو الساكن الذي لا زيادة فيه.

> Al-Khalīl claimed that the *fatḥa*, *kasra*, and *ḍamma* were additions, and they attach to the letter in order to connect it into speech; and [a letter of] the base structure is the *sākin*, which is not an addition. (Sībawayh 1986, IV:241–42)

Al-Khalīl states that the vowels are not inherent to Arabic words, but rather they are added to consonantal structures in order to create speech. Without them, the base consonants are *sākin*. Thus, for Sībawayh, the vowels are the connective energy that allows groups of consonants to form words and speech.

Ibn Jinnī takes up Sībawayh's division between 'movement' and 'stillness' in his tenth-century book on phonology, *Sirr Ṣināʿa al-Iʿrāb* (*The Secret of Making Proper Arabic*). He devotes a great deal of ink to describing the different ways that one can classify the Arabic letters, and one of these divisions is into *sukūn* and *ḥaraka* (Ibn Jinnī 1993, 62). This contrast is particularly apparent in his description of one Arabic letter—the *hamza bayna bayna* 'in-between *hamza*'—which has characteristics of both a vowel and a consonant. Sībawayh uses this term to refer to a weakened *hamza* that functions more like a *mater lectionis* that lengthens a vowel than as a typical consonant (e.g., the *hamza* in *saʾala* 'he asked') (al-Nassir 1993, 81–82). Ibn Jinnī clarifies what he believes Sībawayh meant, writing: "by saying *bayna bayna*, Sībawayh's meaning was that it is weak, not able to be properly pronounced, but not the total loss of the letter which its vowel is from (ومعنى قول سيبويه بينَ بينَ أي: هي ضعيفة ليس لها تمكن المحققة ولا خُلوص الحرف الذي منها حركتها)" (Ibn Jinnī 1993, 49). That is, the *hamza bayna bayna* is pronounced a little like *ʾalif*, *yāʾ*, or *wāw* when they stand for a vowel. However, in Ibn Jinnī's own words, "even though it has approached *sākin*, it is actually *mutaḥarrika*, such that you count it, in the measure of prosody, as a moved letter (وإن كانت قد قُربت من الساكن فإنها في الحقيقة متحركة، أنك تعتدّها حرفاً متحركاً في وزن العروض)" (Ibn Jinnī 1993, 48). The *hamza bayna bayna* in this context becomes nearly motionless (*sākin*), but not completely still like in Sībawayh's conception of the *matres lectionis*, so it retains its status as a vocalised (*mutaḥarrik*) letter at the onset of a distinct syllable.

The explanation of *mutaḥarrik* and *sākin* letters extended
far beyond the Classical Arabic grammatical tradition, with the
same terms occurring in Judaeo-Arabic Masoretic treatises. The
tenth-century *Treatise on the Shewa* sometimes refers to vowels as
ḥarakāt, and speaks of specific vowels with phrases like "the
movement of *pataḥ*" (*ḥaraka pɔtaḥ*) for /a/ or "the movement of
qameṣ" (*ḥaraka qɔmeṣ*) for /ɔ/ (Levy 1936, ג, lines 18–19, and כא,
line 8). The author demonstrates the full range of their Arabic
technical terms in a passage describing the vocalisation of *shewa*
on certain pharyngeal consonants when they close an onset syllable:

> פאמא תחת הדֿה אלארבעה אחרף אעני אחהע פאנה לא יתחרך תחתהא
> בתה לא בפתח ולא בקמץ ולא בתֿנתין ולא בחרכה מן אלחרכאת בל
> תגדה תחתהא אבדֿא סאכן ולא יחרכהא לחן ולא תחרכה גֿעיה ולא שיא
> אכֿר מן אלאסבאב אלמחרכה בתה בל תגדה עלי הדֿא אלחאל דֿאים כקול
> בָּאְשָׁא מַהְרַי מַחְלָה בַּעְלִי נַחְבַּי וגֿירהמא ליס פיהא שיא יתחרך ודֿלך
> ביאנה.

As for [the shewa] beneath these four letters—namely,
ʾaleph, ḥet, heʾ, and *ʿayin*—it is not moved at all, not with
pɔtaḥ nor *qɔmeṣ* nor *ṣere* nor any *ḥaraka.* Rather, beneath
them you will always find a *sākin,* and no accent or *gaʿya*
or anything else among the causes of movement can move
them at all. Instead, they are always found according to
this pattern [with a closed initial syllable], as is said:
bɔʾshɔ, mahray, maḥlɔ, baʿli, naḥbay, and others which lack
anything that is moved. That is its explanation. (Levy
1936, כא, lines 9–14)

As the author explains, in specific words, a *shewa* sign beneath a
pharyngeal consonant always indicates *sākin,* representing silence at a syllable break, and does not move (*lā yataḥarrik*). These

consonants will never take a *ḥaraka*, not even with one of the "causes of movement" (*al-ʾasbāb al-muḥarrika*) that typically "imparts movement" (*yuḥarrik*), such as an accent that elsewhere would change a word's syllable structure and the realisation of the *shewa*.[32]

The above terminology closely resembles that found in *Kitāb Sībawayh* and *Sirr Ṣināʿa al-Iʿrāb*, but the *Treatise on the Shewa* uses this vocabulary for a uniquely Hebrew purpose, applying *mutaḥarrik* and *sākin* to distinguish the types of *shewa*. Broadly speaking,[33] the Tiberian *shewa* comes in two flavours, usually designated in English as 'silent' and 'mobile' (also called 'quiescent' and 'vocalic'). In the Tiberian reading tradition, both types are marked by a vertical pair of dots below a letter, but silent *shewa* indicates the close of a syllable, while mobile *shewa* represents an epenthetic short vowel (usually /a/) (Khan 2020, I:305). Naturally, this fact causes a certain amount of ambiguity, and many Tiberian Masoretes—including the author of the *Treatise on the Shewa*—wrote about how to differentiate the two she-

---

[32] See also, another section of the *Treatise on the Shewa*: "The Rules of *Shewa* and How Accents and *Gaʿyot* Move It" (Levy 1936, ה, from line 7).

[33] See Khan (2020, I:305–421, 486–95). For simplicity's sake, it may be best to follow the dubious recommendation of Thomas O. Lambdin: "...in fact there are several schools of thought on the subject among the traditional Hebrew grammarians. Since it is completely immaterial to the understanding of the language and to translation, we shall not enter into the dispute" (1971, XXVI).

was. In the *Treatise*, they use the same 'silent' and 'mobile' terminology that we use now, albeit as the Arabic words *sākin* and
mutaḥarrik:

> הדֹא אלקסם איצֹא ינקסם עלי קסמין מנה סאכן ומנה מתחרך. ואלסאכן
> מתֹל קולך שְׁמְעוּ שִׁמְעוֹן . . . וקד ביינת לך אן הדֹה אלשואאת כלהא
> אלוסטאניה אנמא פעלהא אן תפצל אלכלמה ותקטעהא עלי מא יגב להא
> מן אלתקטיע ואלתכֹריג. וכל הדֹא אלנוע פליס פיה שיא יתחרך בל אן
> כאנא אתֹנין פאלתֹאני מנהמא הוא אלמתחרך אבדא לאן אלתֹאני הוא
> אלמאלף אבדא ואלתחריך פהו לצאחב אלתאליף ליס לצאחב אלקטע

> This classification is also divided into two groups, includ-
> ing *sākin* and *mutaḥarrik*. The *sākin* is like how you say [the
> *mem* in]: *shimʿu* [and] *shimʿon*... I have specified to you that
> these *shewas* are all internal; one only uses them to sepa-
> rate and split the word, according to what is required for
> it with respect to splitting and pronunciation. Everything
> of this type has nothing moving, unless there are two [*she-
> was*], for then the second of them is always *mutaḥarrik*, be-
> cause the second is always the combiner. Imparting move-
> ment is for the master of combining, not the master of split-
> ting. (Levy 1936, ד, lines 3–8)

The silent *shewa*, which functions precisely like the Arabic *sukūn*,
splits words into syllables, and thus it is deemed *sākin*. Meanwhile, mobile *shewa* is *mutaḥarrik*, combining separate syllables
via movement. Later on, the author even discusses "the *shewa*, its
ḥaraka, and its *sukūn* (אלשוא וחרכתה וסכונה)" (Levy 1936, ז, line
11). Besides *shewa*, nothing in the Hebrew or Arabic linguistic
traditions has this kind of variable phonological nature, so the
Masoretes adapted existing Arabic terminology to describe it.

This association likely began with *mutaḥarrik* describing the status of a consonant with mobile *shewa*, and then shifted to describing the *shewa* itself.

The *Treatise* even applies a Hebrew version of this terminology, suggesting that the Masoretes may have calqued the words *mutaḥarrik* and *sākin* as early as the ninth century (Dotan 2007, 651; Khan 2020, I:116–18). While discussing the pronunciation of conjunctive *waw* with *shewa* but without *gaʿya* (i.e., a type of stress marker), the author writes:

לאנך אן רפעת אלגעיה מן אלואו פהי אבדא מקטעין מתֿל וּשְׁלַח וּסְגֹר
וּזְהַב וּשְׁבֶה להודיעך כי יש שוא הוא אשר יכרות ויפריד לאילו ובא ללמדך
כי השוא המכרת והמפסק אעני השוא העומד יהיה תֿאני לעולם ושוכן
כאשר ביארנו ואינו מתנענע כי זה המתנענע יש לו שני.

Because if you remove the *gaʿya* from the *waw*, then [the word] is always split into two [syllables], like *ushlaḥ*, *usgor*, *uzhab̲*, and *ushbe*. In order to inform you that there is a *shewa* which may cut and separate them, it comes to instruct you that the cutting, stopping *shewa*—I mean, the motionless *shewa*—will always be second. It is as if it clarifies for us, when [the first] is not moved, that the moved one in it is second. (Levy 1936, ו, lines 5–8)

The author explains that there are exceptions to the rule that when there are two consecutive *shewas*, the second one is always mobile. One such exception is when the first *shewa* in a word is on a conjunctive *waw*. In that case, the situation is reversed, and the second *shewa* is actually *ʿomed* 'standing in place, motionless', while the first *shewa* is *mitnaʿaneaʿ* 'moving'. *ʿOmed* and *mitnaʿaneaʿ* are calques of *sākin* and *mutaḥarrik*, respectively. The language here switches from Arabic to Hebrew, probably reflecting the language of a source text that was used in the compilation

of the *Treatise*. This source was most likely ninth-century Masoretic material written in rhymed Hebrew prose, and it suggests
that the Masoretes adapted *mutaḥarrik* and *sākin* to Hebrew prior
to the tenth century, before they switched to writing mainly in
Judaeo-Arabic (see Khan 2020, I:117–18).

The same language appears in other Masoretic treatises
from the tenth and eleventh centuries. For example, T-S Ar.53.1,
a tenth-century *muṣawwitāt* text, introduces all of the Hebrew
vowel signs, then *shewa*, saying, "Additionally the *shewa*, which
is the two standing dots, it exists according to two divisions: *sākin*
and *mutaḥarrik* (ואלשוא והמא אלנקטתאן אלקאימתאן והי תכון עלי קסמין
סאכן ומתחרך)" (Allony and Yeivin 1985, 92, lines 8–11). Similarly,
Abū al-Faraj Hārūn (d. c. 1050) explains one of the rules of Hebrew phonetics in *Hidāya al-Qārī* (*The Guide for the Reader*), writing:

> ואלחרף קד יערי מן נגמה ואלנגמה לא תערי מן חרף לאן אלנטק לא בד
> לה מן סאכן ומתחרך פאלמתחרך לא יתחרך אלא בנגמה ואלסאכן
> מסתגני ען דלך

> A letter may go without a vowel (*naghama*), but a vowel
> may not go without a letter, because articulation must
> have some *sākin* and some *mutaḥarrik*. So the *mutaḥarrik* is
> not moved except by a vowel, but the *sākin* has no need of
> that. (Khan 2020, II:119, lines 676–78)

The *sākin* may not have needed a *ḥaraka*, but the Masoretes certainly did, and they had no problems adapting Arabic linguistic
terminology to their writings on Hebrew phonology. Syriac scholars had the same need, and they also adapted these words to describe the language of their Bible between the ninth and eleventh
centuries.

Some of the earliest evidence of Syriac authors applying the Arabic ideas of *mutaḥarrik* and *sākin* to vocalisation comes from the Syriac-Arabic lexica of ʿĪsā ibn ʿAlī (d. c. 900)[34] and Ḥasan bar Balul (fl. 942–968). Both of these authors based their dictionaries on the work of earlier ninth-century lexicographers, particularly the famous translator Ḥunayn ibn Isḥāq (d. 873), and both were revised several times after their deaths (see Butts 2009; Taylor 2011). Both lexica also describe the differences in vocalisation between homographic Syriac words using technical phonological terms, and they indicate that a letter is unvocalised with derivatives of the root *shly* 'being still'. In Bar Bahlul's lexicon, this vocabulary is fairly straightforward. For example, he writes: "ʾabnɔ, according to Ḥunayn, while the *bet* is *shalyɔ* (ܐܒܢܐ ܐܝܟ ܚܘܢܝܢ ܟܕ ܒܝܬ ܫܠܝܐ ܗ̄)" (Duval 1901, 17). That is, ʾabnɔ 'stone' is pronounced with a *bet* that is *shalyɔ*, meaning 'unvocalised'. *Shalyɔ* here is a passive participle, literally 'made still', and it is the most common way to indicate an unvocalised letter in Bar Bahlul's lexicon (e.g., Duval 1901, 34, 398, 417, 429, 440). It is most likely a direct calque of the Arabic *sākin*, another participial form. Interestingly, Bar Bahlul also applies 'stillness' terminology to letters that have some vocalic quality, writing: "bʿɔqɔ, while the *bet* is made still, and the ʿayin and qof are stood upright (ܒܥܩܐ ܟܕ ܒܝܬ ܫܠܝܐ ܘܥܝܢ ܘܩܘܦ ܩܝܡܝܢ ܗ̄)" (Duval 1901, 417).[35] While the initial *bet* in *bʿɔqɔ* 'convulsions' lacks a full vowel and never takes vowel points of any kind, it does require a *shewa*-like vocalisation in speech. Bar Bahlul's

---

[34] Also known as Ishoʿ bar ʿAlī.

[35] 'Stood upright' in this context means that these letters have the vowel *zqɔpɔ* /ɔ/. See below, chapter 4, §2.1.

contemporaries among the Hebrew Masoretes would have de-scribed such a *bet* as having *shewa mutaḥarrika*, but he calls it *shalyɔ* 'made still'. This difference between the two languages may reflect a greater concern among the Tiberian Masoretes for proper biblical recitation and orthoepy (see Khan 2020, I:99–105, 441, esp. 452), at least in comparison to Syriac lexicographers.

Like Bar Bahlul, Ibn ʿAlī appears to use terminology similar to *shalyɔ*, although in his lexicon it occurs as an abbreviation, simply the letter *shin*. For example, one entry reads: "*metqbar*, when the *mem* is constrained, the *taw* and *qof* are made still, and the *bet* is opened (ܒ ܪܬܚܩܘ ܗܡ ܠܗ ܪܥܠܬ ܩ ܪܬܢܐ ܗܕ ܓܚܡܬܢ)" (Hoffmann 1874, 283, line 15). By this description, he means that in the word *metqbar* 'buried', the *mem* is pronounced with /e/, the *taw* and *qof* are pronounced without vocalisation, and the *bet* is pronounced with /a/. The *shin* standing for *shalyɔ* parallels other passive participles that indicate vowels throughout the text (see below, chapter 4, §2.2). Note that like Bar Bahlul, Ibn ʿAlī applies this 'stillness' to both the unvocalised *taw* and to the *qof*, even though the latter must have been articulated with a *shewa*-like vowel to break up the consonant cluster. It thus appears that their descriptions focus more on the graphical appearance of vowel points (or lack thereof) on a fully-pointed letter, rather than on that letter's phonetic realisation. This view explicitly differs from the *Treatise on the Shewa*, where the author asserts that any Hebrew *shewa* at the onset of a syllable must be *mutaḥarrik* (Levy 1936, ה, lines 2–3). As such, if a Masoretic author were vocalising the word *metqbar*, they would read the *qof* with a mobile *shewa*.

In addition to Ibn ʿAlī and Bar Bahlul's descriptive usages, both lexicographers link *shɔlyɔ* and *shalyɔ* to *sākin* and *sukūn* in their lexical entries for the words. Bar Bahlul equates *shalyɔ* with *sākin*, writing: "*Shalyɔ* is *al-sākin*; *shelyɔ*, *shalyutɔ*, according to Zekaryɔ, is *al-sukūn* (السكون اها ܘܡܢ ܓܠܝܬܐ. ܓܠܝܬ .ܓܠܝܬ)" (السكون السكون) (Duval 1901, 1980). He includes these two nominal forms—*shelyɔ* and *shalyutɔ*, apparently equivalent to *sukūn*—on the authority of one Zekaryɔ, most likely the Zekaryɔ Maruzɔyɔ whom Bar Bahlul names among his sources in the lexicon's introduction (Duval 1901, 3, line 3). The exact identity of this Zekaryɔ remains unknown, but he may be identifiable with Ishoʿ of Merv, a ninth-century lexicographer known as a source for Ibn ʿAlī's lexicon (Butts 2011). Ibn ʿAlī himself is less specific about *shalyɔ*, but his text does say: "*Shle* is *sakana*; from it *shelyɔ*, which is *sakīna* and *salām* (والسلام السكينة . ܫܠܝܬ ܘܡܢܗ . سكن . ܫܠܐ)"[36] (Gottheil 1928, II:436, line 3). That is, the verb *shle* means 'to be still', and its derivative noun *shelyɔ* means 'steadiness and peace'.

In contrast to *shalyɔ*, neither Bar Bahlul nor Ibn ʿAlī defines 'movement' as a general term for 'vowel', even though eleventh-century grammarians would come to use the word *zawʿɔ* 'movement' for exactly that purpose. For those later grammarians,

---

[36] Gottheil notes six manuscripts that have two sublinear dots, indicating *shle* here, and one that has a supralinear dot, suggesting *shɔlɔ*. He further notes that the manuscript with *shɔlɔ* has the double-dot mark for /a/ in *shalyɔ*, while other manuscripts leave the latter word unpointed. See Gottheil (1928, II:436, nn. 3 and 4).

zawʿɔ is clearly a calque of the Arabic *ḥaraka*, and they likewise calque *mutaḥarrik* with the Syriac *mettziʿɔnɔ* (Kiraz 2012, I:59). While not specifically defining those terms, Bar Bahlul may allude to this later usage in his broader entry on *zawʿɔtɔ* 'trembling, movement', saying: "*mziʿ*, according to Zekaryɔ, is *yahīj*, *yataḥarrak*; *mziʿɔnɔ* is *muḥarrik*; *mettziʿɔnɔ* is *mutaḥarrik*; *ʾaziʿ*, according to Bar Serosheway, is *ʾuḥarrik* (ܡܙܝܥ ܐܝܟ ܙܟܪܝܐ يهيج يتحرّك. ܡܙܝܥܢܐ مُحرّك. ܡܬܬܙܝܥܢܐ متحرّك. ܐܙܝܥ ܐܝܟ ܒܪ ܣܪܘܫܘܝ احرّك)" (Duval 1901, 681). That is, *mziʿ* 'moving' is 'becoming perturbed' (*yahīj*), 'becoming moved' (*yataḥarrak*), while the *nomen agentis* form *mziʿɔnɔ* 'causer of movement' is an equivalent Arabic active participial form, *muḥarrik*. Then the Syriac participle *mettziʿɔnɔ* 'moved' is *mutaḥarrik*, the same as the calque in the later grammars. *ʾAziʿ* 'I will cause movement', according to the ninth-century scholar Bar Serosheway, is Arabic *ʾuḥarrik*, which has the same meaning. Similarly, the section on the word *zawʿɔ* lists seven types of physical movement, including the last one: "And for whatever is moved and circled in place, even though it is in some respects similar to them, and in other respects distinct: [all of them are] *al-ḥaraka* (ܘܠܗܘ ܕܒܟܠ ܕܘܟܬܗ ܡܬܬܙܝܥ. ܘܡܬܟܪܟ ܐܦܢ ܕܒܡܕܡ ܐܠܐ ܒܡܕܡ فهو الحركة. ܦܪܝܫܐ ܥܡ ܗܠܝܢ)" (Duval 1901, 682). Even without technical grammatical definitions here, *ḥaraka* and *mutaḥarrik* were the default Arabic words to translate *zawʿɔ* in the tenth century.

The more technical Syriac calques of *ḥaraka* and *sākin* become fully evident from the eleventh century, in the Syriac grammars of Elias of Nisibis (d. 1046) and Elias of Ṭirhan (d. 1049). In his *Turrɔṣ Mamllɔ Suryɔyɔ* (*The Correct Form of Syriac Speech*), the Nisibene Elias distinguishes two relevant terms in this arena: *mettziʿonito/mettziʿonuto* 'moved one, vocalised, vowel' and *shlito* 'made still, unvocalised'. His second chapter begins thus:

.ܐܚܪܢܝ ܐܬܘܬܐ ܡܬܬܙܝܥܢܝܬܐ ܘܫܠܝܬܐ

ܐܬܘܬܐ ܗܟܝܠ ܡܬܬܙܝܥܢܝܬܐ ܓܝܪ ܠܘܬ ܥܪܒܝܐ ܠܬܠܬ ܐܕܫܝܢ ܡܬܦܠܓܢ ܘܥܡ ܗܠܝܢ ܡܥܪܒܝܐ ܣܘܪ̈ܝܝܐ ܠܚܡܫܐ ܐܕܫܝܢ. ܥܡ ܕܝܢ ܗܠܝܢ ܕܝܠܢ ܡܕܢ̈ܚܝܐ ܠܫܒܥܐ ܐܕܫܝܢ ܡܬܦܠܓܢ

Now we will speak on the moved and motionless letters:

For the moved letters, among the Arabs, are divided into three types, and among the Western Syrians, into five types. Then among us Easterners, they are divided into seven types. (Gottheil 1887, ܙ, lines 6–9)

By the 'moved letters' (*ʾatwoto mettziʿonyoto*), Elias is clearly referring to his seven vowels of Eastern Syriac, contrasting them with the smaller vowel inventories of Arabic and West Syriac (see below, chapter 4, §2.3). *Mettziʿonito* is a calque of *mutaḥarrik*, but Elias slightly extends its usage, using it both as a descriptor of a letter (i.e., "moved letters") and also as the categorical name for vowels as opposed to consonants (i.e., the "seven types") (see Segal 1953, 7; see also, Kiraz 2012, I:69–74; Knudsen 2015, 91–92; Butts 2016, 89–90). There is some variation between *mettziʿonyoto* (sing. *mettziʿonito*), seen here, and *mettziʿonwoto* (sing. *mettziʿonuto*), which Elias uses in the first chapter (Gottheil 1887, ܘ, line 8), although the two forms seem mostly interchangeable. Conversely, he calques *sākin* using the feminine adjective *shlito*, indicating 'motionless letters' (*ʾatwoto shalyoto*). In precisely the same way as Sībawayh's Arabic, this category encompasses all letters that are not marked with a vowel sign in fully pointed

Syriac writing (Gottheil 1887, ـ, lines 19–21; see al-Nassir 1993, 109).

In his *Memrɔ Gramaṭiqɔyɔ* (*The Grammatical Essay*), Elias of Ṭirhan presents his own understanding of 'moved' and 'motionless' letters in a way that is similar, though not identical, to Elias of Nisibis. In the seventeenth chapter of this grammar, he explains:

ܕܝܩܠܝ ܕܢ ܐܬܬ ܝܕܝܥ .. ܐܬܪܝܓܝܒܢ .. ܕܐܝܟ ܐܝܟ ܢܝܢ .. ܫܘܐܝܐ .. ܩܒܘܪܐ .. ܩܝܢܐ

ܩܛܘܠܝ̈ܗܝ, .. ܩܛܘ̈ܠܝܗܝ .. ܚܝ̇ܐ .. ܘ ܝ ܒ ܫ ܪ ܝ [ܩ] ܛ .. ܘܓܠܝ ܡܚܠܝܢ ..

ܫܡܗܐ

Then [also know] that two [letters] being still is possible, for example: *ḥrure, qbure, priyye,*[37] *qṭulɔy(hy), qṭulu(hy),* etc. The *ḥet, rish, qof, bet, shin, rish,* [*qof*], and *ṭet* are motionless in these nouns. (Baethgen 1880, ܐ–ܒܝ)

Elias suggests that the first two consonants in words like *ḥrure* 'holes' are both motionless (*neshlyɔn*), 'unvocalised', although at first glance this appears impossible. As we have already seen with Bar Bahlul—for whom the first letter of *bʿɔqɔ* was 'made still' (*shalyɔ*)—the initial *ḥet* of *ḥrure* could feasibly be called 'still' in Syriac. On the other hand, the *rish* is most certainly 'moved', at least by all the definitions of vocalic movement that we have discussed thus far, since it immediately precedes a vowel. However, Elias does not seem to be describing phonetics in this instance, but rather he designates 'motion' and 'stillness' according to

---

[37] This word may be mistaken in Baethgen's edition, as Elias' explanation indicates it should begin with the letter *shin*.

graphical vocalisation.[38] In Classical Syriac, the vowels /i/ and /u/ are practically always represented by the *matres lectionis* letters *yod* and *waw*. In contrast to Arabic, when such words are vocalised in Syriac, the vowel sign is placed on the *mater lectionis*, rather than the preceding consonant. As a result, in the fully vocalised form of *ḥrure* (ܚܪܘܪܐ), neither the *ḥet* nor the *rish* has a vowel sign, so Elias can say that they are both 'still'. This explanation is interesting in the context of Sībawayh, who classified all of the Arabic *matres lectionis* as *sākin* due to their lack of vowel signs.

Like Elias of Nisibis, Elias of Ṭirhan also expands the idea of 'movement' while breaking with Arabic grammarians. As we have already seen from his discussion of sounding letters, "the vocalised ones are made known by production from these three sounding ones (ܪܬܐܘܝܬܐ ܐܬܝܕܥܝܢ ܡܢ ܗܠܝܢ ܬܠܬ ܩܠܢܝܬܐ)" (Baethgen 1880, ܢܚ, lines 14–15; see above, present chapter, §1.0). By 'vocalised ones'—*mettziʿonwoto*, literally 'things that are moved'—he means each of the vowel phonemes, specifically as they are combined with consonants to create vocalised syllables. But Elias extends this category of 'moved things' beyond vocalic phonemes to include other non-consonantal modulations of the voice. In his introduction, he writes:

---

[38] It seems that Elias' analysis must be based on the fully pointed forms of words, even if complete vocalisation in Syriac writing was uncommon. Full pointing was most common in bliblical texts, which was likely Elias' main concern when writing this grammar.

ܐܡܪ ܐܢܐ .. ܒܪܫܝܬ ܒܪܐ ܐܠܗܐ. ܝܬ̇ ܫܡܝܐ ܘܝܬ ܐܪܥܐ .. ܘܐܠܘ ܠܐ
ܗܘܐ ܡܬܬܙܝܥܢܘܬܐ ܗܕܐ ܕܐܝܬܝܗ̇ ܬܚܬܝܐ ܘܪܛܡܐ . ܕܩܡ ܡܩܕܡܘܗܝ ܠܐ
ܡܬܝܕܥܢ ܗܘܝܢ ܕܒܪܐ ܐܠܗܐ ܠܫܡܝܐ ܘܠܐܪܥܐ

> If I say: "In the beginning, God created the heaven and the earth"—but without this, this *mettziʿɔnutɔ* that is the *taḥtɔyɔ*, and the *retmɔ* before it—then it would not be indicated that *God* created the heaven and the earth. (Baethgen 1880, ܗ, lines 2–4)

Elias explains that the sentence *brɔshit brɔ ʾalɔhɔ yɔt shmayyɔ w-yɔt ʾarʿɔ* is ambiguous. Due to the verb (*brɔ* 'he/it created') coming before the subject (*ʾalɔhɔ* 'God'), the sentence can be interpreted either as God creating heaven and earth, or as another actor creating God. It is only by the addition of a *mettziʿɔnutɔ* that a speaker indicates that God is definitely the subject. The added 'moved ones' are accent dots—in this case the two accents *taḥtɔyɔ*[39] and *retmɔ*[40]—that change a speaker's inflection to clarify the subject and objects in the sentence. The term *mettziʿɔnutɔ* thus encompasses vowels and accents, including both categories that cause a speaker to modulate their voice between consonants. Segal (1953, 147, n. 9) notes that the later grammarian John Bar Zuʿbi (fl. c. 1200) also uses *mettziʿɔnutɔ* for accents in this way, despite it originally being a term only for vowels.

Returning to *Hidāya al-Qārī*, Abū al-Faraj (a contemporary of both Eliases) makes a similar conflation between accentual

[39] The *taḥtɔyɔ* 'declining' is the oblique pair of dots beside the *ʾalaph* in ܐܠܗܐ., indicating that the reader should pause here before introducing a separate clause. See Segal (1953, 109).

[40] The *retmɔ* 'utterance' is the dot above the *taw* in ܝܬ̇, indicating that the word should be emphasised. See Segal (1953, 84).

modulations and vowels in Hebrew. He first writes on the interactions between the types of *shewa* and the accents:

לו אגתמע אלשוא מן אלקסמין אלמדכורין והמא אלסאכן ואלמתחרך
פאגתמאעה מע אלסאכן לא יתם לאן אלסאכן מן חכמה אן יסכן אלחרף
ולא יצטרב בתה כאלריש מן כרְמי ואלמאם מן זמְרי ואלבא מן עְבְדי
ואללחן ואלכאדם מן שאנהמא אן יחרכא אלחרף ויגעלא פיה נגמה
ונגמאת ואלחרף אלסאכן לא יצח פיה נגמה בתה ואלנגמה הי אלחרכה
פכיף יכון אלסאכן מתחרכא פי חאל ואחד פאליס הדא מנאקצה פקד
אסתחאל דלך

> If one of the two aforementioned types of *shewa*—i.e., the *sākin* and the *mutaḥarrik*—came together [with an accent], then the combination [of the accent] with the *sākin* would not occur, because for the *sākin*, its rule is that it makes the letter still, not shaking at all, like the *resh* of *karmi*, the *mem* of *zimri*, and the *bet* of *ʿaḏi*. But disjunctive and conjunctive accents, by their nature, cause the letter to move. They make a melody or melodies in it, but a *sākin* letter cannot properly have a melody at all, for melody [*naghama*] is *ḥaraka*. So how can the *sākin* be *mutaḥarrik* at the same time? Is this not mutually exclusive? Thus it is impossible. (Khan 2020, II:153, lines 952–59)

Abū al-Faraj's key point is that a single Hebrew letter cannot be read with both a silent (*sākin*) *shewa* and an accent. This explanation hinges on perceived equivalence of the two terms *naghama* 'melody, tone' and *ḥaraka*. The latter, of course, is a vowel, but the former—*naghama*—can mean either a phonemic vowel (as it does in the works of Saadia Gaon; see Skoss 1952) or the vocalic modulation of an accent (as it does here).[41] Abū al-Faraj derives

---

[41] Also compare Dawid bar Pawlos' use of *neʿmtɔ*, the Syriac cognate of *naghama*, in his explanation of how the voice generates 'melodies' and

this equivalence from the fact that any letter with a conjunctive or disjunctive accent must be the onset of a syllable, and therefore pronounced with a vowel. It seems that in this way, the ideas of 'melody' and 'vocalisation' became entangled in the Masoretic tradition.

Abū al-Faraj then differentiates the 'moving' effect of an accent from that of the mobile *shewa*, as he explains:

ליס אלקול באן אללחן יחרך אלחרף יקתצׄי אן תכון חרכתה כחרכה
אלשוא ודׄאך אן אלשוא יחרך אלחרף ויסרע בנטקה חתי לא ימכן אחד
אן ילבת בדׄלך אלחרף כאלבא מן בראשית אדׄי לא יצח מסכה . . . . וליס
כדׄלך אללחן בל הו יחרך אלחרף ויגׄעל פיה נגׄמאת ואלחרף פי מוצׄעה
יתחרך לא ירגׄע אלי כלף ולא אלי קדׄאם מהמא אלחרף ינגׄם אלי תרי כיף
ינגׄם אלריש מן וַיָמַהֲרֹוּ ואלחרף מן מוצׄעה מא ברח וקד חרכה נגׄמה ותנתין
ומא זאד . . . פצׄאר אלשוא יתחרך בסרעה אלי קדׄאם ואללחן יחרך פי
אלמוצׄע בעינה פלו אגׄ[תם]ע לכאן דׄלך מתנאקצׄא פבאן מן דׄלך אן שוא
ולחן לא יגׄתמעא פי חרף ואחד מעא

The statement that the accent moves the letter does not require that its movement be like the movement of the *shewa*, and that is because the [mobile] *shewa* moves the letter and accelerates its pronunciation such that one cannot linger on that letter, like the *bā'* of *bareshit*,[42] where

---

vowels (Gottheil 1893, cxii, line 9). Aharon ben Asher uses the equivalent Hebrew word, *naʿimɔ*, in *Diqduqe ha-Teʿamim* to indicate the 'melody' of the accent *shofar* (Dotan 1967, 107, line 13), to classify the accents more broadly (108, line 23), and to explain the vocalic effect of a *gaʿya* (115, lines 2–3). *Naghama* is also an element in Arabic musical theory and occasionally indicates non-speech sounds, but it is not a term for 'vowel' in Arabic grammar (Morag 1979, 89–90; Talmon 1997, 132).
[42] The default pronunciation of mobile *shewa* in the Tiberian pronunciation tradition was /a/ (Khan 2020, I:305).

holding it would not be proper.... This is not so for the accent, which instead moves the letter and induces melodies
in it, and the letter moves in place without going backward
or forward as long as it is intoned. Do you not see how [the
accent] intones the *resh* of *wa-ymaharú*, yet the letter does
not leave its place? [The accent] has moved it [with] a
melody, or two, or more.... The *shewa* proceeds moving
quickly forward, while the accent imparts movement at its
source. If they were brought together, then that would be
a contradiction, and from that it is clear that a *shewa* and
an accent cannot come together in a single letter. (Khan
2020, II:153–55, lines 962–75)

Abū al-Faraj perceives an innate difference in the realisation of
the 'movement' of vocalic *shewa* in comparison to that of an accent. The *shewa*'s *ḥaraka* is quick, always representing a short
vowel, and it drives inevitably forward to connect one consonant
to the next. By contrast, an accent induces 'melodies' or 'tones'
(*naghamāt*) on a single consonant. The result of this effect is that
a speaker may modulate the pronunciation of the vowel that follows that consonant, modifying its pitch and duration *without*
moving to the next consonant.

These Syriac and Hebrew scholars adapted the Arabic terminology of *ḥaraka* and *sākin* to describe the vowel phonology
and syllable structure of their own languages as they differed
from Arabic. This reanalysis included unique aspects of their
pointing systems, accentuation, and the properties of the *shewa*.
All of this terminology traces back to the earliest records of
ḥaraka to mean 'vowel' in Arabic grammar, and it is likely that
this usage has roots in the late antique ideas of *kinesis* in Greek
grammar and philosophy. But there was another issue that these

Semitic grammarians all had in common, and that they could not
solve with Greek grammar: explaining those *matres lectionis* letters that impart movement to speech. We move now to those letters which could act as both vowels and consonants, and examine
how Arabic, Syriac, and Hebrew linguists all defined their dis-
tinctive properties.

3.0. Duality in the *Matres Lectionis*

Whereas the difference between *ḥaraka* and *sākin* established a
separation between vowels and consonants, the two categories
clash when applied to the *matres lectionis* letters. Due to the lack
of dedicated vowel letters in the Semitic abjad scripts, Arabic,
Syriac, and Hebrew scribes all utilised *matres lectionis* to represent
some of the vowels in their languages (Morag 1961, 20). Depending on their phonological context, these 'mothers of reading'[43]—
usually the consonants ʾ*aleph, yod, waw,* and *he*ʾ—took on an additional role in Semitic writing systems, occasionally standing as
placeholders for vowel sounds. Medieval scholars explained the
dual nature of these letters in a variety of ways, with some saying
that the *matres* were inherently silent, sick, or soft in comparison
to other consonants. This view was consistently part of the Arabic
grammatical tradition, which held that the *matres lectionis* were
the most ephemeral letters. This understanding contrasts the interpretation of 'sounding' letters that we have already seen,

---

[43] This is the English translation of *matres lectionis*, itself a Latin phrase
translated from the Hebrew ʾ*immot qeriʾa* 'mothers of reading'. It is now
the standard English term for consonants that stand for vowels in Semitic orthography.

mainly in the Syriac and Hebrew traditions, which maintained that the vowel letters were more dynamic. Despite these differences, members of all three traditions categorised their vowels by assigning each phoneme to one of the *matres lectionis*.

One of the earliest sources for the phonology of Arabic *matres lectionis* is the lexicon *Kitāb al-ʿAyn* (*The Book of the ʿAyn*), particularly its introduction, attributed to al-Khalīl ibn Aḥmad al-Farāhīdi (d. 786/791). Another early source is Sībawayh's grammar, known as *Kitāb Sībawayh*. Both of these grammarians considered the vowel letters 'weaker' than the consonants, an idea which continued into later works on Arabic phonology like Ibn Jinnī's (d. 1002) *Sirr Ṣināʿa al-Iʿrāb* (*The Secret of Making Proper Arabic*). Certain Jewish sources give similar explanations for the *matres*, including Saadia Gaon's (d. 942) *Commentary on Sefer Yeṣira*, the lexicographical works of Judah ben David Ḥayyūj (d. 1000), and at least one *muṣawwitāt* text. As for Syriac sources, the two most useful for explaining the *matres lectionis* are the grammars of Elias of Nisibis (d. 1046) and Elias of Ṭirhan (d. 1049), who adopt technical language similar to that of the Arabic grammarians while also deliberately challenging them.

Most of the aforementioned authors tended to group their vowels by assigning them to the *matres* letters. The same organisation also appears in al-Khwarizmi's (d. 997) encyclopaedia *Mafātīḥ al-ʿUlūm* (*The Keys to the Sciences*) and Ibn Sīnā's (d. 1037) *Risāla Asbāb Ḥudūth al-Ḥurūf* (*The Treatise on the Causes of the Occurrence of Letters*). This classification system may be related to a similar phenomenon in the Greek grammatical tradition.

3.1. Arabic Matres Lectionis: In Sickness and in Health

Kitāb al-ʿAyn is the first comprehensive Arabic lexicon, and its introduction is one of earliest Arabic sources for explaining the *matres lectionis*. Historically, it has been attributed to al-Khalīl ibn Aḥmad (d. 786/791), an early scholar of prosody and one of the teachers of Sībawayh (d. 793/796).[44] Most of the text was actually compiled after his death by another student, al-Layth ibn al-Muẓaffar (d. c. 803), but the organisation of the lexical portion of the book and parts of the introduction are probably original to al-Khalīl (Talmon 1997, 91–100; Schoeler 2006, 142–63; Sellheim 2012a; 2012b). In the introductory discussion of the letters of the alphabet, the text emphasises the distinction between the *matres lectionis* and the rest of the consonants:

قال الليث: قال الخليل: في العربية تسعة وعشرون حرفاً: منها خمسة
وعشرون حرفا صحاحا لها أحياناً ومدارج، وأربعة أحرف جوف، وهي الواو
والياء والألف اللينة والهمزة وسُمِّيت جوفاً لأنها تخرج من الجوف فلا تقعُ في
مدرجة من مدارج اللسان، ولا من مدارج الحلق، ولا من مدرج اللهاة، إنما
هي هاوية في الهواء فلم يكن لها حيز تُنسب اليه إلا الجوفَ. وكان يقول
كثيرا: الألف اللينة والواو والياء هوائية أي أنها في الهواء.

Al-Layth said: Al-Khalīl said: "In Arabic there are twenty-nine letters. Among them are twenty-five healthy letters,

---

[44] Although they died less than a decade apart, Sībawayh was forty-two years younger than al-Khalīl. Sībawayh died—somewhat mysteriously—when he was just thirty-six. He acquired the nickname 'Sībawayh', which means 'odour of apples' in his native Persian, apparently because of the sweetness of his breath (K. Versteegh 1997, 29). As fruity-smelling breath is a symptom of diabetes, it is not implausible that this contributed to his early death.

which have occasions and steps, and four hollow letters, which are the *wāw*, the *yā'*, and the flexible *'alif*, as well as the *hamza*. They are called 'hollow' because they exit from the hollow [of the mouth], so they do not occur at one of the steps of the tongue, or the steps of the throat, or the step of the palate. Instead, they are airy, in the air, for they do not have a space to attach to besides the hollow. He [al-Khalīl] frequently used to say: the soft *'alif*, the *wāw*, and the *yā'* are airy; that is, they are in the air." (Makhzumi 1985, I:57)

The 'healthy' or 'sound' letters (*ṣiḥāḥ*, sing. *ṣaḥīḥ*) include all of the Arabic letters except for *hamza*, *wāw*, *yā'*, and 'soft *'alif*' (*'alif layyina*), which are instead 'hollow' (*jūf*). The two groups differ in that 'healthy' letters connect to specific articulation points within the mouth, while the 'hollow' letters exist only as streams of air that emanate from the glottis through the entirety of the vocal tract.[45] Al-Khalīl described this quality as being 'airy' (*hawā'iya*, sing. *hāwī*) (see also, Makhzumi 1985, IV:95 and VIII:91).

Rafael Talmon has identified several passages in the lexical portions of *al-'Ayn* that further illuminate eighth-century Arabic perceptions of the *matres lectionis* (Talmon 1997, 134–37). A particularly salient line reads: "The three hollow letters have no voice (*ṣawt*) and no sound (*jars*), and they are *wāw*, *yā'*, and soft

---

[45] Talmon classifies this as 'extra-buccal' articulation (1997, 135). One comment in the lexical portion of *al-'Ayn* notes that "al-Khalīl [said]: the three long ones depend on the hamza (الخليل: المدات الثلاث منوطات بالهمزة)" (Makhzumi 1985, VII: 456; Talmon 1997, 137). This statement corresponds to later Arabic grammarians who indicate that the long vowels begin from the articulation point of *hamza* (see below).

ʾalif; the rest of the letters are sounded (*majrūsa*) (والحروف الثلاثة
الجوف لا صوت لها ولا جرس. وهي الواو والياء والالف اللينة. وسائر الحروف
مجروسة)" (Makhzumi 1985, VI:51). Likewise, the lexicon provides
a specific description for 'soft' (*layyin*) letters, saying: "The soft
letter is weak (*khawwār*) and the most hollow (*ʾajwaf*) (الحرف اللين
خوار اجوف)" (Makhzumi 1985, III:352; Talmon 1997, 135). Both
of these comments reinforce the notion that the *matres* were
somehow defective in comparison to the 'healthy' letters. There
is also some gradience between the two groups, as the letter *yāʾ*
is described as "the most similar of the letters to *hāʾ* (الياء اقرب
الحروف شبهاً بالهاء)," and in terms of prosody, "the *yāʾ*, *wāw*, *ʾalif*,
and *hāʾ* happen to conform in the recitation of poetry (ومن هنالك
صار مجرى الياء والواو والالف والهاء في روي الشعر واحداً)" (Makhzumi 1985,
III:348; Talmon 1997, 143). The text even goes so far as to say
that "the *hāʾ* is the softest of the healthy letters (الهاء ألين الحروف
الصحاح)" (Makhzumi 1985, III:355; Talmon 1997, 136), a fact
which correlates in terms of both its phonetic similarity to the
'airy' sounds pronounced from the site of *hamza* and its ortho-
graphic usage as a de facto *mater lectionis* to represent the nominal feminine ending in Arabic (i.e., as *tāʾ marbūṭa*; see Sībawayh
below).

This 'weakness' of the *matres lectionis* ultimately led to their
classification as 'sick' in contrast to the healthier consonants. For
example, regarding the formation of words with three root letters, the introduction of al-ʿAyn reads:

وتفسير الثلاثي الصحيح أن يكون ثلاثة أحرف ولا يكون فيها واوٌ ولا ياءٌ ولا
ألفٌ⁴⁶ في أصل البناء، لأنّ هذه الحروف يُقالُ لها حروف العلل. فكلما
سلمت كلمة على ثلاثة أحرف من هذه الحروف فهي ثلاثي صحيح مثل:
ضَرَبَ، خَرَجَ، دَخَلَ، والثلاثي المعتلّ مثل: ضَرَا ضَرِيَ ضَرُوَ . . . لأنه جاء
مع الحرفين ألفٌ أو واوٌ أو ياءٌ فافهم.

The explanation of the healthy triliteral word is that it is
three letters, but it does not have *wāw*, *yā'*, or *'alif* in the
basic structure, because these letters are called 'letters of
sickness'. Whenever a word is sound, it is based on three
letters from among these [other] letters, so a healthy triliteral word is like: *ḍaraba, kharaja, dakhala*. But a sick triliteral word is like: *ḍarā, ḍariya, ḍaruwa*... because along with
the two letters comes an *'alif*, *wāw*, or *yā'*, so understand.
(Makhzumi 1985, 59–60)

Like the phonetic difference between 'healthy' and 'airy' letters,
in *Kitāb al-ʿAyn*'s morphological system, words based on triliteral
roots can be separated into 'healthy' and 'sick' categories. A word
becomes sickened (*muʿtall*) if it contains an *'alif*, *wāw*, or *yā'* that
represents a vowel or a glide, and *Kitāb al-ʿAyn* classifies them as
letters of *ʿilal* 'sicknesses' (sing. *ʿilla*). The Arabic *matres lectionis*
are thus less 'substantial', so to speak, than the pure consonants.
They are *layyin* 'soft, flexible' and *hāwī* 'airy', based in *ʿilla* 'sickness, weakness, deficiency', and they spread their infection to
make entire words *muʿtall* 'sickened, defective'. Meanwhile, the

---

⁴⁶ Al-Azharī (d. 980) updated parts of *Kitāb al-ʿAyn* when he produced
his own lexicon, *Tahdhīb al-Lugha* (*The Refinement of the Language*), in
the 970s (Arzandeh and Umar 2011). He emends this section of the text
to read *la 'alif* [*al-layyina wa-la al-hamza*] ('not [soft] *'alif* [and not
hamza]'). Makhzumi includes these emendations in brackets, and I have
omitted them here.

rest of the consonants are decidedly *saḥīḥ* 'healthy, sound', and they convey that feature onto words which contain them (Talmon 1997, 131).

Sībawayh adopts and expands these principles when he explains the *matres lectionis* in the *Kitāb*. First, to describe *ʾalif*, *wāw*, and *yāʾ*, he states:

وهذه الحروف غير مهموسات، وهي حروف لِين ومدٍّ، ومخارجُها متّسعة لهواء الصوت؛ وليس شيء من الحروف أوسَعَ مخارِجها منها؛ ولا أمَدَّ للصوت؛ فإذا وقفتَ عندها لم تَضمَّها بشفة ولا لسان ولا حَلق كضمّ غيرها؛ فيهوِى الصوتُ إذا وجد متّسعاً حتى ينقطع آخرُه في موضع الهمزة. وإذا تَفَطَّنتَ وجدتَ مسَّ ذلك.

These letters are not unvoiced, and they are letters of softness and lengthening. Their articulation points are widened for the air of the sound, and none of the letters are wider than them in terms of articulation point, nor longer for the sound. If you stop [their sound], then you will not press with the lip, tongue, or throat like you press for other [letters], for the sound blows like air when it occurs widened, until its end is cut off at the site of the *hamza*.[47] If you understand, then you will feel the touch of that. (Sībawayh 1986, IV:176)

Like *Kitāb al-ʿAyn*, Sībawayh perceives the vowel forms of the *matres lectionis* as 'softer' than the consonants, and thus they are letters of 'softness' (*līn*). He then gives them a second quality that indicates their 'vowel-ness', calling them letters of 'lengthening' (*madd*) (see also, Sībawayh 1986, IV:419). This feature is based on the idea that one can extend a vowel for any length of time,

---

[47] I.e., at the glottis. See also, Sībawayh (1986, III:544).

at least until the breath is depleted (al-Nassir 1993, 30). However, if one instead chooses to interrupt the flow of air, then the
vowel sound is cut off at the articulation point of the *hamza*. Just
as al-Khalīl said, these letters are "airy, in the air."

Later in his book, Sībawayh refines the usage of some of
the vocabulary that he shares with *Kitāb al-ʿAyn*, writing:

ومنها اللّينة وهي الواو والياء لأن مُخرَجهما يتّسع لهواء الصوت أشدّ من اتّساع
غيرهما كقولك وأيٌّ والواو وان شئت أجريت الصوت ومددت.

ومنها الهاوي وهو حرفٌ اتّسع لهواء الصوتِ مُخرَجه أشدّ من اتّساع مُخرَج
الياء والواو لأنك قد تضمّ شفتيك في الواو وترفع في الياء لسانك قِبَل الحَنَك
وهي الألف.

> Among [the letters] are the soft ones, which are *wāw* and
> *yāʾ*, because their pronunciation is widened for the air of
> the sound, more than the widening of other [letters] be-
> sides them, as you say: "*wa ʾayyⁿ* and *al-wāw*,"[48] but if you
> want, you can make the sound occur with lengthening.

> [Also] among [the letters] is the airy one, which is a letter
> whose pronunciation is widened for the air of the sound
> even more than the widening of the pronunciation of *yāʾ*
> and *wāw*—because you press your lips together for *wāw*,
> and you raise your tongue in front of the palate for *yāʾ*—
> and it is *ʾalif*. (Sībawayh 1986, IV:435–36)

In contrast to *Kitāb al-ʿAyn*, Sībawayh limits the 'airy' (*hāwī*) category of letters to *ʾalif* alone, while he describes *yāʾ* and *wāw* as
the letters which are specifically 'soft' or 'flexible' (*layyin*). Moreover, one can make *yāʾ* and *wāw* "occur with lengthening"
(*madadta*). *Yāʾ* and *wāw* thus have the two features of vowel

---

[48] That is, words with semivowel glides. See al-Nassir (1993, 28).

sounds: *līn* 'softness', which accounts for the wideness of the vocal tract and lack of obstruction when articulating vowels; and *madd* 'lengthening', related to the relatively long amount of time that one can maintain a vowel sound. However, Sībawayh does distinguish between the different types of *yāʾ* and *wāw*. As *layyina* letters, they can represent consonants or semivowel glides, depending on their phonetic context, but if one does lengthen them with *madd*, then they represent the pure long vowels /ī/ and /ū/. There is no need to make these distinctions for *ʾalif*, since *ʾalif* alone cannot represent a consonant or a glide in Arabic. It also differs from *yāʾ* and *wāw* in that the tongue and lips are not required to articulate /a/—only the breath is needed—and as such, Sībawayh's *ʾalif* is his only full *hāwī* letter.

Sībawayh also solidifies the idea of the 'sick' letters, largely in line with al-ʿAyn's interpretation, although with one key difference. He explains that a *muʿtall* 'sickened' word is one that contains a *ḥarf al-ʾiʿtilāl* 'letter of weakening, falling ill', and that such letters are so named because of *ʿilla* 'sickness, deficiency' (Sībawayh 1986, IV:47, 93). Furthermore, he says that a word which has none of these as root letters is 'stronger' (*ʾaqwā*) than a *muʿtall* word (Sībawayh 1986, IV:54). He calls these stronger words *ṣaḥīḥ*, but unlike *Kitāb al-ʿAyn*, Sībawayh never refers to the twenty-five pure Arabic consonants themselves as *ṣaḥīḥ* (al-Nassir 1993, 28). Instead, his primary conceptual distinction between vowels and consonants is that the former have *līn* 'softness', whereas the latter do not.

Sībawayh further elaborates on the idea of 'stillness' in the *matres lectionis*, adding another layer to *Kitāb al-ʿAyn*'s perception of 'insubstantial' vowel letters. Within the *Kitāb*, every letter which precedes a vowel is described as *mutaḥarrik* 'moving, moved', while letters which do not precede a vowel are *sākin* 'still'. This division is normally straightforward, but Sībawayh notes the exception of "three letters: the ʾalif, the yāʾ for which the preceding letter has a *kasra* (/i/), and the *wāw* for which the preceding letter has a *ḍamma* (/u/) (ثلاثة أحرف: الألف والياء التي قبلها حرف مكسور والواو التي قبلها حرف مضموم)" (Sībawayh 1986, IV:156). In such cases, ʾalif, yāʾ, and *wāw* represent the long vowels /ā/, /ī/, and /ū/. These vowel letters cannot be followed by another vowel, so by definition, they cannot be *mutaḥarrik*. Instead, they are *sākin* 'still, unvocalised', despite representing the very thing which causes vocalisation in the first place. Sībawayh even goes so far as to call these motionless letters 'dead' (*mayyit*), stating "[the Arabs] dare to elide the ʾalif only because it is dead, not taking *jarr*, *rafʿ*, or *naṣb* (إنما جسروا على حذف الألف لأنها ميتة لا يدخلها جرّ ولا رفع ولا نصب)" (Sībawayh 1986, III:356; see also, 544). That is, a dead, motionless ʾalif cannot take case vowels. He describes yāʾ and *wāw* in similar terms in the following pages (al-Nassir 1993, 34; Sībawayh 1986, III:356, 360). This classification of *sākin* letters corresponds with Qurʾanic vocalisation and diacritic practices, which place a *sukūn* sign above each *mater lectionis*.

A motionless *mater lectionis* can become *mutaḥarrik*, but in doing so it loses the features which make it a vowel (al-Nassir 1993, 34). For example, if you vocalise a yāʾ, then "it is not a letter of softness (لم تكن حرفَ لين)" (Sībawayh 1986, IV:197), which implies that it acts like a regular consonant. Likewise, when *yāʾ* or *wāw* occurs before a vowel, the form becomes "as if not sickened (شبه غير معتل)" (al-Nassir 1993, 28). On the other hand, *ʾalif* can never be *mutaḥarrik*,[49] and if it is ever in a position where a radical would normally be vocalised,[50] then it loses its *ḥāwī* feature and becomes a *wāw* or *yāʾ* (al-Nassir 1993, 34; Sībawayh 1986, III:548; IV:156). That is, it becomes a different consonant, but cannot become fully strong and consonantal itself like *yāʾ* or *wāw* can. Based on this metric, Sībawayh explains that the 'sick' letters are 'stronger' (*ʾaqwā*) in positions where they can function like normal consonants, and 'weaker' (*ʾaḍʿaf*) in positions where they cannot (Sībawayh 1986, IV:381). Usually, this means that they are strong (i.e., vocalised consonants) near the beginning of words, and weak (i.e., *matres lectionis*) at the end of words. Once again, the exception is *ʾalif*, which is the weakest of all letters because it has no consonantal value (al-Nassir 1993, 34).[51]

One final characteristic that Sībawayh attributes to *ʾalif*, *yāʾ*, and *wāw* is the idea of 'subtlety' (*khafāʾ*),[52] which the *matres*

---

[49] If you see one, it is only the seat for a *hamza*.

[50] For example, in some inflections of hollow roots.

[51] The tenth-century lexicographer al-Azharī (d. 980) offers a similar explanation, which he claims is part of al-Khalīl's teachings that al-Layth did not transmit in *Kitāb al-ʿAyn*. This teaching also divides the letters into 'healthy' (*ṣaḥīḥ*) and 'sickened' (*muʿtall*), with the latter group containing *wāw*, *yāʾ*, *hamza*, and *ʾalif*, and further explains how the *ʾalif* differs from *wāw* and *yāʾ*. In effect, *ʾalif* is too weak to hold a vowel on its own, so it must become one of the 'stronger' weak letters in order to be vocalised (Talmon 1997, 260–61).

[52] 'Subtle' in the sense of 'not apparent' or 'subdued'.

lectionis possess more than any other letters. At the end of his divisions of the alphabet, immediately after the passage about *layyin* and *hāwī* letters, he writes: "These three are the subtlest of the letters due to the widening of their articulation point, and the subtlest and widest of them is *ʾalif*, then *yāʾ*, then *wāw* (وهذه الثلاثة

"(أخفى الحروف لاتّساع مُخرَجها وأخفاهنَ وأوسعهنَ مُخرَجاً الألف ثم الياء ثم الواو)

(Sībawayh 1986, IV:436). 'Subtlety' (*khafāʾ*) is not necessarily unique to vowel letters, but rather it is a quality possessed by letters whose phonetic realisation changes or elides as a result of a relationship to nearby letters. The *matres lectionis* are 'most subtle' because, more than any other letter, they vary between multiple modes of articulation: sometimes vowels, sometimes consonants. Such letters may be called *khafiyya* 'subtle, unapparent', in contrast to others which are 'more clear' (*ʾabyan*) (Sībawayh 1986, IV:161, 164, 177, 181–84).

This subtlety also applies to rare cases in which *hāʾ* acts as a *mater lectionis*. Sībawayh devotes an entire chapter to explaining this (largely theoretical) use of *hāʾ* to represent vowel sounds at the end of words that are typically uninflected.[53] For example, he suggests that when one pronounces a noun with a plural ending (e.g., *muslimūna* 'Muslims') or uninflected particles (*ʾayna, ʾinna, thumma*), there is actually an imperceptible *hāʾ* that facilitates the final vowel (i.e., ثمَّه, انَّه, اينَه, مسلمونَه) (Sībawayh 1986,

---

[53] Excluding what we now refer to as *tāʾ marbūṭa*. Whenever a word has a *tāʾ marbūṭa*, Sībawayh refers to it as *hāʾ*, but he does not consider it a 'soft' letter like *ʾalif, yāʾ*, or *wāw*. The modern *tāʾ marbūṭa* grapheme with two dots was not in widespread use at the end of the eighth century.

IV:161–63). This interpretation correlates with the statements in
Kitāb al-ʿAyn that claimed *hāʾ* is the 'softest' of all the consonants,
and thus most similar to the typical *matres lectionis.*

Sībawayh extends his theoretical usage of *hāʾ* to certain Arabic dialects that pronounce the feminine demonstrative pronoun
hādhihi as *hādhī,* saying:

> ونحو ما ذكرنا قول بنى تميم في الوقف: هذِهْ فإذا وصلوا قالوا: هذِي فلانةُ؛
> لأن الياء خفيّة فإذا سَكَتّ عندها كان أخْفَى. والكسرةُ مع الياء أخفى، فإذا
> خَفِيَتِ الكسرةُ ازدادَتِ الياءُ خفاءً كما ازدادَتِ الكسرةُ؛ فأبدلوا مكانها حرفاً
> من موضع أكثر الحروف به مشابَهة، وتكون الكسرةُ معه أبين.

> As we have mentioned, the speech of Banu Tamim in pause
> is *hādhih,* but when they join [the word in context], they
> say *hādhī fulāna,*[54] because the *yāʾ* is subtle. If you stop
> speaking at its place, then it becomes even more subtle, for
> then the [internal] *kasra* [also] elides, and the *yāʾ* gains
> additional subtlety amounting to what the *kasra* had
> added. So [Banu Tamim] exchange its place [in speech]
> with a letter from the place [in the mouth] of the letter
> that most resembles [*kasra*], and with which the *kasra* is
> clearer. (Sībawayh 1986, IV:182)

The subtle *yāʾ* in this case is an invisible *mater lectionis* that results
from Banu Tamim's elision of the classical Arabic word *hādhihi*
'this' to a vernacular *hādhī.* They end the word on the original
final *hāʾ,* but in context with a following word, that *hāʾ* becomes
silent like a *mater lectionis* and the final syllable resembles a long
yāʾ. Sībawayh interprets the silencing of the *hāʾ* as a lengthening
of the internal /i/ vowel, which is then represented by an unvo-

---

[54] 'This is some woman'.

calised, subtle, *mater lectionis yāʾ* due to its proximity to the articulation point of /i/. In this way, he demonstrates that when
yāʾ—and, by extension, *wāw* and *ʾalif*—function as *matres*, they
actually undergo a sort of elision that changes their quality. The
"widening of their articulation" in order to act as vowels causes
this change, increasing their subtlety, and because they perform
this vowel function so frequently, they are "the subtlest of the
letters."

Sībawayh's interpretations of the *matres lectionis* persisted
after his death, and they appear in the first dedicated phonetic
study of Arabic: Ibn Jinnī's (d. 1002) *Sirr Ṣināʿa al-Iʿrāb* (*The Secret of Making Proper Arabic*). Ibn Jinnī explains that the sounds
of speech occur when a stream of air is cut off at one of the articulation points (*makhraj* or *maqtaʿ*) in the vocal tract. However,
like Sībawayh, he adds that there are some letters for which a
speaker can widen (*ʾittisāʿ*) their articulation point and not dis-
rupt the airstream until it is fully depleted (Ibn Jinnī 1993, 7).
He differentiates them thus:

والحروف التي اتسعت مخارجها ثلاثة: الألف ثم الياء ثم الواو، وأوسعها
وألينها الألف، إلا أن الصوت الذي يجري في الألف مخالف للصوت الذي
يجري في الياء والواو، والصوت الذي يجري في الياء مخالف للصوت الذي
يجري في الألف والواو. والعلة في ذلك أنك تجد الفم والحلق في ثلاث
الأحوال مختلف الأشكال

The letters whose articulation points are widened are
three: *ʾalif*, then *yāʾ*, then *wāw*; and the widest and softest
of them is *ʾalif*. But the sound which occurs with *ʾalif* is
different from that which occurs with *yāʾ* and *wāw*, and the
sound which occurs with *yāʾ* is different from that of *ʾalif*

and *wāw*. The reason[55] for that is the mouth and throat are
in three states with different shapes. (Ibn Jinnī 1993, 8)

Ibn Jinnī arranges the *matres* in order, following their articulation
points from back to front. Later, he also links the articulation
points of *ʾalif, yāʾ*, and *wāw* to the articulation points of the vowels: /a/ is farthest back, in the throat; /i/ is in the middle, inside
the mouth; and /u/ occurs last, at the lips (Ibn Jinnī 1993, 8, 53–
54; see also, Kinberg 1987, 17–18; compare Sībawayh 1986,
IV:101). Furthermore, like al-Khalīl and Sībawayh, Ibn Jinnī recognises *ʾalif* as the least consonantal of the *matres lectionis*, and it
is thus the 'widest' (*ʾawsaʿ*) and 'softest' (*ʾalyan*) of them.

He also adopts the idea of the *matres lectionis* as 'sick' letters
in opposition to the 'healthy' consonants, writing:

وللحروف قسمة أخرى الى الصحّة والاعتلال. فجميع الحروف صحيح إلا
الألف والياء والواو اللواتي هن حروف المدّ والاستطالة، وقد ذكرناها قبل، إلا
أن الألف أشدّ امتداداً وأوسع مخرجاً وهو الحرف الهاوي

The letters have another division, into healthiness and
sickness. All letters are *ṣaḥīḥ* except *ʾalif, yāʾ*, and *wāw*,
which are letters of length and extension. We have mentioned them before, but *ʾalif* is the greatest in terms of
lengthening, and widest in terms of articulation, and it is
the airy one. (Ibn Jinnī 1993, 62; see also, 5)

Once again, this division defines *yāʾ* and *wāw* as partially deficient, while *ʾalif* in particular is entirely non-consonantal and
hāwī 'airy'. Ibn Jinnī also expands on this idea, delineating the
exact relationship between *ʾalif* and *hamza*. Elsewhere, he argues

---

[55] This is a pun on *ʿilla*, which means 'reason' but is also the 'sickness'
inherent to these letters.

that the *ʾalif* at the beginning of the alphabet is actually a representation of *hamza*, because when one says its name (*ʾalif*), it begins with a glottal stop (Ibn Jinnī 1993, 41–42). This *hamza* occurs because one cannot begin an utterance with "an *ʾalif* that is long and motionless, since it is not possible to begin with the motionless (بالألف التي هي مدّة ساكنة، لأن الساكن لا يمكن الابتداء به)" (Ibn Jinnī 1993, 43–44). That is to say, it is impossible to begin an utterance with an unvocalised consonant *or* a long vowel, notably contrasting the Greek and Syriac idea of the 'sounding' vowels, which could be pronounced alone (see above, present chapter, §1.0). In this way, *hamza* acts as the consonantal counterpart of the pure vowel of *ʾalif*. However, unlike *yāʾ* and *wāw*, whose vowel and consonant forms are produced from the same articulation points, Ibn Jinnī says that the articulation point of *hamza* is deep in the chest, while that of *ʾalif* (and thus /a/) is higher, in the throat (Ibn Jinnī 1993, 43).

Kitāb Sībawayh and *Kitāb al-ʿAyn* show that at the end of the eighth century, Arabic grammarians perceived the *matres lectionis* vowel letters as much more ephemeral than typical consonants. They were 'soft' (*layyin*) and 'airy' (*hāwī*); 'sickened' (*muʿtall*) letters that were 'weaker' (*ʾaḍʿaf*) than consonants, which in turn were 'healthy' (*saḥīḥ*) and 'stronger' (*ʾaqwā*) in almost every context. The *matres* were also more prone to elision than all other letters, making them the most 'subtle' and imperceptible (*khafiyya*); and they were 'dead' (*mayyit*) or 'still' (*sākin*) specifically when they represented vowel sounds. Additionally, as the above passages demonstrate, at the end of the tenth century, Ibn Jinnī was well aware of the features that Sībawayh and al-Khalīl attributed to the *matres lectionis*, including: 'widening' (*ʾittisāʿ*), 'softness' (*līn*), 'length' (*madd*), and 'sickness' (*ʾiʿtilāl*); as well as the unique status of *ʾalif* as 'airy' (*hāwī*).

These descriptions contrast starkly with those of eighth-century Syriac grammarians, like Jacob of Edessa (d. 708) and Dawid bar Pawlos (fl. c. 770–800), who espoused a notion of 'sounding letters' (*ʾatwɔtɔ qɔlɔnɔyɔtɔ*). These *ʾatwɔtɔ qɔlɔnɔyɔtɔ* were more sonorous and complete than any of the consonants, which were all inherently 'soundless' (*ʾatwɔtɔ dlɔ qɔlɔ*). To some extent, Syriac grammarians maintained this distinction through at least the eleventh century, but they also adopted a number of Arabic features to describe their *matres lectionis*. Like those Syriac sources, some medieval Jewish authors also adapted Arabic ideas of the *matres* to better describe the phonology of Hebrew.

3.2. *Matres Lectionis* in Syriac and Hebrew

Early Arabic grammarians like Sībawayh and the contributors to *Kitāb al-ʿAyn* set the stage for later analyses of Semitic *matres lectionis*, but Syriac and Hebrew scholars did not always adopt the Arabic explanations in their entirety. Some authors, particularly Elias of Ṭirhan (d. 1049), rejected the idea that the *matres* were 'sick' at all, instead maintaining the strength derived from their 'soundingness' (see above, present chapter, §1.0). Despite this, it was also common for both Christian and Jewish grammarians to adapt the Arabic ideas of stillness (*sukūn*) and subtlety/conceal-ment (*khafāʾ*) in the behaviour of the *matres lectionis* to better explain the orthography of the more diverse vowel inventories in Syriac and Hebrew. Most notable among these are Elias of Nisibis

(d. 1046) and Judah ben David Ḥayyūj (d. c. 1000), although they were by no means alone.

Elias of Ṭirhan, the East Syrian bishop who wrote the *Memrɔ Gramaṭiqɔyɔ* (*The Grammatical Essay*), generally reflects a view of the *matres lectionis* that is similar to Sībawayh and Ibn Jinnī. However, he is also explicit about differences between Syriac and Arabic. Most starkly, Elias challenges the Arabic idea that the *matres lectionis* are somehow 'sick'. At the end of his main chapter on vowels, he writes:

> ܣܘܪ̈ܝܝܐ ܓܝܪ ܛܒ ܫܪܝܪ̈ܝܢ ܡܢ ܐܘܪ̈ܗܝܐ ܘܐܦ ܛܝ̈ܝܐ ܡܢܡܘܣܝܢ ܘܢܩܝܦܝܢ ܠܫܪܪܐ
> ܒܠܫܢܗܘܢ. ܕܒܙܒܢ ܠܐܠܦ ܡܫܩܠܝܢ ܐܝܟ ܗܘܐ.. ܘ.. ܝ.. ܘܦܠܓܘܬ.. ܐ.. ܘ.. ܝ..
> ܩܪܝܢ ܠܗܘܢ ܠܡܬܬܙܝܥܢܘܬܐ ܕܥܠ ܐܬܘ̈ܬܐ ܣܝ̈ܡܢ ܛܝܝܐ ܕܝܢ ܩܪܐ ܠܐܬܘ̈ܬܐ
> ܩܠ̈ܝܬܐ.. ܐ.. ܘ̄ ܝ.. ܐܬܘ̈ܬܐ ܟܪ̈ܝܗܬܐ ܘܕܟܘܪܗܢܐ ܒܐܝܕܐ ܕܠܐ ܡܙܝܥܝܢ ܐܢܝܢ
> ܕܠܫ̈ܡܗܐ ܘܠܡ̈ܠܐ ܟܕ ܗܘܝܢ ܒܗܘܢ. ܐܝܟ ܫܪܟܐ ܕܐܬܘ̈ܬܐ
>
> Syrians, indeed, the most faithful among the Edessans, and also rule-abiding Arabs who adhere to the truth in their language, are such that they sometimes remove *ʾalaph* like *waw* and *yod*, and they call half-*ʾalaph*, *waw*, and *yod* 'vocalisations' which are put upon the letters; while an Arab calls the sounding letters—*ʾalaph*, *waw*, and *yod*—'sick letters' and '[letters] of sickness' on account of the fact that they [the *matres*] do not cause nouns or verbs to move when they are in them, just like the rest of the [letters]. (Baethgen 1880, ܠܒ, lines 3–8)

From this passage, it is clear that Elias considers the 'vowels' or 'vocalisations'—literally, 'those made to move' (*mettziʿɔnwɔtɔ*)—to be aural effects which persist on Syriac consonants, even if no *mater lectionis* is written. Moreover, he is familiar with the Arabic grammatical tradition that refers to *ʾalif*, *wāw*, and *yāʾ* as *muʿtall* 'sickened' and *ḥurūf ʿilla* 'letters of sickness', which he translates as *krihɔtɔ* 'sick' (sing. *krihɔ*) and *d-kurhɔnɔ* 'of sickness' (see also, Kiraz 2012, I:61). He takes issue with this designation:

ܗܢܝ ܗܘܐ ܠܗܘܢ ܐܝܟ ܕܐܬܚܙܝ ܠܝ ܕܟܠܗܝܢ ܐܬܘܬܐ ܟܪܝܗܢ ܠܒܪ ܡܢ ܗܘ ..ܐ ..ܘ .., ..ܘܗ ܐܠܗ ܠܗܘܢ ܚܘܡܐ ܠܐ ܡܫܬܡܥ .ܐܠܐ ܒܝܕܥܐ ܗܘ ܡܢ ܗܠܝܢ ܐܝܬ ܠܗܘܢ

[But] it is right for them, as is clear to me, that all letters are sick *except* for ʾalaph, waw, and yod, because despite a voice sounding them out, [the other letters] cannot be heard except via the movement which is from the sounding ones, which therefore are healthy. (Baethgen 1880, ܟܒ, lines 8–10)

Elias keeps with the old Syriac—and ultimately, Greek—maxim that only sounding letters can be articulated by themselves, while consonants require the help of the sounding ones in order to form syllables. Based on this belief, he concludes that the Arabic classification of 'sick' letters is untenable, and so refers to his own sounding letters as *ḥlimɔn*[56] 'healthy, firm, sound'. This word is a calque of the Arabic *saḥiḥ*, which described regular consonants and words with strong roots in Arabic grammar. Elias of Ṭirhan thus reverses the Arabic opposition of 'healthy' and 'sick' letters, making the consonants the ones that are deficient.

Elias of Nisibis (d. 1046) also adapted a number of Arabic ideas into his understanding of the *matres lectionis*. In the second chapter of the *Turrɔṣ Mamllɔ Suryɔyɔ* (*The Correct Form of Syriac Speech*), he lays out the changes that occur to letters under the influence of each Syriac vowel. He says that East Syriac vowels

---

[56] There is no *seyame* on this word, which is irregular for a plural feminine adjective.

are divided into: "the compressed ones and the opened ones; those which stand before the broadened ones and the narrowed ones; and those which stand before the raised ones and the pressed-together ones (ܩܠܝܨ̈ܬܐ ܗܢܘܢ ܘܡܠܐ ܘܦܬܝܚ̈ܬܐ ܘܦܠ̈ܬܐ ܗܢܘܢ ܘܡܠܐ ܐܠܝܨ̈ܬܐ ܗܢܘܢ ܘܡܠܐ ܡܚ̈ܬܐ ܗܢܘܢ ܘܡܠܐ ܒܬ̈ܝܐ ܐܬ̈ܐ)" (Gottheil 1887, ܚ, lines 26–28).

In these examples, the "compressed ones and opened ones" are letters with the vowels /e/ and /a/, which are normally represented by vowel points in Syriac orthography. By contrast, the phrase "those which stand before the broadened ones" refers to the vocalised letter which precedes a *mater lectionis waw*. That is, the 'broadened one' (*rwiḥtɔ*) is the *waw* itself, and the "one which stands before" is a consonant before the vowel /o/. This wording contrasts the normal construction in Arabic grammars, which would refer to the consonant *before* a vowel as 'opened' (*maftūḥ*) or 'pressed together' (*maḍmūm*). The practical difference is minimal—in both languages the *matres lectionis* simply represent the vocalic sound that follows a consonant—but when that vowel sound changes, it is the Syriac *mater* which undergoes modification,[57] whereas in Arabic it is the preceding consonant that is (perceived as) modified.

At the same time, Elias of Nisibis does explain that the *matres lectionis waw* and *yod* are motionless (*shlitɔ*), just like in Arabic. Paralleling Sībawayh's *mutaḥarrik* and *sākin*, he justifies this description by classifying all letters as either *mettzi'ɔnitɔ* 'moved'

---

[57] Compare Elias of Ṭirhan's statements in Baethgen (1880, ܟܒ, line 19–21).

or *shlitɔ* ‘motionless’, depending on whether or not a vowel immediately follows it (Gottheil 1887, ܠܚ). As a result, Elias says, “every broadened or narrowed *waw*, and every raised-up or pressed-together *yod* (ܘܟܠ ܘܘ ܪܘܝܚܬܐ ܘܐܠܝܨܬܐ. ܘܟܠ ܝܘܕ ܡܬܩܡܬܐ ܘܡܬܟܒܫܬܐ)” is *shlitɔ* (Gottheil 1887, ܠܛ-ܡ). That is to say, every *waw* or *yod* which represents a vowel is motionless and unvocalised. Notably, in contrast to Elias of Ṭirhan, Elias of Nisibis does not refer to any letter as *qɔlɔnɔytɔ* ‘sounding’.

Elias of Nisibis also discusses an idea similar to Sībawayh and Ibn Jinnī’s explanations of the ‘subtlety’ in the *matres lectionis*, highlighting the way that these letters may be elided and ‘suppressed’ (*metgneb*). He begins the seventh chapter of his *Turrɔs Mamllɔ Suryɔyɔ*, saying:

> ܐܬܘܬܐ ܗܟܝܠ ܕܡܬܓܢܒܢ ܐܝܬܝܗܝܢ ܬܠܬ. ܐ ܘ ܝ. ܘܟܠ ܚܕܐ ܡܢܗܝܢ
> ܬܠܬܐ ܙܢܝܐ ܡܬܓܢܒܢܘܬܐ | ܐܘ ܠܒܪ ܡܢ ܟܬܒܐ ܘܩܪܝܢܐ ܡܬܓܢܒܢܘܬܐ. ܐܘ
> . ܡܬܓܢܒܢܘܬܐ ܡܢ ܟܬܒܐ. ܘܡܬܩܪܝܢܐ ܒܩܪܝܢܐ. ܐܘ ܡܬܪܫܡܢܐ ܒܟܬܒܐ
> ܘܡܬܓܢܒܢܐ ܒܩܪܝܢܐ
>
> The letters which are suppressed are three: *ʾalaph*, *waw*, and *yod*. Each one of them has three modes of suppression, either suppressed in both writing and recitation; suppressed in writing but pronounced in recitation; or inscribed in writing but suppressed in recitation (Gottheil 1887, ܢܓ, lines 2–6; compare Baethgen 1880, ܠ, lines 6–12, and ܠܐ, lines 17–21).

He proceeds by listing words which exemplify each of the three types of ‘suppressing’. First, the *ʾalaph* in the verb *bnɔ* ‘he built’ (ܒܢܐ) is *metganbɔ* ‘suppressed’ in both writing and recitation when inflected for the third-person plural, resulting in *bnaw* ‘they built’ (ܒܢܘ). That is, the written *ʾalaph* is removed and replaced by *waw* in writing, and the pronunciation of the ʾ*alaph* is 'suppressed', changing from /ɔ/ to /aw/. This type of 'suppression' is also quite similar to the description of verbs with III-weak roots in *Kitāb al-ʿAyn* (see above), in which the final letter changes between ʾ*alif*, *yā*ʾ, and *wāw*, depending on the inflected form. It is likely that this Syriac explanation of a letter being *metganbɔ* was derived from this kind of Arabic verbal analysis and the concept of *khafāʾ* 'concealment', possibly translated from a related Arabic term for elision, ʾ*idghām* 'suppression, assimilation' (see al-Nassir 1993, 56).

Elias of Nisibis' third type of 'suppression' includes words like (ʾ)*nɔshɔ* 'person' (ܐܢܫܐ), *qtal(u)* 'they killed' (ܩܛܠܘ), and *karm(i)* 'my vineyard' (ܟܪܡܝ). These words have an ʾ*alaph*, *waw*, or *yod* that is always written, even though it is not pronounced (i.e., 'supressed') in speech. An equivalent phenomenon in Arabic is the otiose ʾ*alif* that occurs at the end of verbs with the third masculine plural ending (e.g., فعلوا *faʿalū* 'they did, made'). I have not examined any medieval sources to determine whether Syriac and Arabic authors shared terminology related to this type of orthography. Elias himself is of little help here, as he concludes the passage by saying: "The reason for each one of these is known to keen interpreters, without us extending the discussion" (Gottheil 1887, ܟܒ, lines 16–17).

Elias' second type of 'suppression' is more interesting. It includes words like *israyel* 'Israel' (ܣܝܪܐܝܠ) and *idɔ*ʿ 'he knew' (ܝܕܥ). He suggests that both words begin with an invisible *alaph* that is 'suppressed' in writing, even though they necessarily begin with a glottal stop in speech. This kind of 'suppression' has no clear

Arabic equivalent, as Arabic orthography would include the letter *hamza* on the seat of an *ʾalif* to represent that glottal stop. Also
in this type are the words *kul* 'all' (كل) and *meṭul* 'because' (مطل),
which both contain invisible 'suppressed' *waws* that are never
written, but which are pronounced as the vowel /u/ (or /o/ in
Eastern Syriac). The most striking parallel to this description of
matres lectionis letters "suppressed in writing but pronounced in
recitation" is actually found in the lexicographical work of the
Andalusī Jewish scholar Judah ben David Ḥayyūj.

    Ḥayyūj (d. c. 1000) was a tenth-century lexicographer who
wrote a dictionary explaining the morphology of Hebrew verbs
with "weak" roots, titled *Kitāb al-Afʿāl Dhuwāt Ḥurūf al-Līn* (*The
Book of Verbs which Contain Soft Letters*). He was a native Arabic
speaker, so he wrote this book in Judaeo-Arabic[58] and adopted
fundamental concepts and terminology from the Arabic grammatical tradition (Basal 1999, 227). In large part, these terms retained their original Arabic meanings (Basal 1999, 227, n. 3), and
they included a number of items related to *matres lectionis*. As
Ḥayyūj explains in the introduction to *Kitāb al-Afʿāl*:

عرضي في هذا الكتاب الإبانة عن حروف اللين والمدّ العبرانية والتنبيه على
أنحائها وتصاريفها فقد خَفِيَ امرُها عن كثير من الناس للينها واعتلالها ودقّة
معانيها

> My goal in this book is the clarification of the Hebrew let-
> ters of softness and lengthening and the instruction of both
> their forms and their inflections, for their status has been
> concealed from many people due to their softness, their

---

[58] Ḥayyūj wrote in Judaeo-Arabic, but Jastrow (1897) transcribed his
edition of *Kitāb al-Afʿal* in Arabic characters. My quotations of this work
follow Jastrow's orthography.

> sickness, and the fineness of their qualities. (Jastrow 1897,
> 1, lines 7–9)

Like the Arabic grammarians, Ḥayyūj classifies the Hebrew *matres lectionis* letters—ʾaleph, waw, yod, and he’ (Jastrow 1897, 3)[59]—as ‘letters of softness and lengthening’ (*ḥurūf al-līn wa-al-madd*). He highlights that these letters complicate Hebrew morphology as a result of their ‘softness’ (*līn*) and ‘sickness’ (*ʾiʿtilāl*), the same defects that al-Khalīl and Ibn Jinnī identified in the Arabic *matres*. He even says that the status of these letters ‘has been concealed’ (*khafiya*) from people, punning on the Sībawayhan concept of *khafāʾ* in the elision of the *matres*. Furthermore, like Sībawayh did for Arabic, Ḥayyūj regularly refers to the *matres* as *sākin* when they serve to represent vowels (Jastrow 1897, 2, lines 6–7). He applies all of this Arabic terminology to classify the functions of the Hebrew *matres*, distinguishing two types: *sukūn ẓāhir* ‘clear stillness’, when a *mater* acts like a normal consonant, and *sukūn khafī* ‘subtle stillness’, when a *mater* is written as a placeholder for a vowel. He emphasises that this second type of *sukūn* is why the *matres* are called ‘letters of softness’, as they ‘soften’ (*talīn*) until they ‘become subtle’ (*takhfā*) and lose their ‘clarity’ (*ẓuhūr*) in speech (Jastrow 1897, 8, lines 1–16).[60] This explanation is similar to that of Elias of Nisibis, who was born in the last few decades of Ḥayyūj’s life.

---

[59] He includes *he’*, since it is one of the Hebrew *matres*, but Arabic grammarians generally did not recognise their *hāʾ* as a *mater*.

[60] Note also that Abū al-Faraj uses the word *ẓuhūr* as an alternative name for *mappiq* marking consonantal *he’* in *Hidāya al-Qārī* (Khan 2020, II:27–28, 161).

Ḥayyūj also adapted Arabic grammatical terminology in order to better describe phenomena which exist in Hebrew but do
not appear frequently in Arabic. Most notably, he created the
concept of the *sākin layyin* 'soft silent' or 'latent quiescent' for
vowels that are pronounced, but not necessarily written with *matres lectionis* (Jastrow 1897, 3, line 6; Basal 1999, 227, 229;
2013). As Nasir Basal explains, the *sākin layyin* is a phonological
entity that extends from a consonant, "but is neither a vowel itself nor precedes one." Instead, "a *sākin layyin* exists in fact or
potentially as a *mater lectionis*, whose presence or absence makes
no difference to the pronunciation" (Basal 2013). For example,
the word *shofɔr* 'horn' (שׁוֹפָר) may be written with *wāw sākin*—
that is, a *mater lectionis waw*—representing /o/, but it may op-
tionally be written without that *waw*. However, even when the
waw is absent, it still exists, at least theoretically, as a *sākin layyin*. Ḥayyūj thus writes: "Know that the Hebrews permit the drop-
ping of the soft silent from writing for the sake of convenience
(اعلم أن العبرانيين اجازوا اساقط السواكن اللينة من الخط استخفافا)" (Jastrow
1897, 9, lines 12–13). He maintains that the sound of a soft silent
remains even if the *mater* itself is removed, just like Elias of Nisibis said for Syriac words in which a *mater* is 'suppressed'
(*metgneb*) in writing (e.g., *kul* and *meṭul*).

These ideas of *matres lectionis* being 'clear' or 'concealed'
when acting as consonants or vowels, respectively, extended beyond Ḥayyūj and Elias, as it also appears in the writings of Saadia
Gaon (d. 942) and some Masoretes. Saadia presents another example of 'concealment' in the *matres* when he describes the nature of Hebrew vowels in his commentary on *Sefer Yeṣira* (*The*

Book of Creation). In the second chapter, he writes, "As for the seven melodies, they are like the air which is uttered between the letters; they become subtle in their concealment and their cover-

ing (واما الٰذ نغمات فانها كالهواء فيما بين الحروف الملفوظ بها تختفى في كنّها

وسترها)" (Lambert 1891, 42). For Saadia, the seven vowels 'become subtle' (*takhtafā*), less substantial than the consonants which they surround. This verb again shares a root with Sībawayh's *khafāʾ* 'subtlety' and parallels his view that the *matres lectionis* were the 'subtlest' (*ʾakhfā*) of all the letters. Saadia does not apply the idea of 'concealment' directly to *ʾaleph*, *waw*, and *yod* here, but his use of this concept indicates a categorical difference between his perceptions of vowel and consonant phonology.

One of the Masoretic *muṣawwitāt* treatises (T-S Ar.31.28) demonstrates an even more explicit understanding of this dual nature of the *matres lectionis*. The text is extant only from a Genizah fragment, probably written in the tenth or eleventh century, and the author is unknown, but it contains a clear division of the Hebrew letters into three groups. It reads:

אעלם באן אלאחרוף אואכרהא עלי ג אקסאם אלאול הם אליח חרף בעד

אויה כלהא גזם אעני שְׁוָא ליס יכרג מנהא שי אלי אלז מלוך

> Know that for endings [of words], the letters are according to three groups. The first is those eighteen besides *ʾaleph*, *waw*, *yod*, and *heʾ*. All of them are *jazm*; I mean, *shewa*.[61] Nothing is pronounced from them towards any of the seven *mulūk*. (Allony and Yeivin 1985, 101–2, lines 53–58)

---

[61] The text which Allony calls *Kitāb al-Muṣawwitāt* also equates *shewa* with *jazm*; see Allony (1965, 138–40).

The author explains that most Hebrew consonants are *jazm* ('cut-ting off'; also the Arabic grammatical term for vowelless 'jussive' endings) when they occur at the ends of words, so if a *shewa* oc-curs on one of the consonants in this position, it is silent. They "cut off" all potential vowels (*mulūk*). The only letters which do not cause *shewa* to be silent in this position are the four *matres lectionis*: *'aleph, waw, yod,* and *he'*, and so the author continues:

> ואלקסם אלב הוא אלאלף מפרד פאנה לא יטהר פי אלפם אדא כאן פי
> אכר אלכלמה ולא יכון גזם ולא במלך כקולאֶךְ בָּרָא קָרָא מָצָא ומא שא
> דלך ולדלך לא יוגד אלף עלי אלף פי אכר אלכלמה אלא . . . פי לשון
> אֲרָמית וקד יכון גזם פי וסת אלכלמה כקולך וְנֶא מַן בֵּיתֶךְ ואנמא פרקתהא
> חתי תתבין אלשוא

> The second division is the *'alif* alone, for it is not apparent in the mouth when it is at the end of the word, and it is not *jazm*, nor is it with [another] vowel, as you say: *bɔrɔ*, *qɔrɔ*, *mɔṣɔ*, and what is like that. Therefore, *'aleph* does not follow *'aleph* at the end of a word, except... in the Aramaic language. It may occur as *jazm* in the middle of a word, as you say: *w-ne' man betkɔ* [2 Sam. 7.16a], and I have only spaced it [*ne'*] [*man*] so that the *shewa* may be distin-guished (Allony and Yeivin 1985, 102–3, lines 70–82).

For this author, *'aleph* is unique among the Hebrew letters in that, when it occurs at the end of a word, it always represents a vowel. This status contrasts the eighteen *jazm* letters which never repre-sent vowels and is similar to the fully-vowel status of the Arabic *'alif* (see above, present chapter, §3.1). Moreover, according to this author, an *'aleph* can sometimes occur as *jazm*, but only with a silent *shewa* in the middle of a word. As such, most of the time *'aleph* 'is not apparent' (*la yaẓhur*) in the mouth, and it thus lacks

a 'clear' or 'apparent' consonantal state in final position. Three
letters yet remain:

ואלקסם ג הם⁶² ג חרוף הוי פאן להא כרוגין אלואחד כפי ואלאכר טאהר
פאמא אלכפי כקולך פי אלהי אשה דָשָׁה חוּשָׁה קשה ואשבאההם פהולי
רָפַיּים ואלקסם אלב הם אלטאהרין יוסמון מַפֵּקין כמא תקול אָוָה אָנָה בזה...
ואמא אלו קולך פי אלבכּפי עלו ופי אלטאהר עָלָיו... ואמא אליוד תקול פי
אלכפי קָדְשִי ופי אלטאהר קָדָשַי

> The third group are three letters, *he'*, *waw*, and *yod*, and
> they have two pronunciations: one is subtle, and the other
> is clear. As for the subtle, it is as you say, with *he'*:
> *ishshɔ(h)*, *dɔshɔ(h)*, *ḥushɔ(h)*, *qɔshɛ(h)*, and what is like
> them; they are *rɔfayim*. The second type are the clear ones,
> which they call *mappqin*, as you say: *'iwwɔh, bizzɔh*... As for
> the *waw*, it is as you say, for the subtle: *'alu*, and for the
> clear: *'ɔlɔw*... And as for the *yod*, you say for the subtle:
> *qɔdshi*, and for the clear: *qɔdɔshay* (Allony and Yeivin 1985,
> 103–4, lines 83–104).

The author assigns two contrastive qualities to each of the *matres
lectionis*, with 'subtle' (*khafi*) and 'clear' (*ẓāhir*) indicating their
vowel and consonant states, respectively. These terms again correspond to Sībawayh's notion of the *matres lectionis* being the
most subtle (*'akhfā, khafiyya*) letters. This passage also equates
the words *ẓāhir* and *khafi* with the Aramaic Masoretic terms

---

⁶² This word is written with what may be the Babylonian vocalisation
sign for /u/ (a miniature *waw*) above the *he'* and *mem*. The use of this
sign could indicate an Iraqi origin for the manuscript. See Khan (2013);
Dotan (2007, 630–31).

mappiq[63] 'sending out, pronounced' and *rafe* 'relaxed, softened'. In the later Masoretic tradition, *mappiq* is typically reserved for the consonantal form of the letter *heʾ* alone, but in this case the author applies it to the consonantal form of all three of these dual-function letters. They also apply the idea of *rafe*, which eventually came to be used for the fricative forms of the Hebrew *bgdkpt* consonants, to the 'softened' vowel forms of the *matres*.

The text continues with a discussion of the *matres lectionis* in relation to the *bgdkpt* consonants, which further explains the difference between clarity and subtlety, and reveals more of the author's knowledge of Arabic phonetic terminology. They propose that the reason the vowels of the four Hebrew *matres lectionis* cause the six *bgdkpt* letters to become *rafe* 'relaxed' is as follows:

לתכון כרסם סאיר אלמקרא באן אדא כאנו מֶנדֿמגין[64] (ב) מתצלין והם
גיר טאהרין כאנו מלתזקין בחרוף אלמרפייה אד הוי אלג חרוף ליס הם
אצל מן אלכלמה רָפֿיין ואלאלף פי אכר אלכלמה ישבה אלהֶי אלרפֿי אלדֿי

---

[63] This word only appears here in its plural form, and it is possible that the author read the singular as *mappaq*. It is an Aramaic *ʾaphʿel* participle of the root *npq*, meaning 'to bring out' or 'pronounce'. Syriac grammarians use the same verb to mean 'be pronounced'. Both Aramaic versions are likely related to the Arabic verb *kharaja* 'to go out, be pronounced' in Arabic grammar, which has the same phonetic application (see Wright 1871, א, fol. 1a, col. 1, lines 12–13; ב, fol. 2a, col. 1, line 7 and lines 30–31; ב, fol. 2b, col. 1, line 4 and lines 15–16; מ, fol. 38b, line 8; Baethgen 1880, ܠܓ, line 10, and ܠܚ, line 16; Sībawayh 1986, IV:432–36; Ibn Jinnī 1993, 7–8, 43, 62) The equivalent Hebrew calque מֹוצָא appears in *Diqduqe ha-Ṭeʿamim* (Dotan 1967, 145, line 3).

[64] This is a mistaken spelling of מנדגמין (Allony and Yeivin 1985, 104, n. 95).

פי אכר אלכלמה וכאנו אלו להא כרוגין דגש ואל רפי פכרג אלבׁפִׁי מע
אלכפי לאן אלאצול הי אל [ח]רו[ף] אלטאהרה...

[Because] they are like the principle of the rest of the scripture, in that if they are assimilated to what is connected,
and when they are not clear, then they compel the letters
to be *rafe*. Thus *he'*, *waw*, and *yod* are the three letters
which are not *rafe* in the basic form of a word. *'Aleph* at
the end of a word resembles *he' rafe* at the end of a word.
The six [*bgdkpt*] letters [also] have two pronunciations,
dagesh and *al-rafe*. The subtle is pronounced with the subtle
because the originals [of the *matres*] are the clear letters.
(Allony and Yeivin 1985, 104–5, lines 112–22)

This passage shows the same clear/subtle (*ẓāhir*/*khafī*) contrast
that we have seen for the *matres lectionis*, though in this case *rafe*
functions as a synonym for *khafī*. When the *matres* are not *ẓāhir*
(i.e., when they stand for vowels), they are 'assimilated' to the following consonant, compelling it to become *rafe* like them. This
word for 'assimilated'—*mundagham*—is derived from the Arabic
phonetic term *'idghām* 'assimilation, merging, coalescence', which
refers to a type of elision in which one letter combines with the
next in pronunciation. In this case, the consonantal realisation of
the *mater lectionis* is wholly absorbed by the following consonant.
'Idghām is related to *'ikhfā'* 'concealment',[65] the 'elision' that

---

[65] *'Ikhfā'* refers to a reduction in the realization of a letter (e.g., *wāw*
changing from /w/ to /u/), while *'idghām* usually indicates the total
assimilation (in speech) of one letter into another, resulting in gemina-
tion of the second letter (e.g., the loss of the /n/ of *tanwīn* before a word
beginning with a liquid consonant); see al-Nassir (1993, 56, 119). Note
that the precise meanings of these terms can vary between scholars of

Sībawayh indicated was an inherent feature of the *matres lectionis* when they lose their consonantal function. The use of this term suggests that the author of the *muṣawwitāt* text was familiar with these Arabic concepts. This idea then informs the relationship between the vowels and the *bgdkpt* letters: when the *matres* are *khafī* 'subtle, concealed'—that is, representing vowels—their subtle quality assimilates to a following *bgdkpt* letter, causing it to become *khafī* (i.e., *rafe*) as well.

In this context, the author singles out *heʾ*, *waw*, and *yod* as the only letters which are not naturally pronounced in their 're-laxed' forms. That is, the author believes that all of the *bgdkpt* letters are fricatives (*rafe*) in their most basic forms, and it is only by the addition of a *dagesh* dot that they become plosives. By contrast, *heʾ*, *waw*, and *yod* occur in a vacuum as their 'clear' (*ẓāhir*) consonantal forms, but if their phonetic context causes them to function as vowels, then they relax and become 'subtle' (*khafī*). This arrangement results in an interesting conflation of the terms that indicate the dualities of the *matres lectionis* and *bgdkpt* consonants, with the same idea of 'subtlety' and 'relaxation' applying to both vowel and fricative phonemes that are articulated with continuous airflow. A similar conflation occurs in Saadia's commentary on *Sefer Yeṣira*, where he refers to the plosive *bgdkpt* forms as *khashin* 'rough, coarse', in contrast to the *layyin* 'soft, flexible' fricatives (Lambert 1891, 29). In that case, Saadia uses *layyin*—the Arabic term for the 'soft' *matres lectionis* letters—in much the same way as the author of T-S Ar.31.28 uses

_____

different languages, and the one used in T-S Ar.31.28 seems to differ from that of *Kitāb Sībawayh*.

khafī. Abū al-Faraj makes a similar statement in *Hidāya al-Qārī*, where he specifically cites Judah ben David Ḥayyūj as an authority on why the 'letters of softness and lengthening' (*ḥurūf al-līn wa-al-madd*) also 'soften' (*tulayyin*) adjacent *bgdkpt* letters (Khan 2020, II:93, lines 521–25).

One cannot help but notice a similarity here between these terms, the terms used to describe *bgdkpt* consonants in Syriac, and the *aphōna* letters in Greek. In Syriac, the obvious parallels are *rukkɔkɔ* 'softening' and *qushshɔyɔ* 'hardening', which indicate the fricative and plosive *bgdkpt* pronunciations, respectively. These two phonetic terms are already attested in the late eighth century in the writings of Dawid bar Pawlos (Dolabani 1953, 48, lines 4–7; Rahmani 1904, ܡܒ, lines 19–21).[66] Perhaps coincidentally, but almost certainly not, these terms are cognates with the descriptions of the *bgdkpt* letters given in *Sefer Yeṣira*, where the anonymous Hebrew writer calls them *rak* 'soft' and *qɔshɛ* 'hard' (Hayman 2004, 51, lines 37a–37b).[67] Much earlier, but still relevant, is the *Technē Grammatikē*'s classification of the *aphōna* consonants (i.e., the Classical Greek stops). Dionysius Thrax calls three of them 'smooth' (*fila*; /k/, /p/, /t/) and three 'rough' (*dasɛia*; /kʰ/, /pʰ/, /tʰ/) (Davidson 1874, 6), apparently describing aspiration. There is also evidence that Jacob of Edessa (d. 708)

---

[66] See MS Jerusalem, St. Mark's Monastery (SMMJ) 356, ff. 164v–166r; MS Mardin, Dayr al-Zaʿfarān (ZFRN) 192, ff. 199r–200. On the introduction of the *rukkɔkɔ* and *qushshɔyɔ* diacritic dots, see Segal (1989).

[67] There are two versions of this section in the recoverable text of *Sefer Yeṣira*, and one of them reads *raq* instead of *rak*.

adapted this Greek classification system to divide the Syriac consonants (i.e., *naqdɔtɔ* 'smooth', *meṣʿɔyɔtɔ* 'intermediate', *ʿbyɔtɔ*
'heavy/thick'), although it is not clear that he followed the same
bgdkpt dichotomy of fricatives versus plosives (Talmon 2008,
167–69).[68]

The extent to which any of these concepts may have influenced later medieval descriptions of the *matres lectionis* remains
uncertain. All that can be said for sure is that scholars of Semitic
languages regularly adapted concepts from other linguistic traditions to explain the dual nature of their vowel letters. These relationships are most evident in Syriac and Hebrew linguists' bor-
rowings of Arabic terminology to describe their own languages,
but in each instance, they modified that terminology to better
suit their phonological needs.

3.3. Grouping Vowels with *Matres Lectionis*

One of the most pervasive features of the *matres lectionis* in
the medieval period was their perceived role as the source of
every vowel phoneme. As such, many Arabic, Syriac, and Hebrew
linguists assigned each of their vowels to either *ʾalif, wāw*, or *yāʾ*.
Explicit evidence of this type of division appears early in the Arabic grammatical tradition, including in Sībawayh's *Kitāb*. In a

---

[68] Merx (1889, 53) argues that Jacob's system of division was based on
phonetic voicing and triads of consonants that share articulation points,
whereas Revell (1972, 367–68) argues that the division was based on
fricativisation of the *bgdkpt* consonants in addition to voicing. Talmon
suggests that Merx's approach is more tenable.

section on verbs that contain velar/pharyngeal consonants (i.e.,
hāʾ, *ʿayn*, *ḥāʾ*, *ghayn*, and *khāʾ*), he writes:

وإنّما فتحوا هذه الحروفَ لأنها سَفلتْ في الحلق، وكرهوا أن يتناولوا حركة ما
قبلها بحركة ما ارتفع من الحروف، فجعلوا حركتها من الحرف الذي في حيِّزها
وهو الألف، وانما الحركاتُ من الألف والياء والواو.

> They [the Arabs] only put *fatha* on these letters because
> they occur low in the throat, and they avoid making the
> vowel that precedes [the velar/pharyngeal letters] into a
> vowel of that which is raised above those letters. Thus,
> they make the vowel from the letter in the same space,
> namely *ʾalif*. Indeed, the vowels are from *ʾalif*, *yāʾ*, and
> *wāw*. (Sībawayh 1986, IV:101)

Sībawayh states that the three Arabic short vowels (*ḥarakāt*)—
fatha /a/, *kasra* /i/, and *ḍamma* /u/—are derived from *ʾalif*, *yāʾ*,
and *wāw*. He argues the vowel /a/ tends to occur before pharyngeal consonants because /a/ is part of *ʾalif*, and since *ʾalif* is articulated from the same 'space' (*ḥayyiz*) as the pharyngeals, /a/
is the easiest vowel to pronounce with them. Similarly, Arabic
avoids the vowels /i/ and /u/ before pharyngeal consonants, because they come from the articulation points of *yāʾ* and *wāw*,
which are 'raised above' (*ʾirtafaʿa*; i.e., more fronted) relative to
the throat. The consequence of this linking of /a/, /i/, and /u/ to
the respective articulation points of the *matres* is that Sībawayh
creates a scale by which /a/ is regarded as the lowest, most-
backed vowel, /u/ is the highest, most-fronted vowel, and /i/ is
between them on the tongue. This arrangement runs directly
counter to several other perceptions of phonetic 'height', as we
will see later (chapter 3).

Sībawayh also indicates the relationship between vowels and *matres* on the authority of his teacher, al-Khalīl ibn Aḥmad:

وزعم الخليل أنّ... فالفتحةُ من الألف والكسرة من الياء والضمّة من الواو. فكل واحدة شيءٌ مما ذكرت لك.

Al-Khalīl claimed that... *fatḥa* is from *ʾalif*, *kasra* is from *yāʾ*, and *ḍamma* is from *wāw*, and each one is something which we have already mentioned to you. (Sībawayh 1986, IV:241–42)

Like Sībawayh, al-Khalīl apparently states that the vowels are 'from' *ʾalif*, *yāʾ*, and *wāw*, but neither master nor student explains precisely what that means. ʿAbd al-Salam Harun (the modern editor of *Kitāb Sībawayh*) points out that a later grammarian, Abū Saʿid Ḥasan al-Sīrāfī (d. 979), comments on this passage. He provides a more complete understanding of the relationship between *matres* and vowels than al-Khalīl does. In his book, *Sharḥ Kitāb Sībawayh* (*The Explanation of Sībawayh's Book*), al-Sīrāfī writes:

واستدلّ على ذلك بشيئين أحدهما أنّا نرى أن الضمّة متى أشبعناها صارت واوا في مثل قولنا زيدو والرجلو... والاستدلال الثاني ما قاله سيبويه حين ذكر الألف والواو والياء فقال: لأن الكلام لا يخلو منهنّ أو بعضهنّ.

He [Sībawayh] concluded this by two things: one is that we observe the *ḍamma*, when we make it full, becomes a *wāw*, as we say: *zaydū* and *al-rajlū*... and the second is what Sībawayh said when he mentioned *ʾalif*, *wāw*, and *yāʾ*, for he said: "because speech is not devoid of them, or [at least] a portion of them." (Sībawayh 1986, IV:242, n. 1)[69]

---

[69] This reference is for the al-Sīrāfī quote, which Harun transcribes in his edition of the *Kitāb*. I have not come across this supposed quote from Sībawayh in the *Kitāb* itself, but it is a very long book.

Al-Sīrāfī clarifies that the *ḍamma* differs from a *mater lectionis wāw* only in terms of phonetic quantity, and the 'portion' (*baʿḍ*) can be 'made full' (*ʾishbāʿ*) so that it becomes an entire long vowel. In this way, he argues, al-Khalīl meant that the short vowels are 'from' the *matres lectionis* because they make up a small part of their longer phonemes. Al-Sīrāfī also believes that Sībawayh said speech cannot exist "devoid of them"; that is, speech cannot happen without the letters *ʾalif*, *wāw*, or *yāʾ*, or at least not without a fraction of them. This notion conforms with the statements of early Syriac grammarians—particularly Dawid bar Pawlos—who argued that the consonants could not be pronounced without the aid of the vowels.

The idea that the vowels were related to the *matres lectionis* according to degrees of 'fullness' seems to have been widespread in the Arabic tradition after Sībawayh. In *Sirr Ṣināʿa al-Iʿrāb*, Ibn Jinnī (d. 1002) explains their relative quantities, writing:

اعلم أن الحركات أبعاض حروف المدّ واللين، وهي الألف والياء والواو، فكما أن هذه الحروف ثلاثة، فكذلك الحركات ثلاثة، وهي الفتحة والكسرة والضمّة، والفتحة بعض الألف، والكسرة بعض الياء، والضمّة بعض الواو.

Know that the vowels are portions of the letters of lengthening and softness: *ʾalif*, *yāʾ*, and *wāw*, and just as these letters are three, so too are the vowels three: *fatḥa*, *kasra*, and *ḍamma*. *Fatḥa* is a portion of *ʾalif*, *kasra* is a portion of *yāʾ*, and *ḍamma* is a portion of *wāw*. (Ibn Jinnī 1993, 17)[70]

---

[70] See also, Semaan's (1968, 58–59) translation and discussion of this passage.

Ibn Jinnī recognises a clear equivalency in the quality of the long vowel forms of the *matres lectionis* and the unwritten short vowels,[71] and so argues that the latter are derived from the former. He justifies this connection with a simple explanation, saying: "Your evidence that the vowels are portions of these letters is that when you make one of them full, then after it, the letter of which it is a portion occurs (ويدلّك على أن الحركات أبعاض لهذه الحروف، أنك it is a portion occurs (متى أشبعتَ واحدة منهن حدث بعدها الحرف الذي هي بعضها) (Ibn Jinnī 1993, 18, 23). That is, when one makes a short vowel full (*ʾishbāʿ*), then a long vowel occurs. Because of this relationship, Ibn Jinnī identifies the short vowels as *ḥurūf ṣighār* 'small letters', and explains that some "earlier grammarians" would call *fatḥa*, *kasra*, and *ḍamma* "small (*saghīr*) *ʾalif*, small *yāʾ*, and small *wāw*" (Ibn Jinnī 1993, 18). He does not specify whom he is referring to as 'earlier'. His main source, Sībawayh (d. 793/796), does not use *saghīr* for vowel length. Meanwhile, Ibn Sīnā (d. 1037), who is certainly not 'earlier' than Ibn Jinnī, does refer to "large and small *ʾalif*" (al-Tayyan and Mir Alam 1983, 126; see also, Fischer 1985, 94–97).

This analysis of the short vowels as small letter 'parts' of the long vowel letters and Ibn Jinnī's allusion to earlier sources may reveal yet another connection between the Arabic linguistic tradition and earlier Greek grammatical terminology. C. H. M. Versteegh (1977, 21–22) notes Muḥammad ibn Aḥmad al-Khwārizmī (d. 997)—a contemporary of Ibn Jinnī—as a potential

---

[71] Alfozan notes that some modern linguists argue the long and short vowels differed in both quantity *and* quality (1989, 32–33), but medieval grammarians did not recognise such a difference.

source for a 'Greek' system of vocalic analysis that was known in tenth-century Arabic circles. Al-Khwārizmī was a Samanid scribe who wrote one of the earliest extant Arabic encyclopaedias some-time after the year 977 (Bosworth 1963, 100). In this encyclo-paedia, known as *Mafātīh al-ʿUlūm* (*The Keys to the Sciences*), he compiles a general overview of many different topics that would be useful for an Islamic *kātib* 'secretary, scribe' to know, includ-ing several sections on Arabic grammar (Fischer 1985). One of these sections is titled *Wujūh al-Iʿrāb ʿalā Madhhab Falāsifa al-Yūnāniyyīn* (*The Ways of Inflection According to the School*[72] *of the Philosophy of the Greeks*), which reads:

الرفع عند أصحاب المَنطِق من اليونانيّين واو ناقصة وكذلك الضمّ واخواته
المذكورة والكسر واخواته عندهم ياء ناقصة والفتح واخواته عندهم ألف ناقصة
وإن شئت قلتَ الواو الممدودة اللينة ضمّة مُشبَعة والياء الممدودة اللينة كسرة
مُشبَعة والألف الممدودة فتحة مُشبَعة

Al-rafʿ, according to the masters of logic among the Greeks, is deficient *wāw*, and likewise is *ḍamma* and its aforemen-tioned sisters. *Al-kasra* and its sisters are, according to them, deficient *yāʾ*, while *al-fatḥ* and its sisters are deficient *ʾalif*. If you wish, you may say the soft, lengthened *wāw* is a full *ḍamma*, the soft, lengthened *yāʾ* is a full *kasra*, and the lengthened *ʾalif* is a full *fatḥa*. (al-Khwārizmī 1968, 46, lines 4–8)

The key phonological feature which al-Khwārizmī attributes to the Greeks is the division of the vowels of each *mater lectionis* into 'deficient' (*nāqiṣ*) and 'full' (*mushbaʿ*) qualities according to their length. *Wāw mushbaʿa*, for example, is typically written with the

---

[72] Or 'methodology'. *Madhhab* here does not imply a physical school.

letter *wāw* and represents long /ū/. Meanwhile, *wāw nāqiṣa* indicates a short /u/ typically written without *wāw*. These words— *nāqiṣ* and *mushbaʿ*—also appear in Ibn Jinnī's *Sirr Ṣināʿa* when he describes the differences between short *ḥarakāt* and long vowels (Ibn Jinnī 1993, 23, 26).[73]

Versteegh (1977, 21) notes that this perceived 'Greek' idea of a short vowel being a fraction of a longer vowel stands in contrast to the mainstream Arabic analysis of long vowels as a short vowel plus a 'silent' *mater lectionis*. He theorises that the Arabic explanations of the *ḥarakāt* as 'small' or 'deficient' versions of the *matres* are thus translations of Greek letter names, calqued by translators like Ḥunayn ibn Isḥāq (d. 873) who were familiar with spoken Greek. By this logic, the Greek letters *omega* (/ō/) and *omikron* (/o/) were indeed 'big O' and 'small O' (Fischer 1985, 96), and *mikron* (small) was the source of the *saghīr* descriptor for the short vowels. Then *epsilon* (/e/) and *upsilon* (/u/) are 'simple E' and 'simple U', distinguishing their pure vowels from related diphthongs (i.e., αι /ay/ and οι /oy/), and *psilon* 'bare, simple' was the source of *nāqiṣ* (Versteegh 1977, 23). I am sceptical of this connection on the basis of such tenuous calques, but it is not implausible.

---

[73] Abū ʿAmr al-Dānī (d. 1053) uses similar language, for example discussing the *mushbaʿāt* in his *al-Muḥkam fī Naqṭ al-Maṣāḥif* (al-Dānī 1960, 20b). The word *ʾishbāʿ* is also often used to describe metrical extensions to lengthen the end of a line of poetry (see Versteegh 1977, 20; K. Versteegh 2011).

What does seem clear is the fact that there was some notion of a Greek 'school' or 'methodology' (*madhhab*) of Arabic grammar during the tenth century (Fischer 1985, 95), and the Syriac Christian physician Ḥunayn ibn Isḥāq is the most likely source for al-Khwārizmī's knowledge of this school. Recalling the heading from al-Khwārizmī's section on inflection, the title *Wujūh al-Iʿrāb ʿalā Madhhab Falāsifa al-Yūnāniyyīn* (*The Ways of Inflection According to the School of the Philosophy of the Greeks*) is quite similar to that of Ḥunayn's book on Arabic grammar, *Kitāb Aḥkām al-Iʿrāb ʿalā Madhhab al-Yūnāniyyīn* (*The Rules of Inflection According to the School of the Greeks*) (Merx 1889, 105–6; Vidro 2020a, 32). This work was long thought to be lost, but Nadia Vidro recently recovered several pages of the text from Judaeo-Arabic fragments in the Cairo Genizah (Vidro 2020a; 2020b, 296–300).[74] In them, Ḥunayn does in fact lay out a system for classifying the parts of Arabic speech using terminology translated from the Greek grammatical tradition (Vidro 2020a, 27–29). In the introductory section, he also announces his intention to explain the proper pronunciation of Arabic utterances—including the vowels *fatḥa*, *kasra*, and *ḍamma*—at a later point in the book (Vidro 2020a, 14, 29), but unfortunately this section of the text remains missing. In contrast to Ibn Sīnā and other tenth-century Arabic scholars of Greek logic (see Fischer 1985, 95–97), Ḥunayn (d. 873) does predate Ibn Jinnī (d. 1002) by a wide margin. The recovery of additional folios from this text would shed

---

[74] For additional confirmation of the identity of this text, see Posegay (2021b, 159–60).

more light on the possibility of Arabic authors calquing the names of Greek letters.[75]

Syriac and Hebrew scholars also conceived of the *matres lectionis* as the source of their vowels, even though they did not distinguish between long and short vowel phonemes in the same way that Arab grammarians did. Like Ibn Jinnī and al-Khwārizmī, Elias of Ṭirhan (d. 1049) is definitive in attributing vowels to each of the *matres lectionis*, but his system is more complex due to the larger vowel inventory in Syriac in comparison to Arabic. He lays out the different types of vowels in his *Memrɔ Gramaṭiqɔyɔ*. For clarity, I have added approximate phonetic values to each of Elias' vowel names:

> ܘܙܕܩ ܕܝܢ ܠܡܕܥ ܕܐܬܘܬܐ ܩܠܢܝܬܐ. ܬܠܬ ܐܢܝܢ.. ܗ̄.. ܐ.. ܘ.., ܘܫܪܟܐ ܕܐܬܘܬܐ
> ܐܚܪܢܝܬܐ ܠܗܠܝܢ ܢܩܦܢ.. ܗܠܝܢ ܐܬܘܬܐ ܠܙܘܥܐ ܕܡ̈ܫܚܬܐ ܐܢܘܢ ܩ̈ܠܐ
> ܡܫܡ̈ܗܢܐ ܠܗ ܗܘܝܢܐ ܡܬܬܙܝܥܢܝܬܐ ܐܬܦܪܫܘ ܠܡܠܐܘ ܡܢ ܗܠܝܢ ܬܠܬ
> ܡܠܝܬܐ.. ܡܢ .ܐ. ܦ̈ܬ ܙܩܦܐ... ܘܦܬܚܐ... ܘܥܨܨܐ ܐܘܚܕܬ ܪ̈ܒܨܐ... ܡܢ. ܘ̄.
> ܕܝܢ. ܒ. ܡܬܬܙܝܥܢܝܬܐ.. ܘ.. ܢܚܬܝܐ ܘܐܣܝܪܬܐ.. ܘ.. ܕܡܬܩܪܝܢ ܩܪܝܬܐ ܡܗܡܗܡܐ
> ܘܪܘܚܬܐ.... ܡܢ.. ܘ.. ܬܘܒ ܚܕܐ ܕܡܬܬܙܝܥܢܘܬܐ ܕܐܬܝܬܝܗ̇ ,[76]

It is necessary to know that the sounding letters are three, being *ʾalaph, wāw, yod,* and the rest of the other letters [are pronounced][77] with them. They are the letters for the con-

[75] In fact, this book has considerable potential as a possible 'missing link' between the Greek, Arabic, and Syriac linguistic traditions in the early medieval period. The extant portions now require significant further analysis to build on Vidro's foundation and bring Ḥunayn's ideas into context with current scholarship on Syriac and Arabic grammar.
[76] These Syriac vowel names will be discussed in chapter 4, §2.3.
[77] Baethgen's edition reads ܢܩܦܢ 'they cling to', but this is probably an error for ܢܩܦܢ 'they are pronounced'.

struction of nouns or verbs (which indicate action), the vocalisations made known by production from these three
sounding ones. From *ʾalaph* is what is *zqɔpɔ* /ɔ/... *ptɔhɔ*
/a/... and *sheshlɔ*, that is, *rbɔsɔ* /e/.... Then from *waw* are
two vocalisations: [one] is *hbɔsɔ* /u/... and the other is
called *massaqɔ* and *rwahtɔ* /o/.... Then from *yod* is one vocalisation, which is /i/. (Baethgen 1880, ܠܝ, lines 11–18)

This type of vowel classification likely came naturally to Syriac
grammarians, as standard Syriac orthography nearly always represented /u/, /o/, and /i/ with the letters *waw* and *yod*. Conversely, Elias assigns each of the vowels which are *not* typically
marked by *matres lectionis*—/ɔ/, /a/, and /e/—to *ʾalaph*, the
least-consonantal of his three 'sounding' letters. Elsewhere, he
also refers to all three of these qualities as 'half-*ʾalaph*' (*pelgut
ʾalaph*) (Baethgen 1880, ܒ, lines 1–2). While this description is
reminiscent of Ibn Jinnī's explanation of vowel 'portions' and the
'small' letters, we have already seen that the idea of a 'half-sounding' is most likely derived from *hēmiphōna*, the Greek term for
fricative consonants (see above, present chapter, §1.0). In any
case, Elias has a clear understanding of the three sounding letters
as the sources of all six discrete East Syriac vowel qualities.

As for the Masoretic tradition, the classification of vowels
according to the *matres lectionis* appears explicitly in a short text
known as *Reshimat Munnahim* (*List of Terms*). Richard Steiner
draws attention to this passage:

סֵדֶר הַסִּימָנִים. זֶה סֵדֶר הַסִּימָנִים:
שִׁשָׁה נָעִים הֵם שָׁלוֹש אוֹתִיּוֹת.
לְאָלֶף שְׁנֵי פָנִים אֶחָד קָמֵץ וְאֶחָד פָּתַח...
כְּמוֹת: אָ קָמֵץ אַ פָּתַח.
לוֹ לָוֵו שְׁנֵי פָנִים: אוֹ אֻו.

לְיוֹד שְׁנֵי פָנִים: אִי אֵי.
אֵילוּ הֵן שָׁלוֹשׁ אוֹתִיּוֹת שֶׁבָּהֶן נַעֲשׂוּ.

The Arrangement of the Signs. This is the arrangement of
the signs:

Six movers are three letters.

'Aleph has two forms, one closing and one opening.

That is: 'ɔ is closing, 'a is opening.

Waw has two forms: 'o 'u.

Yod has two forms: 'i 'e.

These are the three letters by which they are made. (Steiner 2005, 379, n. 51; see also, Allony 1986, 123)

This text assigns two 'forms' (*panim*) to each of the *matres*, dis-
tributing six discrete vowel qualities among them. It seems that
this Masorete's recitation tradition (quite likely Palestinian or
Babylonian) did not distinguish between /e/ and /ɛ/, and thus
had one fewer vowel than the standard Tiberian tradition (see
Fassberg 1990, 28–31, 53; Dotan 2007, 625–27, 630–32; Khan
2013; 2020, I:244). Nevertheless, they show a clear conceptual
distinction between three types of vowels according to their respective *matres*. This relationship also occurs implicitly in the orthography of a number of early notes and Masoretic treatises,
where it was common to transcribe vowel sounds with *'aleph* plus
an additional *mater* (e.g., אא או אי), with a preference for *yod* and
waw to indicate /e/ and /o/ (e.g., Steiner 2005, 378; Dotan 2007,
634).[78]

---

[78] See also, T-S Ar.31.28 and T-S Ar.53.1 in Allony and Yeivin (1985);
Allony (1964); Eldar (1981).

This division of vowels with *matres lectionis* was known to many medieval linguists, but it was not universal. A clear contrast to this trend is Jacob of Edessa's (d. 708) *Turrọṣ Mamllọ Nahrọyọ*, in which Jacob invents new letters to represent the Syriac vowels, and abandons the usage of *waw* and *yod* as *matres lectionis*. He does retain *ʾalaph* to represent the vowel /ɔ/, a fact which may result from the idea that *ʾalaph* was the least consonantal of all the letters. Still, Jacob is an exception to the rule.

The practice of vowel classification with the *matres* appears in the Arabic, Syriac, and Hebrew phonological traditions at the same time, and it shows a shared understanding of the Semitic phenomenon of dual-functioning letters that can represent both vowel and consonant phonemes. As we have seen, similar notions crossed religious and linguistic boundaries with regard to the sickness and health of these letters, their clarity and subtlety, and their length, softness, and sonority. These ideas changed according to the needs of three language traditions with different vowel inventories, but it remains possible to detect their common features.

4.0. Summary

The preceding sections have surveyed the three primary frameworks that medieval Semitic linguists used to differentiate the phonetic characteristics of vowels and consonants. In general, it seems that they considered vowels both more energetic and more ephemeral than consonants. Members of all three traditions discussed here repeatedly emphasise that speech can only occur due to the movement and sonority of the vowels, without which the consonants cannot be articulated. One way that they expressed this idea was via the 'sounding' letters which can be pronounced alone. Ultimately derived from earlier Greek tradition, this concept was especially influential for Syriac and Hebrew grammarians, who learned it either through direct contact with Greek sources or via Arabic translations produced after the eighth century. By contrast, the soundingness of vowels was not particularly well-known among Arabic grammarians, who overwhelmingly refer to vocalisation with terms related to 'movement' and 'stillness'. This idea may also have Greek roots in the term *kinesis*, although the evidence is not entirely clear. At any rate, Syriac and Hebrew grammarians also adopted it as a result of their contact with Arabic scholarship. Along with these two main principles, Syriac, Arabic, and Hebrew scholars all contended with the dual nature of the *matres lectionis* that existed in their writing systems, and they developed various ways of explaining their behaviour in speech and writing. The most well-known of these ways is the Arabic concept of 'sick' letters, which sometimes act as vowels, but other times may function like 'healthy' consonants. Some Syriac and Hebrew writers challenged or modified this idea, but in general they developed similar explanations, expressing a marked contrast between the 'clear' and 'concealed' forms of their vowel letters. Taken together, these similarities reveal numerous points of contact among scholars of different Semitic languages, as well as potential pathways by which medieval Jewish, Christian, and Muslim scholars could have exchanged other ideas about their holy languages.

Before moving on to the more specific histories of vocalisation in these three traditions, it is worth remarking on the various other identifications for the category of 'vowels' that we have not covered. We tangentially approached one of these ideas, namely, the description of vowels as 'melodies' or 'tones'. This identification is fairly common among medieval Judaeo-Arabic authors (e.g., see Skoss 1952; Allony 1971, 11-15; Eldar 1981; Khan 2020, II:116;),[79] who refer to the vowels as *naghamāt* 'melodies, tones' in addition to 'movements' and 'sounding' ones. It may also be known in Syriac, as Dawid bar Pawlos refers to the Syriac cognate *neˁmtɔ* 'melody' in the context of the production of speech (Gottheil 1893, cxii, line 9). The idea of vowels as 'melodies' most likely evolved out of the Hebrew and Syriac traditions of biblical recitation, associating vowels with both musical intonation and with the number of syllables in a metre (see Werner 1959, 374). Other terms for 'vowel' are explicitly linked to prosody, most notably the Syriac word *nqɔshtɔ* 'beat' (Gottheil 1893, cxvii, lines 5–12; Segal 1953, 7, 54, 171; Kiraz 2012, I:59), which represents a single syllable in poetic metre. Jewish grammarians also have a unique term for vowels—'kings' (either *mulūk* or *melaķim*)—that was likely derived by analogy with the hierarchy of the Hebrew accents (see Khan 2020, II:267). Furthermore, Masoretes sometimes called the vowels 'signs' (*simanim*), using the same word that they used for the 'mnemonic devices' that helped them recall the fine details of Masoretic recitation (Steiner 2005, 379; Dotan 2007, 619; Khan 2020, I:117).

---

[79] See also, MS Cambridge, T-S NS 301.69.

Perhaps the most regrettable omission here is a thorough
discussion of the Arabic concept of ʾiʿrāb, a term for 'declension'
that literally means 'making Arabic' and may be a calque of the
Greek grammatical term *hellenismos* 'declension, making Greek'
(Versteegh 1977, 62–64; 1993, 23–26, 127–28).[80] As we saw with
the history of *ḥarakāt*, the line between 'declension' and 'vocalisation' became blurred at the ends of words where the Arabic
case vowels occurred. In contrast to Arabic, most grammarians
did not recognise distinct grammatical cases in Hebrew, and consequently some Judaeo-Arabic authors adopted the word ʾiʿrāb to
simply mean 'vocalisation' (e.g., Skoss 1952, 290, lines 15–16;
Khan 2020, II:116). This usage of ʾiʿrāb may have also been a
feature of the eighth-century 'Old Iraqi' school of Arabic grammar (Talmon 2003, 239–40 and 240, n. 1).[81] The closest analogue
in Syriac may be the word *puḥḥɔme* 'comparisons, relationships',
which refers to the systems of vocalisation and reading dots that
indicate syntactic relationships within a Syriac text (Hoffmann
1880, VII–VIV; Segal 1953, 48, n. 3, 59, 172; Posegay 2021b,
156–60),[82] and is sometimes used to translate ʾiʿrāb (Duval 1901,
1502–3; Gottheil 1928, II:246, lines 6–9; see also, Merx 1889,

---

[80] For the early Arabic grammatical usage of the term ʾiʿrāb, see Talmon
(1997, 198).

[81] For example, in the introduction to *Kitāb al-ʿAyn*, either al-Khalīl or
al-Layth classifies *ḍamma*, *kasra*, and *tanwīn* as ʾiʿrāb (Makhzumi 1985,
I:50–51).

[82] See especially, Baethgen (1880, ܡܠ, lines 15–18) and Gottheil (1893,
cxviii, lines 10–12).

143–44). Similar to *ʾiʿrāb*, the word *naḥw* broadly means 'grammar' in Arabic, but is also used to indicate an inflected form of an Arabic word, often emphasising the vowel at the end of that form (e.g., Ibn Jinnī 1993, 53–54). It seems that some Hebrew linguists generalised this word to mean all vowels, including with the plural form *ʾanḥāʾ* 'inflections, vowels' (Eldar 1981, esp. 108; Khan 2020, II:267).

While not the primary methods for conceptualising vowels as distinct from consonants, all of these ideas constitute potential avenues for further studies into the shared history of vocalisation in Syriac, Arabic, and Hebrew. For now, however, we turn to the earliest attempts by Semitic linguists to differentiate the actual qualities of the vowels, beginning with the foundational principle that each vowel can be described according to its relationship with the others.

3. EARLY RELATIVE VOWEL PHONOLOGY

With respect to the position of the points also, every man takes authority to himself to place them as he pleases. (Jacob of Edessa [d. 708], *Letter on Orthography to the Scribes* [trans. Phillips 1869, 8])

Prior to the spread of Arabic as the dominant language in the Middle East, both Syriac grammarians and Hebrew Masoretes arranged vowels according to a relative system, classifying each one based on its relationship to other vowels. They determined these comparative relations by observing the physical processes of articulation, especially noting the amount that the mouth opens when pronouncing each vowel and whether a vowel is articulated from the back or the front of the mouth. To some extent, the two traditions also share terminology connected to their relative vowel systems in the form of *mille⁽el/men l⁽el* (above) and *millera⁽/men ltaḥt* (below) phonetic designations. These ideas connected positional 'height' within the mouth to vowel phonology and informed the placement of the dots in the Syriac and Tiberian Hebrew vocalisation systems.[1] These relative principles most likely began as pedagogical aides used to help new readers master the proper pronunciation of Syriac and Hebrew vowels.

---

[1] A connection of this sort between the Syriac and Hebrew vowel points has been argued (for and against) in various forms since the 1880s (see, for example, Graetz 1881a; 1881b; Blake 1940; Morag 1961, 17–19; Dotan 1974; 2007, 613; Posegay 2020, 193–202; 2021d).

   https://doi.org/10.11647/OBP.0271.03

By the ninth century, both Syriac and Hebrew scholars shifted away from this mindset and reapplied their relative comparisons to develop absolute terms that could designate discrete vowels on a one-to-one basis.

The Arabic traditions of Qurʾānic recitation emerged in the context of these relative vowel systems that Syriac priests and Hebrew Masoretes used to teach and record biblical recitation. In these biblical traditions, contrastive terms like *pɔtaḥ* 'opening' and *qɔmeṣ* 'closing' compared homographs based on relative openness, while terms like *men lʿel* 'above' and *men ltaḥt* 'below' compared backness. Some Arabic vowel names do designate openness (e.g., *fatḥ*, *ḍamm*), but there is also an early pair that contrasted allophonic variants of *ʾalif* using 'height' as a measure of phonetic backness: *ʾimāla* 'bending down, inclining' and *naṣb* 'standing upright'. The earliest explanations of these terms reveal that, like in Syriac and Hebrew, early Arabic vowel phonology included a two-way relative system that did not assign specific names to each vowel sound. However, due to the smaller vowel inventory in Arabic as compared to Hebrew and Syriac, Arabic grammarians developed their absolute vowel naming system without significant expansions to this relative terminology.

1.0. The Hebrew-Syriac Connection

The Syriac and Hebrew theories of relative vocalisation depend on comparisons between different amounts of phonetic openness and backness during the pronunciation of vowels. These principles appear in the grammatical work of Jacob of Edessa (d. 708), most notably in his tractate *On Persons and Tenses* (Phillips 1869,

13–33, ܓܒ–ܓ), as well as Dawid bar Pawlos' (fl. c. 770–800) fragmentary grammar (Gottheil 1893; Farina 2021) and his *scholion*
on *bgdkt* letters.[2] It also appears in early Masoretic homograph
lists and the terminology in the Tiberian *Masora magna* and *parva*.
Remnants of it can even be seen in Judaeo-Arabic Masoretic treatises. Altogether, these sources suggest that there was contact and
intellectual exchange between Syriac grammarians and Hebrew
Masoretes sometime around the eighth century, just as they began shifting from relative to absolute vocalisation. Their shared
principles of relative vocalisation formed the basis of later phonological analyses of vowels and the placement of the vowel
points in both Syriac and Hebrew.

1.1. Syriac Relative Vowel Phonology

Three works by Jacob of Edessa reveal a Syriac scribal and grammatical tradition on the cusp of the transition between relative
and absolute vocalisation. The first is his *Letter on Orthography* to
George of Sarug, in which he berates Syriac scribes who fail to
follow his ideas of proper orthography and diacritic pointing
(Phillips 1869, 1–12, ܐܙ–ܝ; see also, Farina 2018). He stresses
the importance of the Syriac diacritical dot, which could indicate
the vocalisation of a word in comparison to a homograph with

---

[2] MS Jerusalem, Saint Mark's Monastery 356, ff. 164v–166r; see Dolabani (1994) and Farina's (2021) recent edition and translation. This
manuscript is catalogued as SMMJ 356 by the Hill Museum and Manuscript Library (https://www.vhmml.org/readingRoom/view/136521).

Points of Contact

different vowels.³ Jacob's frustration at the mistaken use of this dot is palpable, but his entreaty to George's community did not resolve the issue, as the diacritic dot alone could not precisely disambiguate every vowel in a given word.⁴ Jacob took matters into his own hands later in his career with his third work related to vocalisation (Segal 1953, 40; Talmon 2008, 167), the Syriac grammar *Turrɔṣ Mamllɔ Nahrɔyɔ* (*The Correct Form of Mesopotamian Speech*) (Wright 1871; see also above, chapter 2, §1.0). In order to record the vowels of precise grammatical examples in this book, Jacob designed what is likely the first absolute vocalisation system in Syriac, Arabic, or Hebrew. This system utilised new letters, derived from Greek letters, to represent each Syriac vowel. Jacob insisted that they were only meant for teaching, and they never saw widespread use outside of the *Turrɔṣ Mamllɔ* (Talmon 2008, 164–66; Kiraz 2012, I:73–75).⁵

---

³ The most accessible and up-to-date explanation of this diacritic system is Kiraz (2015, 31–46). Other explanations, in descending order of readability, include: Kiraz (2012, I:12–14, 20–22), Segal (1953, 7–19), and Duval (1881, 61–67).

⁴ This remained the case even as seventh-century scribes began applying the diacritic dots to individual letters (see Segal 1953, 9; Kiraz 2012, I:20, 64).

⁵ The Arabic red-dot system, which is often attributed to Abū al-Aswad al-Duʾalī (d. 686/7), is also an absolute vocalisation system and may perhaps predate Jacob's vowel letters. It appears in the Qurʾān manuscripts known as Marcel 13 and the upper layer of the Sanaʿa Qurʾān, both of which were produced (though not necessarily vocalised) in the late seventh or early eighth century (Abbott 1939, 39; George 2010, 75–79). Of course, these red dots may be later additions.

Neither Jacob's letter nor his larger grammar directly addresses the Syriac relative vocalisation system, but his second text, *On Persons and Tenses,* does. This grammatical tractate was likely written around the same time as the letter to George and contains Jacob's best attempt to explain Syriac vocalisation within the bounds of the seventh-century diacritic dot system. This explanation is one of the earliest discussions of Syriac vowel phonology, predating even the 'sounding' (*qɔlɔnɔyɔtɔ*) terminology that Jacob would later adopt in his *Turrɔṣ Mamllɔ*. In its introduction, he writes:

> ܙ̈ܒܢܐ ܕܝܢ ܬܠܬܐ . ܕܥܒܪ ܘܕܩܐܡ ܘܕܥܬܝܕ : ܘܒܢܬ ܩ̈ܠܐ ܕܥ̈ܒܝܢ ܘܕܢ̈ܩܝܢ ܀ ܬܘܒ
> ܕܝܢ ܟܠ ܦܬܓܡܐ ܐܘ ܟܝܬ ܗܕܡܐ . ܐܡܬܝ ܗܝ ܕܥܒܝܐ ܐܘ ܦܬܝܐ ܒܒܪܬ ܩܠܐ
> . ܬܣܒ ܡܢ ܠܥܠ ܢܘܩܙܐ ܀ ܐܡܬܝ ܕܝܢ ܕܩܛܝܢ ܐܘ ܢܩܕ ܡܢ ܠܬܚܬ ܀ ܐܢ
> ܡܨܥܝܐ ܐܝܬܘܗܝ ܕܩܛܝܢܐ ܘܥܒܝܐ : ܘܐܝܬ ܬܪ̈ܬܝܢ ܐܚ̈ܪܢܝܢ ܕܟܬܝ̈ܒܢ ܠܗ
> ܟܬܝܒܬܐ ܬܪ̈ܬܝܢ ܢܘ̈ܩܙܐ ܢܣܒ ܚܕ ܡܢ ܠܥܠ ܘܚܕ ܡܢ ܠܬܚܬ
>
> Then the tenses are three, past, present, and future, and sounds are thick and thin. Every saying, that is, [every] form, when it is thick or wide with sound, then it takes a point above. But when it is narrow or thin, then below. If it is intermediate, between narrow and thick, and there are two other [words] written the same as it, then it takes two points, one above and one below. (Phillips 1869, ܝ, lines 9–16)

This passage reveals several details about Jacob's perception of vowels. He indicates that every word has 'sounds' (*bnot qɔle*)[6]—that is, one or more vowels—that differ from those of its homo-

---

[6] For the interpretation of *bnot qɔle* as 'sounds', see entries on *ba(r)t qɔlɔ* in Duval (1901, 438) and Payne Smith (1903, 54).

graphs. This difference is not absolute, but rather Jacob compared the vowels of one word to those in another word according
to two measures: 'thickness' and 'wideness'. Based on the examples of homographs that Jacob gives in the tractate, it seems that
these metrics map approximately onto the modern linguistic concepts of phonetic 'backness' and 'openness', respectively (Kiraz
2015, 44–46; Posegay 2021d, 58–59). That is, Jacob would say
that a word with more backed and open vowels is 'thick' (ʿbe)
and 'wide' (pte), while its homograph with relatively fronted and
closed vowels would be 'thin'[7] (nqed) and 'narrow' (qaṭṭin).
Thicker, wider words were marked with a diacritic dot above,
while thinner, narrower words took a dot below. If a reader were
sufficiently adept at Syriac, then they could infer the vocalisation
of any word based solely on the position of a diacritic dot above
or below it, provided that they were familiar with its homograph.
If, however, a reader had an incomplete mastery of Syriac, then
the diacritic dot left some ambiguity, especially in three-way
homographs. The vowel /a/, for example, was 'thicker' (more-
backed) than /e/, but 'thinner' (more-fronted) than /ɔ/.[8] Thus, as
Jacob mentions, Syriac scribes introduced a two-dot sign to mark

---

[7] Alternatively, 'pure' or 'clear'.

[8] Knudsen points out that the rounded /ɔ/ vowel known from early medieval Syriac may not yet have been part of Jacob's vowel inventory.
He may instead have pronounced the vowel which we today call zqɔpɔ
(usually transcribed ɔ or ā) as an unrounded /ɑ/. Since Jacob implies
that this vowel was 'wider' than /a/, I suspect that it cannot involve
much lip rounding, but the exact qualities of all his vowels are not
known definitively (see Kiraz 2015, 45; Knudsen 2015, 90–98, 115;
Butts 2016, 89–90; Posegay 2021d, 59–61).

a word with 'intermediate' (*meṣʿɔyɔ*) vocalisation, using one supralinear dot and one sublinear dot. The key point here is that any vowel which was called *meṣʿɔyɔ* in one context could be called *qaṭṭin* or *pte* in another context.

These five words—*ʿbe* 'thick', *pte* 'wide', *nqed* 'thin', *qaṭṭin* 'narrow', and *meṣʿɔyɔ* 'intermediate'—are not names for vowels, as each one may be applied to words with different vowels depending on their homographic contexts, but they do carry phonological meaning. They also seem to come from two different sources. On one hand, *ʿbe*, *nqed*, and *meṣʿɔyɔ* are Jacob's attempt to map a triad of Greek consonantal categories onto the Syriac vowels. This adaptation of Greek phonology corresponds to the categories that Jacob would eventually use to describe consonants in the *Turrɔṣ Mamllɔ*, but it is not clear that he perceived any specific relationship between the features of those consonantal groups and the vowels (Talmon 2008, 167–69; compare Davidson 1874, 6). More likely, as a result of his affinity for Greek, Jacob was simply trying to force Greek linguistic concepts to fit the Syriac language (Wright 1871, ܠ; Revell 1972, 367; Knudsen 2015, 77–78; Farina 2018, 179–82). On the other hand, *pte* and *qaṭṭin* are likely internal Syriac developments, used to describe the relative amount of opening and closing of the mouth when pronouncing the vowels. This 'wide-and-narrow' type of comparison was fundamental to nearly all Syriac analyses of vowel phonology from this point onwards.

By the end of Jacob's lifetime, Syriac scribes were already shifting away from this relative vocalisation system with individual diacritic dots and towards an absolute vocalisation system with unique vowel signs for every vowel quality (Segal 1953, 26–30, 41–47, 98; Kiraz 2012, I:12, 14, 20–21, 64, 70–71; 2015, 36–37, 44, 94–102). This development led to the decline of relative descriptions for vowel phonology, as each vowel and its sign was eventually assigned an individual name (see below, chapter 4, §2.0). That said, the works of Dawid bar Pawlos in the late eighth century show us that relative vocalisation was not quite dead yet. In the extant fragments of his grammatical writings, Dawid describes the physical process of articulation that results in speech:

> ܘܡܫܬܪ̈ܝܢ ܥܡ ܪܘܚܐ ܒܪܝܫ ܠܫܢܐ ܕܗ̇ܘ ܐܝܬܘܗܝ، ܩܠܝܕܐ ܕܡܡܠܠܐ ܘܩܢ̈ܝܢ ܢܩ̈ܫܬܐ
> ܒܡܦ̈ܩܢܐ ܡܕܡ ܕܢܫܡܬܐ ܘܥܡ ܓܓܪܬܐ : ܒܙܘ̈ܥܐ ܡܕܡ ܕܪܘܚܐ ܢܫܝܒܬܐ :
> ܡܢܒܥܝܢ ܡܥܢܝ̈ܬܐ ܘܢܝܫ̈ܬܐ ܐܟܘܬܐ . ܒܐܐܪ ܕܐܚܝܕ ܒܓܘ ܦܘܡܐ . ܘܡܬܟܪܟܝܢ
> ܥܡ ܫ̈ܢܐ ܘܡܬܥܨܪܝܢ ܡܢ ܣܦ̈ܘܬܐ . ܘܒܩܠܝܕ ܠܫܢܐ ܐܝܟ ܕܝܐܐ : ܒܩܠܝܠ ܕܦܬܚܐ
> ܘܐܚܝܕܐ ܡܬܚܘܝܢܐ ܘܡܫܬܡܥܢܐ . ܘܥܡ ܩܠܐ ܕܝܘܬܪ : ܡܬܚܘܝܢܐ ܠܐܝܠܝܢ ܕܬܪܥܝܬܐ
> ܐܠܝܢ : ܐܢ ܬܠܡܝܕ̈ܬܐ ܐܝܬܝܗܝܢ ܘܐܢ ܒܪ̈ܝܬܐ ܕܗܘܢܐ . ܘܐܢ ܕܟ̈ܝܬܐ
> ܐܝܬܝܗܝܢ ܘܐܢ ܕܓܠ̈ܬܐ : ܘܒܢ̈ܩܫܬܐ ܕܩ̈ܠܐ ܕܠܐ ܐܬܘ̈ܬܐ ܟܬܝ̈ܒܬܐ :
> ܡܬܓܒܠܢ ܘܡܬܪ̈ܟܒܢ . ܒ̈ܢܬ ܩܠܐ ܟܠܗܝܢ ܐ̄ܢܫܝܬܐ

> They [the spoken utterances] are loosed with breath at the tip of the tongue, which is the key to speech, and they gain beats through some exhalation of breath, and with the throat by some buzzings of inhaled air. Hymns and melodies likewise sound out, in the air that is enclosed in the mouth, wrapped around the teeth, and pressed by the lips. And at the key [i.e., the tip] of the tongue, as is proper, by a little opening and contracting that is shown and heard, with a useful sound which is manifested for those things which the mind conceives—whether they be learned or formed of the intellect, or whether they be pure or false—and in the beats of the sounds that are without written letters, all units of human speech are fashioned and combined. (Gottheil 1893, cxii, line 6–cxiii, line 3; see also, Farina 2021)

As discussed above (chapter 2, §1.0), Dawid views 'beats' (*nqɔshɔtɔ*, sing. *nqɔshtɔ*) as the basic unit of poetic metre, and the only letters which can comprise a beat, in and of themselves, are the 'sounding letters' (*'atwɔtɔ qɔlɔnɔyɔtɔ*). Since every beat of poetry contains a vowel, a reader can identify the number of beats in a metre by counting the vowels, and thus the term *nqɔshtɔ* could be rendered as either 'beat' or 'vowel' (see Segal 1953, 7, 54, 171). With this in mind, the above passage explains how vowels are necessary to speech, including in 'hymns' (*qinɔtɔ*) and 'melodies' (*ne'mɔtɔ*). The final statement about "the beats of the sounds that are without written letters" is unambiguous: in the medieval Syriac writing system, the only sounds without written letters are the vowels. In this context, Dawid's use of the words 'opening' (*pɔtaḥ*) and 'contracting' (*'ɔsar*) as articulatory actions is significant for vocalisation. These words would seem to indicate the movement of the lips during articulation, and just as we saw with Jacob of Edessa's 'wide' (*pte*) and 'narrow' (*qaṭṭin*) comparisons, they present a two-way phonetic contrast based on openness. While Dawid's contrastive word choice in this passage may imply a link between him and Jacob of Edessa, it is not definitive confirmation that he employed relative phonology to describe Syriac vowels.

More conclusive evidence of relative terminology appears in Dawid's *scholion*, in which he explains the changes in the realisation of the *bgdkt* letters in different contexts. Until recently, this *scholion* was only extant in unpublished manuscripts held in Middle Eastern libraries. I transcribed the following quotations by comparing MS SMMJ 356 from St. Mark's Monastery in Jerusalem with MS ZFRN 192 from Dayr al-Zaʿfarān in Mardin.[9] The text begins with a heading, reading "The Scholion on Changeable Letters by Dawid bar Pawlos (ܡܦܫܩܢܘܬ݂ ܡܛܠ ܐܬܘܬܐ ܡܫܬܚܠܦܢܝܬܐ ܕܕܘܝܕ ܒܪ ܦܘܠܘܣ)", and then:

> ܡܛܠ ܐܬܘܬܐ ܕܗܠܝܢ ܕܡܬܐܡܪܢ ܡܫܬܚܠܦܢܝܬܐ ܀ ܗܢܘܢ ܡܬܪܟܟܝܢ ܘܡܬܩܫܝܢ
> ܒܦܪܝܫܘܬ ܩܕܡܝܐ ܀ ܐܦ ܟܕ ܫܡܗܐ ܗܠܝܢ ܕܡܩܕܡܝܢ ܐܝܬ ܥܝܕܐ ܠܣܘܪܝܝܐ
> ܕܢܬܪܟܟܘܢ ܐܟܝܢ ܀ ܗܢܘ ܕܝܢ ܒܬܪ ܐܠܦ ܐܚܪܝܬܐ ܕܫܡܐ ܕܩܕܡ ܐܬܘܬܐ ܗܘ̇
> ܡܬܪܟܟܐ ܐܘ ܡܬܩܫܝܐ ܀ ܘܒܬܪ ܘܐܘ ܟܒܝܫܬܐ ܀ ܘܒܬܪ ܝܘܕ ܚܒܝܫܬܐ ܀
> ܘܒܬܪ ܘܐܘ ܦܬܝܚܬܐ ܀ ܘܝܘܕ ܦܬܝܚܬܐ ܗ̄ ܠܐ ܡܬܪܟܟܢ ܕܐܝܬܝܗܝܢ ܕܝܢ ܗܠܝܢ
> ܀ ܕܠܕ ܕܩܕܡ ܫܡܐ ܀ ܘܓܡܠ ܘܒܝܬ ܘܬܘ ܘܟܦ ܀ ܗܠܝܢ ܡܬܪܟܟܢ ܘܡܬܩܫܝܢ
> ܒܐܬܘܬܐ ܕܡܩܕܡܝܢ ܀
>
> Regarding the letters which are called 'changeable': they are softened and hardened according to what precedes. Also, when what precedes them are nouns, it is customary for the Syrians that they be softened. Thus, after an *ʾalaph* that is the end of a noun which precedes the letters, they may be softened or hardened; and after a constrained *waw*, a pressed *yod*, or an opened *waw*. But an opened *yod* is such that [the letter] is not softened. These are [the changeable letters]: *dalat* which is before a noun, *gamal*, *bet*, *taw*, and *kaph*. They are softened or hardened by the letters which precede them. (ZFRN 192 f. 199r, lines 11–18)

---

[9] See MS Jerusalem, St. Mark's Monastery (SMMJ) 356, ff. 164v–166r and MS Mardin, Dayr al-Zaʿfarān (ZFRN) 192, ff. 199r–200r. Both manuscripts are digitised in the Hill Museum and Manuscript Library's virtual reading room (https://www.vhmml.org/readingRoom/, accessed 24 November 2020). See now the recent edition of Farina (2021), which was unavailable before this book went to print.

While Dawid was certainly a Miaphysite, he spent most of his life near Mosul on the Eastern fringe of 'West' Syriac territory (Rahmani 1904, 67–69; Baumstark 1922, 272; Barsoum 1987, 325–29; Moosa 2003, 272–76; Brock 2011), and he seems to describe a more typically 'Eastern' pronunciation system here. He recognises only five Syriac stops that may become fricativised (ܪ ܓ ܒ ܕ ܟ), excepting *pe'* in contrast to the six Western *bgdkpt* consonants (see Nöldeke 1904, §23; Robinson and Coakley 2013, 11, 147; Knudsen 2015, 47). However, he also notes that fricativisation can occur in an initial *bgdkt* letter of a word following the final *'alaph* of a separate noun. This phenomenon of fricativisation across word boundaries is observed mainly in West Syriac (Knudsen 2015, 42, 51). Either way, what concerns us here is Dawid's description of the letters that cause the *bgdkt* letters to become 'softened' (*metrakkak*). Besides the *mater lectionis* letter *'alaph*, which usually represents /ɔ/ or /e/ at the end of a word, Dawid includes *waw 'ṣiṣtɔ* 'constrained *waw*' and *yod ḥbiṣtɔ* 'pressed-together *yod*'. These words—*'ṣiṣtɔ* and *ḥbiṣtɔ*—are formed from the same roots that eventually became absolute names for the vowels /u/ and /i/ in Syriac (see below, chapter 4, §2.0, and Segal 1953, 170–72), and those appear to be the vowel qualities that Dawid means. His examples of 'softening' caused by final *waw 'ṣiṣtɔ* are the phrases *manu ḡer* and *manu ḵay* (ZFRN 192 f. 199r, lines 20 and 23), both of which contain /u/. He does not give specific examples for *yod ḥbiṣtɔ*, but in both codices in which Dawid's *scholion* appears, it is followed by an anonymous *scholion* on the six *bgdkpt* letters (ZFRN 192 ff. 200r–200v and SMMJ 356 ff. 166r–166v). This latter *scholion* supplies phrases

with /i/, like *ṣbi ḵinɔ* and *ṣbi ḏinɔ*, for word-final *yod ḥbiṣtɔ* (ZFRN
192 f. 200v, lines 10–12).

These *ʿṣiṣtɔ* and *ḥbiṣtɔ* modifiers thus designate the rela-
tively-narrow realisations of the *matres waw* and *yod*. That is, /u/
and /i/ were considered relatively closed realisations, presumably in contrast to the relatively open /o/ and /e/. One of these
more 'open' vowels—/o/—eventually gained a name that confirms this relationship (i.e., *rwiḥtɔ* 'spacious, broadened' compared to /u/) (see below, chapter 4, §2.3), but that is not the
word that Dawid uses in his *scholion*. Instead, he contrasts both
ʿṣiṣtɔ and *ḥbiṣtɔ* with the word *ptiḥtɔ* 'opened'. The only example
that he gives for a *yod ptiḥtɔ* is the phrase *ʾitay ger*, and he states
explicitly that this *yod* does not cause the following *gomal* to soften. Instead, it is 'hardened' (*metqashshyɔ*) (ZFRN 192 f. 199r,
lines 21–22). In later Syriac grammatical texts, *ptiḥɔ* and its derivatives (e.g., *ptɔḥɔ*) invariably designate the vowel /a/ or describe a consonant that is followed by the vowel /a/, but here the
pronunciation of *yod ptiḥtɔ* seems to be a diphthong, /ay/. This
realisation differs from what we expected as the 'opened' version
of *yod* (i.e., /e/), but Dawid does specify that the word *ʾitay* does
not induce fricativisation in the next word, so it cannot be a pure
vowel. It may be, however, that Dawid perceived some monoph-
thongisation of word-final /ay/ in certain contexts, with the actual pronunciation approaching /e/. Similar monophthongisa-
tion of /ay/ to /e/ in Syriac is known from other medieval manuscripts, though it occurs primarily in closed syllables (Knudsen
2015, 122). Dawid provides no examples for what he calls *waw
ptiḥtɔ*, but based on analogy with *yod ptiḥtɔ* and given his note

that it *does* cause fricativisation at the end of a word, he likely meant the monophthong /o/. In both of these cases then, the word *ptiḥtɔ* would indicate the relatively open vocalic quality of a *mater lectionis* in contrast to a closed counterpart.

The works of Jacob of Edessa and Dawid bar Pawlos show that the earliest extant phonetic analyses of Syriac vowels relied on relative descriptions that contrasted qualities according to varying degrees of openness and backness. Diacritic dots placed above or below a word graphically depicted these relationships, with the 'dot above' being linked to relatively open, backed vowels, while the 'dot below' indicated relatively closed, fronted vowels. Similar descriptions of relative vocalisation also appear in the early works of the Hebrew Masoretes.

1.2. Early Masoretic Vowel Phonology

Evidence of Masoretic activity dates back as far as the sixth century, when three groups of Masoretes began to emerge: the Tiberians, based in Tiberias; the Palestinians, located elsewhere in Palestine; and the Babylonians, named for their native Iraq. Their work in preserving Hebrew recitation traditions can be divided into several overlapping stages (Khan 2000, 21; Dotan 2007, 648–49), but we are concerned with the period prior to the ninth century, when some of them described vowels according to relative phonology.

In the seventh and eighth centuries, the first Masoretes recorded their oral tradition related to the proper transmission of the Bible (Dotan 2007, 650). They produced numerous notes and lists, such as those compiled in *Okla we-Okla* (Frendsdorff 1864;

see Dotan 2007, 621, 650) and the *Masora magna* (Yeivin 1983, 33, 126–30), containing details about problematic words, grammar, and errors in the scribal transmissions of the Bible (Roberts 1969, 6–7; Dotan 2007, §3). Most of this work was done in Jewish Babylonian and Palestinian Aramaic, which remained spoken vernaculars until at least the ninth century (Khan 2000, 21; see Fassberg 1990). Furthermore, like the Syriac tradition, many of the Masoretic accent and cantillation signs had already emerged by this stage, and possibly earlier. It seems the Masoretes were not concerned with direct notation of vowel sounds before the eighth or ninth century, and in contrast to Syriac scribes, they lacked the single diacritic point which could graphically differentiate vowels on a relative basis (Dotan 1981, 89, 93–94; 2007, 625; compare Segal 1953, 58–67). However, they did employ contrastive language related to openness and frontedness, and remnants of this relative terminology are evident from numerous Masoretic sources.

Phonetic vowel terms based on the roots *ptḥ* 'opening' and *qmṣ* 'closing' predate all other Hebrew vowel names, and in their original forms they distinguished minimal pairs of vowels according to lip movement (Steiner 2005, 379–80). The earliest hint of this type of phonetic description appears to be a non-technical occurrence in the poetry of Eleazar ben Qillir (fl. c. 600) (Encyclopaedia Judaica (Germany) 2007, 743–44), who writes that one should speak with a 'closed lip' (*sɔpɔ qamuṣɔ*) when saying the name of God (Fleischer 1972, 263).[10] A number of scholars

---

[10] Presumably he means *ʾadonɔy* instead of *ʾadonay*, but this is not certain.

have also noted early Masoretic lists of Hebrew homographs that differ by a single vowel, with headings such as *ḥad mɔleʾ we-ḥad qɔmeṣ* 'one fills and one closes' or *ḥad qɔmeṣ we-ḥad pɔtaḥ* 'one closes and one opens'. In these lists, the homograph with a relatively open vowel is classed as *mɔleʾ* or *pɔtaḥ*, while its counterpart with a relatively closed vowel is considered *qɔmeṣ* (Ginsburg 1880, II: §606, and III: §§529a–b; Graetz 1881a; Bacher 1974, 16, n. 6; Dotan 1974, 28–32; Steiner 2005, 379, n. 52; Posegay 2021d, 62). Most likely, these designations began as pedagogical instructions to inform an unsure reader of how to move their mouth when pronouncing particular difficult words, but over time came to describe the words and vowels themselves (Steiner 2005, 375–77, 380). These relative classifications became less relevant as the Hebrew vowel signs were introduced, but remnants of them persisted in the later terminology used to describe absolute vocalisation.

The best example of this 'remnant' relative terminology is the appearance of derivations of the roots *ptḥ* 'opening' and *qmṣ* 'closing' to describe vowels in the Tiberian *Masora*, especially as the Aramaic active participles *pɔtaḥ* and *qɔmeṣ* (Khan 2020, I:245, esp. n. 4). None of the other modern names for vowels (*ḥolem, ṣere, segol*, etc.) occur in the *Masora magna* and *parva*, suggesting that the contrastive 'open-and-closed' terminology predates them (Khan 2000, 24; Steiner 2005, 374, 377–78). Furthermore, in Masoretic notes, besides referring to /a/ and /ɔ/, the words *pɔtaḥ* and *qɔmeṣ* can also mean /ɛ/ and /e/, respectively (Yeivin 1983, 80, 113–14). In these cases, /ɛ/ is relatively 'open' (*pɔtaḥ*) in comparison to the relatively 'closed' (*qɔmeṣ*) /e/. The phrases *pɔtaḥ*

q‍ɔṭon 'small p‍ɔtaḥ' and q‍ɔmeṣ q‍ɔṭon 'small q‍ɔmeṣ' appear in numerous Masoretic sources and apply to /ɛ/ and /e/ in the same
way (see below, chapter 4, §3.1). These terms add another layer
to the older relative system by indicating a pair of 'small' vowels
that were articulated with comparatively less openness than /a/
and /ɔ/. Notably, this q‍ɔṭon 'small' designation is cognate with
Jacob of Edessa's description of relatively-closed vowels (usually
/e/ or similar) as qaṭṭin (see above, present chapter, §1.1, and
Posegay 2021d, 63).

The author of the tenth-century text which Allony calls
Kitāb al-Muṣawwitāt is likewise aware of this older, two-way division of vowels. Near the end of the extant text, they write:

ותסלב [וצ]תוג וונ תופצל תוצל כיף אלמצותאת עלל [וצח.......אב]ב [....]
חד ב׳ ב׳ מן אלמאסראת [פי] מא גמיע וכדלך ואלפצול אלמעני עלי ותדל
או מצאף וגיר ומצאף ומפעול פאעל באב מן כרג קמ׳ וחד פתֿ
ממתחן בתה דלך מן יכלו לא קמ׳ כאנת אדא קמ׳ מתלהא [אלתי..ה]כלמ
דכרהא [עז] [דנא]אח[ו] אלדי אלמאסראת ולוגוד מחרר

S[ection on the][11] clarification of the reasons for the vowels: how they connect or separate, how they assert or ne-
gate, and how they indicate the meanings and divisions.
Likewise, everything in the *māsorāt* is from two: two, one
pt and one *qm*, in the same way as an actor and an acted
upon, a dependent and an independent, or a word [that is
pt],[12] when what is like it is *qm*, if [the] *qm* always occurs

---

[11] Allony suggests that this first word is *bāb* 'chapter, section', in which
case the lacuna would be *b[āb fī] waḍḥ*.

[12] The lacuna here affects the last few words of MS AIU IX.A.24 f.1r.
Allony's reconstruction of *kalima allatī* is probably sound, as the tops of
a *heʔ* and *lamed* are barely visible. Based on the rest of orthography, this
leaves enough space for approximately two letters at the end of the line,

in that which is verified and accurate, on account of the existence of the *māsorāt*, which for brevity we have not mentioned. (Allony 1965, 154, lines 115–22)

In order to explain the "reasons for the vowels (*muṣawwitāt*)," the author states that everything in the *māsorāt* (an Arabic plural of *masora*) is divided into one of two classes: *ptḥ* or *qmṣ*. The rest of the passage is a list of two-way states that are meant to be analogous to the relationship between one *ptḥ* and one *qmṣ*. For example, in grammar, a word can be an 'actor' (*fāʿil*) or 'acted upon' (*mafʿūl*). A word can be 'dependent' (*muḍāf*; usually implying a genitive construction) or 'independent' (*ghayr muḍāf*). These grammatical distinctions are relevant given subsequent examples listed in the text, which include words that vary by a single vowel depending on their context in Tiberian recitation of the Bible. One such example is *mazɔrɛ* (מְזָרֶה; 'scatters' in Prov. 20.26) and *mazɔre* (מְזָרֵה; 'scatters' in Jer. 31.10) (Allony 1965, 156, lines 125–26). The form with /ɛ/ is *pɔtaḥ* while the form with /e/ is *qɔmeṣ*. It follows then that a 'word' (*kalima*) can be *pɔtaḥ* while 'what is like it' (*mithluhā*; i.e., its homograph) is *qɔmeṣ*. It is not

---

with the badly rubbed traces of two partial strokes still visible. There is also a single dot, again badly rubbed, just above the ruled line over the remnants of these letters. This position is consistent with the height of other dots that the scribe used for abbreviations (i.e., פת and קמ). I suspect that the abbreviated word פת used to be here, such that the end of the line was *kalima ʾallatī pt* and the full clause read *ʾaw kalima ʾallatī pt mithluhā qm* 'or a word that is *pɔtaḥ*, when what is like it is *qɔmeṣ*'. This reconstruction makes structural sense, as the clause ought to continue the author's list of two-way relationships that are analogous to "one *ptḥ* and one *qmṣ*."

clear exactly what the author means by the '*māsorāt*' that verify the appearance of *qɔmeṣ*, but they are probably referring to a known corpus of Tiberian texts, including the *Masora magna* and *parva* and perhaps some other 'independent' Masoretic works (see Dotan 2007, 621).

Besides the Tiberian tradition, remnants of the open-and-closed contrastive terminology also appear in the Babylonian naming for /a/ and /ɔ/, and redundancies among the Babylonian terms reveal an older relative system. The Babylonian Masoretes had three names for the vowel /ɔ/: *miqpaṣ pummɔ*, *meṣap̄ pummɔ*, and *ʾimṣɔ*. This first name, *miqpaṣ pummɔ* 'closing the mouth' stands in contrast to one of the names for /a/, *mip̄taḥ pummɔ* 'opening the mouth' in the same way as the equivalent Tiberian terms. Similarly, *ʾimṣɔ* 'closure' opposes the second Babylonian name for /a/, *pitḥɔ* 'opening' (Morag 1974, 71). Morag argues that the remaining term—*meṣap̄ pummɔ* 'caution of the mouth'—is unique among the three, and it refers to the action required to carefully articulate a vowel that falls between /a/ and /o/. As such, it must have come into use after the Babylonian Masoretes had specifically defined the quality of each vowel, at a time when 'closing' was no longer a logical concept to assign to /ɔ/ (Morag 1974, 72). That is to say, *miqpaṣ pummɔ* and *ʾimṣɔ* must have been derived according to contrastive principles prior to the introduction of absolute, one-to-one vowel names. This evolution matches the development of the Tiberian relative vocalisation terminology as well as its subsequent decline with the rise of absolute vowel naming.

These earliest relative descriptions of vocalisation began as contrasts between physical articulatory motions, but both Syriac and Hebrew scholars eventually associated those physical features with phonetic 'height'. This shared association led them to develop notation systems for absolute vocalisation that each encoded vowel phonology according to graphemic principles of dot position.

1.3. Connecting the Dots

Both Syriac and Hebrew scholars created a genre of writings specifically devoted to preserving the integrity of their biblical texts between the eighth and tenth centuries. For Hebrew, we call these scholars Masoretes, referring to those who compiled notes about the Bible from their oral tradition of *masora* 'passing down'. Both East and West Syriac authors wrote similar notes for the study of biblical and patristic texts, and this Syriac genre is known now by the word *mashlmɔnutɔ*, also 'passing down' (Kiraz 2012, I:15). It has also been deemed the 'Syriac Masora', based on direct analogy with the Hebrew tradition (Yeivin 1983, 36; Loopstra 2014, I:I). Despite this comparison, the Syriac authors of these texts refer to them as collections of *shmɔhe* 'nouns' and *qrɔyɔtɔ* 'readings', and they are more pedagogical tools for teaching the reading tradition than anything else (Loopstra 2009, 13–14; 2014, I:V–VI; see also, Hoffmann 1880, V). While in some ways their work was similar to that of the Masoretes, these Syriac teachers did not, for example, attempt to quantify and cross-reference the occurrences of rare words in the Bible. Instead, they produced a corpus of handbooks related to grammatical, ortho-graphic, phonetic, and accentual rules, which a reader could ref-erence in order to interpret difficult words even in an unvocalised text (Loopstra 2009, 15; 2014, I:III–IV; see also, Balzaretti 1997). Consequently, one aspect of these traditions where Syriac and Hebrew scholars overlap is in the practice of writing homograph lists, which they both used to track words that differed only in their vowels (Balzaretti 1997, 75; Dotan 2007, 622–23; Loopstra 2014, I:IV).

In the Hebrew tradition, most of these lists divided homo-graphic pairs according to stress, separating them with the Ara-maic terms *mille'el* 'above' (penultimate stress) and *millera'* 'be-low' (final stress) (Yeivin 1983, 102–3), often with the heading *ḥad millera' we-ḥad mill'el* 'one is below and one is above' (Graetz 1881a, 348; Dotan 1974; 2007, 623–24). Using these lists, Hein-rich Graetz argued for a connection between the Tiberian Maso-retic tradition and Syriac on the basis of diacritic dot positions. He found that in a few of the homograph lists in *Okla we-Okla*, the terms *mille'el* and *millera'* actually distinguished Hebrew hom-ographic pairs that differed by one vowel, rather than by stress (Graetz 1881a; 1881b; Dotan 2007, 622–23). Graetz identified this usage as part of a relative vocalisation system, reflecting a further extension of the early comparative descriptions of He-brew vowel phonology discussed above (Dotan 1974, 32; Steiner 2005, 379). He also hypothesised that *mille'el* and *millera'* origi-nally referred to the locations of diacritic dots that were placed above or below Hebrew homographs to indicate the relative qual-ity of their vowels, just as the diacritic dot functions in Syriac.

However, very few diacritic dots have ever been attested in Hebrew *mille'el* and *millera'* lists, and even in those rare cases, the
dots indicate stress rather than vowel quality (see Morag 1973;
Dotan 2007, 623).[13] As such, Aron Dotan has taken a hard stance
against Graetz's theory, insisting that Syriac had no terms equivalent to *mille'el* and *millera'* that the Masoretes could have borrowed, and that those terms would not have seen continued use
after the supposed 'disappearance' of Graetz's hypothetical and
unattested Hebrew diacritic dots (Dotan 1974, 28; 2007, 622–23;
Posegay 2021d, 64–65).

The following discussion takes a different view, making
three assertions in challenging both Graetz's and Dotan's theories. First, there were, in fact, Syriac linguistic terms similar to
mille'el and *millera'*—specifically attested in Jacob of Edessa's
writings—that Masoretes could have borrowed to describe vocalisation prior to the ninth century. Second, there was never any
diacritic dot in Hebrew that differentiated vowels in the same
way as the Syriac dot. Third, while both Syriac and Hebrew
scribes had knowledge of the same principles of relative vocalisation, they each manifested those principles differently in the
subsequent development of their respective absolute vowel pointing systems.

As previously mentioned, Jacob of Edessa explains how to
point Syriac homographs in his tractate, *On Persons and Tenses*,
where he states: "Every saying, that is, [every] form, when it is
thick or wide with sound, then it takes a point above. But when
it is narrow or thin, then below" (Phillips 1869, ‫ܠ‬; see above,

---

[13] Also note the earlier view of Morag (1961, 17, n. 1).

present chapter, §1.1). A word with 'thick' vocalisation takes a
dot *men lʿel* 'above', while its 'thinner' homograph is *men ltaḥt*
'below'. Most often, that meant that words with more backed
vowels (e.g., /o/, /ɔ/, /a/) took a dot above in comparison to
their homographs with comparatively fronted vowels (/u/, /e/,
/i/) (Kiraz 2015, 44–46; Posegay 2021d, 66). Notably, Jacob
does not repeat the word 'dot' (*nuqzɔ*) in the latter half of his
statement, such that it could be read as a designation of 'thin' or
'narrow' words as phonetically 'below' (*men ltaḥt*). Fronted vowels would thus be considered 'lower' than their 'above' counterparts, which were relatively backed. This usage of *men lʿel* and
men ltaḥt seemingly as phonetic descriptors correlates with Jacob's descriptions of other 'above' and 'below' words elsewhere
in the tractate (Posegay 2020, 198–200). It likely arose from an
implicit association of relatively backed vowels with the 'higher'
position of the supralinear diacritic dot in Syriac. When used in
this type of phonological context, these two phrases—*men lʿel* and
men ltaḥt—are plausible sources for the Masoretic *milleʿel* and *milleraʿ* terms with the same meanings.

In the conclusion of his first article deconstructing Graetz's
theory, Dotan critiques the utility of Jacob of Edessa's phonological analysis as evidence for connecting Syriac and Masoretic
ideas. Quite significantly, he does not seem to have noticed the
appearance of *men lʿel* and *men ltaḥt* in Jacob's tractate, and so
makes the following statement:

> Some Hebrew Masoretic lists of homographs are certainly
> very ancient, but we cannot know the date of their compi-
> lation. Thus much for the common aspects of Hebrew and
> Syriac. As to all the rest, they have nothing in common,

and that, not only in the technical graphic sense of the use of the points, but what is much more important, in the aspect of contrasting the vowels. In Syriac the contrast is generally between forms with what is regarded as "fuller, stronger pronunciation" and forms with a "finer, weaker" one. These notions which cannot and could not be sufficiently defined suffered, therefore, many deviations in application, as Graetz has already pointed out, and rightly so. In Hebrew, however, the contrast is always within the domain of a very clear scale, based on phonetic grounds which hold true even today. (Dotan 1974, 33)

The common use of homograph lists is certainly a potential vector for intellectual exchange between early Masoretes and Syriac grammarians, although it is true that we cannot date them precisely. As we have seen though, there is actually great similarity between the early Syriac and Hebrew relative vocalisation systems. The earliest phonological vowel descriptions in both languages involve comparisons of openness between two vowels. These contrasts occur in Jacob of Edessa's (d. 708) and Dawid bar Pawlos' (fl. c. 770–800) grammatical writings, early Masoretic homograph lists, and the first vowel names of both the Tiberian and Babylonian Masoretes. Dotan's interpretation of the Syriac contrasts between "fuller, stronger" and "finer, weaker" forms is thus misleading. The qualities that Jacob ascribes to the vowels in *On Persons and Tenses* are not based on strength or weakness, but rather are *ʿbe* 'thick', *nqed* 'thin', *pte* 'wide', and *qaṭṭin* 'narrow'. Dotan's misinterpretation may originate with a similar statement by Segal, who characterised the Syriac system as dependant on the dominance and weakening of homographic forms (1953, 11).

The ʿbe and *nqed* terms are borrowed from the Greek grammatical tradition, so while Jacob does describe open vowels as thick or thin, he does so in order to fit Syriac phonology into a Greek-inspired model (Revell 1972, 367; Talmon 2008, 166–67; see also, Knudsen 2015, 77). These two most likely refer to the relative backness of a vowel, which also happens to correlate with relative openness for most Syriac vowels. The other two— *pte* and *qaṭṭin*—are grounded in a conception of 'wide-and-narrow' phonology that explained vowels according to openness. Jacob does not convey any measure of 'strength' or 'weakness' in vowels (nor does Dawid bar Pawlos). Still, Dotan's statement regarding the early Syriac ideas that "could not be sufficiently defined" and thus "suffered... many deviations in application" highlights the problems of ambiguity inherent in a relative vocalisation system. It is for precisely this reason that Syriac scribes completed their absolute vocalisation system with discrete vowel points and names around the end of Jacob's life (Kiraz 2012, I:20–21). This system took the ideas of 'wide-and-narrow' and 'thick-and-thin' phonology, as well as their association with phonetic 'height', as its defining principles.

On the other side, the statement that "in Hebrew... the contrast is always within the domain of a very clear scale" refers to Dotan's observation that the Hebrew *milleʿel* and *millera*ʿ lists are based on comparisons of phonetic backness, with more-back vowels considered 'higher' in the mouth. This is the correct interpretation of the *milleʿel* and *millera*ʿ lists that compare vowels, and Dotan also notes that this type of comparison according to backness is the principle behind the arrangement of the 'vowel

scale' in the fifth chapter of Saadia Gaon's (d. 942) Hebrew grammar, *Kutub al-Lugha* (*The Books of the Language*) (Dotan 1974, 29–
30; see below, chapter 4, §§3.3–4). However, the persistence of
this conception of 'height' from the known early Masoretic lists
up through the tenth century does not indicate that the Hebrew
tradition *always* contrasted vowels according to that scale. Dotan
himself points out that Ginsburg's homograph list with the heading *ḥad qmṣ we-ḥad ptḥ* 'one closes and one opens' (Ginsburg
1880, II:310–11, section 606) is identical to a list from *Okla we-
Okla* that has the heading *ḥad milleʿel we-ḥad milleraʿ* 'one is above
and one is below' (Dotan 1974, 24; see Frendsdorff 1864, no. 5),
which suggests that the idea of comparing relative backness coincided with or superseded an idea of relative openness. This coincidence is not dissimilar to Jacob of Edessa's connections between 'wide' and 'thick' vowels, and could well have evolved
from contact with a Syriac source.

It is impossible to say whether this list that appears with
two different headings was originally written for 'opening-and-
closing' or 'above-and-below' comparisons. Somewhat suspi-
ciously though, all of the examples of *milleʿel* 'above' words in
this list are also relatively *qɔmeṣ* 'closing'. This correspondence
only occurs when the Hebrew vowel /o/ is compared to /ɔ/, /a/,
or /ɛ/; when /ɔ/ is compared to /a/ or /ɛ/; or when /u/ is compared to any vowel besides /o/. In all of these cases, the vowel
which is farther back in the mouth would also be more closed
than the vowel with which it is compared. Consequently, if a
Masorete had a homograph list that was arranged according to
relative openness, but they wanted to re-label it with *milleʿel* and

*millera*ʿ, then they would have to remove any examples with vowel pairs other than the ones mentioned. Those pairs would include: /a/ with /ɛ/, /e/, or /i/; /ɛ/ with /e/ or /i/; /e/ with /i/; and /o/ with /u/. We find that all of these pairings are absent from this list. Moreover, the *milleʿel-millera*ʿ scale model of 'backness as height' does seem to have continued on through the medieval Hebrew grammatical tradition, and certainly into Saadia's grammatical writing.

Bearing all of this in mind, the following is a potential framework for the parallel development of the Syriac and Hebrew relative vowel systems as they transitioned to absolute vowel pointing. In both systems, the association of height with backness directly informed the placement of the vowel points.

In the seventh century, or possibly earlier, Syriac teachers and the first Masoretes began writing homograph lists to keep track of words in the Bible that had identical consonants. They judged these comparisons according to an easily observable phenomenon—relative openness of the mouth—and various groups used different words to describe these differences. In Syriac, Jacob of Edessa called them 'wide' (*pte*) or 'narrow' (*qaṭṭin*), while Dawid bar Pawlos referred to 'opening' (*pɔtaḥ/ptiḥɔ*) and 'contracting' (*ʾɔsar/ḥbiṣɔ/ṣiṣɔ*). Similarly, Tiberian Masoretes used *ptḥ* 'opening' and *qmṣ* 'closing', while their Babylonian counterparts said *miqpaṣ pummɔ* 'closing of the mouth' and *miptaḥ pummɔ* 'opening of the mouth' or *ʾimṣɔ* 'closure' and *pitḥɔ* 'opening'.

Accompanying the Syriac versions of these homograph lists was the diacritic dot system, which used a point 'above' (*men lʿel*) to indicate a word with more open vocalisation, while a point 'below' (*men ltaḥt*) marked the homograph with less open vowels.[14] In the late seventh or early eighth century, the phrases *men l'el* and *men ltaḥt* acquired an additional function, coming to describe the comparative phonetic qualities of words or vowels, rather than just the locations of diacritic dots. The 'more-open' vowels also tended to be 'more-back', and Syriac scholars began to associate dot height with phonetic backness. This principle was foundational to the absolute vowel pointing system in Syriac, which largely stabilised in its final form during the eighth century (Kiraz 2012, I:20–21). In this system, the 'most-above' (thick, backed) vowel, /ɔ/, received two supralinear dots, the 'intermediate' vowel /a/ took one dot above and one below, and the 'below' (thin, fronted) vowel /e/ got two sublinear points (Segal 1953, 26–30; Kiraz 2012, I:12–13, 21, 70–71; 2015, 41–47, 98–101; Posegay 2021d, 67–68). A *mater lectionis yod* usually indicated /i/, but as another 'below' vowel, one or two dots under a *yod* could also represent it. Then the 'above' vowel /o/ took a single supralinear dot—always above a *waw*—while a single dot beneath *waw* indicated its 'below' contrast, /u/. This pointing system remained the standard system for most East and West Syriac scribes until the beginning of the tenth century, and remained in use for East Syriac scribes after that (Coakley 2011; Kiraz

---

[14] Recall that the Syriac diacritic dot system, invented prior to Jacob of Edessa's lifetime, was likely based on a phonetic system in which the vowel now called *zqɔpɔ* was pronounced unrounded (close to /ɑ/), and was thus both more open and more back than /a/ (Kiraz 2015, 45; Knudsen 2015, 90–98, 115; Butts 2016, 89–90).

2012, I:79–80). The authors who applied it to grammatical writing also maintained this connection between height, openness, and backness, and eventually named the vowels according to principles of 'wide-and-narrow' and 'high-and-low' qualities (see below, chapter 4, §2.0).

At roughly the same time—no later than the eighth century—the Tiberian Masoretes adopted the idea of *mille'el* 'above' and *millera'* 'below' vowel phonology. They most likely heard of this concept from Syriac teachers, and like their Syrian counterparts, they associated 'above' and 'below' with phonetic backness. They thus wrote homograph lists that distinguished relative vowel pairs according to that attribute. Crucially, however, they did not at any point adopt the Syriac usage of a single diacritic dot to differentiate homographs. They merely took the *ideas* of *mille'el* and *millera'* (or *men l'el* and *men ltaht*) as descriptions of phonetic backness and applied them to Hebrew accordingly. Eventually, the link between backness and 'height' led to the notion of a full vowel scale, now well-known from later medieval sources, like *Kutub al-Lugha*.

This backness principle also informed the creation of the absolute system of Tiberian vowel points, similar to Syriac's first absolute vocalisation system. However, due to the earlier invention of a Tiberian cantillation system, accent signs filled much of the supralinear space in a Tiberian Bible, so the Tiberian Masoretes favoured sublinear vowel signs (Dotan 1981, esp. 98).[15] As

---

[15] This chronology also matches that of the Syriac tradition, which had a complex system of accent points (or 'reading dots') before an absolute vocalisation system (Segal 1953, 58–78; Loopstra 2019, 161–66).

such, they needed a graphical method for conveying movement along a vertical scale using primarily sublinear dots, and that is precisely what they created. In the Tiberian vocalisation system, each dot represents a step on the *mille'el-millera'* scale (Posegay 2021d, 69–71).

First, /o/, the most-back, and thus most-*mille'el* Hebrew vowel, received a high supralinear dot (א). By maximal contrast, the most-*millera'* vowel, /i/, took a single sublinear dot (א). These two dots represent the two farthest ends of the vowel scale, and correlate conceptually with the single diacritic dots placed above or below a Syriac homograph. In this manner, almost as Graetz hypothesised, the Masoretes did have 'diacritic' dots that functioned like the Syriac relative dot, but they were already absolute vocalisation signs. The reason for this development is that the Tiberian Masoretes introduced these vowel points comparatively later than Syriac scribes, at a time when absolute vocalisation was already replacing relative descriptions, and so they assigned each dot a single phoneme (/o/ or /i/).

After /i/, each step up the scale gains a single dot. The vowels /e/ and /ɛ/ each occupy one or two steps, respectively, above /i/ on the scale, and so take one (א) or two (א) additional dots. Then the signs for /a/ (א) and /ɔ/ (א)—each including a sublinear line segment—are graphically unique in the Tiberian system, and the Masoretes likely prioritised their differentiation in biblical reading due to a lack of distinction between /a/ and /ɔ/ in spoken Jewish Palestinian Aramaic (Fassberg 1990, 28–31, 53; Steiner 2005, 380; Posegay 2021d, 63). These line segments may

have been modified from the sign for /a/ in the Palestinian vocalisation system (א),[16] probably already in use near Tiberias in
the eighth century, which the Tiberians simply shifted to a sublinear position. This comparison also explains the single dot below the line segment for /ɔ/,[17] as it represents a single step up
from /a/, which has no dot.

Furthermore, similar to Syriac, when a *mater lectionis waw*
was present, /u/ only needed to contrast with /o/, so it received
a single dot within the *waw* in the middle of the line. This middle
position represented /u/'s status as more fronted—that is, more
milleraʿ—than /o/, but more *milleʿel* than the rest of the vowels.
Finally, the sublinear three-dot sign for /u/ is somewhat anomalous, but given that it is the second most backed vowel, it ought
to have the most sublinear dots to represent the most 'steps' up
from /i/. It is also the least common vowel sign in Tiberian Hebrew, which may suggest that it was the last to be added to the
system. Notably, later descriptions of the vowel scale actually remove /u/ from its position next to /o/ and place it at the lowest
possible position, outside the mouth.[18]

Once the Tiberian Masoretes had their full absolute vocalisation system, they had no need for relative vowel phonology,
and the terms *milleʿel* and *milleraʿ* became unnecessary for describing vowels. It was at this time that the terms probably gained
their more well-known use for indicating stress positions, as such

---

[16] On this sign, see Dotan (2007, 625–26).

[17] The original *qɔmeṣ* sign was a horizontal stroke with a dot beneath it,
but most modern fonts do not render this form.

[18] See Posegay (2021, 70, n. 72); see also below, chapter 4, §§3.3–4.

distinctions were still useful when reading a vocalised text with no cantillation signs. In this form, the two words were eventually codified into the *Masora* of the Leningrad Codex, and they continue to represent a small hint of the time when Hebrew and Syriac scholars had a mutual understanding of vocalisation.

This proposed development of the Tiberian vocalisation system remains highly speculative, but it is a plausible interpretation of the principles of relative vocalisation and phonetic 'height' that Hebrew Masoretes seem to have shared with Syriac scribes and grammarians. The Tiberians clearly did not borrow the Syriac vowel points for use in their biblical text, but they may have heard of these 'relative' principles or terms like *men lʿel* and *men ltaḥt* from Syriac contemporaries. Intellectual exchange of this type was certainly possible between Jewish and Syriac Christian scholars in the eighth century. Both groups had a long parallel history of scholastic institutions in the East Syrian school systems and the Rabbinic academies (Becker 2003, 387–91; 2006, 16, 18, 219 n. 98; 2010, 98–99, 103–8; see also, Vööbus 1965), they still retained Aramaic (in some form) as a shared vernacular, and a number of early medieval sources report direct contact between Jewish and Christian intellectuals (Siegal 2018; Butts and Gross 2020, 18–23; Posegay 2021d, 75; see also above, chapter 2, §1.0). Even Jacob of Edessa himself mentions Jews in nearby communities a few times in his writings (Hoyland 2008, 17, 20–21), and he seems to have had an affinity for the Hebrew language not seen among other Syriac grammarians (Salvesen 2001, 457–67; Butts and Gross 2020, 17–18).[19]

This kind of intellectual exchange might also explain the relatively sudden appearance in the historical record of the complete Tiberian vocalisation system, without any evidence of prior developmental stages. If the Tiberians intentionally designed a new absolute vocalisation system, and they decided that that new system should encode phonetic height, then we would expect it to be complete and internally consistent from the outset (see Morag 1961, 29). The Tiberian vocalisation system, at least as we know it, fits this description much better than the Palestinian and Babylonian systems, both of which are comparatively inconsistent with longer periods of evolution (Dotan 1981, 87; 2007, 525, 630, 633; Yeivin 1985; Khan 2013). In any case, there is no evidence of a long Tiberian developmental process such as we find in Syriac, with the gradual introduction of signs that evolved organically from earlier, less precise diacritic dots.

Even if this reconstruction of the Tiberian vocalisation system is not sound, the fact remains that both Syriac and Hebrew linguists employed relative terminology based on openness and backness to describe their vocalisation before the introduction of absolute vowel points. At the same time as these Syriac and Hebrew scribes were creating those absolute systems, Qurʾānic vocalisers were also adapting the Syriac diacritic dot to function as an absolute vocalisation system in Arabic. This development was

---

[19] Jacob probably could not actually read Hebrew, and most of his information about the language came from Greek sources. See also, Salvesen (2008).

itself related to the system of diacritic dots that Arabic scribes used to differentiate consonants, which also depend on 'relative' distinctions of phonetic height. Additionally, relative phonetic terminology similar to that discussed above actually appears in eighth-century discussions of Arabic vocalisation, although it applies mainly to allophones, rather than to phonemic vowels.

2.0. Relative Phonology in Arabic

Using principles similar to the early Syriac and Hebrew descriptions of vowel phonology, the first Arabic linguists also applied a relative system to identify the vowels of their recitation tradition. Like seventh- and eighth-century Jews and Christians, Qurʾānic readers first identified some of their vowels using terms derived from connections between backness and height. The earliest Arabic diacritic dots provide evidence for this relative phonology, as they were placed using the same 'high' and 'low' phonetic associations as seen in the Syriac dot systems, albeit for consonants rather than vowels. The concept also carried into the invention of the Arabic red-dot vocalisation system, which took shape around the end of the seventh century. Early Arabic grammatical sources, specifically *Kitāb Sībawayh* and *Kitāb al-ʿAyn*, also preserve two-way contrastive phonetic terminology that, like in Syriac and Hebrew, linked the back of the mouth to phonetic 'height'. This early tradition used *naṣb* 'standing upright' and *ʾimāla* 'bending down, inclining' to describe the various allophones of *ʾalif* in Qurʾānic Arabic, according to their relative points of articulation. Also, as in Syriac and Hebrew, this two-way comparison of vowels contributed to an absolute naming system during the eighth century.

2.1. Inverting the Alphabet: Letters and Dots in Arabic

The earliest Arabic script evolved from Nabatean writing in the fifth and sixth centuries, possibly spurred on by the spread of Christianity in the Arabian Peninsula during the century before Islam (Abbott 1939, 17; George 2010, 21–26; see also, Robin 2006; Hoyland 2008a). This Arabic lacked the diacritic dots and vocalisation marks seen in modern Arabic, but the rise of Islam and the necessity of unambiguously representing the words of the Qurʾan accelerated the development of Arabic pointing systems. The earliest system of Arabic ʾiǧām 'distinguishing dots' emerged by the first half of the seventh century at the latest,[20] consisting of short strokes or ovoid dots that differentiated consonants with similar forms (Abbott 1939, 38; Rezvan 2004, 95; Ghabban and Hoyland 2008; George 2010, 29–31, 51).

E. J. Revell has shown that Arabic scribes did not place these dots arbitrarily, but rather the positions of the dots encode information about the relative phonetic quality of consonants. He identifies three stages of ʾiǧām development, but the first is most pertinent here. In this stage, scribes distinguished consonants which were identical in writing, but had different points of artic-ulation. A consonant articulated farther back in the mouth re-ceived a dot above, while its graphemic twin with a more fronted

---

[20] Though note al-Shdaifat et al. (2017), who argue for the application of a Nabatean diacritic dot in an Arabic inscription that might be from the sixth century.

position received a dot below (Revell 1975, 178–79). For example, medial *nūn* and *bā*' were identical in writing, so the alveolar *nūn* took a dot above (ن) in contrast to the relatively fronted bilabial *bā*' (ب). Likewise, the velar *khā*' (خ) was farther back than the palatal *jīm* (ج). The pair of *qāf* and *fā*' also falls into this category, as early manuscripts show the uvular *qāf* with a single dot above (ڡ), while the labio-dental *fā*' takes a dot below (ٮ) (see Khan 1992, 43; Gruendler 2001).[21] Additionally, some manuscripts distinguish the palatal *shīn* (ش) with three dots above, while the dental *sīn* takes three dots below (ڛ) (Gruendler 2001, 140).[22] The diacritics of these consonant pairs thus reflect an understanding of the back of the mouth as 'higher' than the front.

This correlation of phonetic backness with height mirrors that of the Hebrew and Syriac relative vocalisation systems, discussed at length in the previous section. Revell argues that such ideas about backness led Arabic-writing Christians or Jews to develop these first contrastive *ʾiʿjām* dots in the pre-Islamic period (Revell 1975, 184–85, 190),[23] although none of the dots are attested prior to the advent of Islam (George 2010, 29). Reports

---

[21] This practice of dotting *qāf* and *fā*' has continued in some *maghrebī* scripts up to the present day (George 2015, 12).

[22] Three dots were also necessary to distinguish *sīn* and *shīn* from medial combinations of *bā*', *tā*', *thā*', and *nūn* (see Déroche et al. 2015, 220–21; Witkam 2015).

[23] He also posits that the association of backness and articulation points with height in Arabic, Syriac, and Hebrew is ultimately derived from Indian phonetic concepts. This argument is not necessary to explain the perceived similarities between the Semitic phonological systems, and

within the Arabic linguistic tradition do acknowledge some Syriac influence in the invention of the script, but evidence from early Arabic papyri and inscriptions suggest that the earliest forms of the letters themselves were mainly the result of its Nabatean origins (Abbott 1939, 38; George 2010, 22, 26–27). However, ḥijāzī scripts from the first few decades of Islam do show Syriac calligraphic influences in the thickness and slanting angles of their strokes. They also tend to have ovoid dots for their ʾiʿjām, rather than the slanting strokes which become more prevalent in later Qurʾāns, which may have been an attempt to match the round diacritic dots of Syriac precursors (George 2010, 51–52, 75). They may also have favoured the use of ʾiʿjām on specific difficult words or grammatical categories, following similar tendencies among Syriac scribes to mark only ambiguous homographic forms with the diacritic dot (Kaplony 2008, 101). Furthermore, there is at least one Arabic inscription from the sixth or seventh century that appears to have diacritic dots held over from earlier Aramaic writing systems (al-Shdaifat et al. 2017).

Regarding the connection between phonology and ʾiʿjām dot position, Revell concludes that "once the theory had served its purpose, it was likely forgotten, and never passed on to adherents of Islam" (Revell 1975, 190), but this is not completely true. The same principle persisted in the creation of the first 'red-dot' vowel points applied to the text of the Qurʾān near the end of the seventh century. Nabia Abbott argues that these signs were introduced first in Iraq, where there was less resistance to modifying

---

the connection with Indian linguistic theory is probably a coincidence; see Versteegh (1993, 27–28, 31).

Qur'ānic orthography than in the Hijaz (1939, 21, 59). Extant manuscripts suggest Syria is a more likely location than Iraq, though it is difficult to identify the place of origin with certainty (George 2010, 78; 2015, 7). Either way, the first attested red dots appear in Qur'ān manuscripts from the Umayyad era, including MSS Marcel 13, BNF Arabe 330c, and TIEM ŞE321 (see Déroche 2014, figs. 1–44). While it remains possible that red dots were added some decades or even centuries after the completion of these manuscripts' consonantal texts, their script style is similar to that of the inscriptions on the Dome of the Rock, suggesting they were produced as part of the Caliph 'Abd al-Malik's (d. 705) scribal programmes (George 2010, 75–78). This period corresponds with the timeframe given in traditional Arabic sources for the introduction of the red dots, as the majority of accounts claim that either the Caliph 'Alī (d. 661) or the Iraqi governor Ziyād ibn Abīhī (d. 673) asked the grammarian Abū al-Aswad al-Du'alī (d. 689) to invent a system to preserve the correct recitation of the Qur'ān.[24] Others suggest that it was the governor al-Ḥajjāj ibn Yūsuf (d. 714) who asked the grammarian Naṣr ibn 'Āṣim (d. 707) to create a vowel system, and a few sources give credit to Ḥasan al-Baṣrī (d. 728/9) or Yaḥyā ibn Ya'mar (d. 746) (Abbott 1939, 39).

---

[24] The 'modern' Arabic vocalisation system, with slanted strokes for /a/ and /i/ and a small *wāw* for /u/, does not appear regularly in Qur'ān manuscripts until the tenth or eleventh century. It is attested in non-Qur'ānic texts from the ninth century (Déroche 2003; George 2015, 13–14; Posegay 2021).

While it is possible that Abū al-Aswad was the true 'inventor' of the red-dot system, its creation has been mythologised in the Arabic grammatical tradition. As the Andalusian *tajwīd* scholar Abū ʿAmr al-Dānī (d. 1053) tells it in *al-Muḥkam fī Naqṭ al-Maṣāḥif* (*The Rules for Pointing the Codices*), Ziyād ibn Abīhī asked Abū al-Aswad to make something for the Qurʾān that would prevent the corruption of its recitation. At first, Abū al-Aswad refused, but then:

فوجّه زياد رجلاً، وقال له : اقعد في طريق أبي الأسود، فإذا مرّ بك، فاقرأ شيئاً
من القرآن، وتعمّد اللحن فيه. ففعل ذلك. فلمّا مرّ به أبو الأسود رفع الرجل
صوته، فقال : أنَّ اللهَ بَرِىءٌ مِنَ المُشْرِكِينَ وَرَسُولِهِ. فاستعظم ذلك أبو الأسود،
فقال : عزَّ وجهُ الله أن يبرأ من رسوله.

ثم رجع من فوره إلى زياد، فقال : يا هذا، قد أجبتُك إلى ما سألتَ، ورأيتُ
أن أبدأ بإعراب القرآن، فابعثْ اليَّ ثلثين رجلاً. فأحضرهم زياد. فاختار منهم
أبو الأسود عشرة. ثم لم يزل يختار منهم حتى اختار رجلاً من عبد القيس.

فقال : خذ المصحف وصِبْغاً يخالف لون المداد. فإذا فتحتُ شفتيَّ فانْقُطْ
واحدةً فوق الحرف، وإذا ضممتُهما فاجعل النقطة إلى جانب الحرف، وإذا
كسرتُهما فاجعل النقطة في أسفله، فإن أَتبعتُ شيئاً من هذه الحركات غُنَّةً
فانْقُطْ نقطتين.

Ziyād brought up a man and said to him, "Sit by the path of Abū al-Aswad, and if he passes by you, then recite part of the Qurʾān, but make a mistake intentionally." And he did that. When Abū al-Aswad passed by him, the man raised his voice and said, "God is disassociated from the polytheists and from His messenger."[25] Abū al-Aswad noticed this, and said, "How great can the design of God be, that He would disassociate from His messenger?!"

---

[25] Q. 9:3 (al-Tawba). The man said *ʾanna llāha barīʾun mina l-mushrikīna wa-rasūlihī*, but the proper reading is with *wa-rasūluhū*, i.e., "that God is disassociated from the polytheists, and so is His messenger."

> He went straight back to Ziyād and said, "Now look here: I have an answer for you, to what you requested. I have decided to begin making ʾiʿrāb in the Qurʾān. Bring me thirty men." And Ziyād brought them. Abū al-Aswad selected ten from among them, and he only stopped once he had chosen a man from ʿAbd al-Qays.

> Then he said, "Take a codex and some dye of a different colour than the ink. When I open my lips, make a single dot above the letter. When I press them together, put the dot next to the letter. Then when I break them, put the dot below it. If I follow any of these vowels with a nasal sound, then make two dots" (al-Dānī 1960, 2b–3a).

At the core of this system, a red dot above a letter marked the vowel /a/, a dot to the left marked /u/, and a dot below marked /i/.[26] Two dots marked nunation (*tanwīn*) at the end of a word. Although al-Dānī does not suggest that Abū al-Aswad actually named the Arabic vowels, he does describe the lip movements that happen when one articulates /a/, /u/, and /i/, using verbs that share roots with the Arabic vowels *fatḥa* 'opening', *ḍamma* 'pressing together', and *kasra* 'breaking'. Still, al-Dānī is likely too late a source to know with any certainty what Abū al-Aswad said on the day of the first red dots.[27] Interestingly, the notion that he changed his mind with respect to recording the ʾiʿrāb is reminiscent of his Syriac contemporary, Jacob of Edessa (d. 708), who

---

[26] Other dot colours and diacritic signs could represent additional features (e.g., *hamza* and *shadda*) or record multiple *qirāʾāt* in a single manuscript. See Dutton (1999; 2000) and Muehlhaeusler (2016).

[27] For further analysis on the historical reliability of the tradition behind the dots, see George (2015, 5–7).

reluctantly created Syriac vowel letters after initially believing that they were unnecessary.[28]

While it is difficult to definitively date any vocalised manuscripts to Abū al-Aswad's lifetime (George 2015, 4–5), it is safe to conclude that vowel dots first appeared in Arabic sometime between 675 and 725. This period also coincides with the time prior to absolute Syriac vocalisation, in which the diacritic dot system was at its peak, and overlaps with the end of Jacob of Edessa's life. This coincidence has not gone unnoticed, as Abbott points out that "Arabic traditionists acknowledge the influence of Syriac" in the creation of the red-dot system (1939, 38), and Versteegh remarks that its inventor "borrowed the system of punctuation from the Syrians" (1993, 29). Versteegh further claims that it is "obvious" the red dots were arranged in accordance with the placement of the Syriac diacritic dots (Versteegh 1993, 30; see also, Lipiński 1997, 163), which seems to be accurate. As we have seen with Jacob of Edessa's writings (above, present chapter, §1.0), the seventh-century Syriac diacritic dot system marked vowels by contrasting them between homographs. In general, a supralinear dot marked a homograph with /ɔ/ or /a/, a sublinear dot marked /e/ or /i/, and a supralinear dot with a sublinear dot on the same word marked /a/ (Kiraz 2015, 41–47). Arabic scribes adapted this system for their smaller vowel inventory,[29] taking the dot which *most often* indicated a

---

[28] See above, chapter 2, §1.0, and Wright (1871, ܐ, Bodl. 159 fol. 1a, col. 1).

[29] Medieval Arabic scholars distinguished only three cardinal vowel qualities in Classical Arabic: /a/, /i/, /u/.

type of *a*-vowel—the dot 'above' (*men lʿel*)—for their /a/. Naturally, the dot which most often indicated a type of *e*- or *i*-vowel—
the dot 'below' (*men ltaḥt*)—became /i/. This vocalisation was
first used sparingly, usually on difficult or foreign words and not
to fully vocalise a Qurʾān (Abbott 1939, 39; 1972, 9; Dutton
1999, 123). As Dutton (1999, 117) observes, an account in Abū
Bakr ibn Abī Dāwūd's (d. 929) *Kitāb al-Maṣāḥif* (*The Book of the
Codices*) even suggests that "they were not used for all vowels,
but rather those that indicated grammatical endings, or that distinguished two different words (e.g., *fa-mathaluhu* rather than *fa-
mithluhu*)." That is to say, they were sometimes used to differentiate homographs that differed only in their vowels, exactly like
Syriac.

With dots already accounting for two-thirds of their vowels
(/a/ and /i/), Arabic scribes had no need for an ambiguous relative vocalisation system, and they placed a single intralinear red
dot to the left of a letter to represent /u/. Al-Dānī explains the
intralinear position for /u/ simply because it was the last remaining space (al-Dānī 1960, 20a),[30] and, as far as I know, there is no
evidence for the regular use of a two-dot sign to represent any
vowel in Arabic. There is, however, an anomalous papyrus letter
from the Khalili Collection in which the writer applies an oblique
pair of sublinear dots to designate /i/, or a similarly fronted

---

[30] He also claims that there was once a Hijazi practice that marked /u/
with a supralinear dot, /a/ with an intralinear dot, and /i/ with a sublinear dot, but this system is unattested in manuscripts (al-Dānī 1960,
4b–5a; George 2015, 6, 14).

vowel, in five separate instances (MS Khalili Inv. No. 368). Geoffrey Khan notes that this sign matches the form and usage of the sublinear two-dot sign that represents /e/ and /i/ in Syriac manuscripts from the seventh century onwards, and may be a "loan from Syriac" in the period before the red-dot system stabilised (Khan 1992, 43–44, 234–37).[31] He also highlights a papyrus petition from the same collection in which a dot 'above' marks /ā/ and a dot 'below' marks /ī/, both conspicuously in the same colour as the main script (MS Khalili Inv. No. 69) (Khan 1992, 43, 136–40).[32] This matching colouration is irregular, as medieval Arabic vocalisers explicitly instruct to use different colours for the dots and main script (hence 'red' dots) (al-Dānī 1960, 2b–3a, 9b). It is worth noting that Syriac scribes often used red and black inks for different types of dots in the same manuscript, and their vowel points were usually black or brown (i.e., the same colour as the script). Both of these papyri documents thus reinforce the conclusion that the red-dot system is derived from the Syriac diacritic dots.

This adaptation of the Syriac relative vocalisation system to fit the Arabic language could have occurred in several different ways, including within the scribal bureaucracy of the late Ra-

---

[31] For the function of these particular dots in Syriac, see Kiraz (2012, I:70; 2015, 98–101).

[32] Abbott suspects the Arabic red dots cannot have seen much use in non-Qurʾānic texts, with the system quickly giving way to the modern vocalisation system in works of literature and poetry due to the inconvenience of swapping ink colours (1972, 7–8).

shidun or early Umayyad Caliphate. As Versteegh (1993, 29) remarks, "we know that during the first century of the conquests
Arabs had to rely on Christians to handle the archives of the
newly founded empire." The lack of a complex Arabic bureaucratic system or written literary tradition in the pre-Islamic period prompted the early caliphate to employ non-Arabic scribes,
specifically Greek and Persian, for bureaucratic work until the
reforms of ʿAbd al-Malik at the end of the seventh century (Hoyland 2008b, 13–15). Even into the 690s, many of these scribes
were bilingual Syriac Christians (Hoyland 2008b, 13, n. 6; King
2012, 196–97), and when ʿAbd al-Malik ordered them to begin
keeping records in Arabic, it would have been trivial to transfer
the Syriac dots to a vowelless Arabic script. On the other hand,
with the possible exceptions of the two papyrus documents mentioned above, both the Syriac dots and the Arabic red-dot vocalisation are practically unattested in non-Qurʾānic texts. It is more
likely that the ʾiʿjām entered Arabic from Syriac via this pathway,
as they are attested earlier than the red dots and do appear in
bureaucratic documents (Kaplony 2008).

Another option for the introduction of the red dots is
through pedagogical practices aimed at teaching children to read
Arabic. Several scholars have observed that in Jacob of Edessa's
canons, he accedes that it is permissible for a Christian priest to
teach reading and writing to Muslim (and Jewish) children (Merx
1889, 43; Hoyland 2008b, 17). Versteegh (1993, 29) argues that
such teacher-student relationships must have existed in the late
seventh century, or there would be no need to address such a
question. More than likely, these Syrian teachers were teaching

Arabic reading to Muslim children, and we know from Jacob of Edessa's *Turrọṣ Mamllọ* that vowel marking was a powerful tool for explaining grammar (see above, chapter 2, §1.0). Similarly, in the years following 'Abd al-Malik's reforms, Syriac Christian children would have needed to learn Arabic in order to pursue careers in the scribal bureaucracy. In these scenarios, the introduction of Syriac vowel dots to the Arabic script would have occurred in a pedagogical setting, with Syriac-speaking teachers utilising them to educate Arabic-reading children.

More generally, Arabic vocalisation would have spread after the invention of the red dots as a result of pedagogy. Though much later than Jacob of Edessa, al-Dānī records at least one tradition which forbids vowel pointing, *except* for pedagogical purposes. He writes: "Mālik said... As for the little codices which children learn from, as well as their tablets,[33] I do not think [pointing them] is so bad (قال مالك... وأمّا المصاحف الصغار التي يتعلّم فيها الصبيان وألواحهم فلا أرى في ذلك بأساً)" (al-Dānī 1960, 6a).[34] Drawing a brief modern parallel, also note that children's books are the only Arabic texts besides the Qurʾān that are fully and consistently vocalised.

---

[33] These were wooden tablets with wax surfaces that students could use to practice writing, then scrape clean to use again.

[34] This was also the rule for medieval Hebrew Bible manuscripts. Personal codices and teaching aides could be vocalised, but Torah scrolls meant for use in synagogues could not (Khan 1990, 54; 2020, I:20). For vocalisation in common Bible codices, see Outhwaite (2020).

Still, the red-dot vowel points are not widely attested in non-Qurʾānic texts, so bureaucratic archives and schoolkids' tablets may not be the most likely entry points for Syriac diacritic dots into the Arabic script. Another possibility is implied by several early *ḥadīth* reports that claim seventh- and eighth-century Muslims hired Christian scribes (or recent Christian converts to Islam) to write copies of the Qurʾān for them (Déroche 2004, 263, n. 83; George 2010, 52–53 and nn. 112–16). These scribes would have first learned Syriac calligraphy before adapting to Arabic, and would have had the perfect opportunity to convert Syriac diacritic dots into an Arabic vocalisation system. Such reports also correlate with the observed Syriac influences on the palaeography and codicology of early Qurʾān manuscripts (George 2010, 34–51). Abū al-Aswad and other late seventh- or early eighth-century scholars would have been aware of these practices, or something similar. Some of them may even have learned to read from native Syriac-speakers before adding red dots to the Qurʾānic text themselves. Moreover, it may be that the comparatively early introduction of an absolute vowel pointing system in Arabic actually accelerated the transition to absolute vocalisation in Syriac during the eighth century.

Regardless of the precise origins of the red dots and *ʾiʿjām*, it is clear that their inventor(s) modelled them after the Syriac diacritic dots, thereby importing the concept of 'high' and 'low' phonology into the Arabic writing system. Revell was correct to observe that later Muslim grammarians did not always adopt exactly the same principles to describe Arabic, and the difference may be due to the work of al-Khalīl ibn Aḥmad (d. 786/791). If the older perception of farther-backed articulation points as 'higher' (as evidenced by the *ʾiǧām* positions) became universal in Arabic, then the 'lowest' consonant should always be the bilabial *mīm*. However, the introduction to *Kitāb al-ʿAyn* explains how al-Khalīl rearranged the letters of the Arabic alphabet to ascend in order from back to front:

فأَعْمَلَ فكرَه فيه فلم يمكنه أنْ يبتدىء التأليف من اول ا، ب، ت، ث، وهو الألف. لأن الألف حرف معتلٌّ فلما فاته الحرف الأوّل كَرهَ أن يبتدىء بالثاني—وهو الباء—إلّا بعد حُجّةٍ واستقصاء النَّظَر، فدبَّر ونظر الى الحروف كلِّها وذاقَها [فوجد مخرج الكلام كلَّه من الحلق] فصيَّر أولا بالإبتداء ادخَلَ حرف منها في الحلق.

وإنما كان ذَواقه إيَّاها أنَّه كان يفتح فاهُ بالألف ثم يظهر الحرفَ. نحو اب، ات، اح، اع، اغ، فوَجَدَ العين ادخَلَ الحروف في الحلق، فجعلها أوّلَ الكتاب ثم ما قَرُبَ منها الأرفع فالأرفع حتى أتَى على آخرها وهو الميم.

فإذا سُئِلتَ عن كلمة وأردتَ أن تعرِفَ موضِعَها. فانظرْ الى حروف الكلمةِ فمهما وَجَدتَ منها واحدا في الكتاب المقدَّم فهو ذلك الكتاب.

وقلَّبَ الخليل ا، ب، ت، ث، فوضعها على قدر مخرجها من الحلق وهذا تأليفه: ع، ح، ه، خ، غ ...

So he considered it, for he could not begin his composition from the beginning of the *ʾalif, bāʾ, tāʾ, thāʾ* [alphabet], which is *ʾalif*, because the *ʾalif* is a sick letter. But when he passed the first letter, he was loath to begin with the second (which is *bāʾ*) without pretext and careful consideration. He organised and observed all of the letters; he tested them, [finding the exit of all speech is from the throat]. Thus he made first, at the beginning, the innermost letter among those in the throat.

His test of them was just that he would open his mouth with *ʾalif*, then make the letter appear, for example: *ʾāb, ʾāt, ʾāḥ, ʾāʿ, ʾāgh*. He found the ʿayn was the innermost of the letters in the throat, so he made it the first of the book,

> and then whatever [letter] was next to it was higher, and
> then higher still until he came to their end, which is the
> *mīm*.
>
> So if you were asked about a word and you wanted to know
> its location [in the lexicon], then examine the letters of the
> word, and when you find the one earliest in the book, then
> it is that volume.
>
> And al-Khalīl inverted the *'alif, bā', tā', thā'* [alphabet], and
> he placed them in proportion to [the distance of] their ar-
> ticulation point from the throat. This is his arrangement:
> *'ayn, ḥā', hā', khā', ghayn*.... (Makhzumi 1985, I:47–48)

The narrator of this passage—likely al-Khalīl's student, al-Layth
ibn al-Muẓaffar (d. 803) (Sellheim 2012; Schoeler 2006, 142–
63)—explains that al-Khalīl did not want to arrange his lexicon
in the normal Arabic alphabetical order (*'alif, bā', tā', thā'*), because *'alif* is not a sound root letter. He observed that the throat
is the source of all speech, and so concluded that *'ayn* should be
the first letter because it is produced deepest in the throat.[35]
Then, in contrast to the comparisons found in the relative vocalisation and diacritic systems, al-Khalīl designed a consonantal
scale that moves upwards from the back of the mouth to the front
(see Revell 1975, 183–84, 190 n. 1; Kinberg 1987, 17–18). He
further clarifies this arrangement when he states that the innermost letters are *'ayn*,[36] *ḥā'*, and *hā'*, and that "these three are in

---

[35] This letter's name is the reason why the lexicon is called *Kitāb al-'Ayn*
(*The Book of the 'Ayn*), but al-Khalīl was also punning on the noun *'ayn*,
which means 'source'.

[36] *Hamza* (glottal stop) is actually articulated farther back than *'ayn*
(voiced pharyngeal fricative), but al-Khalīl considered it one of the 'airy'

one space, each one higher than last (هذه ثلاثة أحرف في حيّز واحد
بعضُها أرفع من بعض)" (Makhzumi 1985, 57–58). Similarly, he says,
"*qāf* and *kāf* are both velar-uvular, and the *kāf* is higher (ثم القاف
والكاف لهويتان، والكاف أرفع)" (Makhzumi 1985, 58).[37] That is, *kāf* is
farther forward. This consonantal scale remained the alphabetical order for the lexical entries in *Kitāb al-ʿAyn* even as later scholars compiled it after al-Khalīl's death. The influence of this first
Arabic lexicon may have disrupted the continuity of the earlier
phonological system where 'back' was 'high'.

Al-Khalīl's work was foundational to the Basran school of
grammar (Talmon 2003, 279), and his consonantal arrangement
appears in the *Kitāb* of his student, Sībawayh (d. 793/796).
Sībawayh expands on this notion equating 'height' with frontedness, and he explicitly incorporates the Arabic vowels into the
order of articulation points. In a chapter on verbs of the *faʿala*
pattern containing pharyngeal consonants that inflect with the
vowel /a/, he writes:

وإنما فتحوا هذه الحروفَ لأنها سَفلتْ في الحلق، فكرهوا أن يتناولوا حركة
ما قبلها بحركة ما ارتفع من الحروف، فجعلوا حركتها من الحرف الذي في
حيّزها وهو الألف، وإنما الحركاتُ من الألف والياء والواو.

وكذلك حرَّكوهنَّ إذ كنَّ عيناتٍ، ولم يُفعَل هذا بما هو من موضع الواو والياء،
لأنَّهما من الحروف التي ارتَفعت، والحروفُ المرتفعةُ حيّزٌ على حدةٍ تَتناول
للمرتفع حركةً من مرتفع، وكُره أن يُتناول للذي قد سَفل حركةً من هذا الحيّز.

_____

letters which lacked an articulation point in the mouth (Makhzumi
1985, 58; al-Nassir 1993, 13–14).

[37] *Kāf* never represented a uvular consonant, so al-Khalīl's term *lahawī*
here designates a region around the back of the tongue between the
uvula and the velum (Alfozan 1989, 10–11; al-Nassir 1993, 11, 41; Brierley et al. 2016, 162–63).

> They [the Arabs] only put *fatḥa* on these letters because
> they occur low in the throat, and they avoid making the
> vowel that precedes [the velar/pharyngeal letters] into a
> vowel of that which is raised above those letters. Thus,
> they make the vowel from the letter in the same space,
> namely *ʾalif*. Indeed, the vowels are from *ʾalif*, *yāʾ*, and
> *wāw*.

> They likewise vocalise [these consonants] when they are
> in second position, but this is not done in instances of *wāw*
> or *yāʾ*, because they are both among the letters which are
> raised up. The raised letters are a separate space. For what
> is raised up, you only take a vowel that is [also] from what
> is raised, and taking a vowel from this space for whatever
> is low should be avoided. (Sībawayh 1986, IV:101)

For Sībawayh, since the consonants *hāʾ*, *ʿayn*, *ḥāʾ*, *ghayn*, and *khāʾ*
are articulated far back at the throat, they are the lowest letters.
They frequently take the vowel /a/ because it shares a 'space'
(*ḥayyiz*) with them. More precisely, /a/ shares an articulation
point with *ʾalif* (and thus *hamza*), so it is the vowel that is physically closest to the low consonants. By contrast, if *yāʾ* or *wāw*
occur in these same verbal contexts, they usually take /i/ or /u/.
This tendency occurs, at least according to Sībawayh, because *yāʾ*
and *wāw* are *murtafiʿa* 'raised up', higher in the mouth than the
letters articulated in the throat. These raised letters are farther
forward, and thus it is easier for them to take /i/ and /u/, which
are also 'raised up' at their articulation points (see Kinberg 1987,
16–17). The same explanation appears in Ibn Jinnī's (d. 1002)
Sirr Ṣināʿa al-Iʿrāb, where he places *fatḥa* (/a/) as the lowest
vowel, followed by *kasra* (/i/), and then *ḍamma* (/u/) (Kinberg
1987, 18; Ibn Jinnī 1993, 53–54).

Given the influence that al-Khalīl and Sībawayh's writings had on later Arabic grammarians, it is not surprising that the waters are somewhat muddied with respect to the perceptions of 'high' and 'low' in medieval Arabic linguistics. For indeed, even while al-Khalīl's consonant scale survived in *al-ʿAyn* and the work of some of his successors, there was a concurrent system which considered the velum the highest point in the mouth, and all spaces both in front of and behind it were lower (Kinberg 1987). This system appears much more similar to the *milleʿel-milleraʿ* scale and the Syriac relative vocalisation system, which both identified 'high' vowels as those pronounced farthest back, closest to the velum.

2.2. *Naṣb*, *'Imāla*, and Phonological Height in Arabic

The arrangements of the consonants in the introduction of *Kitāb al-ʿAyn*, Sībawayh's *Kitāb*, and Ibn Jinnī's *Sirr Ṣināʿa al-Iʿrāb* all suggest that they conceived of an ascending scale that located pharyngeals as the 'lowest' letters in contrast to the 'highest' labials (e.g., Ibn Jinnī 1993, 45). However, Naphtali Kinberg has shown that the prevailing perception among Arabic grammarians—including Sībawayh and Ibn Jinnī—is to regard the space between the velum and uvula as the highest point in the mouth. As such, the letters pronounced from articulation points both in front of *and* behind the velum (i.e., palatals, dentals, labials, pharyngeals, glottals) are relatively 'low' (Kinberg 1987, 8). This organisation appears in the work of several later grammarians, but is best summarised by Ibn Jinnī, who classifies all the letters into two groups: *mustaʿliya* 'elevated' and *munkhafiḍa* 'lowered'.

The elevated letters are the velars *khā'*, *ghayn*, and *qāf*, as well as the 'emphatic' pharyngealised consonants *ṣād*, *ḍād*, *ṭā'*, and *ẓā'*. All other letters are lowered, including *hamza*, *ʿayn*, *hā'*, and *ḥā'* (Ibn Jinnī 1993, 62; Bakalla 2011). Two details stand out here. First, *munkhafiḍa* comes from the same root as *khafḍ* 'lowering', the Kufan name for the genitive case and a name for the vowel /i/ until at least the early ninth century (Versteegh 1993, 18–19). Second, Sībawayh uses the same *mustaʿliya* term and group of seven 'elevated' letters to explain the rules which prevent *'imāla* 'bending down, inclination' in the *Kitāb*.

'Imāla in Arabic is a phonetic phenomenon of fronting a vowel so that its pronunciation approaches /i/. Most often, this occurs with long /ā/ represented by *'alif*, resulting in allophonic qualities between /a/ and /i/ (e.g., /ɛ/ or /e/) (Alfozan 1989, 18, 35, 213–16; Levin 2007). Sībawayh's *Kitāb* is the earliest source that describes the comprehensive rules for determining whether or not an *'alif* undergoes *'imāla*, and he devotes several chapters to it (Sībawayh 1986, IV:117–43). The most common cause is /i/ in an adjacent syllable. Throughout this discussion, Sībawayh refers to the default quality of *'alif* (/a/) as *naṣb* 'standing upright' (Sībawayh 1986, IV:123, line 4; Talmon 1996, 291; 2003, 239), while variants in which /a/ is fronted towards /i/ are *'imāla* 'bending down'. He usually does this by saying that a speaker 'bends down' (*yumīlu*) or 'sets upright' (*yanṣibu*) the *'alif* (Sībawayh 1986, IV:123, 125–26, 127, 143). Some later grammarians also delineated two different types of *'imāla*—*'imāla khafīfa* 'light inclination' (likely around /ɛ/) and *'imāla shadīda*

'strong inclination' (closer to /e/ or /i/)[38]—but Sībawayh does not make that distinction in this section (Alfozan 1989, 18, 35–36; Dutton 1999, 121). However, he does say that some instances of ʾimāla are 'weaker' (ʾaḍʿaf) (Sībawayh 1986, IV:122), and he mentions 'strong ʾimāla' in his section on the alphabet (Sībawayh 1986, IV:432), suggesting his idea of ʾimāla encompassed more than one vowel quality. As such, in the *Kitāb* and elsewhere, the term ʾimāla has a relative function, and, depending on context, can indicate multiple fronted allophones of ʾalif (e.g., /ɛ/, /e/).

Naṣb is the name for the accusative case in Classical Arabic, but prior to the ninth century it was also a name for /a/, the vowel that most frequently marks the accusative case ending. Evidence for this usage as a vowel name appears in early Qurʾānic exegesis and the lexical sections of *Kitāb al-ʿAyn* (Versteegh 1993, 125–26; Talmon 1997, 157, 194–97; 2003, 235–40). The identification of /a/ with 'standing upright' indicates that the vowel is articulated higher up in the mouth—that is, not fronted, not ʾimāla 'bending down'. However, besides /a/ and /e/, Sībawayh includes another allophone of ʾalif in this discussion of naṣb and ʾimāla. He states that the seven mustaʿliya letters—khāʾ, ghayn, qāf, ṣād, ḍād, ṭāʾ, and ẓāʾ—prevent ʾimāla when they precede ʾalif (see Kinberg 1987, 8–9), explaining:

وإنما منعت هذه الحروف الإمالةَ لأنها حروف مستعلية الى الحَنَك الأعلى، والألفُ إذا خرجتْ من موضعها استعلتْ الى الحنك الأعلى، فلما كانت مع هذه الحروف المستعلية غلبتْ عليها، كما غلبت الكسرة عليها في

---

[38] Sībawayh does not describe the exact quality of ʾimāla, so we can only estimate here. See discussion in Levin (2007).

مَساجِد ونحوها. فلما كانت الحروفُ مستعليةً وكانت الألف تَستعلى،
وقربتْ من الألف، كان العَمَلُ من وجه واحد أخفّ عليهم...

You prevent ʾimāla for these letters because they are letters
which are elevated towards the upper palate, and the
ʾalif—if it is pronounced from their position—is elevated
towards the upper palate. When [the ʾalif] is adjacent to
these elevated letters, then they overpower it, just as the
kasra overpowers it in masējid and other variations [that
have ʾimāla]. So when the letters are elevated while the
ʾalif elevates, and they are adjacent to the ʾalif, then the
articulation is in a single manner, which is less burdensome for them [the Arabs] (Sībawayh 1986, IV:129).

This passage describes the production of a non-ʾimāla allophone
of ʾalif from the same articulation point as the 'elevated'
(mustaʿliya) letters, so called because the back of the tongue is
'elevated' to the high point between the velum and the uvula (Ibn
Jinnī 1993, 62; see Bakalla 2011). A speaker also retracts the
tongue in order to shift the vowel back towards that point, realising it somewhere between /a/ and /o/ (e.g., /ɑ/ or /ɔ/) (al-
Nassir 1993, 97, 103–4; Bakalla 2011). Sībawayh suggests that
this pronunciation is "less burdensome" because a speaker does
not have to move quickly from the high articulation point of the
mustaʿliya letters to the comparatively low articulation point of a
vowel that has undergone ʾimāla.

Kinberg interprets this passage to mean that the ʾalif rises
towards the velum from a low position in the throat, since that is
the same position as the other munkhafiḍa pharyngeal consonants
and the place which Arabic grammarians indicate for the articulation point of ʾalif (Kinberg 1987, 9). However, this interpretation cannot be correct. When Sībawayh says ʾalif in this passage,

what he is really describing is not the letter itself, but rather the phoneme /ā/ as represented by a written ʾ*alif*. By default, this long vowel has the same quality as /a/, but when it undergoes ʾ*imāla* then it is realised between /a/ and /i/. If Sībawayh perceived the default /a/ as being articulated from low in the throat, then it could not 'bend down' towards /i/—it would either rise or remain level. As such, the 'elevation' of ʾ*alif* in the passage must be from the articulation point of /a/ in the centre of the mouth, between the points of /i/ and the *mustaʿliya* letters, and up towards the velum.[39] This analogy of the transition from a front vowel to a back vowel as movement from a low position to a high position is the same as that seen in Syriac and Hebrew relative vocalisation. In this Arabic system, ʾ*imāla* indicates a downward movement from a default phonemic vowel, while *naṣb* is a comparatively steady or upward movement.

Sībawayh's discussion of ʾ*imāla* with the vowel /u/ reinforces this interpretation. He says that one 'bends down' the second vowel in the word *madhʿūr* 'frightened', with the resulting vowel fronted from /u/ to /ʉ/ (Sībawayh 1986, IV:142–43; Al-fozan 1989, 143; al-Nassir 1993, 102; see also, Ibn Jinnī 1993, 53). Sībawayh's description is a relative comparison of two allophones, with the more-fronted, 'lower' vowel /ʉ/ explained as 'inclined' or 'bent down' in comparison to the 'higher', more-backed /u/. In fact, as Kinberg notes, the articulation point of /u/ is also at the velum—the same as the *mustaʿliya* letters—so it is the 'highest' vowel (Kinberg 1987, 7–8), and any ʾ*imāla* from that

---

[39] Though see al-Nassir (1993, 32–33). Sībawayh may not have had a definite sense of the locations of the articulation points of the vowels.

point results in a relatively-fronted vowel between /i/ and /u/ (i.e., /ʉ/). Further reinforcing this position is a note in *Kitāb al-ʿAyn* that equates *rafʿ* 'rising' with *tafkhīm* 'thickening', the term which Sībawayh applies to the backed realisation of an *ʾalif* in a way that resembles *wāw* (i.e., /o/) (Makhzumi 1985, IV, 281; Sībawayh 1986, IV:432; Talmon 1997, 141). *Rafʿ* was also an early name for the vowel /u/, so called because it indicates the relatively high position of the vowel's velar articulation point. It comes from a separate 'high-and-low' dichotomy in Arabic phonology, contrasting with the fronted 'lowering' of *khafḍ* (/i/) (see below, chapter 4, §1.1). Arabic grammarians eventually combined this pair of terms with *naṣb* as a name for /a/, but only after *naṣb* had been established as the phonetic opposite of *ʾimāla*.

Sībawayh also remarks that the *wāw* in *madhʿūr* does not undergo complete *ʾimāla*, "because it does not resemble *yāʾ*, and if you bend it down, then you [actually] bend down what precedes it, but seeking towards /i/ (ما أَمَلْت ولو أَمَلْتها، الياء تُشبه لا لأنها الكسرة تروم ولكنَّك وقبلها)" (Sībawayh 1986, IV:143; al-Nassir 1993, 102).[40] The implication is that *ʾalif* (and /a/) resembles *yāʾ* (and /i/) more than *wāw* (and /u/), which is why *ʾalif* can undergo more complete downwards inclination. Based on this information, we can estimate that Sībawayh's arrangement of allophonic vowels from low to high would match their approximate order of relative backness: /i/, /e/, /a/, /ʉ/, /ɑ/, /o/, /u/.

At the end of the section on *ʾimāla*, Sībawayh says, "We have heard all that we have mentioned to you, regarding *ʾimāla* and *naṣb* in these chapters, from the Arabs (لك ذكرنا ما جميع سمعنا

---

[40] See discussion of *rawm* 'seeking, desiring' below, chapter 4, §1.2.

(من الإمالة والنصب في هذه الأبواب من العرب)" (Sībawayh 1986, IV:143).
This comment could be read as an indication that all the examples in the preceding chapters—including those with /a/ and
/u/—are classified as either *naṣb* or *ʾimāla*. This usage is actually
inconsistent with the terminology that Sībawayh uses in the rest
of the *Kitāb*. In one of its first chapters, he specifically details a
system to differentiate the vowel names *fatḥ*, *kasr*, and *ḍamm*
from the *ʾiʿrābī* case names *naṣb*, *jarr*, and *rafʿ* (Sībawayh 1986,
I:13; K. Versteegh 2011).[41] This was a novel distinction, as prior
to the *Kitāb*, all of these terms were used interchangeably for both
vowel and case names (Versteegh 1993, 17–19, 125; Talmon
1997, 194–97; 2003, 235–40, 283).[42] Following his own rules,
Sībawayh avoids using *naṣb*, *rafʿ*, and *jarr* to name non-inflectional vowel phonemes the vast majority of the time (Talmon
2003, 238). The section on *ʾimāla* is thus significant for containing an abnormally high density of instances where he describes
the phonology of /a/ and its allophones with terms derived from
naṣb. He seems to be transmitting an inherited tradition (Talmon
2003, 239) in which *naṣb* and *ʾimāla* were binary terms for describing allophonic pronunciations, without always updating it
to match his own terminological system. In this tradition, each
term included a range of possible vowel qualities, depending on
its specific context, with *ʾimāla* 'bending down' indicating relatively fronted 'low' vowels (e.g., /ɛ/, /e/, /æ/), and *naṣb* 'standing

---

[41] On all of these terms as vowel names, see below, chapter 4, §1.1.
[42] Talmon suspects that al-Khalīl created the distinction between vowel
names and *ʾiʿrābī* terms at the end of his career, just before Sībawayhi
wrote the *Kitāb*. See also, Versteegh (1977, 17–18).

upright' indicating relatively 'high' backed vowels (e.g., /a/, /ɑ/, /ɔ/).

Previous scholars have put forth similar explanations for the meaning of these two terms, though they have focused on the idea of *naṣb* as 'stable' in contrast to the 'deviation' of *ʾimāla* (Talmon 2003, 239, n. 2). For example, Morag emphasises the binary relationship between *naṣb* and *ʾimāla*, suggesting that a *manṣūb* allophone is 'stable', while a *mumāl* form is 'deviating' (Morag 1979). This explanation is unconvincing, as *naṣb* means 'standing upright', 'erecting', or even 'elevating' more than 'stabilising' (Kazimirski 1860, 1286; Lane 1863, 2799).[43] If, instead, we take *naṣb* as 'standing upright' to indicate a high position in the mouth, then *ʾimāla* as 'bending down' is the logical antonym for a lower position. Meanwhile, Kinberg (1986, 172) argues that *naṣb* and *ʾimāla* were part of a triad with *tafkhīm* 'thickening, magnifying', indicating either a lack of inclination (/a/), inclination towards the front of the mouth (/e/), or inclination towards the back of the mouth (/o/), respectively. Sībawayh does mention *ʾalif al-tafkhīm* in his account of the alphabet as a variant of *ʾalif* that is opposite to *ʾimāla*. It signifies an apparently Hijazi dialectal shift from /ā/ to /ō/ in the final syllables of *ṣalāt, zakāt,* and *ḥayāt* (all written with *wāw* in the Qurʾan) (Sībawayh 1986, IV:432; Alfozan 1989, 259–60; al-Nassir 1993, 91, 103; Talmon

---

[43] Lane even notes that *naṣb* can be "a kind of song, or chant, of the Arabs, or of the Arabs of the desert, or poetry such as is commonly recited, well-regulated and set to an air, so called because, in singing or chanting it, the voice is raised, or elevated" (Lane 1863, 2799). See also, Talmon (1997, 197).

1997, 141). However, he does not use the word *tafkhīm* in any of his chapters devoted to *ʾimāla*, not even when describing the quality of *ʾalif* after *mustaʿliya* letters. As such, it does not appear that *tafkhīm* originated as part of a conceptual triad with *naṣb* and *ʾimāla*. It may instead be related to Jacob of Edessa's Greek-influenced classification of /ɔ/ and /o/ as 'thick' (ʿbe), in contrast to 'thinner' vowels like /e/ and /i/ (see above, present chapter, §1.1).

A contrastive, binary origin for *naṣb* and *ʾimāla* can be interpreted with the same height-based associations as the Hebrew and Syriac relative vocalisation systems that correlated height with backness. These systems were contemporaneous with the earliest pre-Sībawayhan Arabic grammarians, and those grammarians could have adopted the same explanations for their vowel phonology from a shared source. The most likely possibility would be an element of the Syriac grammatical tradition that was in contact with the 'Old Iraqi' school of Arabic grammarians (Talmon 2003, xi),[44] which included many of Sībawayh's sources, during the late Umayyad or early Abbasid period (see Versteegh 1993, 28; 2003, 32–33; Talmon 2008, 174–76; King 2012, 195–205, esp. 199–201). Like the early Hebrew and Syriac relative vocalisation systems, the terms *naṣb* and *ʾimāla* likely began as part of an oral teaching tradition to instruct the reading and recitation of modified *ʾalif*s, particularly from a Qurʾānic text that

---

[44] This is Talmon's designation for the early milieu of Arabic grammarians in Iraq, prior to the emergence of the distinct 'Kufan' and 'Basran' strains of grammatical thought.

did not have dedicated symbols to represent vowel qualities besides /a/, /i/, and /u/.[45] It seems, then, that Sībawayh recorded,
with only minor updates, part of an early relative system that
used each of these terms to identify multiple allophones: *ʾimāla*
could include /ɛ/ and /e/, while *naṣb* included /a/ and /ɑ/. This
vowel terminology was part of the same overarching phonological system that construed the back of the mouth as 'higher' than
the front, and which informed the placement of the Arabic consonantal diacritic dots and the red-dot vocalisation system.

3.0. Summary

The earliest systems for describing vowels in Syriac, Hebrew, and
Arabic relied on comparisons of vowel qualities, rather than absolute pointing and terminology for indicating each individual
vowel. The first extant evidence of this methodology is the Syriac
diacritic dot system, which appeared at least as early as the fifth
century and distinguished homographic pairs of words according
to the relative quality of their vowels. Syriac scribes placed a dot
above to indicate a word with relatively open and back vowels,
while a dot below marked its homograph with closed and fronted
vowels. By the seventh century, multiple diacritic dots could even

---

[45] There was a rare practice in early Qurʾān manuscripts to indicate
ʾimāla by the addition of a green dot, but it is not widely attested (Dutton 1999, 116). In general, the red-dot system could not explicitly mark
ʾimāla. Later manuscripts include additional symbols for *ʾimāla*, including a *kasra* beneath an *ʾalif* or a small rhombus (Morag 1961, 15, n. 11;
Alfozan 1989, 12, n. 33). See also, Connolly and Posegay (2020, 344–
45).

indicate multiple vowels within a single word. This system led to an association of 'thick' or 'wide' vowels (e.g., /ɔ/, /o/) with the notion of 'above' (*men lʿel*), and 'thin' or 'narrow' vowels (e.g., /e/, /u/) with 'below' (*men ltaḥt*). In the seventh and eighth centuries, these principles informed the final placements of dots in the Syriac absolute vowel pointing system. Around the same time, the phonological ideas of 'above' and 'below' entered the Masoretic linguistic tradition in the form of *milleʿel* and *milleraʿ* homograph comparisons. The Masoretes used these ideas to create a conceptual 'scale' of vowels, placed according to relative backness within the mouth, with the most-back vowels considered the 'highest' or 'most-*milleʿel*'. They did not adopt the Syriac diacritic dot directly, but in the eighth or early ninth century, the conceptual framework of 'above-and-below' phonology also informed the placement of the dots in the Tiberian pointing system.

In the early seventh century, Arabic scribes—likely influenced by Syriac scribal practices—developed a similar system of diacritic dots to differentiate consonants according to their relative 'height' within the mouth. Then, in the late seventh or early eighth century, this principle informed the adaptation of the Syriac diacritic dot system for the Arabic script as the red-dot vocalisation points. Also around this time, Arabic grammarians developed terminology to instruct allophonic variants of vowels that their script and vocalisation system could not represent. Following a similar arrangement to Syriac and Hebrew scholars, they referred to relatively backed 'high' variants of *ʾalif* (/a/, /ɑ/) as *naṣb* 'standing upright', while 'low' fronted allophones (/ɛ/, /e/) were called *ʾimāla* 'bending down'. However, relative terms like these were less prominent in Arabic than in Syriac and Hebrew, as the Arabic script could adequately represent the three main Arabic vowel qualities from an early stage. This situation led to a comparatively early adoption of absolute vowel names in Arabic, though often still rooted in the earlier 'high-and-low' relative terminology. Beginning with these Arabic names, we will now explore the emergence of absolute vowel names in all three traditions.

4. THE DEVELOPMENT OF ABSOLUTE VOWEL NAMING

The vowels have names which are suitable for them, indicating their meanings in the Arabic language, so that they are easy to recognise and clear for the reader. (Anonymous Masorete [c. 10th century]; Allony 1965, 140, lines 28–30)

The idea that particular vowel phonemes might have 'names' developed fairly late in the chronology of Semitic vocalisation traditions, and such names emerged only after the culmination of the early relative vowel systems and the introduction of absolute vowel pointing. Prior to the eighth century, there is little evidence that any Arabic, Syriac, or Hebrew linguists had discrete names like *kasra*, *zqɔpɔ*, or *segol* for their vowels, but rather they relied on relative terms that compared vowel qualities in different contexts. This situation gave way to absolute vowel naming first in the Arabic tradition, likely because the small number of phonemic Arabic vowels—only three, compared to six or seven in Hebrew and Syriac—made the transition from two-way comparative terms to three absolute names fairly simple. Arabic grammarians implemented these vowel terms in the mid-eighth century at the latest, at a time when Syriac and Hebrew scribes were still transitioning from relative to absolute vowel pointing. With the completion of their absolute dot systems, Syriac and Hebrew linguists then began creating unique vowel names, but neither tradition had a full set of names until the late ninth or tenth century. While some of these new terms evolved from the

   https://doi.org/10.11647/OBP.0271.04

earlier relative terminology, some described the vowel dots themselves, and others were adapted from Arabic vowel names.

By examining the chronology of vowel naming in Arabic, Syriac, and Hebrew, it is possible to discern the original meaning of these names, as well as identify further points of contact between the three traditions. For the purposes of this discussion, most vowel names can be classified as one of two main types: graphemic and phonetic. Graphemic names are those which describe the form of a grapheme that represents a vowel in writing (e.g., *mpaggdɔnɔ, segol, zujj*), while phonetic names describe some aspect of the articulatory process required to produce a vowel (e.g., *ptɔḥɔ, ṣiryɔ, ḍamma*).

The conceptual relationship between the Arabic and Syriac phonological traditions is closely intertwined with the development of the Arabic vocalisation system, since the earliest Arabic vowel points—the red-dot system—are a direct import from the Syriac scribal tradition. However, Arabic scribes adopted these dots at the time when the Syriac vocalisation system was still relative and based on comparative diacritical points. Within this context, eighth-century Arabic grammarians developed two separate sets of vowel names: one that described the openness of the mouth during articulation (*fatḥ, ḍamm, kasr*), and another that corresponded to the 'above-and-below' scales of height and backness (*naṣb, rafʿ, khafḍ*). The first set has rough equivalents in both the early Syriac and Masoretic vowel terminology. Meanwhile, the second set evolved from the pre-Sībawayhan tradition of *naṣb* and *ʾimāla* in Qurʾānic recitation, and it later became the source of a few Syriac vowel names (*zqɔpɔ, massaqɔ*) after Syrian scribes completed their own absolute pointing system. In addition to these six names for their three cardinal vowels, some Arabic scholars refined their naming system by adding additional terms for vowels which appear only in specific morphosyntactic contexts.

Besides the few later Arabic calques, most of the vowel names in the Syriac tradition evolved as extensions of the 'wide-and-narrow' relative comparisons of earlier Syriac grammar. One exception is actually the earliest absolute name in Syriac, *mpaggdɔnɔ* 'bridling', which appears in Jacob of Edessa's work at the end of the seventh century. The earliest attested Syriac sources with semblances of absolute vowel naming systems are Dawid bar Pawlos' (fl. c. 770–800) *scholion* on *bgdkt* letters and Ḥunayn ibn Isḥāq's (d. 873) version of *Ktɔbɔ d-Shmɔhe Dɔmyɔye* (*The Book of Similar Words*), although they still only contain partial sets of terms. Other terms appear in the *mashlmɔnutɔ* material of the codex BL Add. 12138, which was completed in 899 but certainly copies from earlier sources. Additional names occur in the Syriac lexica of ʿĪsā ibn ʿAlī (d. c. 900) and Ḥasan bar Bahlul (fl. 942–968), both of whom recorded and transmitted the work of scholars like Ḥunayn, who participated in the Syriac and Arabic translation movements. However, they too lacked names for every discrete Syriac vowel, and it was not until the eleventh-century grammars of Elias of Nisibis (d. 1046) and Elias of Ṭirhan (d. 1049) that complete sets of absolute Syriac vowel names appeared. Even then, the names of the two Eliases differ from one another.

Like in Syriac, the first absolute names in the Hebrew tradition
were based on earlier relative phonology, with *pɔtaḥ* 'opening'
and *qɔmeṣ* 'closing' solidifying as the absolute names for /a/ and
/ɔ/. Then, during the ninth and tenth centuries, four different
conventions emerged that Hebrew linguists used to supplement
pɔtaḥ and *qɔmeṣ*: expansion of the earlier relative terminology,
descriptions of graphemes that represented vowels, descriptions
of articulatory processes, and terminology borrowed from the Arabic grammatical tradition. These conventions overlapped and
mixed with each other, and all four are still present in the modern
names for the Hebrew vowels. Hebrew scholars also took the
unique step of organising their vowels into phonetic groups located along the earlier *milleʿel-milleraʿ* scale, a practice which
spans Masoretic sources in both Hebrew and Judaeo-Arabic and
features in Abū al-Faraj's (d. c. 1050) *Hidāya al-Qārī* (*The Guide
for the Reader*).

1.0. Vowel Names in the Arabic Tradition

The Syriac scribal and grammatical traditions influenced Arabic
linguistics from the earliest period of Qurʾānic vocalisation in the
late seventh and early eighth centuries. While this influence directly affected the introduction of diacritic and vowel points to
the Arabic script, it did not introduce absolute vowel names into
Arabic linguistic vocabulary. Instead, Arabic grammarians developed absolute vowel names at a time when Syriac grammarians
were still using a relative vocalisation system, and most absolute
Syriac vowel names are unattested until at least half a century

after they first appear in the Arabic tradition. That said, the Arabic set of *fatḥa* (/a/), *ḍamma* (/u/), and *kasra* (/i/) (henceforth: 'non-ʾiʿrābī set') is conceptually similar to earlier Syriac descriptions of "wide-and-narrow" vowels. These Arabic names are attested in the earliest sources, and likely saw use in Qurʾānic pedagogy before the first Arabic grammarians put pen to parchment. Additionally, the meanings of the set of *naṣb* (/a/), *rafʿ* (/u/), and *khafḍ* (/i/) (henceforth: 'ʾiʿrābī set') are based on the same principle of phonetic 'height' that determined the position of the diacritic dots and the two-way comparisons of *ʾimāla* and *naṣb*. These terms were names both for vowel phonemes and for the grammatical cases that those phonemes represent from as early as the first half of the eighth century.

In addition to terms for the cardinal vowels, some Arabic grammarians refined their naming system by introducing terminology for vowels produced in specific morphosyntactic contexts. These refinements include allophones of the cardinal vowels as well as different names related to syllable position and length. Our most concise source for this terminology is a list in the encyclopaedia *Mafātīḥ al-ʿUlūm* (*The Keys to the Sciences*) by Muḥammad ibn Aḥmad al-Khwārizmī (d. 997). Many of the terms in this list can be linked to passages in *Kitāb al-ʿAyn* and *Kitāb Sībawayh*, but later sources like Ibn Jinnī's (d. 1002) *Sirr Ṣināʿa al-Iʿrāb* further clarify their usage, and it seems that al-Khwārizmī's vowel 'system' is somewhat idiosyncratic to him.

1.1. Names for Cardinal Vowels

The modern names for the three cardinal Arabic vowels are the
non-ʾiʿrābī set of *fatḥ* 'opening', *kasr* 'breaking', and *ḍamm* 'bring-
ing/pressing together', and all three are attested from the mid-
eighth century onwards (Versteegh 1993, 18, 125–30; Talmon
1997, 194–97).[1] They are phonetic names, each describing a
physical process required to articulate a vowel. *Fatḥ* is the 'opening' of the mouth when saying /a/ while *ḍamm* is the 'pressing-
together' of the lips when saying /u/. The phonetic meaning of
kasr is less certain, and depends on which portion of the vocal
tract it originally meant to describe. For example, in his version
of the story of Abū al-Aswad (see above, chapter 3, §2.1), al-Dānī
(d. 1053) connects the vowels to the movement of the 'lips'
(*shafatān*) (al-Dānī 1960, 2b–3a). By contrast, an earlier record
of the story in Abū al-Ṭayyib's (d. 962) *Marātib al-Naḥwiyyīn* (*The
Ranks of Grammarians*) instructs that the vowels depend on the
movement of the 'mouth' (*fam*). If *kasra* applies to the whole
mouth, then it may describe the 'breaking' of the vocal tract into
two sections by the raising of the tongue towards the palate (al-
Nassir 1993, 33; Versteegh 2011).[2] Alternatively, if *kasr* is derived from the movement of the lips, then it presents a logical
contrast as an antonym of *ḍamm*: 'breaking [apart]' as opposed
to 'pressing together'.

---

[1] They usually appear as *fatḥa*, *kasra*, and *ḍamma* when indicating the
vocalisation sign rather than describing the mode of articulation.

[2] Versteegh's translation of *wa-ʾidha kasartu famī* as 'when [you see me]
folding my mouth', while lexically possible, does not seem plausible to
me.

These names are based on an easily observable physical phenomenon and double as instructions for how a speaker should move their lips to properly articulate a vowel. They also have notable parallels in Syriac and Hebrew. *Fatḥ* (/a/) reflects the same thinking as Jacob of Eddessa's *pte* 'wide' descriptor for relatively-open vowels, while *ḍamm* (/u/) corresponds to his idea of *qaṭṭin* 'narrow' for relatively-closed vowels. Moreover, *fatḥ* is cognate with the *ptiḥtɔ* descriptor for /a/ and the open pronunciations of the *matres lectionis* letters *waw* and *yod* in Dawid bar Pawlos' *scholion* on *bgdkt* letters (see above, chapter 3, §1.1), as well as the common Syriac vowel name *ptɔḥɔ*. The same can be said for *pɔtaḥ* 'opening', the early Masoretic term for relatively-open vowels and later the name for /a/ alone. *Ḍamm* corresponds lexically to several Syriac vowel names, including *ḥbɔṣɔ* (/i/, /u/), *zribɔ* (/e/), *rbɔṣɔ* (/e/), and *ʿṣɔṣɔ* (/u/), all of which indicate some idea of 'compressing' or 'constraining' in the articulation of relatively closed vowels. The same applies to the Masoretic *qɔmeṣ* (/ɔ/), which means 'closing' in reference to the mouth and indicated relatively-closed vowels before stabilising as the Tiberian name for /ɔ/. Then *kasr* may be the source of *ṣere* 'crack, cracking', the Tiberian name for /e/, but it does not seem to have a Syriac parallel. Versteegh has argued that it is related to *ḥbɔṣɔ* 'squeezing, pressing together' (Versteegh 1993, 30; see also Versteegh 2011), but this is not a common definition for *kasr*, and probably not a calque (see Kazimirski 1860, 895–97; Lane 1863, 2610–12; Wehr 1993, 967–68). All of these connections rely on the same principles of opening and closing the mouth that were current in the relative vocalisation systems of the seventh and eighth centuries, and there is no clear way to determine which ones are calques and which are independent derivations based on similar phonological thinking.[3]

As for the *ʾiʿrābī* set, they are best known as the names for the noun cases and verbal moods in Classical Arabic. *Naṣb* 'standing upright' is the name for the accusative case, *rafʿ* 'rising' is the nominative case, and *khafḍ* 'lowering' is well-known as the genitive case in the Kufan grammatical school. Additionally, *jarr* 'dragging, drawing, pulling' is the name for the genitive case in the Basran school (Kinberg 1987, 15; al-Zajjājī 1959, 93; Versteegh 1993, 18). However, as we have seen, prior to Sībawayh's *Kitāb*, these words served interchangeably as both case names and the names for the vowels that most often marked those cases (Talmon 2000, 250). Versteegh identifies a Qurʾānic *tafsīr* by Muḥammad al-Sāʾib ibn al-Kalbī (d. 763) as one of the earliest sources that employs the *ʾiʿrābī* set as vowel names. In it, he uses *fatḥ* and *naṣb* for /a/; *ḍamm* and *rafʿ* for /u/; and *kasr*, *khafḍ*, and *jarr* for /i/; even applying the *ʾiʿrābī* names to internal vowels with no grammatical import (Versteegh 1993, 125–30). The lexical sections of *Kitāb al-ʿAyn* contain further examples of this interchangeability, suggesting it was common in the 'Old Iraqi' school of Arabic grammar some decades before al-Khalīl and Sībawayh (Talmon 1996, 288; 1997, 194–97; 2000; 2003, 159, 235–40). Due to this lack of distinction between these two sets of terms, Versteegh (1993, 126) concludes that "the later terms for the case endings were once part of a system to indicate vowels."

---

[3] Though note Merx (1889, 154), among others, who holds that the Syriac names are the sources of the Arabic names.

The prevailing notion as to the origin of the *ʾiʿrābī* set is that they are calques from Syriac vowel names, possibly also affected by the influence of Greek grammar (Revell 1975, 181; Versteegh 1993, 26–32, 127–29; Talmon 1996, 290–91; 2000, 248–50; Versteegh 2011). Specifically, the thinking goes that *naṣb* and *khafḍ* are calques of the Syriac vowel names *zqɔpɔ* 'standing upright' and *rbɔṣɔ* 'compressing' (although Versteegh and Revell interpret it as 'lowering'). Versteegh and Revell both propose that early Arabic linguists adopted these Syriac names at the same time that they adapted the Syriac diacritical dots to Arabic (Revell 1975, 181 n. 2; Versteegh 1993, 31–32). Talmon generally concurs, but also emphasises that the reconstruction of this borrowing relies on the list of vowel names that Bar Hebraeus (d. 1286) attributes to Jacob of Edessa (d. 708) (see Merx 1889, 50), even though most Syriac vowel names are not actually attested before Ḥunayn ibn Isḥāq's (d. 873) version of the *Ktɔbɔ d-Shmɔhe Dɔmyɔye* (*The Book of Similar Words*) (Talmon 2008, 165; see Hoffmann 1880, 2–49). Meanwhile, the *ʾiʿrābī* names are attested from no later than approximately 750, and *naṣb* may have described relatively-backed allophones of *ʾalif* even earlier.

I previously argued that since *zqɔpɔ* was unattested prior to Ḥunayn Ibn Isḥāq, and since *rbɔṣɔ*, *ḥbɔṣɔ*, and *ṣɔṣɔ* were unattested prior to the eleventh-century Syriac grammars, none of them could be sources of the Arabic vowel names (Posegay 2020, 202–6). However, several of the Syriac terms are actually attested earlier, some even before Ḥunayn ibn Isḥāq's work. Most notable for the discussion of Arabic vowel names is the occurrence of *zqiptɔ* 'stood upright', *ḥbiṣtɔ* 'pressed', and *ṣiṣtɔ* 'constrained' to

describe vowel qualities in the *scholion* on *bgdkt* letters by Dawid
bar Pawlos (fl. c. 770–800).[4] Dawid was a contemporary of
Sībawayh, about 30 years younger than al-Khalīl, and his career
pushes *zqiptɔ* much closer to the presumed introduction of *naṣb*
as a vowel name in first half of the eighth century. Despite this,
the evidence from *Kitāb al-ʿAyn* and other sources of vowel naming in the Old Iraqi school still suggest that the *ʾiʿrābī* names predate Dawid's *zqiptɔ* by several decades at least, and perhaps as
much as 75 years. The fact remains that chronologically, the closest descriptions of Syriac vowels to the introduction of the Arabic
dots are those in Jacob of Edessa's writings, and even at the end
of the seventh century, he describes the Syriac relative vocalisation system without any hint of the later absolute names. Unless
additional early Syriac sources emerge, it remains more likely
that the Arabic *ʾiʿrābī* names are the sources of later Syriac vowel
names, rather than the converse. This chronology correlates with
the adoption of the red-dot absolute vocalisation system in Arabic, which preceded the final developments of absolute pointing
in both Syriac and Hebrew.

Nevertheless, as Revell and Versteegh note, the principles
of phonetic height that determined the placement of the Arabic
diacritic and vowel points do seem to originate with the high and
low homograph comparisons of seventh-century Syriac. It was
those same principles that likely led to the first binary usage of
naṣb 'standing upright' and *ʾimāla* 'bending down' to designate
relatively backed or fronted allophones of /a/ and /ā/ in Arabic

---

[4] MS Mardin, ZFRN 192 f. 199r, lines 11–18 and f. 200r, line 5; MS
Jerusalem, SMMJ f. 166r, line 10. See Farina (2021).

(see above, chapter 3, §2.2). These two terms would have been necessary to teach the recitation of variant vowel qualities that the Arabic script had no way of recording. As the red-dot system spread, *naṣb* became the absolute name for /a/, while the term *tafkhīm* 'thickening' became the standard word for backed allophones, like /o/ in *ṣalāt* 'prayer' and /ɑ/ after *mustaʿliya* letters.[5]

ʾImāla remained in use to indicate fronted allophones like /e/, but it was also associated with the concept of *khafḍ*. This likely resulted in part from grammarians perceiving letters produced in front of the velum as *munkhafiḍa* 'lowered' in contrast to the elevated *mustaʿliya* letters. As we have seen, Ibn Jinnī attests to this contrast in his division of the alphabet (Kinberg 1987, 13; Ibn Jinnī 1993, 4, 62; al-Nassir 1993, 51). When the grammarian Abū al-Qāsim al-Zajjājī (d. 948/949) explains the *khafḍ* case in his *al-Īḍāḥ fī ʿIlal al-Naḥw* (*The Clarification of the Reasons of Grammar*), he says: "And regarding the one called *khafḍ* among the Kufans, they explained it in the same manner as the explanation of *rafʿ* and *naṣb*, for they said [it was] due to the lowering of the lower jaw during its articulation, and its bending toward one of two directions (ومن سماه منهم من الكوفيين خفضاً، فإنهم فسروه نحو تفسير الرفع والنصب فقالوا لانخفاض الحنك الأسفل عند النطق به، وميله إلى إحدى الجهتين)" (al-Zajjājī 1959, 93; see Kinberg 1987, 15). Al-Zajjājī

---

[5] *Fukhkhāma* and the phrase *ʾalif mufakhkhama* appear in the lexical material in *Kitāb al-ʿAyn*, likely stretching back to the period of the Old Iraqi school. This 'thickening' of *ʾalif* is presented as contrasting *ʾimāla* and resembling *wāw* (Makhzumi 1985, III:317; IV:103, 281; Talmon 1997, 136, 141). Note that Sībawayh does not use *tafkhīm* for this purpose, and only applies it to the /ō/ allophone of *ʾalif* in *ṣalāt*, *zakāt*, and *ḥayāt* (Sībawayh 1986, IV:432).

uses the word *mayl* 'bending, inclination' to explain the directionality of *khafḍ*'s articulation, taking the same root as *ʾimāla* to indicate the fronted articulation point and low tongue position of
the vowel /i/. There is also one passage in the lexical sections of
Kitāb al-ʿAyn that presents *munkhafiḍ* 'lowering, lowered' and
māʾil 'bending, inclining' as synonyms when describing the position of a relaxed shoulder, both as opposed to a raised shoulder,
which is called *muntaṣib* 'standing upright' (Makhzumi 1985,
IV:79; Talmon 1997, 139).

This continued association of the front of the mouth with a
comparatively 'low' position led to the addition of *khafḍ* 'lowering' as a name for /i/. Along with *naṣb* for /a/, the only remaining
cardinal vowel was /u/, which was called *rafʿ* 'rising'. This 'rising'
reflects the comparatively-backed position of the velar vowel
/u/, which was 'raised up' with the tongue retracted near the
position of the *mustaʿliya* letters. The lexical material in *al-ʿAyn*
supports this interpretation while defining *tafkhīm*, where it
states: "The *tafkhīm* of speech is magnifying it; *rafʿ* in speech is
tafkhīm; and *ʾalif mufakhkham* resembles *wāw* (.وتفخيم الكلام تعظيمه)
وألف مفخم يضارع الواو .والرفع في الكلام تفخيم)" (Makhzumi 1985,
IV:281; Talmon 1997, 141). Furthermore, the entry on *naṣb* says:
"*Naṣb* is your *rafʿ* [raising] of something, you setting it upright,
standing straight up (والنَصْب—رَفعُك شيئاً تَنصِبُه قائماً منتصباً)" (Makhzumi 1985, VII:136). Al-Azharī's (d. 980) later addition to this
section is similar, as he says: "The *manṣūb* word, its sound is
yurfaʿ [raised up] toward the upper palate (الكلمة المنصوبة يُرفَع
صوتُها الى الغار الأعلى)" (Makhzumi 1985, VII:136). *Al-ʿAyn* further
suggests that *rafʿ* was the natural antonym for *khafḍ*, as the *rafʿ*

entry reads: "*Rafʿ* is the opposite of *khafḍ* (الرفع نقيض الخفض)" (Ma-khzumi 1985, II:125; Talmon 1997, 198). The entry for *khafḍ* then states: "*Khafḍ* is the opposite of *rafʿ* (الخفض نقيض الرفع)" (Ma-khzumi 1985, IV:178). It seems that when Arabic phonologists implemented the absolute *ʾiʿrābī* vowel vowels, they added *khafḍ* and *rafʿ* as a natural binary pair to the pre-existing pair of *naṣb* and *ʾimāla*.

Besides this phonetic meaning, *rafʿ* was also linked to *naṣb* in the grammatical teaching of the Old Iraqi school, where it formed an early distinction between perfect and imperfect verbs in the *ʾiʿrāb* system. Again in the *naṣb* entry of *Kitāb al-ʿAyn*, the text reads: "*Naṣb* is opposed to *rafʿ* in *ʾiʿrāb* (النَصْب ضد الرفع في الإعراب)" (Makhzumi 1985, VII:135), apparently referring to an Old Iraqi method of distinguishing verbal aspects. Talmon notes that despite Sībawayh's instructions to separate the *ʾiʿrābī* and non-*ʾiʿrābī* vowel sets, he also applies the term *naṣb* to the non-inflectional /a/ ending of a few perfect verbs, likely in contrast to imperfect verbs which end in /u/. He thus argues that in this case, Sībawayh "seems to follow an early theorem that considers the *a* vs. *u* contrast in the perfect vs. imperfect verbs a significant *ʾiʿrābī* feature" (Talmon 2003, 238).

In sum, the *ʾiʿrābī* set of vowel names reflects the same prin-ciple of phonetic height that informed the placement of the Syr-iac and Arabic diacritic dots, the Tiberian vocalisation points, and the red-dot vowel system. *Naṣb* 'standing upright' meaning /a/ is a remnant of an earlier system for describing allophones of *ʾalif*, representing relatively 'high' backed vowel qualities in com-parison to the relatively fronted 'low' qualities of *ʾimāla* 'bending down'. The perception among Arabic grammarians of the front of the mouth as low led to the classification of *munkhafiḍ* conso-nants and the use of *khafḍ* 'lowering' as a name for the vowel /i/. They also introduced *rafʿ* 'rising', the logical opposite of *khafḍ*, as a name for /u/, indicating its raised articulation at the top of the mouth near the place of the *mustaʿliya* letters.

Lastly, rather than *khafḍ*, the Basran grammatical school referred to both /i/ and the genitive case as *jarr* 'dragging, draw-ing, pulling'. This term is attested in the same early sources as the other three *ʾiʿrābī* names (e.g., Ibn al-Kalbī's *tafsīr* and *Kitāb al-ʿAyn*'s lexicon), and it can be interpreted as a phonetic name in contrast to *ḍamm* 'pressing together', describing the action of 'pulling' or 'drawing' back the lips to pronounce /i/. However, it may be more likely that the original meaning referred to the ex-tension ('drawing out') of a word by adding /i/ to facilitate the pronunciation of an unvocalised consonant. Talmon argues that this usage of *jarr* is derived from the West Syriac cognate and accent name *gᵊrōrᵊ* (Talmon 1996, 290–91; 2000, 250; 2008, 174), which also means 'drawing' or 'pulling,' and informs a reader to "draw out or prolong in recitation, and hence to stress, the syllable to which it is attached" (Segal 1953, 123). For this explanation, he cites al-Khwārizmī's (d. 997) example of *jarr* in *Mafātīḥ al-ʿUlūm* (*The Keys to the Sciences*), which refers to the /i/

vowel added to the end of a jussive verb to connect it to a subsequent *'alif waṣl* (al-Khwārizmī 1968, 45, lines 7–9; Fischer 1985, 99).[6]

To this evidence we may add a statement from al-Zajjājī, who writes: "As for *jarr*, it is only called that because the meaning of *jarr* is *iḍāfa* [addition]; and that is, the *jārra* letters pull what precedes them, connecting it to what follows them, as you say 'I passed *bi-zayd*[in],' for the *bā'* has connected your passing to Zayd

(وأما الجر، فإنما سمي بذلك لان معنى الجر الإضافة؛ وذلك ان الحروف الجارة تجر ما قبلها فتوصله إلى ما بعدها كقولك مررت بزيد، فالباء أوصلت مرورك إلى زيد)" (al-Zajjājī 1959, 93). For al-Zajjājī here, *jarr* is the /i/ added to the preposition *b-* 'by, with' to connect it to the noun Zayd. In that sense, Talmon's interpretation of the term's meaning seems correct. Moreover, unlike the other Syriac terms that have been proposed as sources for the *'iʿrābī* names, *gɔrorɔ* is actually attested prior to the time of the Old Iraqi school in the accent list attributed to Thomas the Deacon (fl. c. 600) (Martin 1869, ܟ, line 17; see also, Phillips 1869, 77; Segal 1953, 120).

In conclusion, both the *'iʿrābī* (*naṣb, khafḍ, rafʿ, jarr*) and non-*'iʿrābī* (*fatḥ, kasr, ḍamm*) sets of vowel names are attested in the earliest eighth-century Arabic grammatical sources. In this early period, the two sets were used interchangeably, representing both final 'inflectional' vowels and internal vowel phonemes. The non-*'iʿrābī* set shares its meanings with vowel names in both

---

[6] Al-Khwārizmī attributes his list of vowel terms to al-Khalīl, and Talmon treats it as genuinely Khalīlian, but this is not certain (Talmon 2003, 263–65). The vowel list in *Mafātīḥ al-ʿUlūm* is discussed below.

Syriac and Hebrew, but it is not clear whether one tradition borrowed from the others or vice versa. It is equally possible that
'open-and-closed' phonetic naming was a kind of areal feature in
early Islamicate Semitic phonology, and Arabic linguists derived
their vowel names without directly calquing Syriac terminology.
Meanwhile, the *ʾiʿrābī* set (except *jarr*) emerged out of the widespread perception of 'high-and-low' phonology that also permeated the Syriac and Hebrew relative vocalisation systems. These
explanations suffice for the names of the three cardinal vowels in
Arabic, but Arabic grammarians also refined their phonological
vocabulary by creating terms for vocalic allophones and vowels
in specific morphosyntactic positions.

1.2. Refining the Arabic System: Al-Khwārizmī and the Keys to the Sciences

Arabic grammarians and Qurʾān reciters developed numerous
technical terms for addressing the allophonic realisations of vowels in certain contexts, and we have already seen a bit of this
terminology in the analyses of *ʾimāla* and *tafkhīm* (see above,
chapter 3, §2.2). This section will discuss additional pertinent
vowel terminology through the lens of the chapters on grammar
in Muḥammad ibn Aḥmad al-Khwārizmī's (d. 997) encyclopaedia, *Mafātīḥ al-ʿUlūm* (*The Keys to the Sciences*) (see Bosworth
1963; Fischer 1985). Al-Khwārizmī claims to transmit two separate non-standard traditions of *ʾiʿrāb*, one from al-Khalīl ibn
Aḥmad (d. 786/791) and one from "the school of the philosophy
of the Greeks" (al-Khwārizmī 1968, 44–46). Both mention multiple vowel names besides those covered above. The division of the

text suggests that al-Khwārizmī perceived the *ʾiʿrāb* systems of al-Khalīl and the Greek philosophers as different from that of the majority of Arabic grammarians, who essentially followed the system laid out by Sībawayh (al-Khwārizmī 1968, 42–44).

We have already addressed the most likely source for al-Khwārizmī's Greek school—namely, the Arabic grammar of Ḥunayn ibn Isḥāq (see above, chapter 2, §3.3)—but his attribution of information to al-Khalīl is more problematic. First, while al-Khwārizmī was an accomplished encyclopaedist, he was not a grammarian, and several inconsistencies in the text of these chapters suggest he might have made some mistakes (e.g., Fischer 1985, 96, 99). His goal with *Mafātīḥ al-ʿUlūm* was to provide a useful reference book for tenth-century Islamicate scribes, and compiling a wide range of obscure (and perhaps dubious) linguistic terminology may have been preferable to only recording a few terms with well-known meanings. Second, as Wolfdietrich Fischer notes, in more than 550 quotations from the *Kitāb*, Sībawayh never cites al-Khalīl using al-Khwārizmī's terminology (Fischer 1985, 97; see Reuschel 1959). Sībawayh does not quote his teacher in any of his own chapters on phonetics (Troupeau 1958; 1976, 16–17; Versteegh 1993, 16), but many of al-Khwārizmī's 'Khalīlian' terms are not phonetic in nature, so the absence is still striking. Talmon does locate most of the Khalīlian terms in linguistic contexts in the lexical portions of *Kitāb al-ʿAyn*, but besides those names which are shared with the typical *ʾiʿrābī* system, their meanings do not closely match al-Khwārizmī's (Talmon 1997, 264).

Fischer (1985, 98) concludes that "we may regard them as al-Khalīl's true technical terms, until we get proof to the contrary," despite the fact that they suggest al-Khalīl's approach to grammar and *ʾiʿrāb* differed considerably from Sībawayh's (Fischer 1985, 98–101).[7] We know this is not the case (Versteegh 1993, 17; Talmon 2003, 279–80). Talmon is slightly more cautious, but still concludes that

> the list is a unique attempt, probably by al-Khalīl himself, to create a most accurate terminology of the vowel system. This set was probably neglected by the inventor himself, but was recorded by posterity as a curious attempt. It does not undermine the attribution to al-Khalīl of the vowel terminology and related terms, although it does not support it in any significant manner (Talmon 1997, 265).

The present study accepts that many of al-Khwārizmī's 'Khalīlian' terms are undoubtedly based on linguistic terminology from the eighth century, but it remains sceptical that *Mafātīḥ al-ʿUlūm* faithfully transmits their original meanings or that al-Khalīl himself actually employed them as a vowel-naming 'system'. The following discussion refers to them collectively as 'pseudo-Khalīlian'.

Al-Khwārizmī lists 21 items among the pseudo-Khalīllian terms in his encyclopaedia, 18 of which are names for vowels. Seven of these are the *ʾiʿrābī* and non-*ʾiʿrābī* names (see above, present chapter, §1.1), including *jarr*. He describes each of these

---

[7] Specifically, Fischer argues that these terms suggest al-Khalīl did not recognise Sībawayh's fundamental principle of *ʿamal* 'governance' in analysing *ʾiʿrāb*. On this concept, see Rybalkin (2011).

as having essentially the same function as they do in most grammatical texts, albeit with contextual restrictions (e.g., *raf‹* only applies to words with *tanwīn*) (Fischer 1985, 98–100; Talmon 1997, 264).[8] The other 11 have no parallels in the names for cardinal vowels. They are, in the order that they appear: *tawjīh*, *ḥashw*, *najr*, *ʾishmām*, *qaʿr*, *tafkhīm*, *ʾirsāl*, *taysīr*, *ʾiḏjāʿ*, *ʾimāla*, and *nabra* (al-Khwārizmī 1968, 44–46).

Al-Khwārizmī writes that *tawjīh* 'guidance, direction' is "what occurs at the beginnings of words, for example, the *ʿayn* in *ʿumar* and the *qāf* in *qutam* (ما وقع في صدور الكَلِم نحو عين عُمَر وقاف

قُتَم)" (al-Khwārizmī 1968, 44, lines 6–7). That is, *tawjīh* is /u/ that occurs in the first syllable of a word (Fischer 1985, 100). This term does not appear in *Kitāb al-ʿAyn*, but in the context of this list it belongs with *ḥashw* 'stuffing', a name for /u/ in an internal syllable of a noun (e.g., *rajul⁽ᵘⁿ⁾*), and *najr* 'natural form, condition' (Kazimirski 1860, 1202; Lane 1863, 2830), a name for /u/ in the final syllable of a noun (e.g., *al-jabalu*) (al-Khwārizmī 1968, 44, lines 7–8; see Versteegh 1993, 18).[9] Each of these three represents the same vowel in different syllabic positions, a distinction which has little importance in grammar (where *ḍamm* can cover all three), but which would have been useful in analysing poetic metre. Talmon notes that *ḥashw* can refer to any internal letter in *Kitāb al-ʿAyn* (Talmon 1997, 264), but it is also the prosodic term

---

[8] Three further terms are names for 'silence' or 'lack of vowel' (*jazm*, *taskīn*, *tawqīf*) (al-Khwārizmī 1968, 45, lines 9–11). They are related to the *ʾiʿrābī* and non-*ʾiʿrābī* sets of vowel names, but are not analysed here.

[9] Al-Khwārizmī specifies that *najr* does not apply to a word with *tanwīn*.

for a verse's internal feet, excepting the last foot of each hemistich (Abbas 2002, 48).[10] *Tawjīh* is also a technical term in poetry, where it indicates a verse that has two different meanings (Abbas 2002, 300). *Najr* is not a prosodic term, and in general it relates to carpentry, but its meaning of a 'natural form' may indicate the default function of /u/ as the marker of nouns in the nominative case. While it is not clear why al-Khwārizmī connects /u/ to these three terms in particular, it does seem that the tradition which he transmits is somehow derived from prosodic vocabulary. Given al-Khalīl's outsized influence on Arabic prosody (Frolov 2011; Sellheim 2012), al-Khwārizmī's attribution of these terms to him is unsurprising.

The next pseudo-Khalīlian term is *ʾishmām* 'giving a scent', which al-Khwārizmī says is "what occurs at the beginning of deficient words, for example, the *qāf* of *qīla* when it is given a hint of *ḍamma* (ما وقع في صدور الكَلِم المنقوصة نحو قاف قيل اذا أُشِمّ ضَمّةً)" (al-Khwārizmī 1968, 44, lines 10–11). This explanation describes the pronunciation of the long /ī/ in *qīla* 'it was said' as slightly rounded and backed (i.e., /ɨ/), approximating /u/ (i.e., *ḍamma*) (Alfozan 1989, 35; see also, 16, n. 49, no. 2). *ʾIshmām* appears in the lexical portions of *Kitāb al-ʿAyn*, where it indicates "pronunciation of a shade of a vowel," mainly /i/ with shades of /u/ (Makhzumi 1985, VI:224; VIII:13, 92; Talmon 1997, 141, 264). Sībawayh also defines it in his discussion of the endings of words in pausal form (see Hoberman 2011):

---

[10] Cf al-Dānī's (1960, 39, 53–54) usage of *ḥashw* when explaining Qurʾānic pointing.

وأما الإشمام فليس إليه سبيل، وإنما كان [ذا] في الرفع لأنَّ الضمة من الواو،
فأنت تقدر أن تضع لسانك في أيِّ موضع من الحروف شئتَ ثمّ تَضُمّ
شَفَتَيك، لأنَّ ضمَّك شفتيك كتحريكك بعض جسدك، وإشمامك في الرفع
للرُّؤْية وليس بصوتٍ للأُذُن.

As for *ʾishmām*, it is not towards a particular way, but rather it is in *rafʿ* because *ḍamma* is from *wāw*, so you are
able to put your tongue in whatever position of the letters
that you want, and then bring together your lips, since
your bringing together of your lips is like your imparting
movement to part of your body. Your *ʾishmām* in *rafʿ* is visual, not with any sound for the ears. (Sībawayh 1986,
IV:171)

Sībawayh's explanation emphasises that *ʾishmām* is a visual phenomenon that is only possible because *ḍamma* is articulated with
the same lip movement as *wāw*. As such, a speaker can use their
tongue to pronounce another letter at the end of a word in pause
while also pressing their lips together in the shape of *ḍamma*, but
not fully pronouncing /u/. The letter is thus given a 'scent' or
'hint' of *ḍamma*, while not actually being vocalised as such (Alfozan 1989, 16, n. 49, no. 4). This phenomenon contrasts al-
Khwārizmī's explanation, which refers to an internal vowel and
indicates an aural change.

Ibn Jinnī (d. 1002) also uses *ʾishmām* to describe blended
allophones, similar to al-Khwārizmī's mixed vowel. He connects
these allophones to the sense of smell, writing:

وأما الضمة المشوبة بالكسرة فنحو قولك في الإمالة: مررت بمذعور، وهذا
ابن بور، نَحوتَ العين والباء نحو كسرة الراء، فأشممتها شيأ من الكسرة.
وكما أن هذه الحركة قبل الواو ليست ضمة محضة، ولا كسرة مرسلة،
فكذلك الواو أيضاً بعدها هي مشوبة بروائح الياء، وهذا مذهب سيبويه، وهو
الصواب

> As for the *ḍamma* mixed with *kasra*, for example in *ʾimāla*
> as you say '*marrartu bi-madhʿūr^in*' and '*hādhā ibn būr^in*', you
> make the form of the *ḍamma* on the *ʿayn* and the *bāʾ* re-
> semble the *kasra* of the *rāʾ*, so you give it the scent of a bit
> of the *kasra*. Just as this vowel before this *wāw* is not a
> pure *ḍamma*, neither is it a slackened *kasra*, and likewise
> the *wāw* after it is mixed with the odours of *yāʾ*. This is the
> school of Sībawayh, and it is correct. (Ibn Jinnī 1993, 53)

Ibn Jinnī interprets the same example of the *ʾimāla* of /u/ (i.e.,
madhʿūr^in 'frightened') that Sībawayh used in the *Kitāb* (see above,
chapter 3, §2.2), and says that the blending of /u/ occurs when
'you give it the scent' (*ʾashmamtahā*) of /i/. The result is that the
long vowel of the *wāw* takes on *rawāʾiḥ* 'odours' of *yāʾ*, and its
quality is realised as /u/ with a hint of /i/ (i.e., a fronted rounded
vowel). Ibn Jinnī uses the same olfactory language to describe
other vowel blends (e.g., /a/ mixed with /u/ or /i/) (Ibn Jinnī
1993, 53–54), as well as the changing of a particular consonant
to approximate another consonant (e.g., *ṣād* like *zāy*) (Ibn Jinnī
1993, 51; see Alfozan 1989, 16, n. 49, no. 1).

Al-Khwārizmī also gives a second description of *ʾishmām*,
this time from the "school of the philosophers of the Greeks."[11]
According to them: "*Rawm* and *ʾishmām* are to the *ḥarakāt* as the
ḥarakāt are to the letters of lengthening and softness; I mean, *ʾalif*,
wāw, and *yāʾ* (الرَوم والإشمام نسبتهما الى هذه الحركات كنِسبة الحركات الى)
والياء (حروف المدّ واللين اعنى الألف والواو والياء)" (al-Khwārizmī 1968, 46, lines
8–10). In this 'Greek' analysis of vowels, the *ḥarakāt*—the 'short'
vowels—each have reduced quantity in comparison to the length
of the *matres lectionis*. Al-Khwārizmī suggests that by the same

---

[11] 'School' as in 'doctrine, methodology'. The Arabic word is *madhhab*.

reckoning, *rawm* and *ʾishmām* are each a portion of the quantity of a *ḥaraka*. This quantitative interpretation of *ʾishmām* seems to have nothing to do with the long blended *ʾishmām* vowel that he said is in *qīla*, but it does relate to Sībawayh's description of *ʾishmām*, by which a speaker articulates only the slightest amount of /u/ while stopping on a letter. Sībawayh also mentions *rawm* as a reduced vowel and another way that a word in pause can end:

وأما الذين راموا الحركة فإنّهم دعاهم إلى ذلك الحِرْصُ على أن يُخرجوها من حال ما لزمه إسكانٌ على كلِّ حال، وأن يُعْلِموا أنَّ حالها عندهم ليس كحال ما سَكَنَ على كلِّ حال. وذلك أراد الذين أشمّوا؛ إلّا أنَّ هؤلاء أشدُّ توكيداً.

As for those who desire [i.e., make *rawm*] the vowel, they are motivated by that desire to pronounce something when normally it must be silent, to make known that its condition for them is not like what was normally silent. That is also what those who did *ʾishmām* intended, except that they were more strongly restrained. (Sībawayh 1986, IV:168)

Sībawayh's *rawm* 'seeking, desiring' is similar to *ʾishmām*, in that it is a partial vowel pronounced instead of *sukūn* on a letter at the end of a word in pause, but it is stronger, in that it is not just a visual phenomenon. Instead, a speaker pronounces an ultra-short vowel, 'seeking' towards a complete *ḥaraka*, but only reaching a fraction of its length (Hoberman 2011). It is not limited to /u/, and can also occur as a shortened /a/ or /i/ at the end of a word that is *naṣb* 'accusative' or *jarr* 'genitive' (Sībawayh 1986, IV:171). This *rawm* is distinct from *ʾishmām* for Sībawayh, but al-Khwārizmī does not attempt to distinguish the two in the *ʾiʿrāb* of the Greeks, and he does not list *rawm* among the pseudo-Khalīlian vowel terms.

The next pseudo-Khalīlian term is *qaʿr* 'lowest depth, depression', "which occurs at the beginnings of words, like the *ḍād* of *ḍaraba* (ضَرَبَ ضاد نحو الكَلِم صدور في وقع ما)" (al-Khwārizmī 1968, 45, line 1). Like *naṣb* and *fatḥ*, *qaʿr* refers to the vowel /a/, although it only applies to the first syllable of a word. Like *tawjīh* and *ḥashw*, this feature may indicate that it was originally a term used in the analysis of prosodic metre. Its meaning is likely related to the association of /a/ with the articulation point of *hamza*, deep in the throat, and hence at the lowest depth of all the vowels (see Kinberg 1987 and above, chapter 3, §2.2). The term may also be connected to the anatomical description of the 'laryngeal prominence',[12] for which Ibn Sīnā (d. 1037) says: "its *taqʿīr* 'depressing, deepening' is inwards and backwards (إلى تقعيره خلف إلى و داخل)" (al-Tayyan and Mir Alam 1983, 64; see also, Lane 1863, 2546). Given that al-Khwārizmī's only example of *qaʿr* is a *fatḥa* on the *mustaʿliya* letter *ḍād*, he might also be alluding to a degree of velarisation in the articulation of /a/.

After *qaʿr* is *tafkhīm* 'thickening', a common term that appears as early as *Kitāb al-ʿAyn* to indicate the allophonic realisation of *fatḥa* as /ɔ/ or /o/, especially in contrast to *ʾimāla* (i.e., /e/) (al-Nassir 1993, 103–4; Talmon 1997, 264; see above, chapter 3, §2.2). It was certainly in use from the earliest stages of Arabic linguistics to describe variations in recitation that could not be marked by the vowel points, but there is no reason to associate it specifically with al-Khalīl. It is also lexically similar to

[12] The Adam's apple.

Jacob of Edessa's vowel descriptor ʿ*be* 'thick', which he applied to relatively-backed Syriac vowels like /ɔ/ and /o/ in the second half of the seventh century. That said, al-Khwārizmī does not demonstrate this usage of *tafkhīm*. Instead, he writes: "*Al-Tafkhīm* is what occurs in the middles of words on *ʾalif* with *hamza*, for example, *saʾala* (سأل نحو المهزومة الالفات على الكَلِم أواسط في وقع ما) (al-Khwārizmī 1968, 45, lines 1–2). The vowel on the *hamza* in *saʾala* is a regular *fatḥa* (/a/),[13] so it is not clear what distinction al-Khwārizmī is trying to make. He may mean a vernacular pronunciation of the medial *hamza* in which long /ā/ replaces the glottal stop (*sāla* instead of *saʾala*). This specific usage of *tafkhīm* as the vowel of a medial hamza does not occur in *Kitāb al-ʿAyn*.

The next pseudo-Khalīlian vowel is *ʾirsāl* 'unbinding, easing, slackening', which al-Khwārizmī says is "what occurs at the ends [of words] on *ʾalif* with *hamza*, for example, the *ʾalif* of *qirʾa* (قراة الف نحو المهموزة الالفات على اعجازها في وقع ما)" (al-Khwārizmī 1968, 45, lines 2–3).[14] This vowel, too, is /a/, corresponding to the *fatḥa* before *tāʾ marbūṭa*, and again it seems that al-Khwārizmī may be alluding to a vernacular pronunciation in which the glottal stop is lost (thus *qirā* or the like). Talmon reports that in *Kitāb al-ʿAyn*, *ʾirsāl* denotes short /a/ in contrast to the lengthening of *madd*, but his only example states that for the *yāʾ* (i.e., the *ʾalif*

---

[13] Or a *hamza bayna bayna*; see above, chapter 2, §2.2.

[14] The reading of *qirʾa* 'endemic disease' is based on the orthography as given by Van Vloten, which is قراه or قرأة (al-Khwārizmī 1968, 45, n. G). Talmon (1997, 264) suggests that this word should instead be read *qaraʾ(a)*. It may also be a defective spelling of *qirāʾa* 'reading, recitation'.

maqṣūra) at the end of the word *al-marʿizzā* 'fine-haired' (المَرْعِزّى),
"they hang the *yāʾ* as *mursila* [slackened] (عَلّقوا الياء مرسلة)" (Makhzumi 1985, II:334; Talmon 1997, 264). This line corresponds
with al-Khwārizmī's definition of *ʾimāla* 'bending down, inclination', which reads: "*ʾImāla* is what occurs on the letters before
slackened *yāʾ*s, for example, *ʿĪsā* and *Mūsā*; and *tafkhīm* is opposed to it (ما وقع على الحروف التي قبل الياءات المرسلة نحو عيسى وموسى
وضِدّها التفخيم)" (al-Khwārizmī 1968, 45, line 12, to 46, line 1).
Here he does recognise that *tafkhīm* is opposed to *ʾimāla*, and he
identifies the "slackened *yāʾ*s" of *ʿĪsā* and *Mūsā* (pronounced *ʿĪsē*
and *Mūsē*) as indicators of the /e/ allophone of *ʾalif*.

The concept of *ʾirsāl* thus seems to indicate two related phenomena: the long vowel that results from the 'slackening' of a
glottal stop in the final syllable of words like *qirʾa*,[15] and the long
ʾimāla vowel represented by 'slackened' *ʾalif*s that hang below the
line as *ʾalif maqṣūra*. However, Ibn Jinnī also uses *mursila* to designate a type of *kasra* that is *not* blended with /u/. Writing again
regarding the *wāw* of *madhʿūr*, he says: "Just as the vowel before
this *wāw* is not a pure *ḍamma*, neither is it a slackened *kasra* (وكما
أن هذه الحركة قبل هذه الواو ليست ضمة محضة، ولا كسرة مرسلة)" (Ibn Jinnī
1993, 53). This description may be a reference to *ʾimāla* (and /e/)
as a type of *kasra* blended with *fatḥa* instead of *ḍamma*.

Taysīr 'facilitation, simplification, making easy' is one of
the few pseudo-Khalīlian terms that does not appear at all in
Kitāb al-ʿAyn, though Talmon (1997, 264) suggests it comes from
the vocabulary of Qurʾānic recitation. Al-Khwārizmī says that "it

---

[15] Perhaps notably, if pronounced without the glottal stop, then the long
/ā/ in *qirā* could also undergo *ʾimāla*.

is the *ʾalifs* which are removable from the ends of words, like the saying of God most high, *fa-aḍallūnā al-sabīlā* [Q. 33.67] (هي -al) "(الالفات المستخرجة من اعجاز الكلم نحو قول الله تعالى فَأَضَلُّونا السَّبِيلا) Khwārizmī 1968, 45, lines 3–5). He is referring to the *ʾalif* at the end of *al-sabīlā* 'the path', which is a *mater lectionis* representing the /a/ of the accusative case ending. Typically, a *fatḥa* alone marks the accusative, so this orthography is extremely irregular. This verse is the only instance in the Qurʾān where the case ending of *al-sabīl* is written *plene*. Al-Khwārizmī apparently considers this *ʾalif* 'removable' (*mustakhraja*); it could be deleted without changing the meaning of the verse. Exactly how this property relates to *taysīr* is not clear, but perhaps al-Khwārizmī means that it 'facilitates' the reading of the final /a/ (notably at the end of the verse), or that the removal of this *ʾalif* would 'simplify' the orthography.

Al-Khwārizmī lists *ʾiḍjāʿ* 'laying something down, lowering something' as the name for /i/ in a medial syllable, giving the example of the *bāʾ* in *ʾibil* 'camels' (al-Khwārizmī 1968, 45, line 7). Talmon notes one line from *Kitāb al-ʿAyn*'s entry on the root *ḍjʿ*, which reads: "*ʾiḍjāʿ* is in the rhymes which you make *ʾimāla* (والإضجاع في القوافي أن تُميلها)" (Makhzumi 1985, I:212; Talmon 1997, 264), which seems to indicate that *ʾiḍjāʿ* has a similar quality to the approximate /e/ of *ʾimāla*. It also suggests that the term's origin is in the technical vocabulary of prosody, which is appropriate given al-Khwārizmī's attribution of it to al-Khalīl and his note that it only occurs in specific syllables.[16] *ʾIḍjāʿ* appears

---

[16] See *tawjīh* discussion above and Fischer (1985, 100).

among the other terms for /i/ in the pseudo-Khalīlian list (including *kasr*, *khafḍ*, and *jarr*), and Lane (1863, 1769) has already observed that its meaning relates to the phonetic 'inclination' and 'lowering' of *ʾimāla* and *khafḍ*. This connection tracks with the idea of 'bending down' towards the front of the mouth as a phonetic feature of /i/ and /e/.

The last pseudo-Khalīlian term is *nabra* 'rising outward, raising the voice, swelling', which al-Khwārizmī says is "the *hamza* that occurs at the ends of verbs and nouns, like *sabaʾ*, *qaraʾa*, and *malaʾ* (الهمزة التي تقع في أواخر الأفعال والاسماء نحو سبأ وقرأ وملأ)" (al-Khwārizmī 1968, 46, lines 1–2). *Nabra* does mean *hamza* at least once in the lexical portion of *Kitāb al-ʿAyn*, and Talmon suspects that it comes from a non-technical usage (Talmon 1997, 264; see also, Makhzumi 1985, VIII:269), perhaps related to *hamza* 'rising outward' from the lowest articulation point in the throat or chest (Sībawayh 1986, IV:101, 176, 433; Ibn Jinnī 1993, 7, 43). Al-Khwārizmī may be stressing that a speaker raises the intensity of the voice to articulate full glottal stops for the *hamzas* of *sabaʾ* 'Sheba', *qaraʾa* 'he read', and *malaʾ* 'assembly',[17] rather than eliding them into a vernacular pronunciation with long final /ā/.

Al-Khwārizmī's definitions and evidence from other Arabic linguistic texts suggest that the vowel names which he attributes to al-Khalīl come from a variety of disparate sources. Besides the seven *ʾiʿrābī* and non-*ʾiʿrābī* names—all of which likely predate al-Khalīl—the other 11 pseudo-Khalīlian terms are a mixture of

---

[17] The three examples are unvocalised in Van Vloten's edition.

items from prosody (*tawjīh, ḥashw,* perhaps *najr* and *ʾidjāʿ*), phonology (*ʾishmām, tafkhīm, ʾimāla,* perhaps *nabra*), and Qurʾānic
recitation (*taysīr,* perhaps *ʾirsāl*). It might be correct to connect a
few of the prosodic terms to al-Khalīl, but even then, many of al-
Khwārizmī's definitions do not match the usage of these words in
other contexts. Fischer (1985, 100) remarks that "undoubtedly,
the list of technical terms attributed al-Khalīl is very incomplete,
and does not allow one to conclude a consistent concept of his
grammatical ideas from it." However, it seems that this chapter
is merely a collection of miscellaneous words that al-Khwārizmī
recognised as related to grammatical inflection or other spoken
phenomena, the technical nuances of which he did not always
understand. As such, there is no grammatical system to discern,
save perhaps one that al-Khwārizmī himself construed to supplement the more mainstream *ʾiʿrāb* analysis in his preceding chapter. This 'system' cannot be linked to al-Khalīl with any degree of
confidence. Nevertheless, many of the vowel names given in
Mafātīḥ al-ʿUlūm, especially the ones found in other philological
sources (e.g., *rawm, ʾishmām, tafkhīm, ʾimāla, ʾirsāl, ʾidjāʿ*), represent genuine innovations to describe the phonology of non-cardinal vowels, whether for linguistic analysis, prosody, or Qurʾānic
recitation.

2.0. Vowel Names in the Syriac Tradition

In the third chapter of the most recent edition of *Robinson's Paradigms,* J. F. Coakley records the Syriac vowel names *zqɔpɔ* (/ɔ/),
ptɔḥɔ (/a/), *rbɔṣɔ* (/e/), *ḥbɔṣɔ* (/i/), and *ʿṣɔṣɔ* (/u/) (Robinson and
Coakley 2013, 13, n. 5; see also, Nöldeke 1904, §9). These names

are based on the thirteenth-century terminology of Bar Hebraeus, and some scholars have suggested that they are the sources of Arabic vowel terminology (Hoffmann 1880, XV–XVI; Merx 1889, 50; Versteegh 1993, 29–31). However, as we have seen, the earliest Syriac grammatical tradition did not have specific names for each vowel, instead describing them in terms of relative openness and backness with terms like 'wide' (*pte*), 'narrow' (*qaṭṭin*), 'thick' (*ʿbe*), and 'thin' (*nqed*). The following section traces the development of Syriac vowel names from their conceptual origins in the 'wide-and-narrow' language of Jacob of Edessa through to the eleventh-century grammars of the Eliases of Nisibis and Ṭirhan.

This development begins with the first hints of absolute naming in the *scholion* on *bgdkt* letters by Dawid bar Pawlos (fl. 770–800) before progressing to the more complete systems attested by Ḥunayn ibn Isḥāq's (d. 873) *Ktɔbɔ d-Shmɔhe Dɔmyɔye* (*The Book of Similar Words*) and the late ninth-century *mashlmɔnutɔ* manuscript BL Add. 12138 (Loopstra 2014; 2015). Evidence from the Syriac-Arabic lexica of ʿĪsā ibn ʿAlī (d. c. 900) Ḥasan bar Bahlul (fl. 942–968) reinforces this progression, showing a transition from partial sets of names to the complete—albeit unstandardised—sets in the grammars of Elias of Nisibis (d. 1046) and Elias of Ṭirhan (d. 1049). This history is also intertwined with parallel developments in the Arabic linguistic tradition, but even in its latest stages, Syriac grammarians maintained their basic principles of the early 'wide-and-narrow' comparative analysis.

2.1. The Earliest Sources for Absolute Names

The first Syriac term that might be considered an absolute vowel name comes from Jacob of Edessa's (d. 708) grammatical tractate, *On Persons and Tenses*. He refers to the pair of a supralinear dot plus a sublinear dot that represents the "intermediate" vocalisation of a three-way homograph as *mpaggdɔnɔ* 'bridling' (Phillips 1869, ܝ, line 15). It is apparently a graphemic name, comparing the two points on opposite sides of a word with the ends of a bridle on the sides of a horse's mouth. Theoretically, this term can indicate any vowel between two other vowels on the Syriac scale, but it almost always applies to a word with /a/. It is thus a *de facto* absolute name in most cases, even though Jacob of Edessa did not use it exactly as such.[18] Some later grammarians (c. thirteenth century) and modern(ish) scholars refer to *mpaggdɔnɔ* with the related term *pugɔdɔ* (Hoffmann 1880, XVI; Segal 1953, 23, n. 16, 172), but this form of the word does not appear in Jacob of Edessa's grammatical works.

After Jacob, the next source of vowel names is Dawid bar Pawlos (fl. 770–800), although we have seen that some of his terminology was still transitioning between relative and absolute vocalisation (see above, chapter 3, §1.1). He utilises four terms that approximate some absolute vowel names found in later

---

[18] See discussion in Segal (1953, 23). It should be noted here that the 'vowel diagram' in the appendix of Segal's book is misleading. Even though the Syriac authors in the diagram appear to represent an evolutionary trajectory, Segal does not list them chronologically. He also 'modernises' some of the names to match the *ptɔhɔ* pattern (i.e., *CCɔCɔ*), even when they do not appear in that form in the Syriac sources.

sources, including: *zqiptɔ* 'stood upright', *ptiḥtɔ* 'opened', *hbiṣtɔ* 'pressed together', and *ʿṣiṣtɔ* 'constrained'.[19] His *hbiṣtɔ* and *ʿṣiṣtɔ* describe the letters *yod* and *waw* realised as /i/ and /u/, respectively. *Ptiḥtɔ* then indicates a letter with /a/, though it also seems to be a relative term that can describe relatively-open realisations of *yod* and *waw*.[20] Meanwhile, Dawid applies *zqiptɔ* only to letters with /ɔ/.

As addressed above (present chapter, §1.1), this earliest attestation of *zqp* 'standing upright' to indicate /ɔ/ post-dates the first usage of the *ʾiʿrābī* term *naṣb* 'standing upright' to name the Arabic /a/ by at least several decades. Recall that this term eventually became the name for the Arabic accusative case, but prior to Sībawayh's (d. 793/796) *Kitāb* it commonly referred to both the case and the vowel. Moreover, some grammarians—most notably, the Kufan al-Farrāʾ (d. 822) in his *Maʿānī al-Qurʾān* (*The Meanings of the Qurʾān*)—continued to name vowels with the *ʾiʿrābī* terms even in the first half of the ninth century (Owens 1990, 59; Versteegh 1993, 18–19). As a result, the use of *naṣb* as an Arabic name for /a/ was still current during the entire lifetime of Dawid bar Pawlos and the early career of Ḥunayn ibn Isḥāq (d. 873), who likewise refers to /ɔ/ with *zqp*. Furthermore, even as late as Sībawayh, *naṣb* could also designate relatively backed allophones of *ʾalif*, approximating /ɑ/ and /ɔ/, in contrast to the

---

[19] MS Mardin, ZFRN 192 f. 199r, lines 11–18, and f. 200r, line 5; MS Jerusalem, SMMJ f. 166r, line 10. See Farina (2021). These forms are feminine past participles because they describe 'letters', which are feminine in Syriac (*ʾɔtɔ*, pl. *ʾatwɔtɔ*).

[20] Either as /e/ and /o/ or as diphthongs (see above, chapter 3, §1.1).

fronted allophones of *ʾimāla* (/ɛ/, /e/) (see above, chapter 3, §2.2).

This usage of *naṣb* is the most likely source of *zqp* for the Syriac name for /ɔ/. It appears that when Syriac grammarians began naming vowels in their absolute system, they followed their fundamental principles of 'wide-and-narrow' phonology, so *ptḥ* 'opening' was an obvious term for /a/. This association would have been reinforced by the cognate Arabic name *fatḥ* 'opening', which referred to Arabic /a/ from at least the early eighth century. Then when Syriac grammarians needed a name to describe /ɔ/, their secondary *a*-vowel, they calqued *naṣb* 'standing upright', the second Arabic name for /a/ which also covered backed allophones similar to /ɔ/.

The next earliest evidence of absolute vowel terms comes from the work of Ḥunayn ibn Isḥāq (809–873), an Arab Christian physician who lived in Abbasid Baghdad and played a critical role in the ninth-century translation movement (Talmon 2008, 165). He expanded the lexicographical text known as *Ktɔbɔ d-Shmɔhe Dɔmyɔye* (*The Book of Similar Words*), which was originally written by the seventh-century monk, ʿEnanishoʿ (Childers 2011, 144; see edition of Hoffmann 1880, 2–49). The bulk of the vowel terminology within was added as part of Ḥunayn's ninth-century recension (Hoffmann 1880, XIII), but, despite his fame in both Syriac and Arabic history, this text has been somewhat neglected in studies that discuss Syriac vocalisation. Kiraz does not deal with it, and Segal mentions it only in passing (see Kiraz 2015, 94–113; see also, Segal 1953, 32, n. 1, 52, n. 1). Revell and Versteegh likewise do not mention it in their comparisons of the

Arabic and Syriac phonological traditions, even though it is pertinent to their proposed chronologies of vowel naming (Revell
1975, 181, n. 2; Versteegh 1993, 29–32; see above, present chapter, §1.1). In this expanded version of *Ktɔbɔ d-Shmɔhe Dɔmyɔye*,
Ḥunayn distinguishes six vowel qualities of Eastern Syriac—/ɔ/,
/a/, /e/, /i/, /o/, and /u/[21]—using a combination of phonetic
and graphemic descriptors.

Ḥunayn consistently indicates /a/ either by saying that a
letter is *ptiḥɔ* 'opened' (Hoffmann 1880, 6, lines 18–19, 14, lines
21–23, 33, line 22), or that "you *pɔtaḥ* [open] the [letter]" (Hoffmann 1880, 15, lines 1–2), where 'opening' is the act of adding
/a/ to a consonant. This second construction also appears in a
section of the text attributed to ʿEnanishoʿ (Hoffmann 1880, 18,
lines 6–8), suggesting that if Ḥunayn's transmission is reliable,
then the use of *pɔtaḥ* to describe Syriac /a/ may have begun as
early as the seventh century. Such an early usage could predate
even the 'wide-and-narrow' terminology used by Jacob of Edessa
(d. 708). Although less frequent than /a/, Ḥunayn designates /ɔ/
by saying that a letter is *zqipɔ* 'stood upright' (Hoffmann 1880,
10, line 13, 14, line 21), or that "you *zɔqep* [stand up] the [let-
ter]" (Hoffmann 1880, 14, line 23). He never uses the comparatively modern nominal forms *zqɔpɔ* or *ptɔḥɔ*.

Ḥunayn also refers to the two supralinear dots that indicate
/ɔ/ as *sheshltɔ* 'chain' (Hoffmann 1880, 6, line 13). In contrast to
the phonetic terms of 'opening' and 'standing upright', this is a
graphemic name that describes the appearance of the oblique
vowel points, which look like a 'chain' above the letter. *Sheshltɔ*

---

[21] On the Eastern vowel inventory, see Knudsen (2015, 90–91).

is a cognate of the Tiberian Hebrew accent *shalshelet,* and *zɔqep* is a cognate of the Hebrew accent with the same name (see Dotan 2007, 638–39). It remains to be seen whether these similarities are simply coincidences or evidence of a greater conceptual connection.

Pɔtaḥ (/a/) and *zɔqep* (/ɔ/) are Ḥunayn's only terms that are similar to those listed by Bar Hebraeus, but they function more as adjectives that describe effects on letters than as independent names. As for /e/, Ḥunayn instructs to "put 'two dots' (*treyn nuqze*) below the [letter]" (Hoffmann 1880, 6, lines 18–19, 21, lines 16–17, 30, line 22, 31, lines 14–15), with horizontal and vertical pairs indicating variations of the vowel's quality.[22] He does not specifically describe /i/, and while he does not have explicit phonological terms for /o/ and /u/, he does write:

ܦܘܿܫ ܐܒ̈ܩܐ ܬܗ ܒܓܘ̈ܢܝ ܣܒ ܡܕܝ̈ܘܣܝܐ ܡ̈ܕ ܐܢܘܣܐ ܪ̈ܫ̈ܐ. ܩ̈. ܗ. ܕܗ̈ܐ ܐ̈ܦܠ̈ܐ ܪ̈ܫ̈ܐ

Also, distinguish *maruhin* from *mrɔwḥin* by this sign: the one whose *mim* is opened relates to relief, which is said to be from evils or miseries. The rich give relief to the poor and do good to them. As for the one whose *mim* is not opened, but rather has the *sheshltɔ* [i.e., *zqɔpɔ*] on the *rish*: it relates to those who open wide a gate or house or some cleft, and it is said that they endow them with, as it were,

---

[22] On such variation, see Segal (1953, 28–32), Kiraz (2012, I:70–71), and Knudsen (2015, 112–14).

breadth and wideness, which they did not have before.
(Hoffmann 1880, 33, line 17 to 34, line 2)

This passage offers a mnemonic device for remembering the difference between the homographs *maruḥin* 'relieving ones' and *mrɔwḥin* 'widening ones'. Ḥunayn says the first word "relates to relief (*ʿal rwaḥtɔ*)," specifically relief "from evils (*bishɔtɔ*) or miseries (*ʾulṣɔne*)." But *rwaḥtɔ* has a double meaning here: besides 'relief', it also means 'space'. The phrase *ʿal rwaḥtɔ* can thus be read as 'against space'. Similarly, *men ulṣɔne* can be interpreted as 'from/among narrow things'. In this way, Ḥunayn indicates that *maruḥin* has the lexical meaning of 'those giving relief', but on a phonological level, it is 'narrow' with respect to 'space'. That is, its vowel is the narrow /u/. Meanwhile, its homograph (*mrɔwḥin*) has the comparatively open /ɔw/,[23] approximating the rounded back vowel /o/. As we will see, the Eliases of Nisibis and Ṭirhan eventually used the roots of *ʾulṣɔne* and *rwaḥtɔ* when naming the vowels /u/ and /o/ (*ʾalɔṣɔ* and *rwaḥɔ*), likely due to a familiarity with Ḥunayn's mnemonic device or a related concept.

As for *mrɔwḥin*, Ḥunayn says it "relates to those who open wide a gate or a house," bestowing them with 'breadth' (*shṭiḥutɔ*) and 'wideness' (*ptɔyutɔ*). Here we again see combined lexical and phonological meanings, as the articulation of /ɔw/ (or /o/) requires the opening the mouth and granting of 'wideness', at least in comparison to /u/. The word *ptɔyutɔ* even shares a root with what Jacob of Edessa called *pte* 'wide' vowels. These links suggest that that this line of 'wide-and-narrow' phonological thinking

---

[23] On representations of this diphthong in Syriac, see Knudsen (2015, 115, 135).

persisted within the Syriac tradition from Jacob of Edessa, through Ḥunayn ibn Isḥāq, and into the eleventh century.

Similar mnemonic devices are found in Masoretic explanations of homographs. In fact, the Masoretes refer to such mnemonics as *simanin* 'signs' (Dotan 2007, 619), just as Ḥunayn remarks that the reader will distinguish these Syriac homographs 'by this sign' (*b-nishɔ hɔnɔ*). Steiner notes an example of a Masoretic mnemonic, writing:

> Another Masoretic note, preserved only in later sources,[24] provides even clearer support: דאכיל פתח פומיה ודלא אכל קמץ פומיה. This note refers to the contrast between Ezekiel 18:11 אֶל־הֶהָרִים אָכָל/עַל־הֶהָרִים לֹא אָכָל and Ezekiel 18:6, 15. Its literal meaning is: "He who eats opens his mouth; he who does not eat closes his mouth." As a directive for reading, it means: "He who reads *ʾkl* opens his mouth (in the final syllable); he who reads *lʾ ʾkl* closes his mouth (in the final syllable)." (Steiner 2005, 376)

This *siman* equates 'eating' (*ʾɔ̯kal*) with 'opening' (*pɔtaḥ*) the mouth, because אָכָל 'eating' in Ezek. 18.11 is pronounced with /a/. By contrast, it equates 'not eating' (*lo ʾɔkɔl*) with 'closing' (*qɔmeṣ*) the mouth, because לֹא אָכָל 'not eating' is pronounced with pausal /ɔ/ in Ezek. 18.6. This explanation parallels the one that Ḥunayn gives for *maruḥin* and *mrɔwḥin*, incorporating both lexical and phonological information into a single line of instructions.

Another source of vowel names is the Eastern *mashlmɔnutɔ* manuscript BL Add. 12138. However, while the scribe Babai completed this codex in 899, he did not provide any vowel names

---

[24] This one is from a fourteenth- or fifteenth-century source.

himself, and the names that do appear are in marginal notes that were mostly added by later hands (Loopstra 2015, II:XXXVII). Jonathan Loopstra (2015, II:XXXVIII–XXXIX, 439) identifies several examples of vowel terminology from *zqp* (/ɔ/) and *ptḥ* (/a/) among these notes, including imperative forms like *zqup* 'stand upright' and *lɔ teptaḥ* 'do not open' to instruct the vocalisation of particular words. While these instructions are the results of later emendations to the codex after 899, such terms correspond with Ḥunayn ibn Isḥāq's vocabulary, and would have been current in the late ninth and early tenth centuries. This connection implies that these notes are not *necessarily* much later than Babai, though they certainly could be. The only other vowel name in BL Add. 12138 is in six separate notes containing the active participle ʿɔṣṣ and the noun ʿṣɔṣɔ 'constraining', all of which indicate /u/ (Loopstra 2015, II:439). This term shares its root with Dawid bar Pawlos' term for describing a *mater lectionis* letter *waw* that represents /u/, as well as the name which Bar Hebraeus would eventually give to /u/. None of the notes in BL Add. 12138 provide additional explanations for the usage or pronunciation of the East Syriac vowels, and as Loopstra points out, no treatises on them are extant from before the eleventh century. There are, however, further sources for the names of the vowels prior to that time; specifically, the extant Syriac-Arabic lexica written in the wake of the ninth-century translation movements.

2.2. Vowel Names in Syriac-Arabic Lexica

Ḥunayn ibn Isḥāq was one of the most prolific scholars of the early Islamicate translation movement, and throughout this career he amassed knowledge of many Arabic, Syriac, and Greek technical terms. He compiled much of this information into a Syriac-Arabic lexicon, but his original text is no longer extant (Brock 2016, 11–12; see also, Versteegh 1977, 3), and its contents survive only via the work of later lexicographers. One such lexicographer was Ḥunayn's student, ʿĪsā ibn ʿAlī (d. c. 900),[25] another Christian physician who compiled a Syriac-Arabic *Lexicon* in the latter half of the ninth century (Hoffmann 1874; Gottheil 1908; 1928; Butts 2009, 59–60). In the preface to this lexicon, Ibn ʿAlī explains that he based his book on the lexica of Ḥunayn and another scholar, Ishoʿ of Merv, expanding their work with additional words (Hoffmann 1874, 3, lines 3–7; Butts 2009, 61). This text seems not to have been considered a closed corpus, and was expanded in at least four recensions after Ibn ʿAlī completed the original version. It is not clear precisely when all of these recensions occurred, but at least one happened near the end of the ninth century (Butts 2009, 61–62), and the following discussion assumes that most of the others took place before the Eliases of Nisibis and Ṭirhan completed their grammars in the first half of the eleventh century. This assumption is based on the fact that

---

[25] Also known as Ishoʿ bar ʿAlī. There is some confusion among both medieval and modern sources that conflate this individual with other medieval scholars who have similar names. Butts (2009) has shown that the author of this lexicon is most likely the ʿĪsā ibn ʿAlī who was the student of Ḥunayn.

Ibn ʿAlī's *Lexicon* does not define any of the technical terms that the eleventh-century Eliases use to name vowels, but does describe vocalisation using phonetic participles like Ḥunayn did. Furthermore, this discussion relies on the editions of Hoffmann and Gottheil. The former published a handwritten version of the first half of the *Lexicon* (*ʾalep–mem*) in 1874, based a single recension, while the latter published a critical edition of the second half as two volumes in 1908 (*nun–ʿayn*) and 1928 (*pe–taw*) (see Butts 2009, 59).

As a source for technical definitions of vowel names, Ibn ʿAlī's *Lexicon* is surprisingly unhelpful. None of the entries on words from the roots *ptḥ*, *zqp*, *rbṣ*, *ḥbṣ*, or *ʿṣṣ*, nor any of the roots used for vowel names in other sources, contain a definition that explains a technical linguistic term. However, the text does indicate the proper pronunciation of certain words by describing their letters with passive participles, specifically: *zqipɔ* 'stood upright', *ptiḥɔ* 'opened', *ḥbiṣɔ* 'pressed-together', *rbiṣɔ* 'compressed', and *zribɔ* 'narrowed, contracted'. Each of these terms may also be abbreviated (e.g., *zr* and *zri*), rather than written with full orthography. They occur infrequently, but when they do appear, it is usually after the text introduces a new word, using the construction: "[lexeme], while [participle] is [letter]." This construction matches that in Ḥunayn's *Ktɔbɔ d-Shmɔhe Dɔmyɔye*.

For example, with *zqipɔ* 'stood upright', the *Lexicon* reads: "*ɔwkel*, while the *ʾalaph* is *zqiptɔ* (ܐ ܐܟܘܠܐ ܗܕ ܐܟܘܠܐ)" (Hoffmann 1874, 16). That is, for the word *ɔwkel*, the initial letter *ʾalaph* is 'stood upright', indicating that it is pronounced with /ɔ/. *Ptiḥɔ* 'opened' occurs more frequently in the text than *zqipɔ*, but it follows the same construction: "*'alep*, while the *'alaph* is *ptiḥɔ* (ܐܠܦ ܗܘ ܦܬܝܚ)" (Hoffmann 1874, 31).[26] This line means that in the word *'alep*, the letter *'alaph* is pronounced with /a/. *Ḥbiṣɔ* 'pressed together' is the rarest of the five vowel terms in the lexicon, but in at least one instance, the text has: "*zirɔ*, while the *yod* is *ḥbiṣɔ* (, ܐܝܢܐ ܕܝ ܕ ܚܒܝܨ)" (Hoffmann 1874, 126). In accordance with Jacob of Edessa's original principles of 'wide-and-narrow' vowels, *ḥbiṣɔ* here describes the closure of the mouth when articulating /i/. However, in contrast to the descriptions of *a*-vowels—which are not written with *matres lectionis*—rather than *ḥbiṣɔ* modifying the consonant *zayin*, here it is the *mater* letter *yod* that is 'pressed together'. *Ḥbiṣɔ* is also the first of the *Lexicon*'s terms that does not appear in *Ktɔbɔ d-Shmɔhe Dɔmyɔye*, as Ḥunayn used no specific term for /i/.

The *Lexicon*'s two terms *rbiṣɔ* 'compressed' (e.g., Hoffmann 1874, 23, 31) and *zribɔ* 'contracted, narrowed' (e.g., Hoffmann 1874, 16, 26, 29, 31, 32) also do not occur in *Ktɔbɔ d-Shmɔhe Dɔmyɔye*. Both describe letters with *e*-vowels, clearly contrasting the relative closedness of their articulation with the openness of /a/, but their exact nuance is difficult to determine. It seems that they are broadly interchangeable, or at least that the person who added them (either Ibn ʿAlī himself or a redactor) perceived them as representing the same vowel quality (/e/). A more extensive study is needed to determine their precise applications. It may simply be that the instructions with *zribɔ* and *rbiṣɔ* are the prod-

---

[26] Note the abbreviated Syriac ܦܗ for *ptiḥɔ*.

ucts of separate recensions of the *Lexicon* by editors who preferred different terminology. In any case, it is significant that the
literal meaning of both terms for *e*-vowels indicate 'narrowed'
articulation in contrast to the 'wider' *a*-vowels. This contrast is a
clear continuation of Jacob of Edessa and Dawid bar Pawlos' earlier relative vowel comparisons even after the Syriac absolute vocalisation system had solidified.

   Rbiṣɔ here is also our first hint of a vowel name (the later
rbɔṣɔ) that has caused some confusion in the realm of Syriac and
Arabic vocalisation. Revell and Versteegh suggest that *rbɔṣɔ* is
lexically equivalent to *khafḍ* 'lowering', an Arabic name for /i/,
and thus *khafḍ* is a potential calque of *rbɔṣɔ* (Revell 1975, 181, n.
2; Versteegh 1993, 30–31).[27] Such a calque would imply that
eighth-century Arabic grammarians borrowed a Syriac vowel
name for use in Arabic. However, vowel terminology derived
from *rbṣ* is not attested prior to the ninth-century *Lexicon* of Ibn
ʿAlī, far too late for it to have been adopted by pre-Sībawayhan
Arabic grammarians.[28] The proposed calque is also lexically untenable. *Khafḍ* does mean 'lowering', and as we have seen, it occurs in the Arabic grammatical tradition to indicate the relatively
'low' position of the front of the mouth in contrast to the 'higher'
positions of *naṣb* 'standing upright' (/a/) and *rafʿ* 'rising' (/u/).[29]
By contrast, *rbɔṣɔ* means 'compressing', 'confining', 'gripping', or
'squeezing' (R. Payne Smith 1879, 3801; J. Payne Smith 1903,

---

[27] For *khafḍ* as a vowel name in Arabic, see §4.1.1.
[28] Compare Posegay (2020, 210), which is mistaken.
[29] See §3.2.2 and §4.1.1.

527; Sokoloff 2009, 1430). The same root can indicate 'depressing' only in the sense that compressing an area of ground will create a 'depression',[30] and it is from this sense that Revell and Versteegh seem to have come up with the glosses of 'depressing' or 'lowering'.[31] Instead of stretching for this less common definition, it is simpler to interpret *rbɔṣɔ* as the 'compressing' movement of the lips while articulating /e/ relative to more-open vowels like /a/. This interpretation is wholly unrelated to *khafḍ* and follows the logic of the 'wide-and-narrow' convention that pervades practically all other Syriac vowel naming.

The second major extant Syriac-Arabic dictionary is the *Syriac Lexicon* of Ḥasan bar Bahlul (fl. 942–968), a tenth-century lexicographer who compiled his work from the earlier lexica of translators like Ḥunayn ibn Isḥāq and Ḥenanishoʿ bar Serosheway (d. c. 900). We have already seen him as a key link for connecting the idea of *muṣawwitāt* 'sounding' letters between the Syriac, Arabic, and Hebrew traditions (see above, chapter 2, §1.0), and his *Lexicon* also provides information for the use of Syriac absolute vowel names in the mid-tenth century. However, like Ibn ʿAlī's lexicon, Bar Bahlul's book underwent several revisions after his death, and Duval's edition contains some additions that are at least as late as the thirteenth century (Taylor 2011).

---

[30] This gloss is confirmed by the medieval lexica (Duval 1901, 1868; Gottheil 1928, II:376).

[31] A confounding factor may be R. Payne Smith's (1879, 3801) entry on the Syriac verb *rbaṣ*. He begins it by listing the apparent Arabic etymological cognate *rabaḍa*, which does mean 'to lay down', but this meaning does not apply to the Syriac verb.

Also like Ibn ʿAlī, Bar Bahlul does not give many explicit definitions of technical linguistic terms, and instead only explains the literal meaning of words that are used as vowel names in other sources. Nevertheless, his entry on *zqipɔ* does hint toward the use of the Arabic *ḍamma* (/u/) to name at least one vowel, and he connects the word *sheshlɔ* with *jarr*, an Arabic name for /i/. More often, he uses the passive participle terms to describe the pronunciation of particular words, including: *zqipɔ*, *ptiḥɔ*, *rbiṣɔ*, and *zribɔ*. *Ḥbiṣɔ* may also occur, though much less often than these other four terms. I have only noticed it in a single footnote, where Duval (1901, 385, n. 1) claims it appears in one manuscript instead of *zribɔ*. I have searched approximately one fifth of Duval's edition, but the text is over 2000 pages and it is inevitable that some terms evaded me. I have found no evidence of terms for /o/ and /u/, which notably are (almost) always written with a *mater lectionis* in Syriac.

Zqipɔ is the most frequent term that occurs in this text (e.g., Duval 1901, 45, 385, 401, 404, 406, 408, 417, 438, 448, 449, 1452), followed by *ptiḥɔ* (e.g., Duval 1901, 28, 398, 406, 408, 413, 432, 518). Like Ibn ʿAlī, Bar Bahlul uses these passive participles as attributes of consonants with the vowels /ɔ/ and /a/, respectively. He even follows the same syntax as Ibn ʿAlī, including lines like: "*baliʿ* (خلبـ), while the *bet* is *ptiḥɔ*" (Duval 1901, 398). *Rbiṣɔ* (e.g., Duval 1901, 9, 45, 438) and *zribɔ* (e.g., Duval 1901, 385, 418, 441) are much less common than *zqipɔ* and *ptiḥɔ*, which again makes it difficult to determine their exact functions, but they both indicate some type of *e*-vowel.

In addition to the regular use of the aforementioned Syriac terms, in his entry on the lexeme *zqipɔ*, Bar Bahlul includes the line: "The *zɔqupe* set up a finger. I say one should not give *al-ḍamma* (الضمّة أقول لا يعطى ᵃᵐᵉᵈ ᵢᵈⱼ ᵃᵐᵉᵈ ᵃᵐᵉᵈ)." *Al-ḍamma* 'pressing together' is the Arabic name for /u/, so this sentence seems to suggest that, at least according to Bar Bahlul, one should not pronounce /u/ in the word *zɔqupe* 'crucifiers'. His implied preference would be an East Syriac pronunciation with /o/: *zɔqope*. I have found no evidence in the *Lexicon* of other names that refer to /u/, so in this case Bar Bahlul may have adopted an Arabic vowel name to supplement his Syriac terminology. It is also worth noting that the lexical meaning of *ḍamma* overlaps with two other Syriac names for /u/, *'ṣɔṣɔ* 'contracting, constraining' and *'alɔṣɔ* 'narrowing, pressing, crowding', although neither occurs as a vowel name in Bar Bahlul's *Lexicon*.

Furthermore, Bar Bahlul (or at least, the copyist of the manuscript for Duval's edition) makes an interesting statement in a lexical entry on *sheshlɔ* 'chain', the same word as the term that referred to the two-dot vocalisation points in Ḥunayn's *Ktɔbɔ d-Shmɔhe Dɔmyɔye* and would eventually come to mean /e/ in the eleventh-century grammars. They write, "*Sheshlɔ*, in another manuscript, is *jarr*, that is, the letter when it is 'dragged' (*jurra*) (الحرف اذا جُرّ jarr اعنى ᵈⱼ ᵃᵐᵉᵈ)." This line seems to identify *sheshlɔ* with *jarr* 'dragging, pulling', an Arabic name for the genitive case that also served as an early name for /i/ (see Versteegh 1993, 125–30; Talmon 1997, 194–97).[32]

---

[32] See also, al-Zajjājī and al-Khwārizmī's discussions of *jarr* above, present chapter, §§1.1–2.

While Dawid bar Pawlos' (fl. 770–800) *scholion* on *bgdkt* letters and Ḥunayn Ibn Isḥāq's (d. 873) *Ktɔbɔ d-Shmɔhe Dɔmyɔye* are the earliest extant sources for Syriac absolute vowel terminology, the Syriac-Arabic lexica of Ibn ʿAlī (d. c. 900) and Bar Bahlul (fl. 942–968) provide an important link between their earlier naming conventions and those of later grammarians. Like Ḥunayn, these two lexicographers applied the convention of describing vocalisation with passive participles, but they also expanded on Ḥunayn's terminology with the addition of *ḥbiṣɔ* 'pressed together', *rbiṣɔ* 'compressed', and *zribɔ* 'narrowed'. These terms all have similar meanings, and they deliberately contrast the Syriac *e*- and *i*-vowels as relatively 'closed' in comparison to the relatively 'open' *a*-vowels. This contrast echoes the earlier 'wide-and-narrow' relative comparisons of Jacob of Edessa and demonstrates a continuity in the Syriac conceptions of vowel phonology between the seventh and eleventh centuries. Still, none of Dawid, Ḥunayn, Ibn ʿAlī, and Bar Bahlul had full sets of terms that named every Syriac vowel. Such a set is not attested until the eleventh-century grammars of the Eliases of Nisibis and Ṭirhan.

2.3. Absolute Naming in the Eleventh-century Grammars

The two most prominent representatives of eleventh-century Syriac grammar are Elias of Nisibis (d. 1046) and Elias of Ṭirhan (d. 1049) (Merx 1889, 109, 137, 154; Teule 2011b; 2011a), two bishops who inherited the terminological conventions of earlier Syriac vocalisation. They were both bilingual and well-versed in

Arabic and Syriac grammar, and many of their works are either in Arabic or tailored for Arabic-speaking audiences. Through these works—particularly their respective Syriac grammars—it is clear that they described vowels in much the same way as Ibn ʿAlī and Bar Bahlul, but they also adapted terms from the Arabic grammatical tradition to name the Syriac vowels. Their vowel names approach the forms of the names that appear in Bar Hebraeus and modern Syriac grammars, but they do not exactly match these later terms (Segal 1953, 32–33). Perhaps more interestingly, the Eliases' vowel names do not even match each other, and each must be explained by different interpretations of the 'wide-and-narrow' or 'high-and-low' principles of earlier Syriac vowel phonology.

Elias of Nisibis was born in northern Iraq in 975, and he became the Metropolitan of Nisibis in 1008 (Bertaina 2011, 198). In the second chapter of his *Turrɔṣ Mamllɔ Suryɔyɔ* (*The Correct Form of Syriac Speech*), Elias discusses the 'moved letters' (ʾatwɔtɔ mettziʿɔnyɔtɔ), by which he means the vowels (see above, chapter 2, §2.2). He begins by comparing the Arabic and Syriac vowel inventories:

ܐܘܟܪܐ ܗܟܢ ܡܬܦܫܩܬܐ ܒܝܢ ܐܬܘܬܐ ܐܠܗܐ ܡܬܙܝܥܢ ܘܩ̈ܝܡ ܣܘܪ̈ܝܝܐ ܡܥܪ̈ܒܝܐ ܠܚܡܫܐ ܐܠܗܐ ܙܢ̈ܝܐ. ܘܒܝܢ ܐܢ ܗܢ ܐܠ̈ܠ ܐܢ ܚܕ ܡܢ ܡ̈ܕܢܚܝܐ ܀ ܠܥܠ ܐܠܗܐ
ܡܬܦܫܩܢ

Then the moved letters, among the Arabs, are divided into three types, and among the Western Syrians, into five types. Then among we Easterners, they are divided into seven types. (Gottheil 1887, ܐ, lines 20–25)

Being an Eastern Metropolitan himself, Elias apparently attached some level of prestige to larger vowel inventories, and from here we must proceed with caution. He does name seven vowels, but that does not necessarily mean that he also distinguished seven discrete vowel qualities in his pronunciation of Syriac. Instead, he may be preserving a historical classification of a seventh vowel as a point of pride; as we will see, his Eastern contemporary, Elias of Ṭirhan, distinguishes only six vowel qualities (Segal 1953, 33; Loopstra 2015, II:XXXVII).

Elias of Nisibis proceeds with a simple list, writing:

> ܠܙܩܝ̈ܦܬܐ ܐܡܪܢܐ. ܘܠܪ̈ܒܝܨܬܐ ܘܠܦܬ̈ܝܚܬܐ. ܘܠܗܠܝܢ ܕܩܕܡ ܪ̈ܘܝܚܬܐ. ܘܠܗܠܝܢ ܕܩܕܡ ܐ̈ܠܝܨܬܐ. ܘܠܗܠܝܢ ܕܩܕܡ ܡ̈ܣܩܬܐ. ܘܠܗܠܝܢ ܕܩܕܡ ܚ̈ܒܝܨܬܐ
>
> I say: the *zqipɔtɔ*, the *rbiṣɔtɔ*, and the *ptiḥɔtɔ*; those which are before the *rwiḥɔtɔ* and those before the *ʾaliṣɔtɔ*; those before the *massqɔtɔ* and those before the *ḥbiṣɔtɔ*. (Gottheil 1887, ܣ, lines 25–28; see also, Merx 1889, 112)

Elias uses feminine plural passive participles for each vowel term, with the implication that they describe 'letters' (*ʾatwɔtɔ*) in the same way as earlier writers like Ḥunayn, Ibn ʿAlī, and Bar Bahlul who said *zqipɔ* and *ptiḥɔ*. However, Ibn ʿAlī and Bar Bahlul's lexica each only had Syriac terms for four or five vowels, and they did not name the vowels that are typically represented by *matres lectionis*. By contrast, Elias does refer to those vowels here. For example, when he says "those before the *ḥbiṣɔtɔ*" he means letters which come immediately before a *yod* that represents the vowel /i/. This construction implies that the *mater lectionis* itself is the letter which is *ḥbiṣtɔ* 'squeezed, pressed together'.

Elias then describes each vowel individually, including information on their function and their graphemes. He begins with *zqipɔtɔ* 'ones stood upright', saying that they include the *ʾalaph* and *dalat* in *ʾɔdɔm* 'Adam', and the *lamad* and *heʾ* in *ʾalɔhɔ* 'God'

(Gottheil 1887, ܗ, lines 29–30). Additionally, a letter which is *zqiptɔ* is marked by *treyn nuqze* 'two dots' "placed one over the other in a straight line above the letter, and they are called *sheshlɔ da-lʿel* 'a chain above' (ܩܕܡ ܠܥܠ ܐܝܢ̈ܐ ܐܚ̈ܝܢܐ ܣܡ̈ ܠܥ ܠ ܣܘ ܚܘܫܒܬܗ̈ ܘܡܬܩ̈ܪܝܢ ܫܫܠܬܐ. ܕܐ̈ܚܝܢ)" (Gottheil 1887, ܠ, lines 6–8). Both of these descriptions have parallels in *Ktɔbɔ d-Shmɔhe Dɔmyɔye*, where Ḥunayn ibn Isḥāq also referred to letters with /ɔ/ as *zqipɔ* and to the two-dot supralinear sign of this vowel as a *sheshltɔ* 'chain' (see above, present chapter, §2.1). Elias also quotes at least two of Ḥunayn's other books in this grammar and in the sixth dialogue of his *Kitāb al-Majālis* (*The Book of Sessions*) (Gottheil 1887, 36, n. 49, 29*–30*, no. 49; ܚ, line 32; Bertaina 2011, 202–3; see Samir 1975), reinforcing the possibility that they had access to the same pedagogical tradition of vowel naming.

Next, the *rbiṣɔtɔ* 'compressed ones' are like the *ḥet* in *ḥelmɔ* 'dream' (Gottheil 1887, ܗ, lines 30–31). Like in the tenth-century lexica, and even extending as far back as Jacob of Edessa's *pte* 'wide' and *qaṭṭin* 'narrow' comparisons, this 'compression' is most likely a description of the relative closedness of the mouth when articulating /e/, in contrast to more open vowels like /a/. This vowel is marked by 'two dots' (*treyn nuqze*) straight below a letter, called *sheshlɔ da-ltaḥt* 'a chain below' (Gottheil 1887, ܠ, lines 9–10). In contrast to Ḥunayn, who only used *sheshltɔ* for the supralinear sign of /ɔ/, Elias adopts *sheshlɔ* as the name for any vertical two-dot vocalisation sign, regardless of its position.

The next vowel is on letters that are *ptiḥɔtɔ* 'opened', which Elias says is the *ʾalaph* in *ʾalɔhɔ* and the *ʿayin* in *ʿaprɔ* 'dust'

(Gottheil 1887, ܚ, lines 31–32). Like his predecessors, Elias' use
of this term again maintains the contrast between the 'openness'
of the mouth when articulating /a/ and the 'compression' of /e/.
He states that the sign for this /a/ is two dots, with one above
and one below the letter (Gottheil 1887, ܠܛ, lines 11–13). These
first three terms—*zqipɔ*, *rbiṣɔ*, and *ptiḥɔ*—form an important triad
for Elias, as they are the vowels that do not typically occur with
a *mater lectionis* in Syriac orthography.

Elias' fourth vowel is on letters which come before the
rwihɔtɔ 'broadened ones', like the *ʾalaph* in *ʾo* 'or' and the *kaph* in
ʾarkonɔ 'magistrate'. The 'broadened one' in each of these cases
is the *mater lectionis* letter *waw*, which signifies the vowel /o/ on
the consonant that precedes it. The term itself describes the
'broadening' of the mouth during the articulation of /o/ in contrast to the closedness of /u/, the other vowel which a *waw* can
represent in Syriac. The term *rwiḥɔ* shares a root with *rwaḥtɔ* 'relief, space', the word that Ḥunayn used as part of his mnemonic
device to explain the difference between the homographs
maruḥin 'relieving ones' and *mrɔwḥin* 'widening ones' (Hoffmann
1880, 33, line 17, to 34, line 2; present chapter, §2.1). Elias may
have adopted a term for /o/ specifically related to 'space' due to
familiarity with this mnemonic from Ḥunayn's work, or a related
pedagogical source in the same vein. He further notes that the
sign of *waw rwiḥtɔ* is a single dot placed above *wāw* (Gottheil
1887, ܠܛ, lines 13–14).

The fifth vowel is on letters that are before the *ʾaliṣɔtɔ* 'narrowed ones', meaning instances where a *mater lectionis waw* represents /u/, like the *nun* in *nurɔ* 'fire'. These *waws* are 'narrowed'

specifically in contrast to the 'broadened' /o/. Compared to every other vowel, /o/ would be considered more 'closed', and /u/ alone requires more closure during its articulation. The two terms *rwiḥɔ* and *ʾaliṣɔ* thus make sense in the context of each other— and in context of their shared *mater lectionis*—by maintaining the principle of relative comparisons that extends back to Jacob of Edessa. *ʾAliṣɔ* also shares a root with *ʾulṣone* 'miseries, narrow things', another word from Ḥunayn's mnemonic which he associated with *maruḥin* (with /u/), rather than *mrɔwḥin* (with /ɔw/). The sign for this vowel is *waw* with a dot below it (Gottheil 1887, ↳, lines 14–15).

Elias' sixth vowel is on letters before the *massqɔtɔ* 'raised ones',[33] which are instances where a *mater lectionis yod* represents /e/. He gives examples of the *ʾalaph* in *ʾel* 'El' and the *bet* in *bel* 'Jupiter' (Gottheil 1887, ↳, lines 1–2), and here we see a problem reminiscent of the *rbiṣɔ-zribɔ* distinction in the tenth-century lexica. By the eleventh century, the East Syriac quality of the vowel in both of these words was probably the same as the first vowel in *ḥelmɔ* (see Knudsen 2015, 91–92); that is, the vowel which Elias described as *rbiṣɔ* (/e/). Based on his citations of *ʾel* and *bel*, the only apparent difference between a letter which is before a *yod massaqtɔ* and a letter which is *rbiṣɔ* is the presence of a *mater lectionis yod*, though it may also be relevant that both of these examples are non-Syriac loan words. It would seem then that Elias differentiates *rbiṣɔ* and *yod massaqtɔ* solely on the basis of orthography, even though they likely sounded the same in his

---

[33] This term is distinct from the accent dot with a similar name (Loopstra 2015, II:XLI, n. 142).

speech, and it is this distinction that allows him to count seven vowels in the Syriac of the 'Easterners'. He notes that the sign of this vowel is two dots below the letter which precedes the *yod massaqtɔ* (Gottheil 1887, ܠ, lines 15–16).

The phonetic meaning of *massaqɔ*[34] 'raised up' here is not based on the wide-and-narrow comparisons of the other vowel names. It is a C-stem participle from the root *slq* 'raising', which stands out from the G-stem participles that Elias uses to describe the other vowels. This discrepancy suggests that it came into use separately from the other terms. It is not a technical term in the earlier lexica, nor is there a similar name in the works of Ḥunayn, Dawid bar Pawlos, or Jacob of Edessa, so it is most likely a tenth- or eleventh-century innovation. Its closest analogue in Syriac linguistics might be the early relative use of *men lʿel* 'above', which indicated that a word's vowels were pronounced farther back than those of its homograph (see above, chapter 3, §1.1). Elias likely had sufficient knowledge of Jacob of Edessa's work to make this same analysis, as he cites Jacob's *Turrɔṣ Mamllɔ Nahrɔyɔ* in the introduction of his own *Turrɔṣ Mamllɔ Suryɔyɔ* (Gottheil 1887, ܘ).

By analogy with Elias' description of the two vowels that *waw* represents (i.e., /o/ and /u/), his *massaqɔ* (/e/) should be understood in relation to the second vowel which *yod* can represent: /i/. In that sense, /e/ is indeed the more-backed of the pair, and is thus 'raised' above the position of /i/. As we will soon see with Elias of Ṭirhan, it is also likely that *massaqɔ* is a calque of

---

[34] Never *ʾassɔqɔ*, despite what Merx (1889, 157, n. 2) and Segal (1953, 33) suggest.

the Arabic inflectional term *marfūʿ* 'raised up', (i.e., given /u/), likewise related to a 'high' backed position (see above, chapter 3, §2.2). While it is not clear that Elias of Nisibis is actually calquing *marfūʿ* here, it is certain that he could have, as he displays a proficient understanding of the Arabic inflectional system in the sixth dialogue of his *Kitāb al-Majālis* (Samir 1975, 634–49).

Elias' seventh and final vowel is on letters before the *ḥbiṣɔtɔ* 'squeezed, pressed-together ones', which include the *ʾalaph* in *ʾidɔ* 'hand' and the *dalat* in *zaddiqɔ* 'righteous' (Gottheil 1887, ܠ, lines 2–3). The *ḥbiṣtɔ* in this case is a *yod* acting as a *mater lectionis* for /i/, which corresponds to the rare occurrences of *hbiṣ* in the Syriac-Arabic lexica. It is clearly another phonetic description, meant to contrast the closedness of /i/ with the comparatively open articulation of /a/ and /ɔ/, and in some more precise sense Elias may have considered it a greater indicator of closure than *rbiṣɔ* 'compressed' (i.e., /e/). Its sign is a *yod* with a sublinear dot (Gottheil 1887, ܠ, lines 17–18).

At the end of his list of vowels, Elias also introduces nominalised forms of the Syriac vowel terminology, naming *ʾaliṣutɔ* 'narrowing' (/u/), *rawiḥutɔ* 'broadening' (/o/), *massɔqutɔ* 'rising' (/e/), and *ḥabiṣutɔ* 'squeezing, pressing together' (/i/) (Gottheil 1887, ܠ, lines 4–5). These four vowels are notably the ones represented by the *matres lectionis waw* and *yod*, and they are the four vowels which do not have names (or, for *ḥbiṣɔ*, is named only rarely and dubiously) in the aforementioned works of Ḥunayn, Ibn ʿAlī, and Bar Bahlul. These nominal forms may well be Elias of Nisibis' own innovations from the first half of the eleventh century. They do not appear in the grammar of Elias of Ṭirhan, but this second Elias brought innovations of his own.

Like Elias of Nisibis, Elias of Ṭirhan (d. 1049) was an East Syriac bishop who lived in an increasingly Arabicised linguistic world, so he produced his own Syriac grammar, the *Memrɔ Gramaṭiqɔyɔ* (*The Grammatical Essay*) for an Arabic-speaking audience. He uses various vowel terms throughout this text, and he names six discrete qualities in its twenty-seventh chapter: *zqɔpɔ* (/ɔ/), *ptɔhɔ* (/a/), *rbɔṣɔ* or *sheshlɔ* (/e/), *massaqɔ* or *rwahtɔ* (/o/), *hbɔṣɔ* (/u/), and *yod* (/i/) (Baethgen 1880, ܠܝ, lines 15–18). He also periodically describes letters with certain vowels by using passive participles from these roots, including: *rbiṣɔ* (/e/), *rwihɔ* (/o/), and *hbiṣɔ* (/u/) (e.g., Baethgen 1880, ܠ, lines 1–6). Broadly speaking, these terms match the more modern Syriac vowel names, although when paired with their phonemes they do not all correspond with the modern terminology. Most strikingly, the names for /u/ and /o/ conflict with the vowel list in Elias of Nisibis' grammar, and /i/ has the same name as its *mater lectionis*. These discrepancies reveal that Syriac vocalisation terminology was still in flux during the first half of the eleventh century, even while individual grammarians remained internally consistent with respect to the Syriac tradition of 'wide-and-narrow' comparisons.

Zqɔpɔ and *ptɔhɔ* here refer to /ɔ/ and /a/, respectively, exactly as expected, and in line with the vowel terminology of Ḥunayn ibn Isḥāq, the lexicographers, and Elias of Nisibis. However, for Elias of Ṭirhan, these names are distinct nominal forms, rather than passive participles that describe vocalised consonants. Meanwhile, he refers to /e/ with both *rbɔṣɔ* and *sheshlɔ*, although he prefers *rbɔṣɔ*. Apparently, he worked within a grammatical tradition in which the graphemic name for a two-dot sign—*sheshlɔ*—had lost its meaning related to /ɔ/, and now referred only to the sublinear two-dot sign of /e/. This term thus became interchangeable with *rbɔṣɔ*, the phonetic description of that vowel (Baethgen 1880, ܠܐ, line 21, to ܠܒ, line 8, ܠܓ, lines 18–22). This usage contrasts Elias of Nisibis, who used *sheshlɔ da-lʿel* and *sheshlɔ da-ltaḥt* to describe the shape and position of the two-dot signs for /ɔ/ and /e/.

While Elias favours these nominalised vowel terms, he does occasionally describe individual letters or words with /e/ and /a/ by means of other participial forms. For example, in his twenty-fourth chapter, he explains the inflection of *ʾetpʿel* verbs in the imperative, saying:

> ܗܟܝܠ ܝܕܥ ܕܟܠ ܡܠܬܐ ܕܡܬܪܒܨܐ ܠܬܚܬ ܒܩܪܝܬܗ̇ . ܒܡܫܬܘܕܥܢܘܬܐ ܒܝܢܐ
> ܦܣܘܩܐܝܬ ܡܢ ܡܫܬܚܠܦܐ ܠܦܬܚܘܬܐ ܕܐܝܟ ܐܡܪ .. ܐܣܬܡܟ ܐܣܬܡܟ
> ܐܬܓܗܢ ܐܬܓܗܢ .. ܐܬܢܨܒ ܐܬܢܨܒ .. ܐܬܪܟܢ ܐܬܪܟܢ .. ܐܬܬܟܠ
> ܐܬܬܟܠ .
>
> You should know that every verb which is 'compressed downward' (*metrabṣɔ ltaḥt*) in its reading in the indicative, in the imperative form it is changed to 'opening', like so: *ʾestmek*, *ʾestamk*; *ʾetghen*, *ʾetgahn*; *ʾetnṣeb*, *ʾetnaṣb*; *ʾetrken*, *ʾetrakn*; *ʾettkel*, *ʾettakl*. (Baethgen 1880, ܠܗ, lines 10–12)

Metrabṣɔ 'compressed' here is a passive participle that describes a word with *rbɔṣɔ* (/e/), indicating the result of the relative 'compression' required from the lips to produce /e/ compared to /a/. Meanwhile, *ltaḥt* 'downwards' may indicate the position of the sublinear dots that represent /e/, the relatively-fronted position of /e/ on the scale of vowels within the mouth, or even the direction of airflow during the articulation of fronted vowels (or all three).[35] As Elias explains, when ʾetpʿel verbs with this /e/ are made imperative, the vowel in the second syllable becomes /a/. He indicates this /a/ as the verb becoming *puttɔhɔ* 'opening'.

Elias also has two nominalised terms for /o/, naming it both *massaqɔ* 'raised up' and *rwahtɔ* 'broadening'. *Rwahtɔ* corresponds to Elias of Nisibis' *rawihutɔ*, indicating that the articulation of /o/ is relatively open in comparison to /u/, and may derive from the mnemonic device that Ḥunayn used to explain the difference between *maruhin* and *mrɔwhin*. On the other hand, Elias of Ṭirhan's use of *massaqɔ* for /o/ contrasts Elias of Nisibis, who applied that name to /e/. Nevertheless, both Eliases use this term within the context of a single *mater lectionis*, both following the older Syriac principle of relative backness. For Elias of Nisibis, /e/ was 'raised up'—that is, farther back—in comparison to /i/, the other vowel which a *mater lectionis yod* may represent. For Elias of Ṭirhan, /o/ is 'raised up'—again, relatively backed— in comparison to /u/, the second vowel that *waw* can represent. Elias of Ṭirhan's application of this name to a *u*-vowel, rather than an *i*-vowel, is probably due to an understanding of *massaqɔ* as a translation of the Arabic inflectional term *marfūʿ* 'raised up', which usually described words that ended with /u/. This usage would have been comparatively pragmatic for Elias of Ṭirhan, as

---

[35] On directionality and airflow in vocalisation, see the discussion of Saadia Gaon's vowel names, below, present chapter, §3.3.

he designed the *Memrɔ Gramaṭiqɔyɔ* specifically for an Arabic-speaking audience.

Elias of Ṭirhan then refers to /u/ as *ḥbɔṣɔ* 'squeezing, pressing together', a term that again contradicts Elias of Nisibis, but also again shows how the two Eliases' systems are logically consistent. For Elias of Ṭirhan, this term indicates the phonetic action of articulating /u/, which requires the lips to be pressed together. In this context, *ḥbɔṣɔ* is a clear calque of *ḍamma* 'pressing together', the Arabic name for the same vowel (compare Versteegh 1993, 30). It is also a relative term in Syriac, describing /u/ as relatively closed in comparison to /o/, the other vowel marked by *waw*.[36] In the same way, when Elias of Nisibis said that a *yod* was *ḥbiṣɔ*, he meant that it represented /i/, relatively-closed in comparison to /e/.

We see here a mixture of multiple phonological concepts in the Eliases' terminology for /e/, /i/, /o/, and /u/. It seems that Elias of Ṭirhan calqued the Arabic terms *ḍamma* 'pressing together' and *marfūʿ* 'raised up', both of which indicated /u/ in Arabic, as *ḥbɔṣɔ* and *massaqɔ*. He applied *ḥbɔṣɔ* to the equivalent Syriac vowel, /u/. Then, in a process akin to the likely adoption of *zqɔpɔ* as a calque of *naṣb* (above, present chapter, §2.1), he applied a new Syriac vowel name (*massaqɔ*) based on an Arabic inflectional name (*marfūʿ*) for Syriac's secondary *u*-vowel, /o/ (which did not exist phonemically in Classical Arabic). This adaptation of Arabic terminology supplemented the name *rwaḥtɔ*

---

[36] Recall, however, that Dawid bar Pawlos used *ḥbiṣɔ* to describe *yod* representing /i/ (see above, chapter 3, §1.1). *Ḥbɔṣɔ* was also Bar Hebraeus' term for /i/.

'broadening' (/o/), which Elias likely already knew from the tradition of Ḥunayn ibn Isḥāq, and served the practical purpose of making his Syriac grammar more palatable to Arabic-speaking readers. Elias of Nisibis, on the other hand, seems to have been more concerned with ensuring that East Syriac had a larger vowel inventory than Arabic and West Syriac. In service of this goal, he needed seven discrete terms, and could not afford to apply multiple names to the same vowel. Since he likely already had *rwiḥɔ* 'broadened' (/o/) and *ʾaliṣɔ* 'narrowed' (/u/) from the tradition of Ḥunayn's mnemonic device, he applied *massaqɔ* and *ḥbiṣɔ* to /e/ and /i/, respectively, using the fundamental Syriac principles of relative height and openness.

The two Eliases do not represent the culmination of vowel naming in the Syriac phonological tradition, but their grammars do mark the first time that Syriac linguists had complete sets of terms that could name every Syriac vowel on an absolute basis. These absolute sets developed organically during the ninth and tenth centuries, as translators and lexicographers adopted new terminology based on the relative 'wide-and-narrow' comparisons of the first Syriac grammarians. The earliest sources for such terms are Dawid bar Pawlos' (fl. 770–800) *scholion* on *bgdkt* letters and Ḥunayn ibn Isḥāq's (d. 873) version of *Ktɔbɔ d-Shmɔhe Dɔmyɔye*, which describe /a/ using participles from the root *ptḥ* 'opening'. They contain similar descriptions for /ɔ/, using participles of the root *zqp* 'standing upright', and most likely calquing Arabic *naṣb* 'standing upright' (/a/, /ɑ/). Shortly after Ḥunayn, the lexicographers Ibn ʿAlī and Bar Bahlul included additional 'wide-and-narrow' participles in their dictionaries, including *rbiṣɔ* 'compressed' (/e/), *zribɔ* 'contracted, constrained' (also /e/), and possibly *ḥbiṣɔ* 'pressed together' (/i/). The eleventh-century Eliases then supplemented these terms with even more 'wide-and-narrow' descriptors, taking forms of *rwḥ* 'broadening' (/o/) and *ʔlṣ* 'narrowing' (/u/). They also calqued terms from Arabic grammar, yielding *massaqɔ* 'raised up' (/o/ or /e/) and *ḥbɔṣɔ* 'pressing together' (/i/ or /u/).

Syriac vowel terminology continued to evolve after the Eliases, eventually reaching the forms found in modern grammars. Notably, *ṣɔṣɔ* 'constraining' only occurs in Dawid bar Pawlos' *scholion* (as the participle *ṣiṣɔ*) and the marginal notes of BL Add. 12138, with no trace of it among Ḥunayn, the lexicographers, or the Eliases, even though it appears for /u/ in Bar Hebraeus' (d. 1286) grammar. There is also hardly any sign in our sources of *zlɔmɔ* 'inclining', which occurs as a name for /e/ in Ishoʿyahb bar Malkon's (fl. c. 1200) *Mṣidtɔ d-Nuqze* (*The Net of Points*) (Merx 1889, 113; Talmon 1996, 291; Van Rompay 2011).[37] Moreover, none of the aforementioned authors have systematic terminology to indicate vowel length, even though such terms eventually appear in Bar Hebraeus' vowel system (Merx 1889, 50; Versteegh 1993, 29–30). These developments require more careful analysis in the context of twelfth- and thirteenth-century Arabic and Hebrew linguistic sources, but such a study is beyond the scope of this book. Instead, we now turn back to the Hebrew tradition, and examine how it evolved alongside Syriac between the time

---

[37] Bar Malkon also refers to /u/ as *rbɔṣɔ*, applying yet another interpretation of 'compressing' to the relatively-closed vowel belonging to the *mater lectionis waw* (Merx, *Historia*, 113).

of its earliest relative vowel terminology and its first sets of absolute names.

3.0. Vowel Names in the Hebrew Tradition[38]

Like in the Syriac grammatical tradition, the first Masoretic
vowel names emerged from the comparative context of 'open-
and-closed' comparisons, with the early relative terms *pɔtaḥ* and
qɔmeṣ eventually stabilising as terms for specific vowels (namely
/a/ and /ɔ/) (see Khan 2020, I:245). However, also like in Syriac,
this type of comparison did not become the universal principle
for defining Hebrew vowels. Masoretes and grammarians referred to the Tiberian vowels /ɛ/, /e/, /i/, /o/, and /u/ by many
different names between the ninth and eleventh centuries, including: modifications to the relative terminology; the number,
shape, and position of the vowel points; descriptions of the mouth
during articulation; and the addition of Arabic grammatical
terms to Masoretic vocabulary. Taking note of these different
terms, Israel Yeivin (1983, 80) has suggested that the variation
is the result of different 'schools' of linguistic thought that maintained different naming conventions, all in use at roughly the
same time (Dotan 2007, 634). Each of these conventions has its
roots in the relative naming of *pɔtaḥ* and *qɔmeṣ*, but different authors supplemented these names with additional descriptions of

---

[38] Some passages in this section were previously published in Posegay
(2021a). They appear here re-edited with expanded discussion.

graphemes, phonetic terminology, and names from Arabic grammar.[39]

The expanded usage of the relative terms as vowel names is evident in a few anonymous Masoretic treatises, as well as in Aharon ben Asher's (d. c. 960) *Diqduqe ha-Ṭeʿamim* (*The Fine Details of the Accents*) and Judah ben David Ḥayyūj's (d. c. 1000) early work *Kitāb al-Tanqīṭ* (*The Book of Pointing*). Some of this usage appears in the *Treatise on the Shewa* and other *muṣawwitāt* texts, but those sources also count the number of dots in each vowel sign or utilise Arabic phonetic terminology. The earliest datable text that approximates the 'modern' vowel names *ḥolem* (/o/), *shuruq* (/u/), *ṣere* (/e/), and *ḥiriq* (/i/) is Saadia Gaon's (d. 942) Hebrew grammar, *Kutub al-Lugha* (*The Books of the Language*), but it is not certain how he vocalised those names. A number of undated fragments from the Cairo Genizah imply that they were initially segolate nouns in Hebrew, and two *muṣawwitāt* texts cite clear Aramaic forms for each vowel, suggesting that the terms predate Saadia. Ḥayyūj also mentions Saadia's vowel names in his book on Hebrew verb forms, *Kitāb al-Afʿal Dhuwāt Hurūf al-Līn* (*The Book of Verbs with Soft Letters*), but he generally prefers Arabic vowel names over Hebrew ones. Whatever their source, these 'modern' names did not immediately take hold in the Hebrew tradition, and certain scholars continued identifying vowels by other methods even into the eleventh century.

---

[39] Brief treatments of the vowel names appear in Gesenius (1910), Haupt (1901), Dotan (2007), and Khan (2020, I:245–46, 256–65).

3.1. Expanding the Relative System

In his exploration of early Hebrew relative vowel phonology (see above, chapter 3, §1.2), Steiner identifies several Masoretic vowel lists which contain names from the roots *ptḥ* 'opening' and *qmṣ* 'closing', but do not have phonetic terms for the other Hebrew vowels. This convention is found in a number of other Masoretic texts, including Aharon ben Asher's tenth-century *Diqduqe ha-Ṭeʿamim* (*The Fine Details of the Accents*) and some of the additional notes published in Baer and Strack's book of the same name, *Dikduke ha-Ṭeʿamim* (1879).

It is worth pausing here to reiterate the relationship between these two books. Aharon ben Asher wrote his *Diqduqe ha-Ṭeʿamim* in the first half of the tenth century as a guide to the rules of the Tiberian Hebrew accent system. The text is mainly in rhymed Hebrew prose, and from time to time it describes Hebrew vocalisation in addition to cantillation marks. In 1879, Baer and Strack published the first edition of Ben Asher's book along with many shorter Masoretic texts in the second part of the same volume. However, the version of *Diqduqe ha-Ṭeʿamim* that they compiled contained a number of sections that were not part of Ben Asher's original work. Dotan (1967) identified these sections and published a new edition of *Diqduqe ha-Ṭeʿamim* based only on Ben Asher's writings. As such, some passages which appear to be part of *Diqduqe ha-Ṭeʿamim* in Baer and Strack's volume—and are cited under that title—are in fact from other Masoretic works.

Returning to the vowel names, Steiner (2005, 378–79) finds three Masoretic vowel lists that use just *ptḥ* and *qmṣ* in their phonetic descriptions. Each list applies these terms to /a/ and

/ɔ/, and then uses other methods to define the other five vowels. The first is a passage from Baer and Strack's *Dikduke ha-Ṭeʿamim* (1879, 11, lines 23–28; Steiner 2005, 378). After /a/ and /ɔ/, it calls /ɛ/ and /e/ *pɔthɔ qtannɔ* 'small opening' and *qɔmṣɔ qtannɔ* 'small closing', respectively, indicating that /ɛ/ is relatively open in comparison to /e/. Steiner (2005, 379) takes the lack of vowel names derived from phonetic descriptions, besides *pth* and *qmṣ*, as a remnant of the earlier relative phase in which those two terms alone could refer to any vowel, preserved now in the transition towards absolute vowel names. That is, /a/ became *pɔtah* 'opening' because it was once considered more open in relation to /ɔ/, which accordingly was more *qɔmeṣ* 'closing'. In fact, the author of this passage even describes *qɔmṣɔ* by saying: "first is *qɔmṣɔ*, with mouth gathered together (ראשונה היא קָמְצָה בפה היא קבוצה)." They use the word *qbuṣɔ* 'gathered, pressed together', which would eventually come to mean /u/ due to the compression of the lips (see below, present chapter, §3.4).

What Steiner does not notice is that *qtannɔ* 'small' is also a phonetic term in this context. It indicates that /ɛ/ and /e/ are relatively closed in comparison to /a/ and /ɔ/, their parallel pair of 'open-and-closed' vowels. This description is precisely the same as what we might expect from Jacob of Edessa (d. 708), who considered /e/ *qaṭṭin* 'narrow' relative to the more *pte* 'wide' /ɔ/ and /a/.[40] This secondary relative relationship strengthens

---

[40] Recall that Jacob pronounced an unrounded /ɑ/ as his reflex of the later Syriac and Tiberian /ɔ/, and thus he classified it as 'wider' (more-open) than /a/.

Steiner's argument that these terms are a remnant of the earlier
relative stage of Masoretic phonology.

The second vowel list is also from one of Baer and Strack's
additional notes, with the heading *Nequdot Omeṣ ha-Miqrɔ* (*The
Dots of the Greatness of the Scripture*) (1879, §36, 34, lines 5–9). It
spells out most of the vowels with *matres lectionis* (i.e., *ʾey, ʾow,
ʾiy, ʾuw*), and Dotan (2007, 634) argues that such phonetic spellings are among the earliest methods for naming vowels, most
likely predating the vocalisation signs themselves. However, the
list also includes the terms *pɔthɔ* and *qɔmṣɔ*, which Steiner again
takes as evidence that these two preserve the phonological features of an earlier stage. This note also shows how late that 'early'
stage remained influential in Masoretic vocalisation, as it was
found in the Masoretic material of the Leningrad Codex, completed in 1008, and the subsequent section contains a vowel scale
that appears to be divided using calques of Arabic grammatical
terminology (see below, present chapter, §3.4 and Eldar 1983,
43). Steiner's (2005, 379, n. 51) third list is from the text known
as *Reshimat Munnaḥim* (*List of Terms*) (see also, Allony 1986, 123;
above, chapter 2, §3.3). In addition to two names from *pth* and
qmṣ, it associates each of the Hebrew vowels with one of the *matres lectionis*: *ʾaleph, waw*, and *yod*. Again, Steiner takes the two
phonetic terms as evidence of the relative system that predates
the other vowel names.

Ben Asher's *Diqduqe ha-Teʿamim* uses this same vowel classification system, with only two main phonetic terms that are derived from *pth* and *qmṣ*. Ben Asher consistently refers to the vowel
/a/ with *pɔtaḥ* and *pɔthɔ* (Dotan 1967, 131, line 5, 133, lines 1–

2, 144, line 1), and he describes the Tiberian vocalic *shewa* using the same root (Dotan 1967, 140, lines 2–3, 141, line 1), including with the verbal form *yip̄taḥ* 'one would open' (Dotan 1967, 115, lines 3–5). Similarly, he indicates /ɔ/ with *qɔmeṣ* and *qɔmṣɔ* (Dotan 1967, 119, lines 2–3, 138, line 2), as well as the passive participle *qɔmuṣ* (Dotan 1967, 144–45, lines 2–3). He is also familiar with the secondary relative usage, using *qɔmeṣ qɔṭon* 'small *qameṣ*' for /e/ (Dotan 1967, 137, line 2). As Steiner (2005, 379) emphasises, Ben Asher does not use any of these words as relative terms. Instead, each defines a specific vowel quality, showing remnants of relative vocalisation fossilised in the absolute system.

Judah ben David Ḥayyūj (d. c. 1000) also makes use of the expanded relative naming in his early work, *Kitāb al-Tanqīṭ* (*The Book of Pointing*) (Nutt 1870, I–XV). While this text is mostly in Arabic, Ḥayyūj uses the Hebrew terms *qɔmeṣ gadol* 'large *qameṣ*' and *pɔtaḥ gadol* 'large *pataḥ*' for /ɔ/ and /a/, respectively (Nutt 1870, I, lines 5–7 and III, lines 5–6, lines 12–14), and likewise applies *qɔmeṣ qɔton* and *pɔtaḥ qɔton* to /e/ and /ɛ/ (Nutt 1870, VIII, lines 14–22, X, lines 19–21, and XI, lines 6–10). This contrast of 'big' and 'small' vowels may also be connected to similar descriptions of *matres lectionis* found in the work of Ḥayyūj's Arabic contemporaries, Ibn Jinnī (d. 1002) and Ibn Sīnā (d. 1037), and ultimately related to Greek phonetics (see above, chapter 2, §3.3). Notably, however, Ḥayyūj abandons this system for his later works on irregular verbs, *Kitāb al-Afʿal Dhuwāt Ḥurūf al-Līn* (*The Book of Verbs Which Have Soft Letters*) and *al-Qawl fī al-Afʿāl Dhuwāt al-Mathalayn* (*The Discourse on Verbs Which Have Two of the Same*) (Jastrow 1897, 220). In those texts, even though he expresses knowledge of other Hebrew vowel names, he prefers names from the Arabic grammatical tradition (e.g., *fatḥa*, *kasra*, *ḍamma*) to describe Hebrew phonology. The same expanded relative names also appear in T-S Ar.5.57, a Judaeo-Arabic fragment of a Hebrew grammatical text from the Cairo Genizah. It (T-S Ar.5.57 f. 1v, lines 5–6) discusses how certain forms of the root *ʾkl* have *qɔmeṣ qɔton* (/e/) or *qɔmeṣ gadol* (/ɔ/).

3.2. Graphemic Vowel Names

Hebrew scribes seem to have first supplemented the *ptḥ* and *qmṣ* vowel names by counting the dots in the Tiberian vowel signs. As such, they often called /i/ (אִ) and /o/ (אֹ) 'one dot', /e/ (אֵ) 'two dots', and /ɛ/ (אֶ) and /u/ (אֻ) 'three dots'. These names were still insufficient to name all the vowels absolutely, so some Masoretes—most notably the *Treatise on the Shewa*'s author—applied additional descriptors related to the position, location, and shape of the signs.

Ben Asher refers to several vowels according to numbers of dots in *Diqduqe ha-Ṭeʿamim*. When comparing different ways that one can vocalise כל (*kol* or *kɔl*), he writes: "But if it is cut off, not combined with its neighbour, it is free of *qɔmṣɔ*, and one dot is required (ואם הוא חתוך עם שכנו לא פתוך, מקמצה הוא רש ונקודה אחת נדרש)" (Dotan 1967, 119, lines 2–3). Similarly, he explains that the suffix *-hem* "is *qɔmeṣ qɔton* in every case, with two dots (הֶם בכל מקום קמץ קטן בשתי נקודות),", except in the context of a few letters, "which occur with three dots [/ɛ/] (בשלש נקודות מצויות)" (Dotan 1967, 137, lines 1–2). In stating that 'two dots' (*shte nequdot*)

accompany the *qɔmeṣ qɔton* (/e/) in -*hem*, but also that -*hɛm* occurs with 'three dots' (*shɔlosh nequdot*), Ben Asher links the vowel
points to the relative phonology of the term *qɔmeṣ*. This mixture
of terms is interesting, as it does not presuppose that the reader
already associates the *qɔmeṣ qɔton* with 'two dots'. This may in
turn imply that referring to a vowel by the number of its dots was
a recent development in Ben Asher's time. In any case, he is
aware of some convention that indicates /o/, /e/, and /ɛ/ according to the form of their Tiberian graphemes.

The descriptions of vowel points in two of Steiner's vowel
lists reflect terminology similar to Ben Asher's numeration. The
first refers to /e/ as *qɔmṣɔ qtannɔ*, but clarifies that it occurs with
shte nequdot. It then identifies /o/ as "one dot, placed all alone
(נְקֻדָּה אַחַת לְבַאד מוּנחת)," and /u/ as "the *ʾu* of the middle (או
האמצעית)" (Baer and Strack 1879, 11, lines 23–28), referring to
the intralinear position of the Tiberian vowel point. This last description incorporates the location of a point as an identifying
feature of a vowel phoneme, a concept which is more fully developed in *The Treatise on the Shewa* (see below). Steiner's second
list calls /ɛ/ *shɔlosh nequdot* 'three dots', but otherwise applies no
numbering conventions (Baer and Strack 1879, 36, lines 2–6).

Numerical vowel names also appear frequently in linguistic
texts from the Cairo Genizah, though the precise age of these references is difficult to determine. For example, T-S NS 301.37, a
fragment of a Judaeo-Arabic Karaite grammatical text, explains
the vocalisation of verbs that contain *al-nuqṭatayn* 'the two dots'
(T-S NS 301.37, recto line 10 and verso line 13). It also still vo-
calises *pth* as an Aramaic active participle, *pɔtaḥ* (פָּתַח) (T-S NS

301.37, verso line 2), which may suggest that it is relatively old.
T-S NS 301.48, another fragment of a grammatical text, refers to
/e/ and /ɛ/ as *al-nuqtatayn* 'the two' and *al-thalātha* 'the three',
respectively. It includes Arabic plural forms of *pɔtaḥ* and *qɔmeṣ*:
al-pātiḥāt and *al-qāmiṣāt* (T-S NS 301.48, f. 2 recto, line 24–25).
Although Arabic forms, these too are active participles, perhaps
translated from an earlier Aramaic source, and again may point
to a relatively early date. Unfortunately, the fragment is too
badly rubbed to decipher the rest of the text. Additionally, T-S
Ar.5.8 refers to *ptḥ mukhaffaf* 'lightened opening' and *nuqtatayn*
for /a/ and /e/ (T-S Ar.5.8, f. 1 verso, lines 4–5). This fragment
is vellum, has frequent *plene* spellings for Judaeo-Arabic words
(though not for the definite article with sun letters), and is in a
horizontal book format, all of which point to an early date (c.
tenth century).[41]

Naming vowels according to the graphemic appearance of
points was clearly not rare in the medieval Hebrew linguistic tradition, but the *Treatise on the Shewa* shows an especially developed application of this convention. Likely from the tenth century (Khan 2020, I:117–18), this text is a portion of a larger Masoretic treatise on Hebrew accents and vocalisation. It may be considered another *muṣawwitāt* text, and it refers to the category of
the seven Hebrew vowels using that term (Levy 1936, א; see
above, chapter 2, §1.2). The extant portion is a chapter on the

---

[41] On Judaeo-Arabic orthography, see Blau and Hopkins (1984) and
Khan (2018). On horizontal vs. vertical format in Islamicate codicology,
see Déroche (1992, 17–18), James (1992, 14), and Gruendler (2001,
142).

shewa—hence the modern title—which describes the various phonetic situations in which *shewa* can occur. The anonymous author writes mainly in Judaeo-Arabic, but they often switch into partially-rhymed Hebrew prose, including for some descriptions of the format of the treatise itself and the history of earlier Masoretes (Levy 1936, ה, line 3, ט, line 5, to י, line 9). This inconsistency suggests that the author drew on ninth-century Hebrew sources when writing the *Treatise*. The language variation also grants insight into the author's terms for vowels, as they provide their own Arabic translations for Hebrew terms that describe the appearance of vocalisation points.

Like most Hebrew scholars, the author of this text retains the roots of the old relative terms *ptḥ* and *qmṣ* and uses them to indicate /a/ and /ɔ/ (Levy 1936, י, line 10). For example, they say for *shewa*, "at the beginning of words, it is always *mutaḥarrik*, and its vocalisation and pronunciation are with *fātiḥa* 'opening' (פי אול אלתבות והו אבדא מתחרד ותחריכה וכרוגה יכון בפאתח)" (Levy 1936, ח, lines 2–3). Then, after a string of examples of words with vocalic *shewa*, the text reads, "all of them are opened in the recitation with *ptḥ* (גמיעהם ינפתחוא פי אלקראה בפתח)" (Levy 1936, ח, lines 4–5). These constructions are used practically interchangeably throughout the text to indicate that a vocalic *shewa* is pronounced as /a/, sometimes saying that its vocalisation is "with *ptḥ*" and other times "with *fātiḥa*" or "with *fatḥa* (פתחה)" (Levy 1936, ד, lines 12–13, יד, lines 13–14). However, in general, it

seems that *pth*[42] is the author's name for the vocalisation sign itself, because they refer several times to 'the vowel of *patah*'
(*haraka pth*) or 'the vowel of *qames*' (*haraka qms*)" (Levy 1936, ג,
lines 18–19, and כא, line 8). Moreover, they say that for a particular *'aleph* that has a *hatef patah*[43] sign (אֲ), "beneath the *'aleph* is
shewa and *pth* (ותחת אלאלף שוא ופתח)" (Levy 1936, יב, lines 2–3),
suggesting that the *pth* is the sublinear horizontal stroke itself. By
contrast, the Arabic forms *fātiha*, *fatha*, and *maftūh* 'opened' are
taken directly from the Arabic verb *fataha* 'to open' (Levy 1936,
יח, line 5, ט, line 5), which indicates the phonological process
that a *shewa* undergoes to acquire vocalic status. This usage
matches the way that Arabic grammarians describe the addition
of /a/ to a consonant (see above, chapter 2, §2.2), despite *shewa*
not being a full letter.

   As for the Tiberian *e*-vowels, the *Treatise on the Shewa* only
uses terms based on the number of dots for /e/ and /ɛ/. The author lists them alongside *pth* and *qms* with the Judaeo-Arabic
forms *thnatayn* 'two' (Levy 1936, כא, line 8) and *al-thalātha* 'the
three' (Levy 1936, י, lines 10–11), and in another section as *thnatayn nuqat* 'two dots' and *thalātha nuqat* 'three dots' (Levy 1936,
יח, line 14, and כ, lines 19–20). The author also denotes /e/ with
the Arabic dual form *al-nuqtatayn* 'the two dots' (Levy 1936, כ,
line 20). Similarly, the text describes what is now known as *hatef*

---

[42] Likely vocalised like the Aramaic active participle *pɔtah*, but the text
only gives the consonants.

[43] The text does not use this precise term, although it does use the *htp*
root in several instances to describe shortened vowels. See Levy (1936,
י and כה, lines 5–6).

segol with the phrase *al-thalātha shewa* 'the three-*shewa*(?)', using their name for /ɛ/ as an attribute of a vocalic *shewa*. Finally, in another instance where the author shows the differences in their various source materials, they explain how to pronounce *shewa* in forms of the Hebrew verb *ʾɔkal*. Beginning in Hebrew, they write, "every variant of *ʾɔkila*, if it is with *shɔlosh nequdot*... (כל לשון אכילה אם בשלושה נקודות)" (Levy 1936, ל, line 8), and then explain the effect of /ɛ/ on *shewa*. They then continue, now in Arabic: "but if *nuqṭayn*[44] is after the *shewa*... (ואדא כאן בעד אלשוא נקטין)" (Levy 1936, ל, lines 10–11), before explaining the impact of /e/ on *shewa*. It seems that the author is either combining passages from separate Hebrew and Arabic works or composing additional Arabic sentences to expand an earlier Hebrew text. As a result, the Arabic term *nuqṭayn* 'two dots' appears here beside the Hebrew *shɔlosh nequdot* 'three dots', even though the author has already used a Hebrew term for 'two dots'—*shte nequdot*—earlier in the text (Levy 1936, יז, line 10).

None of these terms for *e*-vowels vary substantially from those in *Diqduqe ha-Teʿamim* or other Masoretic texts that also count dots, but the *Treatise on the Shewa* distinguishes itself by implementing additional names based on the location of the dots. When indicating /o/, the text reads: "as for the symbol of the upper one, I mean, the upper dot (ואמא סימן העליוני אעני אלנקטה אלפוקא)" (Levy 1936, טז, line 15). The author uses the Hebrew phrase *siman ha-ʿelyoni* 'the symbol of the upper one', applying a nominal form related to the Hebrew preposition *ʿal* 'over, above'

---

[44] This spelling might be a mistake for *nuqṭatayn* 'two dots', but it could also be an intentional dual form of *naqṭ* 'pointing'.

(see Dotan 2007, 634; Khan 2020, I:263). They translate this term
with the Arabic phrase *al-nuqṭa al-fawqā* 'the upper dot', using a
nominalised form of the Arabic preposition *fawqa* 'over, above'.
Then for /i/, they write, "as for the lowered symbol (פאמא אלסימן
אלתחתוני)" (Levy 1936, י׳, lines 1–2), again using a noun (*al-
taḥtoni* 'the lowered one') formed from a Hebrew preposition
(*taḥat* 'under, below'), although this time prefixing it with the
Arabic (rather than Hebrew) definite article. Later, they give additional Arabic calques of the Hebrew terms, referring to *al-siman
al-fawqānī* 'the upper symbol' and *al-saflānī* 'the lower [symbol]'
(Levy 1936, יט׳, line 1). In all of these cases, the word *siman* 'symbol' suggests that these locative terms are names for the dots
themselves. Nevertheless, a deliberate association of 'upperness'
and 'lowerness' with the vowels /o/ and /i/, respectively, is precisely the type of description that would be expected in a graphical system that evolved from a relative system that connected
phonetic backness to a height-based scale (see above, chapter 3,
§1.3).

In addition to the 'above' and 'below' terms, the text sometimes refers to /i/ and /o/ by simply counting their dots, just as
for /e/ and /ɛ/. For example, the author indicates /i/ by saying
that a word is read with *nuqṭa wāḥida* 'one dot' (Levy 1936, יט׳,
lines 14–15), trusting that the reader can tell from context that
they mean a dot below (/i/) rather than a dot above (/o/). Additionally, when listing the vowels that have reduced forms (i.e.,
ḥaṭef vowels), the author explains that they are only "*ptḥ, qmṣ,*
and *al-thalātha nuqaṭ*, but not *al-nuqṭatayn*, or one *min fawqa* or
min ʾasfal" (Levy 1936, ב, lines 18–21). That is, *shewa* can reduce

/a/, /ɔ/, and /ɛ/, but not /e/, /o/, or /i/. These last two are
called 'one above' (*wāḥid min fawqa*) and 'below' (*min 'asfal*), respectively, paralleling the construction of *milleʿel* 'above' and *milleraʿ* 'below' found in earlier Masoretic sources.

Lastly, the *Treatise on the Shewa* includes multiple ways to
indicate the vowel /u/, which is unique in the Tiberian pointing
system in that it has two different graphemes: one dot within a
mater lectionis waw (וּ) or three oblique dots below a consonant
(אֻ). The author accounts for this fact at the end of one of their
vowel lists, describing /u/ as "the three which are pronounced
with ʾu, which they call *al-zujj* (אלתלתה אלתי תכרג באוּ אלדׁין יסמונהא
אלזֻג)" (Levy 1936, יׁ, lines 1–2). 'The three' here refers to the
three sublinear dots of the second sign for /u/, but the author
explains the phonetic quality of this sign by spelling out the
sound, using a *waw* with a single dot (אוּ). As for *zujj*, in Classical
Arabic, it refers to a physical 'tip' or 'point', usually of something
that pierces, like an arrow or spear (Kazimirski 1860, 973; Lane
1863, 1215). *Al-zujj* thus describes the 'piercing' of a *wāw* by the
intralinear dot that represents /u/. This name also occurs in two
eleventh-century Karaite texts, namely *Hidāya al-Qārī* (*The Guide
for the Reader*) by Abū al-Faraj Hārūn and the anonymous *Kitāb
al-ʿUqūd fī Taṣārīf al-Lugha al-ʿIbrāniyya* (*The Book of Rules Con-
cerning the Grammatical Inflections of the Hebrew Language*) (Vidro
2013, 2–3, 395; Khan 2020, II:17). Besides *zujj*, the *Treatise on
the Shewa* still identifies /u/ by counting the dot in a *mater lectionis waw*. For example, they instruct that if a *waw* with a *shewa*
precedes *bet*, *mem*, or *peʾ*, then "never point with a *shewa*, but
rather with one dot (לא תנקט בשוא לעולם בל בנקטה ואחדה)" (Levy

1936, כו, lines 16–17). Likewise, those same *waws* are "pointed and recited with a dot in the heart of the *waw* (ינקט ויקרא בנקטה בגוף אלואו)" (Levy 1936, כז, lines 17–18).

To summarise, the *Treatise on the Shewa* follows the basic Hebrew vowel naming conventions inherited from the early relative vocalisation system, and also uses one of the most developed sets of Masoretic vowel names based on graphemic descriptions. Like most Hebrew linguists, the author refers to /a/ and /ɔ/ using the older relative terms from the roots *ptḥ* 'opening' and *qmṣ* 'closing'. Like *Diqduqe ha-Ṭeʿamim*, T-S NS 301.37, and T-S NS 301.48, they supplement these two names by counting dots. The result is vowel numerical terminology in both Hebrew (*shte nedudot, shɔlosh nequdot*) and Arabic (*al-nuqṭatayn, thnatayn nuqaṭ, al-thalātha, thalātha nuqaṭ*) for the vowels /e/ and /ɛ/. Accordingly, the author calls both /o/ and /i/ *nuqṭa waḥida*, assuming that the reader can differentiate them from context, but also gives them names related to their position, again in both Hebrew (*ha-ʿelyoni, al-taḥtoni*) and Arabic (*al-nuqṭa al-fawqā, al-fawqānī, al-saflānī*). Finally, /u/ is both *nuqṭa wāḥida* (ו) and *al-thalātha* (א), depending on its grapheme, and also takes the Arabic name *al-zujj* 'piercing', referring to the physical form of a single dot within a *mater lectionis waw*.

Many Hebrew linguists continued using vowel terms based on the physical appearance of graphemes, even into the eleventh century (Khan 2000, 24; Dotan 2007, 634). However, while Ben Asher was writing about *qɔmeṣ qɔṭon* and 'the two dots', other scholars were implementing vowel names as phonetic descriptions of articulation.

3.3. Phonetic Vowel Names

The 'modern' Hebrew vowel names are almost all phonetic names, derived from the descriptions of articulatory actions that produce them, but they did not all develop from the same source. Like the expanded relative system and the naming conventions based on graphemes, the phonetic names for /a/ and /ɔ/ remained *pataḥ* 'opening' and *qameṣ* 'closing', or minor variations thereof. At some early stage (c. ninth century), Masoretes assigned the remaining vowels Aramaic names based on the roots *ḥlm* 'closing firmly' (/o/), *ṣry* 'crack, rift, splitting' (/e/), *ḥrq* (/i/) 'gnashing, grinding the teeth', and *shrq* 'whistling' (/u/), each corresponding to physical motions involved in articulation. The main exception to this convention is the term for /ɛ/, which goes by the name *segol* 'a bunch of grapes' in most phonetic vowel lists, probably based on an analogy with the accent sign of the same name and shape (*segoltɔ*: אֱ) (see Dotan 2007, 637).

The earliest dated list of phonetic vowel names comes from the fifth chapter of Saadia Gaon's *Kutub al-Lugha* (*The Books of the Language*), titled *al-Qawl fī al-Nagham* (*The Discourse on Melody*), which he wrote sometime between 913 and 931 (Lambert 1891, 76, n. 1 [French]; Malter 1921, 44, n. 57).[45] This chapter is thus one of the earliest explanations of Hebrew vowel phonology that goes beyond basic instructions for recitation. In the text, Saadia places the Hebrew vowels on a vertical scale that follows the phonetic hierarchy of the *mille'el* and *millera'* homograph

---

[45] Saadia completed his earliest work, the poetic dictionary *Agron*, when he was twenty years old in 913. He completed his *Commentary of Sefer Yeṣira*, which cites *Kutub al-Lugha*, in 931. See Brody (2016, 79).

272   *Points of Contact*

comparisons, judging those which are pronounced farther back
in the mouth to be 'higher' than those pronounced near the front
(see above, chapter 3, §§1.2–3). He explains how the vowels are
arranged according to the place at which one interrupts their airflow, writing:

ואמא שרח אלבאב אלתאלת אלדי הו מערפה אמאכנהא פי אלפם
ומראתבהא פאנא נקול אדא אכתאר אן יפצל נגמתה פי אול מוצע ימכנה
קטעהא פיה בעד תרקיתהא מן אלחלק פאנה יטהר אלחלם וקותה
סאלכה אמאמה גיר חאידה אלי פוק ולא אלי אספל ואן שא אן יתגאוז
בהא הדא אלמוצע תם יפצלהא טהרת קוה אלקמץ וכאנת חרכתה אלי
אעלי אלחנך כאצה

As with the explanation of the third chapter, which was
the knowledge of the places in the mouth, and their levels,
we say then: if someone chose to interrupt their melody at
the first point, they could cut it off after its ascension from
the throat; then *al-ḥlm* would appear, with its force proceeding ahead of it, not wavering upwards or downwards.
But if one wanted to take [the melody] past this point, then
they would interrupt it, the force of *al-qmṣ* would appear,
and its movement is specifically towards the top of the palate. (Skoss 1952, 292, lines 7–13)

This passage shows the extent to which Saadia was familiar with
the Arabic grammatical tradition, as his progression through the
'points' (*mawāḍiʿ*) and 'levels' (*marātib*) of the mouth mirrors the
language of al-Khalīl ibn Aḥmad (d. 786/91) and Sībawayh (d.
793/6) in their rankings of the Arabic articulation points in *Kitāb
al-ʿAyn* and *Kitāb Sībawayh*. Also note the similarity between Saadia's description of /ɔ/ and Sībawayh's description of the allophones of *ʾalif* following *mustaʿliya* letters (i.e., /ɑ/, /ɔ/)
(Sībawayh 1986, IV:129; see above, chapter 3, §2.2). On the

other hand, while the precise definition of 'force' (*quwwa*) in this text is not entirely clear, it seems to refer to the stream of air that emits during the articulation of a vowel. Saadia applies it to explain the ways in which one can manipulate the direction of airflow to produce different phonemes. This meaning of *quwwa* differs from that found in *Kitāb Sībawayh*, where the word instead indicates the 'strength' of phonological elements (al-Nassir 1993, 121).

More importantly for our current discussion, this passage also explains how *ḥlm* (/o/) and *qmṣ* (/ɔ/) are 'cut off' (*faṣala*; *qaṭaʿa*) as the first two vowels on the Hebrew scale. That is, they are articulated farthest back in the mouth, with *ḥlm* occurring as close as possible to the throat, and *qmṣ* occurring just ahead of it at 'the top of the palate' (*ʾaʿlā al-ḥanak*). Moreover, while the 'force' (*quwwa*) of the *qmṣ* requires some 'movement' (*ḥaraka*) up towards the palate, the *quwwa* of *ḥlm* does not turn 'upwards' (*ʾilā fawq*) or 'downwards' (*ʾilā ʾasfal*) at all. This perception of /o/ as 'unwavering' (*ghayr ḥāʾida*) is unique to the Hebrew linguistic tradition, and does not occur in phonological descriptions of Syriac or Arabic vowels. It also shows that the direction of airflow during articulation was a significant phonetic feature for Saadia, and he uses that feature throughout this section to differentiate vowels.

It is sometimes difficult to determine how exactly Saadia, or indeed any medieval Hebrew grammarian, would have pronounced their vowel terms. While most of the names in this text appear to have Hebrew forms, *qmṣ* was probably still pronounced close to the older Aramaic participial form *qɔmeṣ* 'closing'. However, Saadia also refers to /ɔ/ as *qamṣa* (קמצה) (Skoss 1952, 296, line 17, and 314, line 1),[46] possibly on analogy with the pattern of the Arabic vowel names (*fatḥa, kasra, ḍamma*). As for *ḥlm*, it was not until the eleventh century that Hebrew grammarians began adding 'symbolic' vowels to the first syllable of vowel names to match the phonetic qualities which those names denoted (i.e., *ḥolem, shuruq, pataḥ*, etc.) (Steiner 2005, 380; Dotan 2007, 634), so Saadia probably pronounced *ḥlm* like a Hebrew segolate noun.[47] The vocalisation *ḥelɛm* (חֶלֶם) does appear in Skoss' manuscript of *al-Qawl fī al-Nagham* (Skoss 1952, 292, line 27, footnote), and it also occurs in other Masoretic works (Steiner 2005, 377; Khan 2020, I:263).[48] As we will see, that Hebrew form is probably derived from an earlier Aramaic term, meaning 'closing firmly', indicating the near-total closure of the lips when articulating /o/.

Stepping down the scale and away from the most-backed vowels, Saadia then describes the intermediate /a/ and /ɛ/:

> ואן שא אן יתג̇אוז בהא הד̇א אלמוצ̇ע ת̇ם יקטעהא עלי מא בעדה ט̇הרת
> אלפתחה וקותהא סאירה עלי סטח אללסאן מנחדרה אלי אלספל. ואן
> אכ̇תאר אן יבקיהא פי הד̇ה אלמוצ̇ע לכנה ימלא מנהא ג̇אנבי פמה
> אלספליין ט̇הר אלסגול וקותה משתמלה עלי נצף אלפם אלאספל

---

[46] Alternatively, *qāmiṣa* or *qɔmṣɔ*, though Skoss transcribes it with defective spelling and a final *tāʾ marbūṭa*.

[47] That is, a noun of the form *CvCvC* with stress on the onset syllable, usually containing two *e*-vowels, and ultimately formed from the historical bases *qaṭl/qiṭl/quṭl*.

[48] See also, the Genizah fragment T-S NS 301.69, recto, line 5.

> If one wanted to also pass this point, then they would cut
> off [the melody] at what is beyond it, and *al-fatḥa* would
> appear, its force progressing along the surface of the
> tongue, descending towards the bottom. Then, if they
> chose to keep it at that point, but also fill both bottom sides
> of their mouth, *al-sgwl* would appear, and its force would
> be completely upon the lower half of the mouth. (Skoss
> 1952, 292, lines 14–18)

Saadia indicates that /a/ is *fatḥa* 'opening', adopting the name
for the same vowel in the Arabic grammatical tradition, although
later on he does refer to it with just *ptḥ* (likely pronounced *pɔtaḥ*)
(Skoss 1952, 294, line 1).[49] He again describes the motion of the
vowel's *quwwa*, noting that the *quwwa* of *fatḥa* moves downward
(*munḥadira ʾilā al-safl*) along the tongue. This contrasts the *quwwa*
of *qmṣ*, which moved up towards the velum.[50] *Al-Qawl fī al-
Nagham* thus indicates that the articulation point (*mawḍiʿ*) of /a/
is in the space 'past' the point of /ɔ/ (i.e., more fronted), and its
airflow has a comparatively downward trajectory.

According to Saadia, the vowel *segol* (/ɛ/) occurs at the
same location in the mouth as /a/, but its *quwwa* moves in a different direction. Rather than passing over the surface of the
whole tongue, *segol*'s *quwwa* only manifests in 'the lower half of
the mouth' (*niṣf al-fam al-ʾasfal*). The speaker compresses it into
this lowered position by 'filling' (*yamlaʾu*) the sides of the mouth,

---

[49] This form (פתח) could also be the Arabic word *fatḥ*, and it raises the
question of whether some Hebrew linguists said *patḥa* for /a/.

[50] Compare this language with the words associated with 'high' and
'low' positions in Arabic grammatical texts; see Kinberg (1987, 8) and
above, chapter 3, §2.2.

indicating a slight contraction of the cheeks and the sides of the lips. Unlike the rest of the names in this chapter, the Aramaic word *segol* 'a bunch of grapes' is a graphemic term designating the physical shape of its vowel sign (אֶ), rather than any phonetic feature. The source of this name is most likely the Aramaic name of the Hebrew accent sign *segol/segoltɔ*, which consists of a similar supralinear cluster of three dots (אֵ) (Dotan 2007, 637). This sign and its name likely predate the vocalisation points and the use of *segol* to mean /ɛ/.

Saadia continues his descent, moving down to the two most fronted vowels on the Hebrew scale:

ואן גֿאז בהא הדֿא אלמוצֿע תֿם קרב טרף אללסאן אלי אסנאנה ולם
יטבקהא טֿהר אלצֿירי ואן הו אטבקהא צֿהר אלחרק והתאן אלנגמתאן
תגֿאור אלאסנאן מן דאכֿלהא

If one passed this point with [the melody], and then the tip of the tongue drew near to their teeth, but did not cover them, then *al-ṣyry* would appear; and if it did cover them, then *al-ḥrq* would appear. These two vowels are adjacent to the interior side of the teeth (Skoss 1952, 292, lines 18–21).

Ṣyry (/e/) and *ḥrq* (/i/) occur past the point of /a/ and /ɛ/, at the theoretically 'lowest' position near the front of the mouth. *Ḥrq* requires a slightly lower placement of the tongue than *ṣyry*. Each of these vowel names is a description of a phonetic process (Dotan 2007, 634). In Aramaic, *ṣyry* 'crack, rift, splitting' indicates the narrow fissure between the lips during the articulation of /e/. Meanwhile, the verb *ḥraq* 'to gnash the teeth' would describe the overlapping motion of the teeth in producing /i/. In this instance, *ḥrq* is written without any *matres lectionis*, which again suggests a vocalisation like a Hebrew segolate noun (e.g., *ḥereq* 'gnashing the teeth').

Saadia's scale skips /u/, even though earlier Masoretic homograph lists judged it to be *milleʿel* 'above' in comparison to /ɔ/, and should thus precede *al-qmṣ* as the more-backed vowel. Instead, he writes:

ואן גֿאוז בהא גֿמיע אלמואצֿע אלמדֿצורה חתי תכֿרג עז אלאסנאן טהר
אלשרק וקותה פי מא ביז אלאסנאן ואלשפתין

If one took [the melody] past all of the aforementioned points, until it exited from the teeth, then *al-shrq* would appear, and its force would be in between the teeth and the lips (Skoss 1952, 292, lines 21–22).

Saadia removes *al-shrq* (i.e., /u/) from the mouth entirely, placing it at the lowest point on his scale, with its *quwwa* moving specifically through the teeth and lips. Noting this odd placement, Dotan points out that /u/ must be at this low point on the scale in order to justify later claims that Saadia makes about Hebrew morphology (Dotan 1974, 28–30). After defining the scale in this section, Saadia spends the second half of the chapter explaining this theory of morphology, which is based on the idea that when a word is inflected or its pronunciation changes due to its context in recitation, the vowels in the that word generally shift to the step immediately above or below it on the scale (Skoss 1952, 300–2). For example, the first vowel in the singular noun *ʿomɛr* 'sheaf' in עֹמֶר הַתְּנוּפָה (Lev. 23.15) is /o/, but in the plural form *ʿɔmɔrim* of בֵּין הָעֳמָרִים (Ruth 2.15), that first vowel moves one step down to /ɔ/ (Skoss 1952, 304, lincs 5–6).

Saadia continues in this manner as he records numerous possible vowel changes in Hebrew, describing shifts from a lower to a higher vowel as 'rising' (*rafʿ*; notably the name of the Arabic nominal case), and from a higher to a lower vowel as 'descending' (*habūṭ/ḥaṭṭ/naql*) (Skoss 1952, 302–14). However, he does not find any instances of /u/ 'rising' to another vowel, and only finds three cases total where another vowel—always /o/—'descends' to /u/. As such, he cannot reconcile his theory of morphology based on single-step vowel increments with the phonetic arrangement of the *milleʿel-milleraʿ* scale. According to his morphological theory, if /u/ were truly one phonetic step beneath /o/, then words with /o/ (e.g., *ʿomɛr*) should descend to /u/ (i.e., *ʿumɔrim*, which does not occur). Likewise, words with /ɔ/ would ascend to /u/, and they do not. Faced with a choice between being wrong about morphology or rearranging the scale, Saadia rearranges the scale, concluding:

פאד̇ קד תממנא הד̇ה אלמרכבאת פינבגי אן נאתי בעדהא בשרח אלבאב אלכ̇אמס אלד̇י הו מערפה הבוט אלנגמאת מן דרג̇ה אלי אכ̇רי ונקול איﬨ נגמה מן הד̇ה אלסת אלתי דאכ̇ל אלפם ונעזל אלשרק אד̇ [הו] כ̇ארג̇ אלפם אעני אן קותה באלשפתין פאנה לד̇לך לא מדכ̇ל לה מע הד̇ה אלסת אלא פי שי שאד̇ נד̇כרה [לא]חקא.

Now that we have come to the end of these combinations, we must next set forth the explanation of the fifth chapter, which is the knowledge of the descent of the vowels from one level to another. We speak on any of these six vowels which are inside the mouth, and we remove *al-shrq*, since it is outside the mouth. That is, its force is at the lips, and therefore it is not included among these six, except in an irregular case, which we will mention afterwards (Skoss 1952, 300, line 23, to 302, line 5).

With /u/ now outside the mouth, Saadia has no problems: his principles of morphological ascent and descent hold for all vowels within the mouth. His justification for removing /u/ may also be bolstered by an idea from Arabic phonetics, specifically as we have seen in *Kitāb Sībawayh* and Ibn Jinnī's *Sirr Ṣinā'a al-I'rāb*, wherein every vowel shares an articulation point with its *mater lectionis* (Sībawayh 1986, IV:101; Kinberg 1987, 16–18; Ibn Jinnī 1993, 8, 53–54; see also above, chapter 2, §3.3, and chapter 3, §2.2). The articulation point of /u/ is thus at the same place as the bilabial *wāw*. It is worth noting that this rearrangement—and probably the morphological theory—may predate Saadia, as several other Masoretic sources (e.g., the two *muṣawwitāt* texts that follow) also put /u/ at the end of their vowel lists.

Despite this morphological pontification, when Saadia does describe the phonetic shift from /o/ to /u/, he still regards it as 'descent' (*ḥaṭṭ*) from *ḥlm* to *shrq* (Skoss 1952, 308, lines 11–12). Additionally, in his *Commentary on Sefer Yeṣira*, written several years after *Kutub al-Lugha*, Saadia explains that there are gradients which occur between the seven vowels, including ones that are between "*al-qamṣa* and *al-fatḥa*" as well as between "*al-ḥlm* and *al-shrq*" (Lambert 1891, 43, lines 7–9). This explanation further suggests that, even though Saadia needs /u/ to be at the bottom of the scale for his morphological system to work, he still acknowledges that it is phonetically nearer to /o/, and thus would have a place within the mouth.

Finally, we come to the word *al-shrq*, Saadia's term for /u/. This name, likely pronounced *shɛrɛq*, means 'whistling', comparing the shape of the lips to the articulation of /u/. Like

ḥlm, *ṣyry*, and *ḥrq*, it is ultimately based on an Aramaic word indicating the phonetic action required to produce the vowel, but
it appears here as a Hebrew segolate. This name encompasses
both the sign with a single dot inside a *waw* and the sublinear
sign with three oblique dots, as Saadia makes no distinction between them.

Besides this list of names from *Kutub al-Lugha*, Saadia provides another list in his *Commentary on Sefer Yeṣira*, and it shows
that his seven vowel terms remained static between the times
that he completed the two works. In the *Commentary*, he includes
the vowels with an account of the alphabet, saying:

يبتدئوا بهذه الـدَّدَ ويضمّون اليها الـأ المضاعف ويضيفون اليها الـأ نغمات
اعني قمץ وفتح وחلم وסגול וחرق وצרי ושرق فتصيرلا

> They begin with these twenty-two, and they bring them
> together with the seven doubles, and then they add the
> seven vowels, I mean, *qmṣ*, *ptḥ*, *ḥlm*, *sgwl*, *ḥrq*, *ṣry*, and *shrq*,
> and they make thirty-six. (Lambert 1891, 42, lines 8–10)

The vowel names in this text are essentially identical to those in
Kutub al-Lugha. Besides minor variations with the endings on *qmṣ*
and *ptḥ*, the phonetic terms tend to appear without *matres lectionis*, once again suggesting that they were pronounced as segolates. Some manuscript variants of this list also contain *ḥyrq*, *ṣyry*,
or *shyrq* (Lambert 1891, 42, nn. 3–5; see also, Steiner 2005, 380–
81), showing that while a shift from normal segolates to terms
with an initial 'symbolic' vowel (i.e., *ḥireq* for /i/, /ḥolem/ for /o/)
certainly occurred, the first vowel was not always the one that
the term represented (e.g., *shirεq* or *sherεq* for /u/). Moreover, in
their original forms—before Saadia and prior to their status as

Hebrew segolates—the phonetic vowel names *ḥlm, ḥrq, ṣry,* and *shrq* all existed as Aramaic nouns.

Two *muṣawwitāt* texts use phonetic terminology similar to Saadia, but rather than Hebrew segolates, their vowel names are distinct Aramaic nominal forms. The extant manuscripts of these two texts are also notable in that their scripts are quite similar. They may have been copied by the same scribe or by two scribes trained in the same unique style, even though one is square format on parchment (T-S Ar.53.1) and the other is vertical on paper (T-S Ar.31.28).[51] If the copyist was also the author of these texts, then it is clear they held a single systematic conception of the vowel names in Aramaic. On the other hand, they may merely have reproduced two earlier Masoretic treatises with similar terminology. Either way, these two manuscripts were probably produced during a single lifetime around the tenth century. The text from T-S Ar.53.1 begins quite succinctly:

אעלם באן אלמצותאת ז מן סוא אלשוא אלאול חלמא והו או אלב קָמֵץ
והו אָא אלג פתח והו אא אלד סגול והו אֶי אלה צריא והו אֵי אלו חרקא
והו אִי אלז שרקא והו או ואלשוא והמא אלנקטתאן אלקאימתאן. . .

> Know that the vowels are seven, excluding the *shewa*. The first is *ḥlm*ʾ, and it is ʾo. The second is *qɔmeṣ*, and it is ʾɔ. The third is *ptḥ*, and it is ʾa. The fourth is *sgwl*, and it is ʾɛ. The fifth is *ṣry*ʾ, and it is ʾe. The sixth is *ḥrq*ʾ, and it is ʾi. The seventh is *shrq*ʾ, and it is ʾu. And then *shewa*, which is

---

[51] Square and horizontal format Genizah manuscripts are generally earlier than vertical formats, and parchment Genizah manuscripts are generally older than paper. My thanks to Ben Outhwaite for pointing out the similarity of the scribal hands.

the two standing dots.... (Allony and Yeivin 1985, 91, line
1, to 92, line 9)

Several details stand out from this passage. First, *qɔmeṣ* is vocalised as an active participle, still in its original Aramaic form, and
presumably *pɔtaḥ* would have been as well. Second, the author
spells out all the vowel sounds phonetically (*ʾa, ʾe*, etc.), a practice which predates the naming of any vowels, and probably predates the creation of the pointing system. Third, the name for the
"two standing dots" is vocalised as either *shewa* or *shewɔ* 'equal,
levelling', another Aramaic form.[52] Fourth, the author describes
the shape of the *shewa* grapheme (*al-nuqtatān al-qāʾimatān*), but
not the vowel signs, suggesting that either the name *shewa* or the
sign itself had only recently been introduced, at a time when the
vowel points had already been well established (Dotan 2007,
634). Finally, the author gives the four phonetic vowel names as
ḥlmʾ (/o/), *ṣryʾ* (/e/), *ḥrqʾ* (/i/), and *shrqʾ* (/u/). These all appear
to be Aramaic emphatic nominal forms, probably *ḥelmɔ, ṣeryɔ,
ḥerqɔ*, and *sherqɔ*, but they are unvocalised in the manuscript.

The second text, from T-S Ar.31.28, provides more information for the internal vocalisation of these Aramaic terms. It
begins with a *lacuna*, but the ensuing discussion includes: "*al-ʾo*,
which its name is *ḥlmʾ* (אלאו אלדֿי אסמה חלמא);" "*al-qɔmeṣ* (אלקֶמֶץ);"
"*al-fatḥa* (אלפתחה);" and "*shrqɔ* (אלשרקָ[א])" (Allony and Yeivin
1985, 99, lines 5–9). Later in the manuscript, the author lists:

אלוֹ מלוך והם אלחלמא אעני או ואלקמצה אעני אָ ואלפתחה אעני אָ...
ואלסֶגול והו אָ ואלצֶרֶיָא והו אָ ואלחרקא והו אָ ואלשרקא והו אָ

---

[52] On a potential link between *shewa* and Syriac accents, see Dotan
(1954).

> ...the seven *mulūk*, and they are *al-ḥlmɔ*, I mean *ɔo*, *al-qmṣa*,
> I mean *ɔɔ*, *al-ptḥa*, I mean *ɔa*, *al-segwl*, I mean *ɔɛ*, *al-ṣiryɔ*, I
> mean *ɔe*, *al-ḥrqɔ*, I mean *ɔi*, and *al-shrqɔ*, I mean *ɔu*. (Allony
> and Yeivin 1985, 102, lines 58–64; see also, present vol-
> ume, cover image)

Once again, the vowels are spelled out phonetically, and the author names /o/, /e/, /i/, and /u/ with Aramaic emphatic nouns
that end in *ɔaleph*. However, in contrast to those four vowels,
qmṣa (/ɔ/) and *ptḥa* (/a/) are spelled with final *heɔ*.[53] This difference makes sense, as the names of /ɔ/ and /a/ were derived separately based on early relative terminology, and here they seem
to be either Arabicised forms (like *fatḥa*, *kasra*, *ḍamma*) or retain
an older style of Aramaic orthography. The term from the root
ṣry also stands out, as it is completely vocalised, giving the form
ṣiryɔ. It may be possible to extrapolate this vowel pattern onto
the other unvocalised names (i.e., *ḥilmɔ*, *ḥirqɔ*, *shirqɔ*), but it is
perhaps more likely that *ṣiryɔ* was unique in having an initial /i/.
This /i/ may have been contextually conditioned by harmony
with the *yod* in the second syllable, while the other names had
/e/ or /a/ (*ḥelmɔ*, *ḥerqɔ*, *sherqɔ*) like most Aramaic nouns of this
pattern.

The vowel names in these two *muṣawwitāt* texts are almost
certainly older than those of *Kutub al-Lugha*. Given that these
works are all written in Judaeo-Arabic, it is not surprising that
they contain some Hebrew and Aramaic technical terms. That
said, since Saadia wrote *Kutub al-Lugha* in the early tenth century,

---

[53] Though note the name *ptḥɔ* (פתחא), spelled with *ɔaleph* at least once
in *Diqduqe ha-Teʿamim* (Dotan 1967, 114, line 5).

if its apparent Hebrew segolate terms (ḥelɛm, ṣyry, ḥrq, shrq) are the original forms of the phonetic vowel names, then it would be likely that he or someone shortly before him had deliberately created them as Hebraisms to name the Tiberian vowels. If this development occurred, then the authors of T-S Ar.53.1 and T-S Ar.31.28 would have had to take those Hebrew terms and convert them to Aramaic forms (ḥelmɔ, ṣiryɔ, ḥerqɔ, and sherqɔ) for use in otherwise Arabic texts. It is unlikely that tenth-century Arabic-speaking Masoretes would have calqued Hebrew technical terms into Aramaic in this manner. Much more likely, these Aramaic forms are remnants of an earlier stage of linguistic activity, probably from the second half of the ninth century, when the Masoretes still wrote in Aramaic (see Khan 2020, I:246).

Accordingly, all four of the phonetic names are best understood as Aramaic descriptions of articulation: closing firmly (ḥelmɔ; /o/); splitting (ṣiryɔ; /e/); gnashing (ḥerqɔ; /i/); and whistling (sherqɔ; /u/). Then, in the first quarter of the tenth century, some linguists (perhaps Saadia was the first) rendered them with Hebrew segolate forms, creating vowel names like ḥelɛm or ḥɛlɛm. These segolates gradually gave way to names with 'symbolic' first vowels, as later grammarians adopted the practice of putting the vowel that a term represented into the term itself (e.g., ḥolem, qɔmeṣ, pataḥ, sɛgol, ṣere, ḥireq, shureq) (Steiner 2005, 380; Dotan 2007, 634).

Finally, qibbuṣ, the 'modern' name for the three-dot sign of /u/, is the last Hebrew vowel term that has its roots in a phonetic description. It is not derived from the same relative terminology as *pɔtaḥ* and *qɔmeṣ*, nor was it originally an Aramaic term. Instead, *qibbuṣ* is most likely calqued from *ḍamm*, a by-product of contact between the Hebrew and Arabic grammatical traditions in the period after Saadia and Aharon ben Asher. Evidence of this contact is not limited to *qibbuṣ* alone, and although the phonetic vowel names eventually became the Hebrew standard, tenth- and eleventh-century grammarians also utilised a range of vowel names from the Arabic grammatical tradition.

3.4. Names from Arabic Grammar and the Division of the Vowel Scale

Besides the Aramaic phonetic terms, some tenth- and eleventh-century Hebrew linguists adapted Arabic terms to describe the Tiberian vocalisation system. These Masoretes and grammarians supplemented the basic relative pair of *ptḥ* and *qmṣ* with the names for vowels and cases in the Arabic grammatical tradition. One important example of this phenomenon is the anonymous *muṣawwitāt* text that Allony first identified as *Kitāb al-Muṣawwitāt* (Allony 1964; 1965; 1983; see above, chapter 2, §1.2), which uses a combination of the expanded Hebrew relative names and the Arabic case names to list all of the Tiberian vowels. Similarly, the Masoretic texts *Nequdot Omeṣ ha-Miqrɔ* (*The Dots of the Greatness of the Scripture*) (Baer and Strack 1879, §36, 34, lines 5–9) and *Kitāb Naḥw al-ʕIbrānī* (*The Book of Hebrew Inflection*) (Eldar 1981) show that some scholars modified the *milleʕel-millerɑʕ* scale by dividing the vowels into groups according to Arabic case names. Abū al-Faraj Hārūn made comparable modifications to the scale in his classification of vowels in *Hidāya al-Qārī* (*The Guide for the Reader*) (Khan 2020).

The *muṣawwitāt* text composed of the fragments T-S Ar.32.31 and AIU IX.A.24 (and probably T-S Ar.33.6)[54] uses a unique combination of Hebrew and Arabic vowel terminology. It classifies every vowel in the context of its role in Hebrew grammar, generally by identifying the types of words which most commonly contain each one. Throughout the extant text, the author abbreviates *pɔtaḥ* and *qɔmeṣ* to *pt* (פת) and *qm* (קמֹ), though this in itself is not remarkable, as they also abbreviate other common words to save space (Allony 1983, 88). These abbreviations are included in the complete vowel list, which begins:

אלמצותאת באסמא לאיקה בהא דאלה עלי מעאניהא בלגה ערביה ליכון
סהל עלי אלנאטֹר ובין ללקארי והי אלמצותאת סבעה אחדהא אלקמֹ
אלכבירה

The vowels have names which are suitable for them, indicating their meanings in the Arabic language, so that they are easy to recognise and clear for the reader. The vowels are seven, and the first of them is *al-qm al-kabīra*. (Allony 1965, 140, lines 28–30)

The first of the 'vowels' (*muṣawwitāt*) is /ɔ/, called *al-qm al-kabīra* large *qameṣ*, following the expanded relative naming convention

---

[54] See Allony (1983). He argues that the content of T-S Ar.33.6 is most likely part of the *muṣawwitāt* text in T-S Ar.32.31 and AIU IX.A.24, but the order of the material in this new fragment does not slot neatly into the text of the other fragments. It does contain several passages that match the other almost exactly. At best, we can be sure that one author was copying sections from another, or that two authors were both copying from the same common source.

that uses 'large' to differentiate /ɔ/ from the 'small' *qameṣ*, /e/. The author's second vowel is indeed /e/, which they call *al-qm al-ṣaghīra* 'small *qameṣ*' (Allony 1965, 140, line 35).

Third and fourth are *al-pt al-kabīra* 'large *pataḥ*' and *al-pt al-ṣaghīra* 'small *pɔtaḥ*' (Allony 1965, 142, lines 38–41), which are /a/ and /ɛ/, respectively. They follow the same large-small pairing as /ɔ/ and /e/. Allony's additional fragment (T-S Ar.33.6), which may contain another portion of this text, also uses Arabic versions of the expanded relative terms. After explaining how different uses of /e/ and /ɛ/ are known from the *Mishna*, it reads:

פאן קאל קאיל מא אלמעٓ פי תקצّי דלך פי אלבֿ ואלגֿ אלתי הי אלפֿת
אלצגירה ואל קםٓ אלצגירה קיל לה אן בינהמא פצל בّין כקולנא...

> If someone said, "What is the meaning of you decreeing this, for the two and the three, which are the small *pataḥ* and the small *qameṣ*?" It would be said to him that a distinction is made between them, as we say... (Allony 1983, 110, line 54, to 112, line 56).

The text cuts off at that point, but the author seems to be explaining, to a hypothetical reader who pronounces 'the two [dots]' and 'the three [dots]' the same way, that they are actually distinct phonemes. It also deliberately connects the names 'small *pataḥ*' and 'small *qameṣ*' to the graphemes of /ɛ/ and /e/, although apparently mixed up here, which may indicate that the author had difficulty separating the two sounds. This detail may hint toward the text's regional origin, but is not enough information to determine a definitive provenance. In any case, it is clear that this Masorete named /ɔ/, /e/, /a/, and /ɛ/ by modifying *pataḥ* and *qameṣ* in Arabic.

The fifth vowel in this text is /u/, which the author refers to as *al-ḍamma* 'bringing together, pressing together', using the name for the same vowel in Arabic grammar (Allony 1965, 142, line 43; see above, present chapter, §1.1). They also do not distinguish between the oblique three-dot sign and the single dot in a *mater lectionis waw*, classifying them both as *ḍamma* regardless of their appearance. Despite its Arabic origin, this term is still a basic phonetic descriptor, similar to the Aramaic and Hebrew phonetic vowel names used by Saadia and the relative terminology of the earlier Masoretes. It eventually received a Hebrew calque as the vowel name *qibbuṣ* (later with symbolic vowel, *qubbuṣ*), though not until at least the eleventh century (Dotan 2007, 634).

After /u/, the author goes into greater detail with the phonology of the sixth vowel, /i/. They say, "The sixth is *al-khafḍa*, which is bent to a degree of inclination according to its speaker. It establishes the role of the noun (ואלסדסה אלכֿפצֿה והי אלמנעטפה עלי קאילהא אנעטאפא יקום מקאם אלאסם)" (Allony 1965, 142, lines 45–46). It is unclear precisely what this sentence means. The name *khafḍa* is simple enough: it comes from *khafḍ* 'lowering', the Arabic grammatical term for the genitive case, which is usually marked by /i/. It also served as a name for the phoneme /i/ itself at least as late as the first half of the ninth century (see above, chapter 4, §1.1). The author of this text probably added the feminine suffix *-a* on analogy with the other Arabic vowel names (*fatḥa*, *kasra*, *ḍamma*). Then the phrase "bent to a degree of inclination (*ʾinʿiṭāf*)" evokes the Arabic phonological concept of *ʾimāla* 'bending down, inclination', which grammarians used

to describe the fronting of /a/ towards /i/ with 'degrees' of inclination around /ɛ/ and /e/ (Levin 2007). In the earliest Arabic
tradition, this *ʾimāla* was a 'low' classification for fronted allophones of /a/, whereas *naṣb* 'standing upright' indicated 'higher'
allophones produced in the back of the mouth (/a/, /ɑ/) (see
above, chapter 3, §2.2). Most likely, this duality followed the
same identification of backness with 'height' as that found in the
early relative Hebrew and Syriac traditions (see above, chapter
3, §1.0).

   An analogy with *ʾimāla* is probably at play here, but the
'inclination' that the author indicates with *ʾinʿiṭāf* may also describe of the directed movement of airflow—the *quwwa*, in Saa-
dian terms—during the articulation of /i/. That is, the airflow of
/i/ is angled downward in comparison to that of other vowels,
and this motion further corresponds to the lexical meaning of
khafḍ 'lowering'.[55] The author even ends up calling it "*al-muṣawwita al-munkhafiḍa*, that is, *ʾi* (אְעָני אִי אלמנכׄפצׄה אלמצותה)" (Allony
1965, 144, line 53). This means 'the lowered vowel' and uses the
same term that Ibn Jinnī applied to the 'low' consonants articulated away from the 'high' point of the velum (Kinberg 1987, 13).
Finally, the line "it establishes the role of the noun" also seems
to be a reference to Arabic grammar, as only nouns can be in the
khafḍ 'genitive' case.[56]

---

[55] For the potential connection between the Arabic case names and directions of airflow, see Eldar (1983, 45–46).

[56] Perhaps compare Abū al-Faraj's attempts to link the Hebrew vowels
to the Arabic cases in *Hidāya al-Qārī* (Khan 2020, II:124–32).

The author concludes the list with /o/, which they also describe in terms of directed airflow and Arabic grammar. They
name it *al-naṣba*, "which is the marker for past verbs, and it sta-
bilises an inclined characteristic, according to a marker of inclination, establishing the role of the verb (והי אלואצפה ללאפעאל
אלמאציה ואלתאבתה וצפא מנעטפא עלי ואצפה אנעטאפא יקום מקאם
אלפעל)" (Allony 1965, 142–44, lines 48–50). In Arabic grammar,
naṣb 'standing upright' is the name of the accusative case, and as
late as the ninth century it could also indicate the vowel /a/. The
author emphasises how *naṣba* is a 'stabiliser' (*thābita*) that ne-
gates 'inclination' (*ʾinʿiṭāf*), apparently applying the same concept
of directed airflow that led Saadia to conclude that /o/ turns neither upwards nor downwards. It also corresponds to Sībawayh's
usage of *naṣb* to mean a realisation of /a/ without the 'inclining'
allophone of *ʾimāla*, including if that /a/ were backed further to
/ɑ/ or /o/ (i.e., *tafkhīm*, 'thickening') (see above, chapter 3,
§2.2).[57]

The names for the vowels /ɔ/, /e/, /a/, and /ɛ/ are all
based on the expanded relative system, and they seem to have
been well-established in the Hebrew tradition by the time this
muṣawwitāt text was written. By contrast, the text's names for
/u/, /i/, and /o/ do not have direct Masoretic Hebrew equivalents, and the author gives lengthier phonological explanations
to /i/ and /o/. They even phonetically spell out *ʾu* and *ʾi*, revert-
ing to the most basic practice for identifying vowel phonemes.

---

[57] For the relationship between *ʾimāla* and *tafkhīm*, see Talmon (1997,
136, 141) and Makhzumi (1985, III:317; IV:103, 281). See also above,
chapter 3, §2.2, and chapter 4, §1.1.

This factor reinforces the conclusion that these three names were adopted later than the others. The author's choice to name /u/ (*ḍamma*), /i/ (*khafḍa*), and /o/ (*naṣba*) with Arabic vowel terms is thus a way for them to supplement the expanded relative system, in the same way that other Masoretes supplemented *ptḥ* and *qmṣ* with graphemic and phonetic names. This addition of Arabic case names to fill out the set of Hebrew names parallels the Syriac tradition, where some authors adopted calques of *naṣb* (*zqɔpɔ*; /ɔ/) and *rafʿ* (*massaqɔ*; /o/) to identify their vowels (see above, present chapter, §2.0). It may also be relevant that while /ɔ/ remained a distinct phoneme in East Syriac, it shifted to /o/ in West Syriac (Knudsen 2015, 92). West Syrians still called this vowel *zqɔpɔ* 'standing upright', so if any Masoretes in Syria or Palestine translated that term for their /o/, then *naṣba* would have been the logical calque.

This vowel list diverges considerably from the one in Saadia's *Kutub al-Lugha* and does not follow the expected scale order at all. However, the use of *naṣba* and *khafḍa* and the idea of *ʾinʿiṭāf* do seem to describe articulation points and directions of airflow for certain vowels, similar to Saadia's explanations of the vowels' *quwwa*. This similarity suggests that the concept of directed airflow as a phonological feature of vowels existed in the Hebrew linguistic tradition outside of (and possibly prior to) Saadia's description of the vowel scale, although it is not clear whether this *muṣawwitāt* text is itself older than *Kutub al-Lugha*.

The use of Arabic case names to describe Hebrew vowel phonemes is also not limited to this *muṣawwitāt* text, as similar interpretations appear in other sources from the tenth and eleventh centuries. Two of these sources are the Masoretic texts known as *Nequdot Omeṣ ha-Miqrɔ* (*The Dots of the Greatness of the Scripture*) and *Kitāb Naḥw al-ʿIbrānī* (*The Book of Hebrew Inflection*), both of which divide the Hebrew scale into groups based on the Arabic case names. *Nequdot Omeṣ ha-Miqrɔ* comes from the Masoretic material attached to the Leningrad Codex, although parts of the text are also known from other sources (see Eldar 1983), and Baer and Strack first published it as an appendix to their edition of *Diqduqe ha-Ṭeʿamim* (1879, §36, 34–36). Then *Kitāb Naḥw al-ʿIbrānī*, which is extant from the Cairo Genizah, includes a Judaeo-Arabic explanation of the vowel scale. Ilan Eldar first published two fragments of this text in 1981, arguing that the first one contained either a summary or extract of *al-Qawl fī al-Nagham*, the fifth chapter of Saadia's *Kutub al-Lugha* (Eldar 1981; see Dotan 1997, I:114–15; Khan 2020, I:265–66). However, *Kitāb Naḥw al-ʿIbrānī* does not use any of the phonetic vowel names that Saadia uses in *al-Qawl fī al-Nagham*, even though both texts contain complete vowel lists. Instead, the section on the vowel scale in *Kitāb Naḥw al-ʿIbrānī* bears such a striking resemblance to *Nequdot Omeṣ ha-Miqrɔ* in its terminology, format, and word order that its Judaeo-Arabic author must have had access to that Hebrew text. As we will see, the vowel scale in *Kitāb Naḥw al-ʿIbrānī* is actually a translation of a passage from *Nequdot Omeṣ ha-Miqrɔ*, and its author attempts to clarify some omissions in that original Masoretic version. Both versions apply a description of a vowel scale that is similar to the scale in *Kutub al-Lugha*, but they divide that scale with the names of the Arabic grammatical cases.

As discussed above, *Nequdot Omeṣ ha-Miqrɔ* begins by listing the seven Tiberian vowels, using terms from *pth*, *qmṣ*, 'three dots', and phonetic transcriptions of vowel phonemes. After this initial list, the text then reads:

פתרונם אגידה וְצֵרופם אחודה דרך הרוּם או אוּ שתים נחויות ודרך מטה
אֵי אִי מנויות והשלוש להציב עשׂויות אָה אֶה אֶי הראויות ואחת סתם
כלויות לא תצא בכל פעם בפיות

And their interpretation, I will tell it; their combination, I will unite it: to the way upwards, both ʾ*o* and ʾ*u* are led; and the way downwards, ʾ*e* and ʾ*i* are counted. [As for] the three which are made to stand upright, ʾ*ɔ*, ʾ*a*, and ʾ*ɛ* are the right ones; and one stops up completely, not pronounced in any instance in the mouths. (Baer and Strack 1879, 34, lines 9–12)

Eldar has also identified this passage as particularly important for understanding Hebrew vocalisation, and argues that it describes a theory of vowel phonology based on directions of airflow (1983, 43–46). He suggests that these three phonetic groups—*rum* 'rising', *maṭṭah* 'descending', and *lehaṣṣiḇ* 'standing upright' (from *nṣb*)—are calques of the Arabic *rafʿ*, *khafḍ*, and *naṣb* (Eldar 1983, 46).[58] He further argues that the names of each of these groups corresponds to the direction of airflow during the articulation of its vowels. That is, the airflow of /o/ and /u/ is angled upwards, that of /e/ and /i/ is downwards, and /ɔ/, /a/,

---

[58] He also notes that instead of *maṭṭah*, another version of this passage has *shahiyyɔ* 'bending down, depressing' (Eldar 1983, 43), which could even be a calque of ʾ*imāla*. See also, Revell (1975, 188, n. 2).

and /ɛ/ are relatively straight.[59] By the same token, the one that
'obstructs' or 'stops up completely' (i.e., the *shewa*) cuts off the
flow of air. It is equivalent to Arabic *waqf* 'stopping' or *jazm* 'cutting off', both of which indicate silence on a consonant. The *leḥaṣṣiḇ* group also contains the same triad of vowels that Elias of
Ṭirhan associated with *ʾalaph* (zqɔpɔ, /ɔ/; ptɔḥɔ, /a/; rbɔṣɔ, /e/),
and corresponds to the allophones of *ʾalif* from *Kitāb Sībawayh*
(*tafkhīm/naṣb*, /ɑ/ or /ɔ/; *fatḥ*, /a/; *ʾimāla*, /ɛ/ or /e/) (see Khan
2020, I:267). This correlation further shows how an idea of *a*-
vowels 'standing upright' (*leḥaṣṣiḇ*, zqɔpɔ, *naṣb*) existed, in some
form, in all three traditions.

   Kitāb Naḥw al-ʿIbrānī offers a similar description of the phonetic vowel groups, and in fact its language is so similar to
Nequdot Omeṣ ha-Miqrɔ that one of these authors must have had
access to the other's work. The first part reads:

קאל מכֿתצר הדֿא אלכתאב אן ללגה אלעבראניה חֿ נגמאת נחו והי
אתנתאן פי אלרפע ואתֿנתאן פי אלכֿפץֿ ותֿלתֿה פי אלנצב וואחדה הי
אלגֿזם פנגמתי אלרפע הי אלאׂ ואלואוׂ ונגמתי אלכֿפץֿ אלאׁי ואלאׁי ותֿלת
נגמאת אלנצב הי אלקמצה ואלפתחה ואלתֿלתֿ נקט ונגמה אלגֿזם הי
אלשוא

   The abridger of this book said that the Hebrew language
   has eight melodies of inflection, and they are two in rising,
   two in lowering, three in standing upright, and one which
   is cutting off. The two melodies of rising are ʾo and ʾu, the
   two melodies of lowering are ʾe and ʾi, the three melodies
   of standing upright are *qamṣa*, *fatḥa*, and the three dots,

---

[59] There is some evidence that certain Arabic scholars—primarily Ibn
Sīnā (d. 1037)—also understood vowel phonology in this way (Eldar
1983, 46–47; al-Tayyan and Mir Alam 1983, 84–85).

and the melody of cutting off is the *shewa*. (Eldar 1981, 116, lines 1–6)[60]

This Masorete calls the vowel groups *al-rafᶜ* 'rising', *al-khafḍ* 'lowering', *al-naṣb* 'standing upright', and *al-jazm* 'cutting off', using the Arabic terms for the nominative, genitive, and accusative cases as well as the name for the jussive mood. In the early Arabic linguistic tradition, these *ʾiᶜrābī* terms could also refer to /u/, /i/, /a/, and vowellessness, respectively, based on the most common inflectional endings for each grammatical case (Versteegh 1993, 16–20; see above, present chapter, §1.1). It is clear that this author chose these words to classify Hebrew 'inflection' due to a familiarity with Arabic grammar. However, it remains uncertain whether the author of *Kitāb Naḥw al-ᶜIbrānī* selected Arabic terms to match a pre-established phonetic division of the Hebrew vowels—perhaps one that was originally defined in *Nequdot Omeṣ ha-Miqrɔ*—or if the author of *Nequdot Omeṣ ha-Miqrɔ* first defined the groups in Hebrew according on their own interpretation of the Arabic *ʾiᶜrāb* system.

Besides the lexical connections to Arabic, this three-way division of vowels from *Nequdot Omeṣ ha-Miqrɔ* seems to apply a variation of the 'directed airflow' concept that Saadia used to describe vowels on his scale. While Saadia defined vowel quality primarily according to relative backness in the mouth and along the vertical vowel scale, the motion of a vowel's *quwwa* 'force' was partially responsible for determining quality. *Nequdot Omeṣ*

---

[60] Eldar's edition is based on the Genizah fragment MS Cambridge, T-S Ar.5.46, although the caption with the plate in his article incorrectly identifies it as T-S Ar.5.48.

ha-Miqrɔ's author follows the same scale, and they also seem to group the vowels according to their directions or 'ways' (*derɔkim*) of motion (Eldar 1983). However, while this author decides that /o/ has an upward movement, Saadia determined that /o/ was 'unwavering', proceeding straight ahead, in contrast to /ɔ/ and /a/, which moved either up or down. Similarly, the author of the *muṣawwitāt* text in T-S Ar.32.31 and AIU: IX.A.24 refers to /o/ as *naṣba*, suggesting that even though the direction of airflow was important to some tenth-century Hebrew phonologists, its application was not standardised. The extant version of *Nequdot Omeṣ ha-Miqrɔ* was not completed until 1008, but given that it is written entirely in Hebrew, its version of the airflow concept may actually predate the Judaeo-Arabic material found in Saadia's scale and the *muṣawwitāt* text.

The next section of *Nequdot Omeṣ ha-Miqrɔ* reinforces its connection to the ideas in *Kutub al-Lugha* and reveals its true relationship to *Kitāb Naḥw al-ʿIbrāni*. The text continues by describing a vowel scale:

ולאלה המלכים דרכים נסוכים אחת באחת נסמכים. ראשונה דרך רוּמָה
והיא אוֹ הנאומה ולמטה ממנה קָמצה והיא במצב הגדול במחצה ולמטה
ממנה פָּתחה לחריצה ו[היא] במצב האמצעי למליצה ולמטה ממנה שלוש
נקודות לאמיצה ולמטה ממנה שלישית תפיצה והיא נקודה אחת מחוצה.
[או] לבדה נשארה לא תמנה עם אלה בספירה לעֻלָה גדולה ויתרה אותה
אזכירה ועניינה אבארה.

And these vowels have various ways; each one comes next to another. First is the way upwards, and it is spoken ʾo. Then below it is *qɔmṣɔ*, which is in the large grade at the partition; then below it, *patḥɔ* is for its slot, which is at the intermediate grade for its interpretation. Below it, three dots are for its appointment; and it [*patḥɔ*] disperses to

third below, which is one dot squeezed. [$'U$][61] alone yet
remains, not counted with these in the account, for a great
and abundant reason, [which] I will mention, and its issue,
I will explain it. (Baer and Strack 1879, 34, line 12, to 35,
line 1)

This scale follows the same vertical arrangement as the one in
Kutub al-Lugha, although it has some variations. The 'way upwards' (*dɛrɛk rumɔ*) is /o/. Below that is /ɔ/ (*qɔmsɔ*), 'at the partition' (*b-meḥiṣṣɔ*) between the 'way upwards' and the intermediate positions. Following /ɔ/ is /a/ (*patḥɔ*), and these two are
united in that they are both at a *maṣṣaḇ* 'grade, rank, position', a
noun of place derived from the same root as the *leḥaṣṣiḇ* classification earlier in the text (and *naṣb*, for that matter). The author
adds that the *maṣṣaḇ* of /ɔ/ is 'large' (*gadol*), while that of /a/ is
'middle' (*'emṣɔʕi*). Interestingly, they do not also specify /ɛ/
('three dots') as being at another *maṣṣaḇ*, nor do they give it a
size characteristic like the other members of the *leḥaṣṣiḇ* group,
though they do say that it is below /a/. Then after /ɛ/, there is
the notable omission where we might expect to find /e/. It is as
if there is a missing line which should say "and second below it
is two dots." The author instead says "it [*patḥɔ*] disperses to third

---

[61] Baer and Strack suggest that 'one dot' here should be interpreted as
/u/ (i.e., Ɪ), while the final, excluded vowel should be /i/. However,
they note that there is variation between the extant versions of this text,
and one manuscript has /u/ for this excluded vowel. Based on a comparison with the vowel scale in *Kutub al-Lugha* and the Arabic translation of this passage in *Kitāb Naḥw al-ʿIbrānī*, it seems that the final vowel
here should be /u/, and I have rendered it as such in [brackets]. See
Baer and Strack (1879, 34, nn. C, c, and V, 3).

below it (*lemaṭṭɔh mi_mɛnɔh shelishit tapiṣɔh*)," counting three steps down from /a/ to /i/. They specify this vowel as 'one dot squeezed' (*nequdɔ ʾaḥat meḥuṣɔ*). *Meḥuṣɔ* 'squeezed, crushed' here likely indicates the closing of the mouth when articulating /i/ in contrast to the openness of /a/, applying a description similar to what we have seen for /i/ and /u/ in Syriac sources.[62] Finally, this scale specifically excludes /u/, just as Saadia placed it outside of the mouth at the bottom of his scale.

Using the same organisational structure, *Kitāb Naḥw al-ʿIbrānī* likewise follows its initial list of four groups with an explanation of the positions of the vowels, seemingly translating and amending the scale passage from *Nequdot Omeṣ ha-Miqrɔ*. It reads:

ולהדֹא אל[זֹ] נגמאת דרגֹאת מרתבה אלוֹאחד פוק אלאכֹרי פנדֹכרהא
ונקול אן אלדרגֹה אלעוליא הי דרגֹה אלרפע אלאכבר והי אלאוֹ ודונהא
דרגֹה אלקמצה והי אלנצב אלכביר ודונהא דרגֹה אלפתחה והו אלנצב
אלאוסט ודונהא דרגֹה אלתֹלתֹה והי {דרגֹה אלתֹלתֹה והי דרגֹה} [אלנצב
אלאצגר ודונהא דרגֹה אלאֵי והי דרגֹה אלכֹפֿץֹ אלאצגר ודונהא דרגֹה]
אלנקטה אלוֹאחדה והי אלכֹפֿץֹ אלאכבר ותבקא נגמה אלאוֹ מפרדה לא
תדכֹל פי תרתיב אלדרגֹאת ולדֹלך לעלה סאצפהא פי מא יסתאנף

These [seven] melodies have levels, arranged one above another, and we will mention it and say that the top level is the level of the greater *rafʿ*, and it is the *ʾo*. Below it is the level of the *qamṣa*, and it is the great *naṣb*, and below it is the level of the *fatḥa*, and it is the intermediate *naṣb*. Below it is the three, and it is {the level of the three, and

---

[62] E.g., *ḥbɔṣɔ* (/i/, /u/), *ʿṣɔṣɔ* (/u/), *zribɔ* (/e/). See above, present chapter, §2.0.

it is the level}⁶³ [of the lesser *naṣb*, and below it is the level
of the ʾe, and it is the level of the lesser *khafḍ*. And below
it is the level of the]⁶⁴ single dot, and it is the greater *khafḍ*.
The melody of the ʾ*u* alone remains, not entering into the
arrangement of the levels, and that is because of a reason
which I will describe in what remains. (Eldar 1981, 116,
line 1, to 118, line 15)

In this scale, the vowel pronounced farthest back in the mouth
(/o/) is deemed the 'greater *rafᶜ* (*al-rafᶜ al-ʾakbar* 'greater rising')
aligning the Arabic term for /u/ with the highest position in the
vowel scale. *Naṣb* 'standing upright', an Arabic name for /a/, then
correlates to the middle positions of /ɔ/ and /a/, though /ɔ/ is
the 'large' (*kabīr*) *naṣb*, while /a/ is 'middle' (ʾ*awsaṭ*). In opposition to the topmost 'greater *rafᶜ*', the lowest vowel /i/ is *al-khafḍ
al-ʾakbar* 'greater lowering', using the Arabic name for /i/ that is
associated with low positions in the mouth (see above, present
chapter, §1.1).⁶⁵ As we have seen time and again, backed vowels
are perceived as 'high' while fronted vowels are 'low'.

Eldar assumes that the passage's text in {curled brackets}
is an error that should be omitted. He then inserts the text in
[square brackets], adding what he assumes to be a 'lesser *naṣb*'
designation for /ɛ/ and a contriving a separate 'lesser *khafḍ*'
clause to define /e/. He is probably correct that the scribe made

---

⁶³ Eldar interprets the text in {curled brackets} as a mistaken reduplica-
tion.
⁶⁴ The text in [square brackets] is Eldar's insertion, which does not appear in the manuscript.
⁶⁵ See also, Dotan (1997, I:113–15), Khan (2020, I:265–66), and Posegay (2020, 221–22).

some kind of mistake in writing "the level of the three, and it is
the level of... (*daraja al-thalātha wa-hiya daraja...*)." However, his
insertion then assumes that the manuscript's lack of a description
for /e/ is also an error, but this is not the case. Together, these
'mistakes' suggest that this passage is translated directly from
Nequdot Omeṣ ha-Miqrɔ, which awkwardly includes the word
shelishit 'third' in the clause after *shɔlosh nequdot* 'three dots'; does
not assign a *maṣṣab* to /ɛ/; and entirely omits /e/. *Kitāb Naḥw al-
ʿIbrānī*'s line about excluding /u/ from the arrangement, and how
they will explain it later, is also a translation of the corresponding
sentence in *Nequdot Omeṣ ha-Miqrɔ* (Baer and Strack 1879, 34,
line 17, to 35, line 1), albeit without some of the payyeṭanic flair.
Finally, rather than using a superlative adjective to describe /ɔ/
(as they do for *al-khafḍ al-ʾakbar*), the author of *Kitāb Naḥw al-
ʿIbrānī* refers to *qamṣa* as *al-naṣb al-kabīr* 'large *naṣb*', literally
translating the basic Hebrew adjective in *Nequdot Omeṣ ha-Miqrɔ*'s phrase *maṣṣab gadol* 'large grade'. This last detail is especially important, as it strongly indicates that *Kitāb Naḥw al-ʿIbrānī*
is a translation of *Nequdot Omeṣ ha-Miqrɔ*, not the other way
around.

Based on this comparison of the structure and omissions in
these two texts' vowel scales, it is highly likely that the author of
Kitāb Naḥw al-ʿIbrānī had access to *Nequdot Omeṣ ha-Miqrɔ* and
converted its somewhat vague poetic Hebrew into clearer Arabic
prose. This conclusion casts doubt on Eldar's initial claim that
Kitāb Naḥw al-ʿIbrānī is an abridgement of the fifth chapter (*al-
Qawl fī al-Nagham*) of Saadia's *Kutub al-Lugha*, and has implica-

tions for the origin of the vowel scale itself. This doubt is reinforced by the fact that *Kitāb Naḥw al-ʿIbrānī* and *Nequdot Omeṣ ha-Miqrɔ* use essentially the same vowel names (*ʾo, qamṣa, fatḥa*, 'the three', 'one dot', and *ʾu*), but neither uses Saadia's phonetic vowel names (*ḥelɛm, ḥerɛq, shɛrɛq, ṣere*). The section explaining the scale in *Kitāb Naḥw al-ʿIbrānī* should thus be understood as a recension of the vowel scale given in *Nequdot Omeṣ ha-Miqrɔ*, not *al-Qawl fī al-Nagham*.

Kitāb Naḥw al-ʿIbrānī's scale also provides details that may influence the interpretation of *Nequdot Omeṣ ha-Miqrɔ*. First, Eldar's emendations notwithstanding, neither version of this scale explicitly classifies /ɛ/ as one of the *naṣb* vowels, although such a grouping may be implied. Second, the author of *Kitāb Naḥw al-ʿIbrānī* resolves the ambiguity in the Hebrew and makes clear that /i/ is 'the one dot', while /u/ is the vowel which is outside the mouth. Third, because the Judaeo-Arabic description of this vowel scale is a translation of the Hebrew, it is *not* certain that the author of the Hebrew version in *Nequdot Omeṣ ha-Miqrɔ* actually modelled the three-way *rum-maṭṭah-lehaṣṣiḇ* division of the vowels on the Arabic case names *rafʿ, naṣb,* and *khafḍ*. Instead, the author of *Kitāb Naḥw al-ʿIbrānī* may have rendered an earlier Hebrew concept of vowel grouping to fit known Arabic phonological terms. That said, it is also not obvious why a Masorete would have divided the seven vowels of the original *milleʿel-millera*ʿ scale into these three groups (see Khan 2020, I:267), at least without Arabic influence.

There is one more notable division of the vowel scale, found in Abū al-Faraj's (d. c. 1050) *Hidāya al-Qārī*. He also incorporates Arabic grammatical terminology, but his vowel names differ from those discussed above (see Khan 2020, I:266; II:112–32). Abū al-Faraj writes:

אלרפע פי לגה אלעבראני דכל תחתה נגמתאן והמא או ואו ואלנצב ידכל
תחתה ג נגמאת אלפתחה אלכברי והי אַ ואלפתחה אלוסטי והי אֶ
ואלפתחה אלצגרי והי אָ ואלכפץ ידכל תחתה נגמתאן והמא אֵי אִי.

> *Rafʿ* in the Hebrew language includes two melodies: ʾo and
> ʾu. *Naṣb* includes three melodies: the greater *fatḥa*, which
> is ʾa, the middle *fatḥa*, which is ʾɛ, and the lesser *fatḥa*,
> which is ʾɔ. *Khafḍ* includes two melodies: ʾe and ʾi. (Khan
> 2020, II:125–27, lines 739–44)

Rafʿ 'rising' includes the two 'highest', most-backed vowels, /o/ and /u/, following the logic of the *milleʿel-milleraʿ* scale. It may also correlate to the angled direction of the airstream during the articulation of each vowel (see Eldar 1983), though we again recall Saadia and the *muṣawwitāt* author who identified /o/ with *ghayr ḥāʾida* 'unwavering' and *naṣba* 'standing upright'. As expected, Abū al-Faraj's antonym for *rafʿ* is *khafḍ* 'lowering', which includes the two most-fronted vowels, /e/ and /i/.

Abū al-Faraj suggests that all three vowels of the *naṣb* 'standing upright' group are types of *fatḥa* 'opening', including /a/, /ɛ/, and /ɔ/. He qualifies these *fatḥas* according to varying degrees of openness: /a/ is *al-fatḥa al-kubrā* 'the greater opening', /ɛ/ is *al-fatḥa al-wusṭā* 'the middle opening', and /ɔ/ is *al-fatḥa al-sughrā* 'the lesser opening'. This description contrasts the vowel scale in *Kitāb Naḥw al-ʿIbrānī*, where /ɔ/ was 'large' (*kabīr*) rather than small, and the 'sizes' (i.e., ʾakbar, ʾasghar) of vowels correlated with backness rather than openness. Abū al-Faraj maintains this difference later in the chapter when he refers to these vowels as *al-naṣb al-ṣaghīr* 'the small *naṣb*' (/ɔ/) and *al-naṣb al-kabīr* 'the large *naṣb*' (/a/) (Khan 2020, II:129, line 773, 131, line 779), apparently exchanging *naṣb* for *fatḥa* without accounting for the relative backness of the two *a*-vowels. Interestingly, he does not name /ɛ/ using *naṣb* in this way (Khan 2020, II:131, line 782), a detail which matches the descriptions of /ɛ/ in *Nequdot Omeṣ ha-Miqrɔ* and *Kitāb Naḥw al-ʿIbrānī*.

These divisions of the vowel scale reveal the extent to which medieval Hebrew linguists adapted Arabic ideas about grammar and phonology to better explain the language of the Bible. They also represent the culmination of the *milleʿel-milleraʿ* scale,[66] which earlier Masoretes used to compare vowel qualities on a relative basis. These comparisons coincided with the use of relative vowel terminology, like *pɔtaḥ* and *qɔmeṣ*, that could indicate multiple different vowels, depending on their context. As absolute vowel pointing gained popularity, Hebrew scholars began to apply these two relative terms to the vowels which they most often described, namely /a/ and /ɔ/. They then supplemented these two terms with a variety of other absolute naming conventions, including expansions to the relative system (e.g., *pɔtaḥ qɔton* for /ɛ/) and the association of vowel phonemes with the appearance of their vocalisation signs (e.g., *al-thalātha* for /ɛ/; *al-taḥtonī* for /i/). Others introduced names connected to the articulatory processes involved for each vowel, first as Aramaic

---

[66] For additional medieval descriptions of this scale, see Neubauer (1891, 15–16) and Allony (1971, 11).

nouns, then as Hebrew segolates, and finally as Hebrew names with 'symbolic' vowels that matched their quality (e.g., *ḥelmɔ, ḥelɛm, ḥolem* for /o/). Finally, a few authors also adopted Arabic grammatical terminology, both as vowel names (e.g., *naṣba* for /o/) and to divide the vowels into groups. This history of vowel naming is thus a record of the transition from relative to absolute vocalisation, crosscutting Masoretic pedagogy, Hebrew scribal practices, and Arabic grammar in the linguistic science of the early medieval period.

4.0. Summary

The phenomenon of assigning unique names to individual vowel phonemes is common to the Arabic, Syriac, and Hebrew linguistic traditions. As members of all three groups created absolute vocalisation systems to record their vowels, they also developed new terminology to discuss the vowel phonemes that did not have dedicated letters in their writing systems. These new terms were derived gradually over the course of multiple centuries, often as the result of contact between different strains of phonological thought within a single linguistic tradition, or from contact between different languages. In almost all cases, the core elements of these naming systems descended from earlier terminology that first described relative features of vocalisation.

The earliest absolute vowel names emerged in the Arabic linguistic tradition, where eighth-century grammarians created two sets of terms for their three vowels: *fatḥ* (/a/), *kasr* (/i/), *ḍamm* (/u/); and *naṣb* (/a/), *khafḍ* (/i/), *rafʿ* (/u/) (also *jarr*, /i/). Neither set clearly predates the other, but the first—the 'non-

ʾiʿrābī set—describes the phonetic action required to articulate each vowel, while the second—the 'ʾiʿrābī set'—indicates the relative 'height' position in the mouth where a vowel was articulated. This latter set was most likely an expansion on an earlier two-way contrastive pair, in which *naṣb* 'standing upright' indicated relatively-backed allophones of *ʾalif* in Qurʾānic recitation (i.e., /a/, /ɑ/) and *ʾimāla* (bending down) represented relatively-fronted allophones (/ɛ/, /e/). This comparison was based on a perception of the back of the mouth as 'high' while the front was 'low', a principle which mirrors the 'above-and-below' relative comparisons of early Syriac and Hebrew homograph lists. Al-Khwārizmī also transmits a list of supplementary terms that describe Arabic vowels in specific morphosyntactic positions. Some of these additional names are linguistic terms, but others come from the vocabulary of prosody and Qurʾānic recitation, and while al-Khwārizmī attributes them to al-Khalīl ibn Aḥmad, there is little reason to think that they comprised a single coherent system in the eighth century.

Despite what has been suggested in previous scholarship, all seven of the Arabic names for cardinal vowels are attested before absolute vowel terms appear in the Syriac linguistic tradition, and thus they cannot be calques of Syriac terminology. More likely, Syriac writers like Dawid bar Pawlos (fl. 770–800), Ḥunayn ibn Isḥāq (d. 873), and Elias of Ṭirhan (d. 1049) calqued the Arabic terms *naṣb* 'standing upright' and *rafʿ* 'rising' to name Syriac vowels which had no equivalent Arabic phonemes: *zqɔpɔ* 'standing upright' (/ɔ/) and *massaqɔ* 'raised up' (/o/ or /e/). However, other Syriac vowel terms—*ptɔḥɔ, zribɔ, rbɔṣɔ, sheshlɔ,* rwɔħɔ, ʾalɔṣɔ, ħbɔṣɔ, ʿɔṣɔ—are likely native Syriac inventions, all derived from the relative comparisons of openness first explained by Jacob of Edessa (d. 708). Participial forms from *ptħ, zqp, ħbṣ,* and *ʿṣṣ* appear as early as Dawid bar Pawlos' *scholion* on *bgdkt* letters, while *zribɔ* and *rbiṣɔ* are first attested in the Syriac lexica of ʿĪsā ibn ʿAlī (d. c. 900) and Ḥasan bar Bahlul (fl. 942–968). *Rwɔħɔ* and *ʾalɔṣɔ* first occur definitively as vowel names in the eleventh-century grammars of Elias of Nisibis (d. 1046) and Elias of Ṭirhan (d. 1049), although they may be linked to an earlier tradition of Ḥunayn ibn Isḥāq.

Several different vowel naming conventions developed within the Hebrew Masoretic and early grammatical tradition prior to the eleventh century, four of which contributed to the set of absolute names that eventually became standard. The earliest of these four includes *pɔtaḥ* 'opening' and *qɔmeṣ* 'closing', which solidified as absolute names for /a/ and /ɔ/ with the decline of the relative vocalisation, likely around the time that the Tiberian vowel points were invented. Then, during the ninth and tenth centuries, Hebrew scholars described their other five vowels using graphemic descriptions (e.g., *nuqtatayn, zujj, segol*), phonetic descriptions (*ḥelmɔ, sherqɔ, ṣiryɔ, ḥerqɔ*), and Arabic grammatical terminology (*naṣba, khafḍa, ḍamma/qibbuṣ*). Following the tradition of earlier *milleʿel* 'above' and *milleraʿ* 'below' relative comparisons, Saadia Gaon (d. 942) and other linguists also placed the Hebrew vowels on a scale, corresponding to their relative 'height' within the mouth. Some writers even divided this scale into sections based on the Arabic case names.

The absolute vowel naming traditions in Arabic, Syriac, and Hebrew could not exist, at least as we know them, in isolation. Each one evolved in the context of the other two, continuously absorbing and adapting new terms and principles as a result of intellectual and scholastic contact. The previous sections have shown the extent to which the principles of relative and absolute vocalisation connect these three traditions, but in truth, they only begin to scratch the surface. Besides the connections between the terms discussed above, there are also vowel names which are cognates with accent names in other traditions; for example: Syriac *zqɔpɔ* and Hebrew *zɔqep̄*; Syriac *massaqɔ* and Hebrew *silluq*; Syriac *sheshltɔ/sheshlɔ* and Hebrew *shalshelet*; Syriac *mpaggdɔnɔ* and Hebrew *meteg*;[67] and Arabic *jarr* and Syriac *gɔrorɔ* (see Talmon 1996, 290–91; 2000, 250; 2008, 174; and above, present chpater, §1.1). Undoubtedly, vocalisation and vowel phonology are closely related to concepts of accentuation and cantillation, and future studies must combine the history of vocalisation with that of cantillation to reveal a more complete picture of connections between the medieval Arabic, Syriac, and Hebrew recitation traditions.

---

[67] These two are not cognates, but they both mean 'bridling'.

5. CONCLUSION

Now that we have shown all the sections on pointing, based on the rules which we have set for it with regard to reasons and meanings, and having reached the limit in specifying that, according to the sayings of tradition, the schools of recitation, the way of language, and the model of Arabic, I believe we are at the end of our book. (Abū ʿAmr al-Dānī [d. 1053], *The Rules for Pointing the Codices* [1960, 87a–87b])

The history of Semitic vocalisation is the shared history of Christians, Muslims, and Jews in their attempts to preserve the recitation of their holy texts. It is a history of mutual innovations, adaptations, and intellectual exchanges over the course of hundreds of years, beginning with the first Syriac relative diacritic dots in the fifth century and reaching its zenith with the absolute vocalisation systems of the eleventh century. This book has examined that history with an emphasis on the phonological ideas that medieval Syriac, Arabic, and Hebrew scholars developed to explain their new technologies of vowel pointing. The foundation for this analysis was a survey of the ways that Semitic scholars differentiated vowels from consonants, enabling them to better describe the phonetics of vocalisation (chapter 2). That survey equipped us with the vocabulary and phonological understanding needed to trace the development of relative vocalisation in Syriac, Hebrew, and Arabic up through the eighth century (chapter 3). We then explored the ways that relative vocalisation and phonology gave way to absolute pointing, specifically focusing on the development of discrete names for the vowels in Semitic linguistic traditions between the ninth and eleventh centuries (chapter 4).

     https://doi.org/10.11647/OBP.0271.05

Our survey of medieval linguistic texts identified three primary concepts that Semitic scholars used to distinguish the phonology of vowels from consonants: 'sounding' letters (chapter 2, §1.0), 'movements' (chapter 2, §2.0), and the dual nature of the *matres lectionis* (chapter 2, §3.0). The sounding letters descended from the Greek grammatical concept of *phōnēenta* 'sounding, voiced', a word applied to the vowels as a result of their continuous airflow and their ability to be pronounced alone. By contrast, the *aphōna* 'soundless' consonants were stop-plosives that required the assistance of vowels to be articulated. Relying on the Greek *Technē Grammatikē* of Dionysius Thrax (c. second century BCE), Jacob of Edessa (d. 708) adapted this dichotomy for Syriac with the calques *qɔlɔnɔyɔtɔ* 'sounding', which included all the vowels, and *dlɔ qɔlɔ* 'without sound', which encompassed the consonants. His conception of the sounding ones persisted in the Syriac linguistic tradition, with some modifications, through Dawid bar Pawlos (fl. c. 770–800) and up to the eleventh-century grammar of Elias of Ṭirhan (d. 1049). Early Arabic grammarians were also aware of the Greek sounding letters, but they did not apply the concept to vowels before approximately the tenth century. Instead, early scholars like al-Farrāʾ (d. 822) used the Arabic calque *muṣawwit* 'sounding' to describe groups of consonants with continuous airflow.

It was not until the Greek-Syriac-Arabic translation movement in the ninth century that an Aristotelian view of *phōnēenta* vowels penetrated the Arabic scholastic tradition, and non-grammarians like Abū Bishr Mattā (d. 940) and Ibn Sīnā (d. 1037) began to apply the concept to Arabic. They adopted the word *muṣawwitāt*, most likely a direct calque of *qɔlɔnɔyɔtɔ* based on Syriac-Arabic lexicography. This translation also allowed Arabic-speaking Hebrew Masoretes to study 'sounding' phonology, and they applied *muṣawwita* to the category of the seven Tiberian vowels. The term is especially common in a subgenre of Judaeo-Arabic Masoretic treatises that emerged around the tenth century. These have come to be known as *muṣawwitāt* texts due to their emphasis on explaining the Hebrew vowels.

Rather than sounding letters, Arabic grammarians over-whelmingly preferred the idea of 'movement' to describe vowels, naming them *ḥarakāt* 'movements'. This term somehow indicated the vocalic energy required to move between the consonants of a word. Its antonym was *sākin* 'still', which instead applied to unvocalised consonants. *Ḥaraka* is attested from the earliest Arabic grammatical sources in the eighth century, but the origin of the term is unclear. It is most likely a calque of the Greek word *kinesis*, which has the occasional use of referring to inflectional vowels at the ends of Greek words in *scholia* of Dionysius Thrax's *Technē*. It may also be related to the early Syriac accent names *zawʕɔ* 'move-ment' and *mziʕɔnɔ* 'mover', which both predate the earliest men-tions of *ḥaraka* in Arabic grammar, but this connection is uncer-tain. What is clear is that later Syriac grammarians, like Elias of Ṭirhan (d. 1049) and Elias of Nisibis (d. 1046), calqued the Arabic words *ḥaraka* and *mutaḥarrik* 'moved, vocalised', referring to Syr-iac vocalisation (and sometimes accents) with *zawʕɔ* and *mettziʕɔnutɔ* 'moved, vocalised'. Hebrew scholars, like the author of the *Treatise on the Shewa* and Abū al-Faraj Hārūn (d. c. 1050), also utilised *ḥaraka*, *mutaḥarrik*, and *sākin*. They retained the original meanings of these words while simultaneously adapting them to better describe the mobile and quiescent forms of *shewa*.

Syriac, Arabic, and Hebrew scholars all dealt with the twin functions of the *matres lectionis*, which were letters that could represent vowels or consonants depending on their context. These letters functioned as a modicum of 'vocalisation' prior to the invention of the vowel points, and their dual nature provoked complex analyses of their phonological features. The earliest descriptions of these letters in Arabic come from al-Khalīl ibn Aḥmad's (d. 786/791) introduction to *Kitāb al-ʿAyn*, the lexical material compiled in subsequent sections of that book, and the *Kitāb* of al-Khalīl's student, Sībawayh (d. 793/796). They indicate that the *matres lectionis* are the most ephemeral of all the letters, calling them 'soft' (*layyin*), 'subtle' (*khafī*), 'airy' (*hāwī*), and 'sick' (*ḥurūf ʿilla*). These attributes apply because grammarians perceived the function of the *matres lectionis* letters to represent vowels as a type of elision (*ʾikhfāʾ* lit. 'concealment'), and the changeability between consonantal and vocalic forms made the letters weaker than the rest of the consonants. Several Masoretic *muṣawwitāt* authors adopted similar language, describing the multiple phonetic realisations of the *matres* in similar terms to the multiple realisations of the 'relaxed' (*rafe*) and 'pronounced' (*mappiq*) *bgdkpt* letters.

The Hebrew lexicographer Judah ben David Ḥayyūj (d. c. 1000) was especially familiar with Arabic conceptions of the *matres*, and he adapted their vocabulary to describe the *sākin layyin* ('soft silent' or 'latent quiescent'). He used this principle to explain how some Hebrew vowels are pronounced even when they are not written *plene* with a *mater lectionis*. Similar discussions of the *matres* appear in the work of Elias of Nisibis, who seems to calque the Arabic concept of *ʾidghām* 'suppression, assimilation' with the Syriac term *metgneb* 'suppressed' to explain the defective spellings of certain words. At the same time, his contemporary, Elias of Ṭirhan, explicitly rejected the Arabic analysis of 'sick' *matres lectionis* letters, instead invoking the principle of 'sound-ingness' to insist that the *matres* were the only letters that were *not* sick, since they could be pronounced alone.

Furthermore, members of all three traditions divided their vowel inventories into groups according to the *matres lectionis*, assigning each of their vowel phonemes to a particular letter. This practice was simplest for Arabic, where each *mater* was responsible for just a single vowel, but Syriac and Hebrew writers expanded the concept for their larger vowel inventories. Some evidence from Ibn Jinnī's (d. 1002) *Sirr Ṣināʿa al-Iʿrāb*, al-Khwārizmī's (d. 997) *Mafātīḥ al-ʿUlūm*, and Ḥunayn ibn Isḥāq's (d. 873) *Kitāb Aḥkām al-Iʿrāb ʿalā Madhhab al-Yūnāniyyīn* suggests that part of this shared tradition of grouping vowels may be connected to the Greek names for vowel letters (*omega*, *omicron*, etc).

Our exploration of the vowel qualities themselves began by examining the concept of 'relative' vocalisation (chapter 3), which refers to methods that medieval scholars used to indicate vowels based on their relationship to other vowels. These include the Syriac diacritic dot system and the Masoretic practice of differentiating vowels as *milleʿel* 'above' or *milleraʿ* 'below', both of which were connected to ideas of phonetic 'height' and eventually informed the placement of the Syriac and Hebrew vowel points (chapter 3, §1.0). A similar concept appears in the Arabic terminology of *naṣb* 'standing upright' and *ʾimāla* 'bending down', which also connected vowels to 'height' and described the relative qualities of allophones of /a/ and /ā/ (chapter 3, §2.0).

The Syriac diacritic dot system is the primary graphical example of relative vocalisation. The grammatical works of Jacob of Edessa (d. 708) describe vowels as either 'thick' and 'wide' or 'thin' and 'narrow'. The former were generally more backed and open, while the latter were more fronted and closed, but each of these adjectives described the vowels of a word only in relation to those of its homographs. Syriac scribes indicated these relationships by placing a diacritic dot above a word to indicate relatively 'thick' or 'wide' vowels, while that word's homograph with comparatively 'thin' or 'narrow' vowels took a dot below. This practice led to an association of the vowel phonology of homographs with 'height', as backed vowels were considered 'above' their fronted 'below' counterparts. We saw that Jacob refers to these homographs as *men lʿel* 'above' and *men ltaḥt* 'below', and it seems that these phrases are the source of the Masoretic terms with the same meanings: *milleʿel* and *milleraʿ*. Early Masoretes applied these two words to differentiate Hebrew homographs that differed by a single vowel, taking up the idea of 'backness' as 'height' and creating a vowel 'scale'. However, they did not adopt the Syriac diacritic dot directly. Instead, the phonological principles of 'above' and 'below' vowels informed the later positioning of the absolute vowel points in both Syriac and Tiberian Hebrew. For Syriac, these points evolved gradually over several centuries of scribal developments. By contrast, it seems the

Tiberian Masoretes invented their system all at once, consistently analysing the hierarchy of the vowel scale to determine the number and position of the points in their vocalisation signs.

Classical Arabic had a much smaller inventory of vowel qualities than Syriac and Hebrew—only three, compared to their six or seven—so Arabic scribes did not need a relative vocalisation system to indicate cardinal vowels. Instead, Arabic scholars applied the principles of 'height' as 'backness' to their analysis of vocalic allophones. Likely in the late seventh or early eighth century, they introduced the pair of terms ʾimāla 'bending down' and naṣb 'standing upright', describing relatively fronted (e.g., /e/, /ɛ/) and backed (e.g., /a/, /ɑ/, /ɔ/) allophones of /a/, respectively. These terms would have been useful for describing allophonic pronunciations in Qurʾānic recitation that could not be represented by the Arabic script or the red-dot vocalisation system. Naṣb then became a name for the cardinal vowel /a/, at least until the early ninth century. Meanwhile, ʾimāla remained in use for fronted allophones (/e/) in opposition to tafkhīm 'thickening' (/ɔ/, /o/).

In chapter 4 we followed the transition from relative to absolute vocalisation by tracing the introduction of absolute vowel names to Arabic (chapter 4, §1.0), Syriac (chapter 4, §2.0), and Hebrew (chapter 4, §3.0) phonology. Arabic grammarians had two sets of absolute names for their cardinal vowels by the first half of the eighth century at the latest. One of these, the ʾiʿrābī set, evolved from the perception among Arabic grammarians that the back of the mouth (or more precisely, the velum) was the highest articulation point, and thus velarised sounds were 'elevated' (*mustaʿliya*). Accordingly, the front of the mouth was 'lowered' (*munkhafiḍa*), and the idea of *khafḍ* 'lowering' became associated with the front vowel /i/. Its antonym was *rafʿ* 'rising', a term which correlates with the 'high' velar pronunciation of /u/, and these two names supplemented *naṣb* to form a complete set of absolute vowel names. These *'iʿrābī'* terms also became the names of the grammatical cases, connecting them to the vowels that most often occurred in each inflectional ending.

At least as ancient as the *'iʿrābī* set is the 'non-*'iʿrābī*' set, including *fatḥ* 'opening' (/a/), *kasr* 'breaking' (/i/), and *ḍamm* 'pressing together, bringing together' (/u/). These describe the opening and closing of the mouth or lips when articulating each vowel. They share this descriptive concept with vowel names in both Syriac and Hebrew, but the idea of 'wide-and-narrow' phonology is so widespread that it is not clear whether any one linguistic tradition calqued their terms from the others.

The first hints of absolute vowel terminology in Syriac follow a similar 'wide-and-narrow' model. Dawid bar Pawlos writes about the different qualities of the *matres lectionis* letters *waw* and *yod* as *ptiḥɔ* 'opened' (likely /o/ and /e/ or /ay/), *ṣiṣɔ* 'constrained' (/u/), and *ḥbiṣɔ* 'squeezed, pressed-together' (/i/). He also refers to letters with /a/ and /ɔ/ as *ptiḥɔ* 'opened' and *zqipɔ* 'stood upright', respectively. This term from the *zqp* root is most likely a calque of the Arabic *naṣb*, a name for /a/ that could also indicate /ɑ/ after a *mustaʿliya* letter. Ḥunayn ibn Isḥāq (d. 873) identifies the vowels more directly in *Ktɔbɔ d-Shmɔhe Dɔmyɔye*, where he describes letters as *zqipɔ* or *ptiḥɔ*. He also introduces the term *sheshlɔ* 'chain' to name the two-dot supralinear vocalisation sign that represents /ɔ/. The lexicographers ʿĪsā ibn ʿAlī (d. c. 900) and Ḥasan bar Bahlul (fl. 942–968) use the same type of participial terminology to designate vowels in their Syriac-Arabic lexica, including *zqipɔ* and *ptiḥɔ* plus *rbiṣɔ* 'compressed' (/e/), *zribɔ* 'contracted, narrowed' (/e/), and possibly *ḥbiṣɔ* (/i/). Besides *zqipɔ*, all these terms relate to the relative openness or closedness of a vowel, representing a direct conceptual evolution from Jacob of Edessa's earlier *pte* 'wide' and *qaṭṭin* 'narrow' comparisons.

Syriac linguists reached complete sets of absolute vowel terms only around the eleventh century, as evidenced by the grammars of Elias of Nisibis (d. 1046) and Elias of Ṭirhan (d. 1049), who also introduced nominalised forms of the vowel names. However, these two scholars did not always agree on which vowels their terms represented. The Nisibene Elias lists *zqiptɔ* (/ɔ/), *rbiṣtɔ* (/e/), *ptiḥtɔ* (/a/), *rwiḥtɔ* 'broadened' (/o/), *ʾaliṣtɔ* 'narrowed' (/u/), *massaqtɔ* 'raised' (/e/), and *ḥbiṣtɔ* (/i/). Again, most of these rely on 'open-and-closed' comparisons of vowels. The *zqp* term is still an exception, but so is *massaqtɔ*—likely a calque of Arabic *marfūʿ* 'raised up, given /u/'—which seems to indicate that /e/ is 'higher' (i.e., more-backed) than /i/. By contrast, Elias of Ṭirhan names the vowels *zqɔpɔ* (/ɔ/), *ptɔḥɔ* (/a/), *rbɔṣɔ* or *sheshlɔ* (/e/), *massaqɔ* or *rwaḥtɔ* (/o/), *ḥbɔṣɔ* (/u/), and *yod* (/i/). For him, *massaqɔ* represents the 'raised' backed position of /o/ relative to /u/, while *ḥbɔṣɔ* seems to be a calque of Arabic *ḍamm* 'pressing together' (/u/). These differences show that the East Syriac vowel names were not standardised even at the end of the period covered in this book.

Hebrew absolute vowel terminology was equally varied, as Masoretes and grammarians developed four conventions to name their vowels between the ninth and eleventh centuries. All four began with the old relative terms from *pth* 'opening' for /a/ and *qmṣ* 'closing' for /ɔ/, and then supplemented them by various means. The first, known from Masoretic notes and the work of Aharon ben Asher (d. c. 960), was an expansion to the relative terminology, contrasting /ɛ/ and /e/ as 'small *pth*' and 'large *qmṣ*', respectively. Second, some Masoretes, like the author of the *Treatise on the Shewa*, named vowels according to the number and position of the Tiberian vocalisation points. Third, ninth-century Masoretes introduced Aramaic 'phonetic' names that described the physical processes of articulating vowels, including *ḥelmɔ* 'closing firmly' (/o/), *sherqɔ* 'whistling' (/u/), *ṣiryɔ* 'cracking, splitting' (/e/), and *ḥerqɔ* 'gnashing the teeth' (/i/). These names later took Hebrew segolate forms (*ḥelɛm*, etc.), which appear in Saadia Gaon's (d. 942) presentation of the old *mille'el-millera'* vowel scale in *Kutub al-Lugha*. Finally, as evidenced by the treatise which Allony called *Kitāb al-Muṣawwitāt*, some Hebrew scholars adapted Arabic grammatical terminology to name their vowels. These included Arabic inflectional terms such as *naṣba* (/o/) and *khafḍa* (/i/), as well as *qibbuṣ* 'bringing together' (/u/), which is ultimately a calque of Arabic *ḍamm*. These linguists used Arabic terms not just as absolute vowel names, but some—like Abū al-Faraj Hārūn (d. c. 1050) and the anonymous author of

Kitāb Naḥw al-ʿIbrānī—also adapted them to divide the Hebrew vowel scale into phonetic groups.

This book presents a history of Semitic vocalisation, but it is not, as Shelomo Morag contemplated, the "complete history" (1961, 5). It compares the ways the Syriac, Arabic, and Hebrew linguists faced the shared challenges of preserving their religious recitation traditions in an increasingly Islamicised and Arabicised—but also multicultural and multi-ethnic—medieval Middle East. It is a proof of concept that simultaneous close readings of sources from different religious and linguistic traditions can yield valuable insights into the historical contexts of the people who produced them. Such comparisons highlight the points of contact between diverse communities and allow for the reconstruction of more complete intellectual histories for each group involved. However, this comparative methodology also highlights its own weaknesses, since there are many topics that we cannot fully incorporate.

As a result, we are still quite a way from a complete history of Semitic vocalisation, but the path forward is clearer than ever before. Besides the primary frameworks outlined above, the other methods by which Semitic linguists differentiated the phonetic categories of vowels and consonants require further examination. Such research would include comparisons of the ways that Syriac and Hebrew scholars utilised the cognate terms *neʿmɔtɔ* 'melodies' and *naʿimot/naghamāt* 'melodies, tones' (see Allony 1971), as well as the ways that they interpreted the Arabic terms *ʾiʿrāb* 'making Arabic' and *naḥw* 'grammar, form' (see chapter 2, §4.0). Related research might include a systematic comparison of the phonological meanings of the Syriac and Hebrew accent names in relation to the vowels, building on the work of Eric Werner's *The Sacred Bridge* (1959), which I have not dealt with here. I have also not examined many of the Hebrew and Aramaic notes found in Ginsburg's *Massorah* (1880) or Baer and Strack's appendices to *Dikduke ha-Teʿamim* (1879), but it would not be surprising if some of them contain technical vocabulary that also appears in the Syriac tradition (e.g., qɔlɔnɔyɔtɔ 'sounding ones'). Further analysis of the technical terms related to vocalisation in Arabic *tajwīd* scholarship would also prove illuminating (see Nelson 2001; Gade 2003; Khan 2020, I:100, n. 123, 440, n. 183).

Besides Syriac, Arabic, and Tiberian Hebrew, there are other aspects of the history of vocalisation that only studies of additional systems can reveal. For example, we have not examined to what extent the Palestinian and Babylonian vocalisation systems are related to the Tiberian tradition and Arabic grammar, especially in terms of their technical vocabulary (see Morag 1961, 30–41; Dotan 2007, §§5.1–2). The same can be said for Samaritan Hebrew, which is surely relevant to the medieval relationship between Arabic and Hebrew linguistics (Morag 1961, 41–44).[1] We have also not addressed the fourth major tradition of Semitic vocalisation, which of course appears in the Ethiopic writing system. This tradition is unique among Semitic languages, as rather than the free-floating vowel points and strokes, it utilises an alphasyllabic system in which vowel 'diacritics' are

---

[1] A possible starting point would be the discussion of Samaritan grammarians and phonology in the introduction to Ben-Ḥayyim and Tal (2000). See also, Dotan (2007, §5.6).

bound directly to consonantal bases. This Ethiopic alpahasylla-
bary appeared at least as early as the fourth century, apparently
under the influence of Greek, and well before the vocalisation
systems in Syriac, Arabic, and Hebrew (Ullendorff 1951). At least
on the surface, this system is more reminiscent of the South Asian
Indic alphasyllabaries than other Semitic scripts.[2] Finally, the history of Coptic linguistics is also relevant to Semitic vocalisation.
We have already noted that Coptic grammarians may have been
aware of the concept of 'sounding' letters (chapter 2, §1.2),[3] and
the Greek-derived Coptic alphabet is among the few Middle Eastern scripts that actually indicates vocalic phonemes with letters
on par with the consonants. Jacob of Edessa invented the same
type of vowel letters for use in Syriac, and although it is assumed
that he based his letters on the Greek alphabet (Merx 1889, 51;
Segal 1953, 42), he also studied in Alexandria and would have
been exposed to Coptic in the Christian community there (Hoyland 2008, 20–21). If we are ever to reach a complete history of
Semitic vocalisation, then each of these other systems must be
brought into the proper context with the languages discussed
here. It is hoped that this book provides a firm foundation to an-
chor future comparative studies of vocalisation, especially for ex-
perts in adjacent fields.

We may at last recall ʿAbd Allah ibn Ṭāhir, the ninth-century governor of Khurasan, who held a hard line against any kind

---

[2] This may be an opportunity to revisit Revell's hypothesis of Indian
influence on the early arrangement of Arabic consonantal phonology
(1975).

[3] See Bauer (1972, 147–48) and Versteegh (2011).

of pointing in Qurʾān manuscripts. He lamented the addition of dots: "How beautiful this would be, if there were not so much coriander seed scattered over it!" (Hughes 1895, 686). We now see that he represents just a single opinion in a varied history of linguistic traditions that grew and evolved together over hundreds of years. In the end, it turns out, the study of vocalisation required many different points of view.

6. GLOSSARY OF SELECTED VOCALISATION TERMINOLOGY

The following brief definitions appear here as a reference. Each term receives a more detailed discussion in the main text.

ʾ*akhras*: 'mute'; al-Farrāʾ's categorical term for plosive consonants, indicating the lack of continuous airflow during their articulation; calque of Greek *aphōna* and antonym of *muṣawwit*.

ʾ*aliṣtɔ*/ʾ*aliṣutɔ*: 'narrowed, narrowing'; Elias of Nisibis' descriptor for a letter pronounced with the vowel /u/. The nominal form ʾ*aliṣutɔ* is his name for /u/.

aphōna: 'soundless, mute'; a Greek term for stop-plosive consonants, indicating the lack of continuous airflow during their articulation and their inability to be pronounced alone. Entered the Semitic grammatical traditions via Dionyisus Thrax's *Technē Grammatikē* (*The Art of Grammar*) and translations of Aristotle's *Poetics*.

ʿ*be*: 'thick'; Jacob of Edessa's descriptor for a word with relatively backed vowels in comparison to a homograph (primarily /o/ and /ɑ/). Antonym of *nqed*.

ḍamm/*ḍamma*: 'bringing together, pressing together'; an Arabic name for the vowel /u/, describing the movement of the lips during articulation. Attested from the earliest grammatical sources. The form *ḍamma* usually denotes the vowel sign that represents /u/.

 https://doi.org/10.11647/OBP.0271.06

dlɔ qɔlɔ: 'without sound, soundless'; a Syriac designation for the phonetic category of consonants in contrast to the 'sounding' vowels, attested in Jacob of Edessa's *Turrɔṣ Mamllɔ Nahrɔyɔ* and Dawid bar Pawlos' fragmentary grammar. Calqued from Greek *aphōna* and the antonym of *qɔlɔnɔyɔtɔ*.

ʿelyoni: 'upper one'; a Hebrew name for /o/ in the *Treatise on the Shewa*, describing the supralinear position of the Tiberian *ḥolem* dot. Calqued into Arabic as *fawqānī*.

fatḥ/fatḥa: 'opening'; an Arabic name for the vowel /a/, describing the movement of the lips during articulation. Attested from the earliest grammatical sources. The form *fatḥa* usually denotes the vowel sign that represents /a/. Cognate with Syriac *ptɔḥɔ* and Hebrew *pɔtaḥ*.

ḥaraka: 'movement'; the most common term for 'vowel' in Arabic grammar, often specifically designating a short vowel (i.e., *fatḥa, kasra, ḍamma*). Likely a calque of Greek *kinesis*.

ḥashw: 'stuffing'; a name for /u/ in an internal syllable of a noun, according to al-Khwārizmī's *Mafātīḥ al-ʿUlūm* (*The Keys to the Sciences*).

ḥāwī: 'airy'; al-Khalīl's term for describing how the vowel forms of the *matres lectionis* are produced entirely as streams of air emanating from the glottis. Ibn Jinnī restricts this quality to the letter *ʾalif*.

ḥbɔṣɔ/ḥbiṣtɔ/ḥabiṣutɔ; 'squeezed, pressed together'; *ḥbiṣtɔ* is first attested in the grammatical *scholion* on *bgdkt* letters by

Dawid bar Pawlos to describe /i/ as the relatively-closed pronunciation of Syriac *yod* (contrasting /e/). Elias of Ṭirhan applies the nominal form *ḥbɔṣɔ* as a name for /u/, while Elias of Nisibis uses *ḥabiṣutɔ* to name /i/.

ḥiriq/ḥerqɔ: 'gnashing the teeth'; a Masoretic name for the vowel /i/, highlighting the overlapping motion of the teeth during its articulation. Originally an Aramaic nominal form (*ḥerqɔ*) as found in *muṣawwitāt* texts.

hēmiphōna: 'half-sounding'; a Greek term for continuant consonants, indicating the partial obstruction of airflow during their articulation, which can be produced but not fully pronounced without a vowel. Entered the Semitic grammatical traditions via Dionyisus Thrax's *Technē Grammatikē* (*The Art of Grammar*) and translations of Aristotle's *Poetics*.

ḥolem/ḥelmɔ: 'closing firmly'; a Masoretic name for the vowel /o/, describing the compression of the lips during its articulation. Originally an Aramaic nominal form (*ḥelmɔ*) as found in *muṣawwitāt* texts.

ḥurūf al-madd wa-al-līn/ḥurūf al-līn wa-al-madd: 'letters of lengthening and softness'; an epithet for the *matres lectionis* in the Arabic linguistic tradition, as well as in Judah ben David Ḥayyūj's lexicon of Hebrew verbs with weak roots, *Kitāb al-Afʿāl Dhuwāt Ḥurūf al-Līn* (*The Book of Verbs which Contain Soft Letters*).

ḥurūf ṣighār: 'small letters'; a categorical term that Ibn Jinnī applies to the Arabic short vowels in his *Sirr Ṣināʿa al-Iʿrāb*, possibly related to the names of the Greek vowel letters (i.e., *omikron*, 'small O').

ʾidjāʿ: 'laying something down, lowering something'; a name for /i/ in a medial syllable, according to al-Khwārizmī's *Mafātīḥ al-ʿUlūm* (*The Keys to the Sciences*).

ʾiʿjām: 'distinguishing dots'; the name for the diacritic dots that differentiate Arabic consonants with the same shape (e.g., *bāʾ* and *tāʾ*).

ʿilla: 'sickness, illness, deficiency'; a quality possessed by the Arabic *matres lectionis* that causes them to change during inflection depending on their morphophonetic context. Letters with ʿilla are not *ṣaḥīḥ*.

ʾimāla: 'bending down'; an Arabic term describing the contextual fronting of /a/ towards /e/, classifying the fronted articulation point as relatively 'low'. Antonym of *naṣb*.

ʾimṣɔ/miqpaṣ pummɔ: 'closing/closing the mouth'; Babylonian Masoretic names for the vowel /ɔ/, describing the movement of the lips in contrast to /a/.

ʾishmām: 'giving a scent'; an Arabic term describing either the blending of two vowel sounds (e.g., in Ibn Sīnā's *Sirr Ṣināʿa* and al-Khwārizmī's *Mafātīḥ al-ʿUlūm*) or the slight pressing of the lips as if to pronounce /u/ at the end of a word in pause (e.g., in *Kitāb Sībawayh*).

jazm: 'cutting off'; an Arabic term for a vowelless inflectional ending and the jussive mood, attested from the earliest grammatical sources.

jarr: 'dragging, drawing, pulling'; the 'Basran' name for the Arabic genitive case, but also a name for the Arabic vowel /i/

until at least the ninth century, possibly describing the pulling apart of the lips when pronouncing /i/ in contrast to /u/. Cognate with and possibly adapted from the West Syriac accent name gɔrorɔ, which relates to 'drawing out' the pronunciation of a syllable.

jūf: 'hollow'; a descriptor which al-Khalīl applies to the Arabic *matres lectionis* and *hamza*, apparently because they exit from the 'hollow' of the mouth are not articulated from any specific point. This group contrasts with the other twenty-four consonants, which al-Khalīl calls *ṣaḥīḥ*.

kasr/kasra: 'breaking'; an Arabic name for the vowel /i/, probably describing the separation of the lips during articulation in comparison to /u/. Attested from the earliest grammatical sources. The form *kasra* usually denotes the vowel sign that represents /i/.

khafāʾ/khafī/khafiyya: 'subtlety, inconspicuousness'; Arabic terms that highlight the quality of the *matres lectionis* to change their pronunciation depending on their morphophonetic context, particularly with the perceived 'elision' of the consonantal form of a *mater* when it functions to represent a vowel. Adapted to describe Hebrew phonology in some *muṣawwitāt* texts.

khafḍ/khafḍa: 'lowering'; the 'Kufan' name for the Arabic genitive case, but also a name for the Arabic vowel /i/ until at least the ninth century, indicating its relatively low articulation point in comparison to /u/. Antonym of *rafʿ*. *Khafḍa* is a name for the Hebrew vowel /i/ in at least one *muṣawwitāt* text.

layyin: 'soft, flexible'; a descriptor for the Arabic *matres lectionis*, designating the relative lack of obstruction for the airstream in the vocal tract when they are realised as vowels.

leḥaṣṣib: 'standing upright'; a Hebrew term calqued from Arabic *naṣb* that designates the phonetic group of /ɔ/, /a/, and /ɛ/ in *Nequdot Omeṣ ha-Miqrɔ*, possibly due to the relatively level movement of the airflow produced during their articulation.

madd: 'lengthening'; a quality which Arabic grammarians ascribe to the *matres lectionis*, indicating their function to represent long vowels that can be extended in duration.

massaqɔ/massaqtɔ/massɔqutɔ: 'raised up, rising up'; Elias of Nisibis describes letters with the vowel /e/ as *massaqtɔ*, indicating the 'raised up' (i.e., backed) pronunciation of Syriac *yod* (contrasting /i/). He also uses *massɔqutɔ* to name /e/. Elias of Ṭirhan applies the nominal form *massaqɔ* as an alternate name for /o/, indicating the 'raised up' (i.e., backed) pronunciation of Syriac *waw* (contrasting /u/).

maṭṭah: 'descending'; a Hebrew term calqued from Arabic *khafḍ* that designates the phonetic group of /e/ and /i/ in *Nequdot Omeṣ ha-Miqrɔ*, possibly due to the relatively upwards movement of the airflow produced during their articulation.

men lꜥel-men ltaḥt: 'above-below'; two Syriac phrases which Jacob of Edessa uses to describe the location of the diacritic dot in the Syriac relative vocalisation system, and by extension designations for the relative 'height' of vowels according to their level of backness in the mouth.

meṣʿɔyɔ: 'intermediate'; Jacob of Edessa's descriptor for a word with relatively 'intermediate' vowels in comparison to the other two members of a three-way homograph. Usually refers to a word with /a/.

metgneb: 'suppressed'; Elias of Nisibis' term for a letter which is removed from a word in writing or pronunciation. Probably calqued from Arabic *ʾidghām/mundagham*.

mettziʿɔnɔ/mettziʿɔnitɔ/mettziʿɔnutɔ: 'moved, moved one'; Syriac descriptors for unvocalised consonants, their 'movement' in contrast to 'still' unvocalised letters. Attested in the Syriac-Arabic lexica of Ibn ʿAlī and Bar Bahlul as well as the eleventh-century Syriac grammars. *Mettziʿɔnitɔ* and *mettziʿɔnutɔ* can also refer to vowel phonemes, and Elias of Ṭirhan uses *mettziʿɔnutɔ* to designate both vowels and accents as 'modulations' of the voice. Antonym of *shalyɔ/shlitɔ*.

milleʿel-milleraʿ; 'above-below'; two Aramaic Masoretic terms that most commonly indicate the position of stressed syllables in pairs of homographs, but in early Masoretic lists also differentiate homographs that differed by a single vowel according to their level of backness within the mouth. These relative comparisons gave rise to the Hebrew 'vowel scale'. Likely adapted from *men lʿel-men ltaḥt*.

meṣap̄ pummɔ: 'caution of the mouth'; Babylonian Masoretic name for the vowel /ɔ/, apparently highlighting the care needed to pronounce a discrete vowel between /a/ and /o/.

mpaggdɔnɔ: 'bridling'; Jacob of Edessa's term for the Syriac sign consisting of one sublinear dot and one supralinear dot, comparing the points to the ends of a bridle in a horse's mouth. It marks a word as having 'intermediate' (*meṣʿɔyɔ*) vowels compared to the other two members of a three-way homograph. Such words almost always have /a/, so *mpaggdɔnɔ* is also a *de facto* name for that vowel.

mulūk/melakim: 'kings'; a Masoretic term for the category of 'vowels', commonly attested in both Arabic (*mulūk*) and Hebrew (*melakim*).

munkhafiḍa: 'lowered'; Ibn Jinnī's classification for all Arabic consonants produced 'below' the velum, including both in front of and behind it. Antonym of *mustaʿliya*.

muṣawwit/muṣawwitāt: 'sounding, sounding ones'; an Arabic term for 'vowels' or 'vowel letters', calqued either from Greek *phōnēenta* or Syriac *qɔlɔnɔyɔtɔ*, depending on the source. *Muṣawwitāt* appears as the translation of *qɔlɔnɔyɔtɔ* in Bar Bahlul's Syriac lexicon. It is not a common term for vowels in Arabic grammar, but Ibn Sīnā does use it in his *Risāla Asbāb Ḥudūth al-Ḥurūf*. It is more common in the Tiberian Masoretic tradition, where it indicates the category of the seven Hebrew vowels in contrast to the twenty-two consonants.

mustaʿliya: 'elevated'; an Arabic term used by Sībawayh and Ibn Jinnī to classify seven consonants (*khāʾ, ghayn, qāf, ṣād, ḍāḍ, ṭāʾ, ẓāʾ*) produced near the velum, considered the highest articulation point in the mouth. These consonants 'elevate' subsequent vowels by raising their articulation point towards the velum, preventing *ʾimāla* and inducing allophonic realisations of /a/ as /ɑ/ or /ɔ/. Antonym of *munkhafiḍa*.

mutaḥarrik: 'moved'; Arabic descriptor for a vocalised consonant, attested from the earliest grammatical sources. Antonym of *sākin*.

muʿtall: 'sickened'; a term used by al-Khalīl and Sībawayh to describe words formed from roots containing a *ḥarf al-ʾiʿtilāl* (letter of weakening, falling ill); that is, is one of the *matres lectionis*. Antonym of *ṣaḥīḥ*.

nabra: 'rising outward, raising the voice, swelling'; a name for a *hamza* pronounced with /a/ at the end of an Arabic word, according to al-Khwārizmī's *Mafātīḥ al-ʿUlūm* (*The Keys to the Sciences*).

naghama: 'tone, melody'; a Judaeo-Arabic term for 'vowel' in the Hebrew linguistic tradition, appearing in Saadia Gaon's *Kutub al-Lugha*. Abū al-Faraj also uses it as a term for Hebrew accents. Cognate with Syriac *neʿmɔtɔ* in Dawid bar Pawlos' fragmentary grammar and Hebrew *naʿimɔ* in Aharon ben Asher's *Diqduqe ha-Ṭeʿamim*, although neither of those authors use it to mean 'vowel'.

najr: 'natural form, condition'; a name for /u/ in the final syllable of a noun, according to al-Khwārizmī's *Mafātīḥ al-ʿUlūm* (*The Keys to the Sciences*).

naṣb/naṣba: 'standing upright'; the name for the Arabic accusative case, but originally a name for the vowel /a/ and a designation for vowels that have not undergone *ʾimāla*, indicating
the 'high' articulation point relatively-backed allophones. *Naṣba*
is a name for Hebrew /o/ in at least one *muṣawwitāt* text. Antonym of *ʾimāla*.

niṣf al-muṣawwit/niṣf ṣawṭ: 'half-sounding'; Abū Bishr and
Ibn Sīnā's phrases to translate Aristotle's *hēmiphōna* category of
consonants, generally describing continuant consonants in contrast to vowels and plosives.

nqɔshtɔ: 'beat'; a Syriac term for 'syllable' in Dawid bar
Pawlos' fragmentary grammar, and also a term for 'vowel' in
other Syriac sources.

nqed: 'thin, clear'; Jacob of Edessa's descriptor for a word
with relatively fronted vowels in comparison to a homograph
(primarily /e/). Antonym of *ʿbe*.

pɔtaḥ: 'opening'; Tiberian Masoretic name for the vowel
/a/, based on an Aramaic active participle describing the movement of the lips during articulation. Originally a relative term
that indicated a vowel in a word that was more open than a vowel
in the same position in its homograph. Antonym of *qɔmeṣ*. Cognate with Syriac *ptɔḥɔ* and Arabic *fatḥ*.

pɔtaḥ qɔṭon: 'small opening'; a name for the Tiberian vowel
/ɛ/, so called because it is relatively-open in comparison to /e/
and also requires less lip opening than /a/. Attested in *Diqduqe
ha-Teʿamim*, *The Treatise on the Shewa*, Judah ben David Ḥayyūj's

Kitāb al-Tanqīṭ, and other Masoretic notes. Appears as the Arabic calque *pɔtaḥ saghīr* in some *muṣawwitāt* texts.

pɔtaḥ gadol: 'large opening'; a name for the Tiberian vowel /a/, so called because it is relatively-open in comparison to /ɔ/ and also requires more lip opening than /ɛ/. Attested in Judah ben David Ḥayyūj's *Kitab al-Tanqīṭ.* Appears as the Arabic calque *pɔtaḥ kabīr* in some *muṣawwitāt* texts.

pelgut qɔlɔnɔyɔtɔ: 'half-soundings'; Elias of Ṭirhan's term for the vowels /a/, /ɔ/, and /e/, which are not typically represented by *matres lectionis* in Syriac. Calqued from Greek *hēmiphōna*, although Elias changes its technical sense.

phōnēenta: 'sounding ones'; a Greek term for vowels, highlighting their continuous airflow during articulation and their ability to be pronounced alone. Entered the Semitic grammatical traditions via Dionyisus Thrax's *Technē Grammatikē* (*The Art of Grammar*) and translations of Aristotle's *Poetics.*

pitḥɔ/mip̄taḥ pummɔ: 'opening/opening the mouth'; Babylonian Masoretic names for the vowel /a/, describing the movement of the lips in contrast to /ɔ/.

ptɔḥɔ/ptiḥtɔ: 'opening'; a Syriac name for the vowel /a/, describing the opening of the lips during articulation. First attested as a participle (*ptiḥtɔ*) in Dawid bar Pawlos' *scholion* on *bgdkt* letters and Ḥunayn ibn Isḥāq's version of *Ktɔbɔ d-Shmɔhe Dɔmyɔye,* it then appears throughout the Syriac linguistic tradition. The nominal *ptɔḥɔ* form appears at least as early as Elias of Ṭirhan's Syriac grammar. Cognate with Arabic *fatḥa* and Hebrew *pɔtaḥ.*

pte: 'wide'; Jacob of Edessa's descriptor for a word with relatively open vowels in comparison to a homograph (primarily
/ɑ/ and /a/). Antonym of *qaṭṭin*.

puḥḥome: 'comparisons, relationships'; a Syriac term referring to the systems of dots that represent phonetic and syntactic
information in Syriac texts. Depending on the author, it sometimes indicates vowel dots, sometimes reading dots, and sometimes all dots indiscriminately.

qaʿr: 'lowest depth, depression'; a name for /a/ in the first
syllable of a word, according to al-Khwārizmī's *Mafātīḥ al-ʿUlūm*
(*The Keys to the Sciences*).

qaṭṭin: 'narrow'; Jacob of Edessa's descriptor for a word
with relatively closed vowels in comparison to a homograph (primarily /u/, /e/, and /i/). Antonym of *pte*.

qɔlɔnɔyɔtɔ, sing. *qɔlɔnɔytɔ*: 'sounding'; a Syriac designation for the phonetic category of vowels in contrast to the 'soundless' consonants, so called because they can be pronounced and
form complete syllables alone. First attested in Jacob of Edessa's
Turrɔṣ Mamllɔ Nahrɔyɔ as a calque of the Greek *phōnēenta*. Also
appears in Dawid bar Pawlos' fragmentary grammar and Elias of
Ṭirhan's *Memrɔ Gramaṭiqɔyɔ*. Antonym of *dlɔ qɔlɔ*.

qɔmeṣ: 'closing'; Tiberian Masoretic name for the vowel
/ɔ/, describing the movement of the lips during articulation with
an Aramaic active participle. Originally a relative term that indicated that a vowel in a word was more closed than a vowel in the
same position in its homograph. Antonym of *pɔtaḥ*.

qɔmeṣ qɔṭon: 'small closing'; a name for the Tiberian vowel /e/, so called because it is relatively-closed in comparison to /ɛ/ and also requires more lip closing than /ɔ/. Attested in *Diqduqe ha-Teʿamim*, *The Treatise on the Shewa*, Judah ben David Ḥayyūj's *Kitāb al-Tanqīṭ*, and other Masoretic notes. Appears as the Arabic calque *qɔmeṣ saghīr* in some *muṣawwitāt* texts.

qɔmeṣ gadol: 'large closing'; a name for the Tiberian vowel /ɔ/, so called because it is relatively closed in comparison to /a/ and also requires less lip closing than /e/. Attested in Judah ben David Ḥayyūj's *Kitāb al-Tanqīṭ*. Appears as the Arabic calque *qɔmeṣ kabīr* in some *muṣawwitāt* texts.

qɔshɛ: 'hard'; the Hebrew term for the plosive realisation of *bgdkpt* consonants in *Sefer Yeṣira*. Cognate with Syriac *qushshɔyɔ*.

qibbuṣ: 'pressed together, squeezed together'; a Hebrew name for the vowel /u/, first attested in the time of the Qimḥi family. Calqued from Arabic *ḍamm*.

qushshɔyɔ: 'hardening'; the Syriac term for the plosive re-alisation of *bgdkpt* consonants and the supralinear dot that marks such consonants. The term is attested in the works of Dawid bar Pawlos. Cognate with Hebrew *qɔshɛ* as used in *Sefer Yeṣira*.

rak̲: 'soft'; the Hebrew term for the fricative realisation of *bgdkpt* consonants in *Sefer Yeṣira*. Cognate with Syriac *rukkɔkɔ*.

raf^c: 'rising'; the name for the Arabic nominative case, but also a name for the Arabic vowel /u/ until at least the ninth century, indicating its relatively high articulation point in comparison to /i/. Antonym of *khafḍ*. Sometimes associated with *tafkhīm*.

rawm: 'seeking, desiring'; an ultra-short Arabic vowel, shorter than a *ḥaraka*. According to al-Khwārizmī's *Mafātīḥ al-ʿUlūm*, this term belings to the grammatical school "of the philosophers of the Greeks". Sībawayh explains it as an ultra-short vowel related to *ʾishmām* and pronounced at the end of a word in pause.

rbɔṣɔ/rbiṣtɔ; 'compressing, compressed'; *rbiṣtɔ* is first attested in the Syriac-Arabic lexica of Ibn ʿAlī and Bar Bahlul, where it describes /e/ as relatively closed in comparison to *a*-vowels. Elias of Ṭirhan applies the nominal form *rbɔṣɔ* as a name for /e/ in his *Memrɔ Gramaṭiqɔyɔ*.

rum: 'rising'; a Hebrew term calqued from Arabic *rafʿ* that designates the phonetic group of /o/ and /u/ in *Nequdot Omeṣ ha-Miqrɔ*, possibly due to the relatively upwards movement of the airflow produced during their articulation.

rukkɔkɔ: 'softening'; the Syriac term for the fricative realisation of *bgdkpt* consonants and the sublinear dot that marks such consonants. The term is attested in the works of Dawid bar Pawlos. Cognate with Hebrew *rak* as used in *Sefer Yeṣira*.

rwaḥtɔ/rwiḥtɔ/rawiḥutɔ: 'broadened, broadening'; *rwiḥtɔ* is Elias of Nisibis' descriptor for a letter with /o/ as the relatively-open pronunciation of Syriac *wāw* (contrasting /u/). He also uses *rawiḥutɔ* as a name for the vowel /o/. Elias of Ṭirhan applies the nominal form *rwaḥtɔ* to name /o/.

saḥīḥ: 'firm, healthy, sound'; an Arabic term used to describe words formed from roots that do not contain a *ḥarf al-ʔiʿtilāl* 'letter of weakening, falling ill'; that is, is one of the *matres lectionis*. Al-Khalīl describes the consonants as *ṣaḥīḥ* in the introduction to *Kitāb al-ʿAyn*, but Sībawayh only applies it to describe entire words. Antonym of *muʿtall*.

sākin: 'still, unmoving'; Arabic descriptor for an unvocalised consonant, attested from the earliest grammatical sources. Antonym of *mutaḥarrik*.

ṣāmita: 'soundless'; Ibn Sīnā's descriptor for Arabic *wāw* and *yāʔ* when they are pronounced as consonants. Antonym of *muṣawwita*.

sere/ṣiryɔ: 'cracking, splitting'; a Masoretic name for the vowel /e/, describing the separation of the lips during articulation. Originally an Aramaic nominal form (*ṣiryɔ*) as found in *muṣawwitāt* texts.

segol/segoltɔ: 'bunch of grapes'; an Aramaic name for the Hebrew vowel /ɛ/, indicating the shape of the Tiberian triangular three-dot sublinear vowel sign. Most commonly appears with the set of phonetic names *ḥolem, ḥiriq, sere*, and *shuruq*.

shalyɔ/shlitɔ: 'made still'; a Syriac descriptor for an unvocalised consonant, highlighting its 'stillness' in contrast to 'moved' vocalised letters. Attested in the Syriac-Arabic lexica of

Ibn ʿAlī and Bar Bahlul as well as the eleventh-century Syriac grammars. Antonym of *mettziʿɔnɔ/mettziʿɔnitɔ/mettziʿɔnutɔ*.

shelyɔ: 'stillness'; a Syriac term for the absence of a vowel, calqued from Arabic *sukūn*.

sheshlɔ/sheshltɔ: 'chain'; a Syriac term for the two-dot signs that indicate /ɔ/ and /e/, attested in Ḥunayn ibn Isḥāq's version of *Ktɔbɔ d-Shmɔhe Dɔmyɔye* and Elias of Nisibis' *Turrɔṣ Mamllɔ Suryɔyɔ*. Elias of Ṭirhan uses it as an alternate name for *rbɔṣɔ* in his *Memrɔ Gramaṭiqɔyɔ*.

shewa: 'levelling'; an Aramaic Masoretic term for the vertical pair of sublinear dots that represents either an epenthetic short vowel or the lack of a vowel in Tiberian Hebrew.

shewa mutaḥarrik: 'moved *shewa*'; an Arabic Masoretic designation for vocalic *shewa*, adapted from the function of the term *mutaḥarrik* in Arabic grammar; translated into Hebrew as *shewa mitnaʿaneaʿ* (e.g., in *The Treatise on the Shewa*).

shewa sākin: 'still, motionless *shewa*'; an Arabic Masoretic designation for silent *shewa*, adapted from the function of the term *sākin* in Arabic grammar; translated into Hebrew as *shewa ʿomed* (e.g., in *The Treatise on the Shewa*).

shuruq/sherqɔ: 'whistling'; a Masoretic name for the vowel /u/, comparing its articulation to the shape the lips while whistling. Originally an Aramaic nominal form (*sherqɔ*) as found in *muṣawwitāt* texts.

simanim: 'symbols'; a Hebrew term for the category of 'vowels' as well as the term for the Masoretic mnemonic devices used to recall vocalisation.

tafkhīm: 'thickening'; an Arabic term for the pronunciation of a backed allophone of /a/ or /ā/. Sībawayh applies it only to the Hijazi pronunciation of /ō/ in *ṣalāt* and *zakāt*, but for most grammarians it encompassed other backed allophones (/ɑ/, /ɔ/). Often depicted as the phonetic opposite of *ʾimāla* and sometimes associated with *rafʿ*.

taḥtoni: 'lower one'; a Hebrew name for /i/ in the *Treatise on the Shewa*, describing the sublinear position of the Tiberian *ḥiriq* dot. Calqued into Arabic as *saflānī*.

tanwīn: 'nunation'; the addition of a short vowel plus /n/ to the end of an Arabic noun, usually marked by two of the corresponding vocalisation sign.

tawjīh: 'guidance, direction'; a name for /u/ in the first syllable of a word, according to al-Khwārizmī's *Mafātīḥ al-ʿUlūm* (*The Keys to the Sciences*).

taysīr: 'facilitation, simplification, making easy'; a name for a word-final Arabic /a/ when written *plene* with *ʾalif*, according to al-Khwārizmī's *Mafātīḥ al-ʿUlūm* (*The Keys to the Sciences*).

ṣɔṣɔ/ṣiṣtɔ: 'constrained'; *ṣiṣtɔ* is first attested in the grammatical *scholion* on *bgdkt* letters by Dawid bar Pawlos to describe /u/ as the relatively-closed pronunciation of Syriac *waw* (contrasting /o/). The nominal form *ṣɔṣɔ* appears as a name for /u/ in the grammatical work of Bar Hebraeus.

sukūn: 'stillness'; an Arabic term for the lack of a vowel and for the miniature supralinear circle grapheme that marks an unvocalised consonant. Antonym of *ḥaraka*.

ẓāhir/ẓuhūr: 'clear, apparent'; a term used by Judah ben David Ḥayyūj and some *muṣawwitāt* authors to describe the consonantal pronunciation of the *matres lectionis*. *Ẓuhūr* is an alternative name for *mappiq* indicating consonantal *heʾ* in *Hidāya al-Qārī*.

zawʿɔ: 'movement'; a Syriac term for 'vowel', probably calqued from Arabic *ḥaraka* and first widely attested as a vowel name in the grammars of Elias of Nisibis and Elias of Ṭirhan. One West Syriac accent sign is also known as *zawʿɔ* from the seventh century onwards, but it appears to be unrelated to the phonological definition meaning 'vowel'.

zlɔmɔ: 'inclining'; a Syriac name for /e/ attested in Bar Malkon's *Mṣidtɔ d-Nuqze* (*The Net of Points*). Possibly a calque of Arabic *ʾimāla*.

zqɔpɔ/zqiptɔ: 'standing upright'; a Syriac name for the vowel /ɔ/, indicating its relative backness in comparison to /a/, and most likely a calque of the Arabic *naṣb*. First attested as a participle (*zqiptɔ*) in Dawid bar Pawlos' *scholion* on *bgdkt* letters, it then appears throughout the Syriac linguistic tradition. The nominal *zqɔpɔ* form appears at least as early as Elias of Ṭirhan's Syriac grammar.

zribɔ: 'narrowed, contracted'; a Syriac descriptor for letters with the vowel /e/, indicating the relative closedness of the lips in comparison to more open *a*-vowels; common in the Syriac-Arabic lexica of Ibn ʿAlī and Bar Bahlul.

zujj: 'spearpoint, piercing'; an Arabic Masoretic name for Tiberian /u/, indicating the graphic appearance of the *shuruq* sign (ו).

REFERENCES

Abbas, Adnan. 2002. *Arabic Poetic Terminology*. Poznań: Adam Mickiewicz University.

Abbott, Nabia. 1939. *The Rise of the North Arabic Script and Its Ḳurʾānic Development*. Chicago: University of Chicago: Oriental Institute.

———. 1972. *Studies in Arabic Literary Papyri III*. Chicago: University of Chicago Press.

Alfozan, Abdulrahman Ibrahim. 1989. 'Assimilation in Classical Arabic: A Phonological Study'. PhD Thesis, Glasgow: University of Glasgow.

Allony, Nehemia. 1964. 'Kitāb Al-Muṣawwitāt by Moshe Ben Asher: Two Fragments'. *Lěšonénu: A Journal for the Study of the Hebrew Language and Cognate Subjects* 29/1, 9–23. [in Hebrew]

———. 1965. 'Sefer ha-Qolot (Kitāb al-Muṣawwitāt): The text and translation'. *Lěšonénu: A Journal for the Study of the Hebrew Language and Cognate Subjects* 29/3 136–59. [in Hebrew]

———. 1971. 'Ne'ima (Naghmah) in Medieval Hebrew Literature'. *Yuval* II: 8–29. [in Hebrew]

———. 1983. 'Kitāb al-Muṣawwitāt (Sefer ha-Qolot): A New Fragment from the Cairo Geniza'. *Lěšonénu: A Journal for the Study of the Hebrew Language and Cognate Subjects* 47/2, 85–124. [in Hebrew]

———. 1986. *Meḥqere Lashon we-Sifrut*. Jerusalem: Mekhon Ben-Tsevi le-ḥeqer qehilot Yiśraʾel ba-Mizraḥ. [in Hebrew]

Allony, Nehemia, and Israel Yeivin. 1985. 'Four Fragments from Four Muṣawwitāt (Vowels) Works'. *Lěšonénu: A Journal for the Study of the Hebrew Language and Cognate Subjects* 48–49/2–3: 85–117. [in Hebrew]

Arzandeh, Mehran, and Suheyl Umar. 2011. 'Al-Azharī'. In *Encyclopedia Islamica*, edited by Farhad Daftary and Wilferd Madelung, 3:983–88. Leiden: Brill.

Bacher, Willhelm. 1974. *Die Anfänge der hebräischen Grammatik (1895) together with Die hebräische Sprachwissenschaft vom 10. bis zum 16. Jahrhundert (1892)*. Edited by Ludwig Blau. Studies in the History of Language Sciences 4. Amsterdam: John Benjamins.

Badawī, 'Abd al-Raḥmān al-. 1953. *Arisṭūṭālis: Fann al-Šiʿr, Maʿa l-Tarǧamah al-ʿArabīyah al-Qadīmah Wa-Šurūḥ al-Fārābī Wa-Ibn Sīnā Wa-Ibn Rušd*. Dirāsāt Islāmīya 8. Cairo: Maṭbaʿat Dār al-Kutub al-Miṣrīya.

Baer, S., and H. L. Strack, eds. 1879. *Dikduke ha-Teʿamim des Ahron ben Moscheh ben Ascher, und andere alte grammatisch-massorethisch Lehrstücke*. Leipzig: Verlag von L. Fernau.

Baethgen, Friedrich, ed. 1880. *Syrische Grammatik des Elias of Tîrhân*. Leipzig: Hinrichs.

Bakalla, Muhammad Hasan. 2011. 'Tafxīm'. In *Encyclopedia of Arabic Language and Linguistics*. Brill. http://dx.doi.org.ezp.lib.cam.ac.uk/10.1163/1570-6699_e all_EALL_COM_0333.

Baker, Colin F., and Meira R. P. Polliack. 2001. *Arabic and Judeo-Arabic Manuscripts in the Cambridge Genizah Collections: Taylor-Schechter Arabic Old Series (T-S Ar.1a-54)*. Cambridge Genizah Series 12. Cambridge: Cambridge University Press.

Balzaretti, Claudio. 1997. 'Ancient Treatises on Syriac Homonyms'. In *Oriens Christianus*, 73–81. Wiesbaden: Otto Harrassowitz Verlag.

Barsoum, Ignatius Aphram I. 1987. *Al-Luʾluʾ al-Manthūr fī Tārīkh al-ʿUlūm al-Ādāb al-Suriyāniyya*. 5th edition. Aleppo: Silsila al-Turāth al-Suriyānī.

Basal, Nasir. 1999. 'The Concept of Compensation (ʿIwad/Taʿwīḍ) As Used by Yehuda Ḥayyūj in Comparison with Sībawayh'. *Journal of Semitic Studies* 44/2: 227–43.

———. 2013. 'Latent Quiescent (Sākin Layyin)'. In *Encyclopedia of Hebrew Language and Linguistics*. Electronic Edition: Brill. http://dx.doi.org/10.1163/2212-241_ehll_EHLL_SIM_0005 35.

Bauer, Gertrud. 1972. *Athanasius von Qus, Qilādat at-Taḥrīr Fī ʿilm at-Tafsīr: Eine Koptische Grammatik in Arabischer Sprache Aus Dem 13./14/Jahrhundert*. Freiburg: K. Schwarz.

Baumstark, Anton. 1922. *Geschichte der syischen Literatur*. Bonn: A. Marcus & E. Webers.

Becker, Adam H. 2003. 'Beyond the Spatial and Temporal Limes: Questioning the "Parting of the Ways" Outside the Roman Empire'. In *The Ways That Never Parted*, edited by Adam H. Becker and Annette Yoshiko Reed, 373–92. Texts and Studies in Ancient Judaism 95. Tübingen: Mohr Siebeck.

———. 2006. *Fear of God and the Beginning of Wisdom: The School of Nisibis and Christian Scholastic Culture in Late Antique Mesopotamia*. Philadelphia: University of Pennsylvania Press.

———. 2010. 'The Comparative Study of "Scholasticism" in Late Antique Mesopotamia: Rabbis and East Syrians'. *AJS Review* zZ

34/1: 91–113. https://doi.org/10.1017/S036400941000
0243.

Ben-Ḥayyim, Ze'ev, and Abraham Tal. 2000. *A Grammar of Samaritan Hebrew: Based on the Recitation of the Law in Comparison with the Tiberian and Other Jewish Traditions.* Revised. Winona Lake, IN: Eisenbrauns.

Bertaina, David. 2011. 'Science, Syntax, and Superiority in Eleventh-Century Christian–Muslim Discussion: Elias of Nisibis on the Arabic and Syriac Languages'. *Islam and Christian–Muslim Relations* 22/2: 197–207.

Blake, Frank R. 1940. 'The Development of Symbols for the Vowels in the Alphabets Derived from the Phoenician'. *Journal of the American Oriental Society* 60/3: 391. https://doi.org/10.2307/594425.

Blau, Joshua, and Simon Hopkins. 1984. 'On Early Judaeo-Arabic Orthography'. *Zeitschrift für Arabische Linguistik* 12: 9–27.

Bloom, Jonathan. 2010. 'Literary and Oral Cultures'. In *The New Cambridge History of Islam, V: Islamic Cultures and Societies to the End of the Eighteenth Century*, edited by Robert Irwin, 668–81. Cambridge: Cambridge University Press.

Bosworth, C. E. 1963. 'A Pioneer Arabic Encyclopedia of the Sciences: Al Khwārizmī's Keys of the Sciences'. *Isis* 54/1: 97–111.

———. 1982. 'Abdallah B. Taher'. In *Encyclopædia Iranica*, 186–87. London: Routledge & Kegan Paul.

Bravmann, Max. 1934. *Materialien und Untersuchungen zu den phonetischen Lehren der Araber.* Göttingen: Dieterichsche Universitäts Buchdruckerei.

Brierley, Clare, Majdi Sawalha, Barry Heselwood, and Eric At-
well. 2016. 'A Verified Arabic-IPA Mapping for Arabic
Transcription Technology, Informed by Quranic Recitation,
Traditional Arabic Linguistics, and Modern Phonetics'.
Journal of Semitic Studies 61/1: 157–86.

Brock, Sebastian P. 1997. *A Brief Outline of Syriac Literature*.
Mōrān 'Eth'ō 9. Kerala: St. Ephrem Ecumenical Research
Institute.

———. 2011. 'Dawid Bar Pawlos'. In *GEDSH: Electronic Edition*.
Beth Mardutho. https://gedsh.bethmardutho.org/Dawid-
bar-Pawlos.

———. 2016. *An Introduction to Syriac Studies*. 3rd edition. Piscataway: Gorgias Press.

Brody, Robert. 2016. *Sa'adyah Gaon*. Translated by Betsy Rozen-
berg. Liverpool: The Littman Library of Jewish Civilization
& Liverpool University Press.

Browning, Robert, and Alexander Kazhdan. 2005. 'Michael Synkellos'. In *The Oxford Dictionary of Byzantium*. Oxford: Oxford University Press. https://www.oxfordreference.com/
view/10.1093/acref/9780195046526.001.0001/acref-978
0195046526-e-3543.

Butts, Aaron M. 2009. 'The Biography of the Lexicographer Ishoʿ
Bar ʿAli (ʿĪsā b. ʿAlī)'. In *Oriens Christianus*, edited by Hubert
Kaufhold and Manfred Kropp, 59–70. 93. Wiesbaden: Otto
Harrassowitz Verlag.

———. 2011a. 'Ḥunayn b. Isḥāq'. In *GEDSH: Electronic Edition*.
Beth Mardutho. https://gedsh.bethmardutho.org/Hunayn-
b-Ishaq.

———. 2011b. 'Isho' of Merv'. In *GEDSH: Electronic Edition*. Beth Mardutho. https://gedsh.bethmardutho.org/Isho-of-Merv.

———. 2016. *Language Change in the Wake of Empire: Syriac in Its Greco-Roman Context*. Winona Lake, IN: Eisenbrauns.

Butts, Aaron M., and Simcha Gross. 2020. 'Introduction'. In *Jews and Syriac Christians: Intersections across the First Millennium*, edited by Aaron M. Butts and Simcha Gross, 1–24. Texts and Studies in Ancient Judaism 180. Tübingen: Mohr Siebeck.

Childers, J. W. 2011. "Enanisho". In *Encyclopedia of the Syriac Heritage*, edited by Sebastian P. Brock, Aaron Michael Butts, George Anton Kiraz, and Lucas Van Rompay, 144. Piscataway: Gorgias Press.

Coakley, J. F. 2011. 'When Were the Five Greek Vowel-Signs Introduced into Syriac Writing?' *Journal of Semitic Studies* 56/2: 307–25.

Connolly, Magdalen M., and Nick Posegay. 2020. '"An Arabic Qurʾān, That You Might Understand": Qurʾān Fragments in the T-S Arabic Cairo Genizah Collection'. *Journal of Islamic Manuscripts* 11/3: 292–351. https://doi.org/10.1163/1878464X-01103002.

Dānī, Abū ʿAmr al-. 1960. *Al-Muḥkam Fī Naqṭ al-Maṣāḥif*. Edited by ʿIzza Ḥasan. Damascus.

Davidson, Thomas, trans. 1874. *The Grammar of Dionysios Thrax*. St. Louis: R. P. Studley.

Déroche, François. 1983. *Manuscrits musulmans: Les manuscrits du Coran aux origines de la calligraphie coranique.* Vol. I, 1. Catalogue des manuscrits arabes 2. Paris: Bibliothèque Nationale de France.

———. 1992. *The Abbasid Tradition: Qur'ans of the 8th to 10th Centuries A.D.* The Nasser D. Khalili Collection of Islamic Art. Khalili Collections. Oxford: Oxford University Press.

———. 2003. 'Manuscripts of the Qur'ān'. In *Encyclopaedia of the Qur'ān*, edited by Jane Dammen McAuliffe, Claude Gilliot, William A. Graham, Wadad Kadi, Andrew Rippin, Monique Bernards, and John Nawas. Leiden: Brill. http://dx.doi.org/10.1163/1875-3922_q3_EQCOM_00110.

———. 2004. 'Colonnes, vases et rinceaux sur quelques enluminures d'époque Omeyyade'. *Comptes Rendus des Séances de l'Académie des Inscriptions et Belles Lettres*, 227–64.

———. 2014. *Qur'ans of the Umayyads: A First Overview.* Leiden Studies in Islam and Society 1. Leiden: Brill.

Déroche, François, Annie Berthier, Marie-Geneviève Guesdon, Bernard Guineau, Francis Richard, Annie Vernay-Nouri, Jean Vezin, and Muhammad Isa Waley. 2015. *Islamic Codicology: An Introduction to the Study of Manuscripts in Arabic Script.* Edited by Muhammad Isa Waley. Translated by Deke Dusinberre and David Radzinowicz. 2nd edition. London: Al-Furqān Islamic Heritage Foundation.

Dolabani, P. Y. 1953. *Egroteh d-Dawid bar Pawlos d-Metida' d-Bet Rabban.* Mardin: The Syriac Printing Press of Wisdom.

————. 1994. *Catalogue of Syriac Manuscripts in St. Mark's Monastery*. Edited by Gregorios Yuhanna Ibrahim. Mardin: Dar Mardin.

Donnet, Daniel. 1982. *Le Traité de la construction de la phrase de Michel le Syncelle de Jérusalem*. Études de philologie d'archéologie et d'histoire anciennes 22. Brussels: Institut historique belge de Rome.

Dotan, Aron. 1954. 'The Names of Šĕwa at the Beginning of Hebrew Grammar'. *Lĕšonénu: A Journal for the Study of the Hebrew Language and Cognate Subjects* 19: 11–30. [in Hebrew]

————, ed. 1967. *Sefer Diqduqe ha-Teʿamim le-R. Aharon ben Moshe ben Asher*. 3 vols. Jerusalem: Academy of the Hebrew Language.

————. 1974. 'The Beginnings of Masoretic Vowel Notation'. In *1972 and 1973 Proceedings IOMS*, edited by H. Orlinsky, 21–34. Masoretic Studies 1. Missoula, MT: University of Montana.

————. 1981. 'The Relative Chronology of Hebrew Vocalization and Accentuation'. *Proceedings of the American Academy for Jewish Research* 48: 87–99.

————. 1997. *The Dawn of Hebrew Linguistics: The Book of Elegance of the Language of the Hebrews by Saadia Gaon*. 2 vols. Jerusalem: World Union of Jewish Studies.

————. 2007. 'Masorah'. In *Encyclopedia Judaica*, 2nd edition, XIII: 603–56. Detroit: Macmillan Reference USA.

Dutton, Yasin. 1999. 'Red Dots, Green Dots, Yellow Dots and Blue: Some Reflections on the Vocalisation of Early

Qur'anic Manuscripts (Part I)'. *Journal of Qur'anic Studies* 1/1: 115–40.

———. 2000. 'Red Dots, Green Dots, Yellow Dots and Blue: Some Reflections on the Vocalisation of Early Qur'anic Manuscripts (Part II)'. *Journal of Qur'anic Studies* 2/1: 1–24.

Duval, Rubens. 1881. *Traité de grammaire syriaque*. Paris: F. Vieweg.

———, ed. 1901. *Lexicon Syriacum Auctore Hassano Bar Bahlule*. 2 vols. Paris: E Reipublicae typographaeo. http://www.du-khrana.com/lexicon/BarBahlul/index.php.

Eldar, Ilan, ed. 1981. 'Kitāb Naḥw Al-ʿIbrānī: A Treatise on the Changes of Vocalization'. *Lěšonénu: A Journal for the Study of the Hebrew Language and Cognate Subjects* 44: 105–32. [in Hebrew]

———. 1983. 'A New Study of the Question of the Divisions of the Hebrew Vowels into Elevation, Descent, and Standing Upright'. In *Meḥkere lashon mugashim li-Ze'ev Ben-Ḥayim be-hagiʿo la-ševah*, 43–55. Jerusalem: Hotsa'at sefarim ʿa. sh. Y. L. Magnes, ha-Universiṭah ha-ʿIvrit. [in Hebrew]

———. 1986. 'On the Identity of Some Genizah Fragments'. In *Alei Sefer: Studies in Bibliography and in the History of the Printed and the Digital Hebrew Book*, 51–61. Bar Ilan University Press. [in Hebrew]

———. 1988. 'On "The Treatise on the Shewa" and "Seder ha-Simanim"'. In *Studies in Hebrew and Arabic in Memory of Dov Eron*, 127–38. Teʿuda 6. Tel-Aviv: Tel-Aviv University. [in Hebrew]

Encyclopaedia Judaica (Germany). 2007. 'Kallir, Eleazar'. In *Encyclopedia Judaica*, 2nd edition, XI:743–45. Detroit: Macmillan Reference USA.

Farina, Margherita. 2018. 'La linguistique syriaque selon Jacques d'Édesse'. In *Les auteurs syriaques et leur langue*, edited by Margherita Farina, 167–87. Études syriaques 15. Paris: Geuthner.

———. forthcoming 2021. 'Les Textes Linguistiques de David Bar Paulos'. Paris: Geuthner.

Fassberg, Steven. 1990. *A Grammar of the Palestinian Targum Fragments from the Cairo Genizah*. Harvard Semitic Studies 38. Atlanta: Scholars Press.

Fiano, Emanuel A. 2011. 'Dionysius Thrax'. In *GEDSH: Electronic Edition*. Beth Mardutho. https://gedsh.bethmardutho.org/Dionysius-Thrax.

Fischer, Wolfdietrich. 1985. 'The Chapter on Grammar in the Kitāb Mafātīḥ Al-ʿUlūm'. In *Studies in the History of Arabic Grammar—Proceedings of the First Symposium on the History of Arabic Grammar*, 94–103. Zeitschrift für Arabische Linguistik 15. Wiesbaden: Otto Harrassowitz Verlag.

Fleischer, Ezra. 1972. 'An Ancient Grammatical Term in a Poem by Qallir'. *Lěšonénu: A Journal for the Study of the Hebrew Language and Cognate Subjects* 31/4: 263–67. [in Hebrew]

Frendsdorff, Zalman. 1864. *Das Buch Ochlah W'ochlah*. Hanover: Hahn.

Frolov, Dmitry. 2011. 'Meter'. In *Encyclopedia of Arabic Language and Linguistics*. Brill. http://dx.doi.org.ezp.lib.cam.ac.uk/10.1163/1570-6699_eall_EALL_COM_vol3_0212.

Gade, Anna M. 2003. 'Recitation of the Qurʾān'. In *Encyclopaedia of the Qurʾān*. Leiden: Brill. http://dx.doi.org/10.1163/1875-3922_q3_EQCOM_00168.

George, Alain. 2010. *The Rise of Islamic Calligraphy*. London: Saqi Books.

———. 2015. 'Coloured Dots and the Question of Regional Origins in Early Qurʾans (Part I)'. *Journal of Qurʾanic Studies* 17/1: 1–44.

Gesenius, Wilhelm. 1910. *Gesenius' Hebrew Grammar*. Edited by E. F. Kautzsch. Translated by A. E. Cowley. Oxford: Clarendon Press.

Ghabban, ʿAli ibn Ibrahim, and Robert Hoyland. 2008. 'The Inscription of Zuhayr, the Oldest Islamic Inscription (24 AH/AD 644–645), the Rise of the Arabic Script and the Nature of the Early Islamic State'. *Arabian Archaeology and Epigraphy* 19/2: 210–37.

Ginsburg, Christian. 1880. *The Massorah*. 4 vols. Jerusalem.

Gottheil, Richard, ed. 1887. *A Treatise on Syriac Grammar by Mâr Eliâ of Ṣôbhâ*. Berlin: Peiser.

———, ed. 1893. 'Dawidh Bar Paulos, a Syriac Grammarian'. *Journal of the American Oriental Society* 15: cxi–cxviii.

———. 1908. *Bar ʿAli (Ishoʿ): The Syriac-Arabic Glosses (Nun-ʿayn)*. Vol. I. 2 vols. Classe di Scienze Morali, Storiche et Filologiche Ser. 5 13. Rome: Atti della R. Accademia dei Lincei.

———. 1928. *Bar ʿAli (Ishoʿ): The Syriac-Arabic Glosses (Pe-Taw)*. Vol. II. 2 vols. Classe di Scienze Morali, Storiche et Filologiche Ser. 5 13. Rome: Atti della R. Accademia dei Lincei.

Graetz, Heinrich. 1881a. 'Die Anfänge der Vocalzeichen im Hebräischen (pt. I)'. *Monatsschrift für Geschichte und Wissenschaft des Judentums* 30/8: 348–67.

———. 1881b. 'Die Anfänge der Vocalzeichen im Hebräischen (pt. II)'. *Monatsschrift für Geschichte und Wissenschaft des Judentums* 30/9: 395–405.

Griffith, Sidney. 2013. *The Bible in Arabic: The Scriptures of the 'People of the Book' in the Language of Islam*. Princeton: Princeton University Press.

Gruendler, Beatrice. 2001. 'Arabic Script'. In *Encyclopedia of the Qurʾān*, edited by J. D. McAuliffe, I: 135–44. Leiden: Brill.

Haar Romeny, Bas ter, ed. 2008. *Jacob of Edessa and the Syriac Culture of His Day*. Leiden: Brill.

Haupt, Paul. 1901. 'The Names of the Hebrew Vowels'. *Journal of the American Oriental Society* 22: 13–17. https://doi.org/10.2307/592407.

Hayman, A. Peter. 2004. *Sefer Yeṣira: Edition, Translation and Text-Critical Commentary*. Tübingen: Mohr Siebeck.

Hilgard, Alfred. 1901. *Scholia in Dionysii Thracis Artem Grammaticam*. Grammatici Graeci, III. Leipzig: B. G. Tevbneri.

Hoberman, Robert D. 2011. 'Pausal Forms'. In *Encyclopedia of Arabic Language and Linguistics*. Brill. http://dx.doi.org.ezp.lib.cam.ac.uk/10.1163/1570-6699_eall_EALL_COM_vol3_0251.

Hoffmann, Georgius. 1874. *Syrisch-arabische Glossen: Autographie einer Gothaischen Handschrift enthaltend Bar Ali's Lexikon von Alif bis Mim*. Kiel: Schwers'sche Buchhandlung.

———. 1880. *Opuscula Nestoriana*. Paris: Maisonneuvee.

Hoyland, Robert. 2008a. 'Epigraphy and the Linguistic Background of the Qurʾan'. In *The Qurʾan in Its Historical Context*, edited by G. S. Reynolds, 51–69. London: Routledge.

———. 2008b. 'Jacob and Early Islamic Edessa'. In *Jacob of Edessa and the Syriac Culture of His Day*, edited by Bas ter Haar Romeny, 11–24. Leiden: Brill.

Hughes, Thomas Patrick. 1895. *A Dictionary of Islam: Being an Encyclopaedia of the Doctrines, Rites, Ceremonies, and Customs, Together With the Technical and Theological Terms, of the Muhammadan Religion*. London: W. H. Allen & Co.

Ibn Jinnī, Abū al-Fatḥ ʿUthmān. 1952. *Kitāb Al-Khaṣāʾis*. Cairo.

———. 1993. *Sirr Ṣināʿa al-Iʿrāb*. Edited by Hasan al-Hindawi. 2nd edition. Damascus: Dār al-Qalaʿ.

Bekker, Immanuel. 1816. *Anecdota Graeca*. Vol. II. Berlin: G. Reimer.

James, David. 1992. *The Master Scribes: Qurʾans of the 10th to 14th Centuries Ad*. London: The Nour Foundation in Association with Azimuth Editions and Oxford University Press.

Jastrow, Marcus. 1897. *The Weak and Geminative Verbs in Hebrew, by Abû Zakariyyâ Yaḥyâ Ibn Dâwud of Fez, Known as Ḥayyûḡ; the Arabic Text Now Published for the First Time*. Leiden: Brill.

Kaplony, Andreas. 2008. 'What Are Those Few Dots for? Thoughts on the Orthography of the Qurra Papyri (709–710), the Khurasan Parchments (755–777) and the Inscription of the Jerusalem Dome of the Rock (692)', *Arabica* 55/1: 91–112.

Kazimirski, A. de Biberstein. 1860. *Dictionnaire Arabe-Français*. Paris: Maisonneuve.

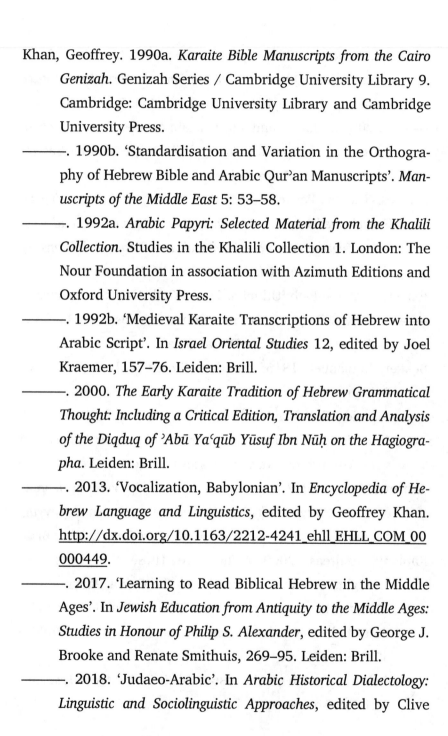

Khan, Geoffrey. 1990a. *Karaite Bible Manuscripts from the Cairo Genizah*. Genizah Series / Cambridge University Library 9. Cambridge: Cambridge University Library and Cambridge University Press.

———. 1990b. 'Standardisation and Variation in the Orthography of Hebrew Bible and Arabic Qur'an Manuscripts'. *Manuscripts of the Middle East* 5: 53–58.

———. 1992a. *Arabic Papyri: Selected Material from the Khalili Collection*. Studies in the Khalili Collection 1. London: The Nour Foundation in association with Azimuth Editions and Oxford University Press.

———. 1992b. 'Medieval Karaite Transcriptions of Hebrew into Arabic Script'. In *Israel Oriental Studies* 12, edited by Joel Kraemer, 157–76. Leiden: Brill.

———. 2000. *The Early Karaite Tradition of Hebrew Grammatical Thought: Including a Critical Edition, Translation and Analysis of the Diqduq of ʾAbū Yaʿqūb Yūsuf Ibn Nūḥ on the Hagiographa*. Leiden: Brill.

———. 2013. 'Vocalization, Babylonian'. In *Encyclopedia of Hebrew Language and Linguistics*, edited by Geoffrey Khan. http://dx.doi.org/10.1163/2212-4241_ehll_EHLL_COM_00 000449.

———. 2017. 'Learning to Read Biblical Hebrew in the Middle Ages'. In *Jewish Education from Antiquity to the Middle Ages: Studies in Honour of Philip S. Alexander*, edited by George J. Brooke and Renate Smithuis, 269–95. Leiden: Brill.

———. 2018. 'Judaeo-Arabic'. In *Arabic Historical Dialectology: Linguistic and Sociolinguistic Approaches*, edited by Clive

Holes, 148–69. Oxford Studies in Diachronic and Historical Linguistics 30. Oxford: Oxford University Press.

———. 2020. *The Tiberian Pronunciation Tradition of Biblical Hebrew*. 2 Vols. Cambridge Semitic Languages and Cultures 1. Cambridge: University of Cambridge and Open Book Publishers.

Khwārizmī, Abū ʿAbd Allāh Muḥammad ibn Aḥmad ibn Yūsuf al-Kātib al-. 1968. *Liber Mafâtîḥ Al-Olûm*. Edited by G. Van Vloten. 2nd edition. Leiden: Brill.

Kinberg, Naphtali. 1986. 'More of the Vowel Concept in Medieval Grammar: To the Understanding of the Term Niṣāb'. *Eshel B'er Sheva* 3: 171–77.

———. 1987. 'The Concepts of Elevation and Depression in Medieval Arabic Phonetic Theory'. *Zeitschrift für Arabische Linguistik* 17: 7–20.

Kindī, Abu Yūsuf Yaʿqūb al-. 1962. *Muʾallafāt Al-Kindī al-Mūsīqiyya*. Edited by Z. Yūsuf. Baghdad: Maṭbaʿat Shafīq.

King, Daniel. 2012. 'Elements of the Syriac Grammatical Tradition as These Relate to the Origins of Arabic Grammar'. In *The Foundations of Arabic Linguistics*, edited by Amal Marogy, 187–209. Studies in Semitic Languages and Linguistics 65. Leiden: Brill.

Kiraz, George A. 2012. *Tūrrāṣ Mamllā: A Grammar of the Syriac Language*. Vol. I. Piscataway: Gorgias Press.

———. 2015. *The Syriac Dot: A Short History*. Piscataway: Gorgias Press.

Knudsen, Ebbe Egede. 2015. *Classical Syriac Phonology*. Perspectives on Linguistics and Ancient Languages 7. Piscataway: Gorgias Press.

Kruisheer, Dirk. 2008. 'A Bibliographical Clavis to the Works of Jacob of Edessa'. In *Jacob of Edessa and the Syriac Culture of His Day*, edited by Bas ter Haar Romeny, 265–94. Leiden: Brill.

Lambdin, Thomas O. 1971. *Introduction to Biblical Hebrew*. Great Britain: Charles Scribner's Sons.

Lambert, Mayer, trans. 1891. *Commentaire sur le séfer yeṣira ou livre de la creation par le Gaon Saadya de Fayyoum*. Paris: Émile Bouillon.

Lane, Edward William. 1863. *Madd Al-Qamus: An Arabic-English Lexicon*. London; Edinburgh: Williams and Norgate.

Levin, Aryeh. 2007. 'ʾImāla'. In *Encyclopedia of Arabic Language and Linguistics*, edited by Lutz Edzard and Rudolf de Jong, II: 311–15. Leiden: Brill. http://dx.doi.org/10.1163/1570-6699_eall_EALL_SIM_vol2_0022.

Levy, Kurt, ed. 1936. *Zur Masoretischen Grammatik: Texte und Untersuchungen*. Bonner Orientalische Studien 15. Stuttgart: W. Kohlhammer.

Lipiński, Edward. 1997. *Semitic Languages Outline of a Comparative Grammar*. Orientalia Lovaniensia Analecta 80. Louvain: Peeters Publishers and Department of Oriental Studies Bondgenotenlaan.

Loopstra, Jonathan. 2009. 'Patristic Selections in the "Masoretic" Handbooks of the Qarqaftā Tradition'. PhD Thesis, Washington, D.C.: The Catholic University of America.

———. 2014. *An East Syrian Manuscript of the Syriac 'Masora' Dated to 899 CE.* Vol. I. Piscataway: Gorgias Press.

———. 2015. *An East Syrian Manuscript of the Syriac 'Masora' Dated to 899 CE: Introduction, List of Sample Texts, and Indices to Marginal Notes in British Library, Additional MS 12138.* Vol. II. Piscataway: Gorgias Press.

———. 2019. 'The Syriac Reading Dot in Transmission: Consistency and Confusion'. In *Studies in Biblical Philology and Lexicography*, edited by Daniel King, 159–76. Piscataway: Gorgias Press.

Makhzumi, Mahdi, ed. 1985. *Kitāb Al-ʿAyn.* 8 vols. Qum: Manshūrāt al-Hijra.

Malter, Henry. 1921. *Saadia Gaon, His Life and Works.* Philadelphia: The Jewish Publication Society of America.

Martin, J. P. P. 1869. *Jacobi Episcopi Edesseni Epistola ad Georgium Episcopum Sarugensem de orthographia syriaca. Eiusdem Jacobi nec non Thomae Diaconi Tractatus de punctis aliaque documenta in eamdem materiam.* Paris: Brockhaus.

———. 1875. *Histoire de la ponctuation ou de la Massore chez les Syriens.* Paris: Impr. Nationale.

Mavroudi, Maria. 2014. 'Greek Language and Education under Early Islam'. In *Islamic Cultures, Islamic Contexts: Essays in Honor of Professor Patricia Crone*, edited by Asad Q. Ahmed, Behnam Sadeghi, Robert G. Hoyland, and Adam Silverstein, 295–342. Leiden: Brill.

Merx, Adalbert. 1889. *Historia Artis Grammaticae Apud Syros.* Leipzig.

Moosa, Matti, trans. 2003. *The Scattered Pearls: A History of Syriac Literature and Sciences*. 2nd revised edition. Piscataway: Gorgias Press.

Morag, Shelomo. 1961. *The Vocalization Systems of Arabic, Hebrew, and Aramaic: Their Phonetic and Phonemic Principles.* Janua Linguarum 13. The Hague, Netherlands: Mouton & Co.

———. 1973. 'Some Aspects of the Methodology and Terminology of the Early Massoretes'. *Lěšonénu: A Journal for the Study of the Hebrew Language and Cognate Subjects* 38/1–2: 49–77. [in Hebrew]

———. 1974. 'On Some Terms of the Babylonian Massora'. In *1972 and 1973 Proceedings IOMS*, edited by H. Orlinsky, 67–77. Masoretic Studies 1. Missoula, MT: University of Montana.

———. 1979a. 'Derekh Niṣåb'. *Lěšonénu: A Journal for the Study of the Hebrew Language and Cognate Subjects* 43: 194–200. [in Hebrew]

———. 1979b. 'Some Notes on Muṣawwitāt in Medieval Hebrew and Arabic Literature'. *Journal of the Ancient Near Eastern Society* 11: 85–90.

Mubarrad, Abū al-ʿAbbās al-. 1965. *Al-Muqtaḍab*. Edited by Muḥammad ʿAbd al-Khāliq ʿUḍayma. Vol. I. Cairo.

Muehlhaeusler, Mark. 2016. 'Additional Reading Marks in Kufic Manuscripts'. *Journal of Islamic Studies* 27/1: 1–16.

Nassir, A. A. al-. 1993. *Sībawayh the Phonologist*. Library of Arabic Linguistics 10. London: Kegan Paul International.

Nelson, Kristina. 2001. *The Art of Reciting the Qurʾan*. Cairo: American University in Cairo Press.

Neubauer, Adolf. 1891. *Petite grammaire hébraïque provenant du Yémen*. Leipzig: Otto Harrassowitz Verlag.

Nöldeke, Theodor. 1904. *Compendious Syriac Grammar*. Translated by James A. Crichton. London: Williams and Norgate.

Nutt, John W. 1870. *Two Treatises on Verbs Containing Feeble and Double Letters, by R. Jehuda Ḥayug; Translated into Hebrew from the Original Arabic, by R. Moses Giḳatilia; to Which Is Added the Treatise on Punctuation by the Same Author, Translated by Aben Ezra: Edited from Bodleian Mss. with an English Translation by John W. Nutt*. London: Asher and Co.

Olszowy-Schlanger, Judith. 2011. 'The Science of Language Among Medieval Jews'. In *Science in Medieval Jewish Cultures*, edited by Gad Freudenthal. New York: Cambridge University Press.

Outhwaite, Benjamin. 2020. 'The Tiberian Tradition in Common Bibles from the Cairo Genizah'. In *Studies in Semitic Vocalisation and Reading Traditions*, edited by Aaron D. Hornkohl and Geoffrey Khan, 405–66. Cambridge Semitic Languages and Cultures 3. Cambridge: University of Cambridge and Open Book Publishers.

Owens, Jonathan. 1990. *Early Arabic Grammatical Theory: Heterogeneity and Standardization*. Amsterdam: John Benjamins.

Payne Smith, J. 1903. *A Compendious Syriac Dictionary*. Oxford: Clarendon Press.

Payne Smith, R. 1879. *Thesaurus Syriacus*. Oxford: Clarendon.

Phillips, George, ed. 1869. *A Letter By Mār Jacob, Bishop of Edessa, on Syriac Orthography: Also a Tract by the Same Author, and a Discourse by Gregory Bar Hebrœus on Syriac Accents.* London: Williams and Norgate.

Posegay, Nick. 2020. 'Connecting the Dots: The Shared Phonological Tradition in Syriac, Arabic, and Hebrew Vocalisation'. In *Studies in Semitic Vocalisation and Reading Traditions*, edited by Aaron D. Hornkohl and Geoffrey Khan, 191–226. Cambridge Semitic Languages and Cultures 3. Cambridge: University of Cambridge and Open Book Publishers.

———. 2021a. 'Hissing, Gnashing, Piercing, Cracking: Naming Vowels in Medieval Hebrew'. In *New Perspectives in Biblical and Rabbinic Hebrew*, edited by Aaron D. Hornkohl and Geoffrey Khan, 29–55. Cambridge Semitic Languages and Cultures 7. Cambridge: University of Cambridge and Open Book Publishers. https://doi.org/10.11647/obp.0250.02.

———. 2021b. 'Men of Letters in the Syriac Scribal Tradition: Dawid Bar Pawlos, Rabban Rāmišoʿ, and the Family of Beṯ Rabban'. *Hugoye: Journal of Syriac Studies* 24/1: 127–86.

———. 2021c. 'The Marking of Poetry: A Rare Vocalization System from an Early Qurʾān Manuscript in Chicago, Paris, and Doha'. *Journal of Near Eastern Studies* 80/1: 73–89. https://doi.org/10.1086/712876.

———. 2021d. 'To Belabour the Points: Encoding Vowel Phonology in Syriac and Hebrew Vocalization'. *Journal of Semitic Studies* 66/1: 53–76. https://doi.org/10.1093/jss/fgaa045.

Rahmani, Ignatius Ephraem II. 1904. *Studia Syriaca: Collectio Documentorum Hactenus Ineditorum Ex Codicus Syriacis*. Sharfeh: Sharfeh Patriarchal Seminary.

Reuschel, Wolfgang. 1959. *Al-Ḫalīl Ibn-Aḥmad, der Lehrer Sībawayhs, als Grammatiker*. Institut für Orientforschung 49. Berlin: Deutsche Akademie der Wissenschaften zu Berlin.

Revell, E. J. 1972. 'The Grammar of Jacob of Edessa and the Other Near Eastern Grammatical Traditions'. *Parole de l'Orient*, Revue semestrielle des études syriaques et arabes chrétiennes 4/2: 365–74.

———. 1975. 'The Diacritical Dots and the Development of the Arabic Alphabet'. *Journal of Semitic Studies* 20/2: 178–90.

Rezvan, E. A. 2004. *The Qurʾān of ʿUthmān: St. Petersburg, Katta-Langar, Bukhara, Tashkent*. St. Petersburg: TSentr Peterburgskoe Vostokovedenie.

Roberts, Bleddyn J. 1969. 'The Old Testament: Manuscripts, Texts and Versions'. In *The Cambridge History of the Bible*. Cambridge: Cambridge University Press.

Robin, Christian. 2006. 'La réforme de l'écriture à l'époque du califat médinois'. *Mélanges de L'Université Saint-Joseph* 59: 319–64.

Robinson, T. H., and J. F. Coakley. 2013. *Robinson's Paradigms and Exercises in Syriac Grammar*. 6th edition. Oxford: Oxford University Press.

Rybalkin, Valeriy. 2011. 'ʿAmal'. In *Encyclopedia of Arabic Language and Linguistics*. Brill. http://dx.doi.org/10.1163/1570-6699_eall_EALL_COM_0013.

Salvesen, Alison. 2001. 'Did Jacob of Edessa Know Hebrew?' In *Biblical Hebrew, Biblical Texts: Essays in Memory of Michael P. Weitzman*, edited by Ada Rapoport-Albert and Gillian Greenberg, 457–69. Journal for the Study of the Old Testament Supplement Series 333. London: Sheffield Academic Press.

———. 2008. 'Jacob of Edessa's Life and Work: A Biographical Sketch'. In *Jacob of Edessa and the Syriac Culture of His Day*, edited by Bas ter Haar Romeny, 1–10. Leiden: Brill.

Samir, Samir Khalil. 1975. 'Deux cultures qui s'affrontent: Une controverse sur l'Iʿrāb au XIe siècle entre Élie de Nisibe et le Vizir Abū l-Qāsim'. *Mélanges de L'Université Saint-Joseph* 49/2: 617–50.

Schoeler, Gregor. 2006. *The Oral and the Written in Early Islam*. Edited by James E. Montgomery. Translated by Uwe Vagelpohl. Routledge Studies in Middle Eastern Literatures 13. London: Routledge.

Segal, J. B. 1953. *The Diacritical Point and the Accents in Syriac*. London: Oxford University Press.

———. 1989. 'Quššaya and Rukkaka: A Historical Introduction'. *Journal of Semitic Studies* 34/2: 483–91.

Sellheim, Rudolf. 2012a. 'Al-Khalīl b. Aḥmad'. In *Encyclopaedia of Islam*, edited by P. Bearman, Th. Bianquis, C. E. Bosworth, E. Van Donzel, and W. P. Heinrichs, 2nd edition. Electronic: Brill. http://dx.doi.org/10.1163/1573-3912_islam_SIM_4161.

———. 2012b. 'Al-Layth b. al-Muẓaffar'. In *Encyclopaedia of Islam*, edited by P. Bearman, Th. Bianquis, C. E. Bosworth, E.

Van Donzel, and W. P. Heinrichs, 2nd edition. Electronic: Brill. http://dx.doi.org/10.1163/1573-3912_islam_SIM_46 55.

Semaan, Khalil I. 1968. *Linguistics in the Middle Ages: Phonetic Studies in Early Islam*. Leiden: Brill.

Shah, Mustafa. 2008. 'Review of The Oral and the Written in Early Islam by Gregor Schoeler'. Translated by Uwe Vagelpohl, Edited and Introduced by James E. Montgomery'. *Journal of Qur'anic Studies* 10/1: 98–128. https://doi.org/ 10.3366/E1465359109000254.

Shdaifat, Y. al-, A. Al-Jallad, Z. al-Salameen, and R. Harahsheh. 2017. 'An Early Christian Arabic Graffito Mentioning "Yazīd the King"'. *Arabian Archaeology and Epigraphy* 28: 315–24. https://doi.org/doi.org/10.1111/aae.12105.

Sībawayh. 1986. *Kitāb Sībawayh*. Edited by ʿAbd al-Salam Harun. 2nd edition. 4 vols. Cairo: Maktaba al-Khanji.

Siegal, Michal Bar-Asher. 2018. 'Judaism and Syriac Christianity'. In *The Syriac World*, edited by Daniel King, 146–56. New York: Routledge. https://doi.org/10.4324/97813157 08195-10.

Skoss, Solomon L. 1952. 'A Study of Hebrew Vowels from Saadia Gaon's Grammatical Work "Kutub al-Lughah"'. *The Jewish Quarterly Review* 42/3: 283–317.

Sokoloff, Michael. 2009. *A Syriac Lexicon: A Translation from the Latin, Correction, Expansion, and Update of C. Brockelmann's Lexicon Syriacum*. Piscataway: Gorgias Press. https://www. gorgiaspress.com/a-syriac-lexicon.

Steiner, Richard C. 2005. 'Påṯaḥ and Qåmeṣ: On the Etymology and Evolution of the Names of the Hebrew Vowels'. *Orientalia, NOVA Series* 74/4: 372–81.

Talmon, Rafael. 1996. 'Review of C. H. M. Versteegh, Arabic Grammar and Qur'anic Exegesis in Early Islam'. *Jerusalem Studies in Arabic and Islam* 20: 287–93.

———. 1997a. 'A Study of the Early History of the Term Muṣawwit and Related Terms in Arabic Linguistic Literature'. *Māssōrōt* 9–11: 209–24. [in Hebrew]

———. 1997b. *Arabic Grammar in Its Formative Age*. Leiden: Brill.

———. 2000a. 'Foreign Influence in the Syriac Grammatical Tradition'. In *History of the Language Sciences: An International Handbook on the Evolution of the Study of Language from the Beginnings to the Present*, edited by E. F. K. Koerner, Hans-Josef Niederehe, and Kees Versteegh, 337–41. Handbooks of Linguistics and Communication Science 18.1. Berlin: De Gruyter.

———. 2000b. 'The First Beginnings of Arabic Linguistics: The Era of the Old Iraqi School'. In *History of the Language Sciences: An International Handbook on the Evolution of the Study of Language from the Beginnings to the Present*, edited by E. F. K. Koerner, Hans-Josef Niederehe, and Kees Versteegh, 245–52. Handbooks of Linguistics and Communication Science 18.1. Berlin: De Gruyter.

———. 2003. *Eighth-Century Iraqi Grammar: A Critical Exploration of Pre-Halîlian Arabic Linguistics*. Winona Lake, IN: Eisenbrauns.

————. 2008. 'Jacob of Edessa the Grammarian'. In *Jacob of Edessa and the Syriac Culture of His Day*, edited by Bas ter Haar Romeny, 159–76. Leiden: Brill.

Taylor, David G. K. 2011. 'Syriac Lexicography'. In *GEDSH: Electronic Edition*. Beth Mardutho. https://gedsh.bethmardutho.org/Syriac-Lexicography.

Tayyan, Muhammad al-, and Yahya Mir Alam, eds. 1983. *Risāla Asbāb Ḥudūth Al-Ḥurūf by Ibn Sīnā*. Damascus: Academy of the Arabic Language.

Teule, Herman G.B. 2011a. 'Eliya I of Ṭirhan'. In *GEDSH: Electronic Edition*. Beth Mardutho. https://gedsh.bethmardutho.org/Eliya-I-of-Tirhan.

————. 2011b. 'Eliya of Nisibis'. In *GEDSH: Electronic Edition*. Beth Mardutho. https://gedsh.bethmardutho.org/Eliya-of-Nisibis.

Troupeau, Gérard. 1958. 'Le commentaire d'al-Sīrāfī sur le chapitre 565 du Kitāb de Sībawayhi'. *Arabic* 5/2: 168–82.

————. 1976. *Lexique-index du Kitāb de Sībawayhi*. Paris: Klincksieck.

Ullendorff, Edward. 1951. 'Studies in the Ethiopic Syllabary'. *Africa: Journal of the International African Institute* 21/3: 207–17.

Van Rompay, Lucas. 2011a. 'Bar Bahlul, Ḥasan'. In *GEDSH: Electronic Edition*, edited by Sebastian P. Brock, Aaron Michael Butts, George Anton Kiraz, and Lucas Van Rompay. Beth Mardutho. https://gedsh.bethmardutho.org/Bar-Bahlul-Hasan.

———. 2011b. 'Isho'yahb Bar Malkon'. In *GEDSH: Electronic Edition*. Beth Mardutho. https://gedsh.bethmardutho.org/Ishoyahb-bar-Malkon.

———. 2011c. 'Yawsep Huzaya'. In *GEDSH: Electronic Edition*. Beth Mardutho. https://gedsh.bethmardutho.org/Yawsep-Huzaya.

Versteegh, C. H. M. 1977. *Greek Elements in Arabic Linguistic Thinking*. Leiden: Brill.

———. 1993. *Arabic Grammar and Qur'anic Exegesis in Early Islam*. Leiden: Brill.

Versteegh, Kees. 1997. *The Arabic Linguistic Tradition*. Landmarks in Linguistic Thought 3. London: Routledge.

———. 2011. 'Ḥaraka'. In *Encyclopedia of Arabic Language and Linguistics*. Brill. http://dx.doi.org.ezp.lib.cam.ac.uk/10.1163/1570-6699_eall_EALL_SIM_vol2_0014.

Vidro, Nadia. 2013. *A Medieval Karaite Pedagogical Grammar of Hebrew: A Critical Edition and English Translation of Kitab al-'Uqud Fi Tasarif al-Luga al-'Ibraniyya*. Études sur se judaïsme médiéval 62. Leiden: Brill.

———. 2020a. 'A Book on Arabic Inflexion According to the System of the Greeks: A Lost Work by Ḥunayn b. Isḥāq'. *Zeitschrift für Arabische Linguistik* 72/2: 26–58.

———. 2020b. 'Grammars of Classical Arabic in Judaeo-Arabic: An Overview'. *Intellectual History of the Islamicate World* 8/2-3: 284–305. https://doi.org/10.1163/2212943X-20201010.

Vööbus, Arthur. 1965. *History of the School of Nisibis*. Corpus Scriptorum Christianorum Orientalium 26. Louvain: American Catholic University and Louvaine Catholic University.

Wehr, Hans. 1993. *The Hans Wehr Dictionary of Modern Written Arabic*. Edited by J. M. Cowan. 4th edition. Urbana, IL: Spoken Language Services.

Werner, Eric. 1959. *The Sacred Bridge: The Interdependence of Liturgy and Music in Synagogue and Church During the First Millennium*. New York: Columbia University Press.

Witkam, Jan Just. 2015. 'The Neglect Neglected. To Point or Not to Point, That Is the Question'. *Journal of Islamic Manuscripts* 6/2–3: 376–408. https://doi.org/10.1163/1878464 X-00602013.

Wouters, Alfons. 1983. 'Review of D. Donnet. Le Traité de La Construction de La Phrase de Michel Le Syncelle de Jérusalem. Histoire Du Texte, Édition, Traduction et Commentaire.' *Scriptorium* 37/2: 321–23.

Wright, William. 1870. *Catalogue of Syriac Manuscripts in the British Museum*. Vol. I. London: Gilbert and Rivington.

———, ed. 1871. *Fragments of the Syriac Grammar of Jacob of Edessa*. Clerkenwell: Gilbert and Rivington.

Yeivin, Israel. 1983. *Introduction to the Tiberian Masorah*. Translated by E. J. Revell. Masoretic Studies 5. Missoula, MT: Scholars Press.

———. 1985. *The Hebrew Language Tradition as Reflected in the Babylonian Vocalization*. 2 vols. Jerusalem: Ha-Akademyah la-Lashon ha-'Ivrit.

Zajjājī, Abu al-Qāsim al-. 1959. *Al-Īḍāḥ Fī ʿIllal al-Naḥw*. Edited by Māzin Mubārak. Cairo: Dār al-Nafāsh.

INDEX

Cambridge Semitic Languages and Cultures

General Editor Geoffrey Khan

Cambridge Semitic Languages and Cultures

About the series

This series is published by Open Book Publishers in collaboration with the Faculty of Asian and Middle Eastern Studies of the University of Cambridge. The aim of the series is to publish in open-access form monographs in the field of Semitic languages and the cultures associated with speakers of Semitic languages. It is hoped that this will help disseminate research in this field to academic researchers around the world and also open up this research to the communities whose languages and cultures the volumes concern. This series includes philological and linguistic studies of Semitic languages, editions of Semitic texts, and studies of Semitic cultures. Titles in the series will cover all periods, traditions and methodological approaches to the field. The editorial board comprises Geoffrey Khan, Aaron Hornkohl, and Esther-Miriam Wagner.

This is the first Open Access book series in the field; it combines the high peer-review and editorial standards with the fair Open Access model offered by OBP. Open Access (that is, making texts free to read and reuse) helps spread research results and other educational materials to everyone everywhere, not just to those who can afford it or have access to well-endowed university libraries.

Copyrights stay where they belong, with the authors. Authors are encouraged to secure funding to offset the publication costs and thereby sustain the publishing model, but if no institutional funding is available, authors are not charged for publication. Any grant secured covers the actual costs of publishing and is not taken as profit. In short: we support publishing that respects the authors and serves the public interest.

Other titles in the series

A Handbook and Reader of Ottoman Arabic
Esther-Miriam Wagner (ed.)
doi.org/10.11647/OBP.0208

Diversity and Rabbinization: Jewish Texts and Societies between 400 and 1000 CE
Gavin McDowell, Ron Naiweld,
Daniel Stökl Ben Ezra (eds)
doi.org/10.11647/OBP.0219

UNIVERSITY OF
CAMBRIDGE
Faculty of Asian and Middle
Eastern Studies

You can find more information about this serie at:
http://www.openbookpublishers.com/section/107/1

CPSIA information can be obtained
at www.ICGtesting.com
Printed in the USA
BVHW031733140722
642166BV00009B/890

9 781800 642966